INDEX LIBYCUS

BIBLIOGRAPHY OF LIBYA

1957-1969

with supplementary material

1915-1956

Compiled
by

Hans Schlüter

G. K. HALL & CO., 70 LINCOLN STREET, BOSTON, MASS.

1972

Library of Congress Cataloging in Publication Data

Schlüter, Hans.
  Index Libycus: Bibliography of Libya, 1957-1969.

    1. Libya--Bibliography. I. Title. II. Title:
Bibliography of Libya, 1957-1969.
Z3971.S36   016.9161'2   72-2779
ISBN 0-8161-0939-7

This publication is printed on permanent/durable acid-free paper.

ISBN 0-8161-0939-7

FOREWORD

The purpose of <u>Index Libycus</u> is to supplement and extend Hill's <u>A Bibliography of Libya</u> of 1959. The period covered by I. L. lies between the publication of Ceccherin's comprehensive <u>Bibliografia della Libia</u> in 1915 and the political upheaval in autumn 1969. A few selected items from later publications have also been included. The collected material is prepared in book form as a short title catalogue. Minor bibliographical data are not given, as many of these on the one hand, (particularly in respect of special reports and publications from Libya itself,) are contradictory or unobtainable or, on the other hand, can easily be obtained from national bibliographies. As far as possible publishers have been named in titles which have appeared since 1945. Each entry appears only once, classified according to its main subject. Titles in Arabic, as well as the numerous translations of law papers, treaties, communications of oil companies and similar pamphlets have not been included.

The aim throughout has been to make a discriminate documentation. Careful selections had to be made in the sections on archaeology, geology, economy and politics due to the vast number of works which have appeared on these subjects since 1957. For this reason, special effort was made to include all the appropriate special bibliographies, library catalogues, etc. The 1915-1956 supplementary entries are principally taken from Italian congress and other academic papers. Here value was laid on Berber studies and contributions from from orientalists. Unfortunately, a large part of the Italian official reports and periodicals, particularly in respect of law, administration, economy, politics, social affairs and medicine has never been indexed. This also applies to the wealth of information contained in periodicals of a more general nature, such as "La Nuova Antologia," "Rassegna Italiana," "Vie del Mondo," <u>et al</u>.

In preparing an index to Hill's bibliography, it was ascertained firstly, that approximately five percent of the material was of little practical use due to defective data and secondly, that the bibliographical state of Italian colonial literature leaves much to be desired and would be a profitable work for the future. A large part of the supplementary material was drawn from the former German Colonial Library, Berlin, which is now housed in the City and University Library, Frankfurt a. M. Entries from Hill's bibliography have not been duplicated.

In gathering contemporary material I received generous support from Prof. Dr. E. Klitzsch, Berlin; Prof. Dr. T. Lewicki, Cracow; Prof. Dr. E. Panetta, Rome; Privatdozent Dr. W. Vycichl, Geneva; P. Ward, Tripoli and Prof. Dr. H. Weis, Vienna. Whereas information from Libya could be obtained only with great difficulty (this is especially regrettable concerning Libyan government publications - <u>v</u>. also Ward's <u>Libyan Research Library Catalogue, 1970</u>) the libraries and documentation centres of international organisations the Istituto Italiano per l'Africa/Rome, have been most cooperative. A special acknowledgement is due to FAO/Documentation Center, ILO/Library and Documentation Branch,

UNESCO/Education Documentation Centre and WHO/Library. In bibliographical research I have constantly received liberal assistance for the Signierdienst and the Inter-library Lending Department of the Stadt- und Universitätsbibliothek, Frankfurt a. M. To Dr. H. Sölken, lecturer of African studies and Privatdozent Dr. J. Obst of the Johann Wolfgang Goethe-Universität, I wish especially to express my gratitude for advice and encouragement. My thanks are due to my wife for English translations, the preparation of the alphabetical index and her support throughout.

I should like here once again to thank the publishers for including the work in their Africana series.

Hans Schlüter
Frankfurt am Main
Stadt- und Universitätsbibliothek

CONTENTS

v

ABBREVIATIONS

AAE	Archivio per l'antropologia e la etnologia.
AAI	Annali dell'Africa italiana.
AAN	Annuaire de l'Afrique du Nord.
AANL	Atti della Accademia Nazionale dei Lincei.
ACGI	Atti del congresso geografico italiano.
ACSC	Atti del congresso di studi coloniali.
AIb	Africa italiana, Bergamo.
AIn	Africa italiana, Napoli.
AIr	Africa italiana, Roma.
AION	Annali del Istituto Orientale di Napoli.
AMS	U.S. Army Map Service.
ASIPS	Atti della Società Italiana per il Progresso delle Scienze.
BAAPG	Bulletin. American Association of Petroleum Geologists.
BfA	Bundesstelle für Aussenhandelsinformation.
BLS	Bulletin de liaison saharienne.
BSGI	Bollettino della Società Geografica Italiana.
BSHN	Bulletin de la Société d'Histoire Naturelle de l'Afrique du Nord.
CGEP	La Cirenaica geografica, economica e politica, a cura di O. Marinelli. Milano 1923.
CHEAM	Centre de Hautes Etudes Administratives sur l'Afrique et l'Asie Modernes.
CR	Compte rendu.
Diss.	Dissertation.
DTLSP	Development of tribal lands and settlements project. Rome: FAO 1969.
EIne	Encyclopaedia of Islam, new edition.
FSL	Field studies in Libya. Durham: Dept. of Geography 1960.
GANC	Geology and archaeology of northern Cyrenaica. Tripoli: PESL 1968.
GAPSF	Geology, archaeology and prehistory of the southwestern Fezzan. Tripoli: PESL 1969.
GPO	U.S. Government Printing Office.
GSGS	Geographical Section of the General Staff.
HBFA	Heinrich Barth. Ein Forscher in Afrika. Wiesbaden: Steiner 1967.
ianc	Individual articles not catalogued.
IdO	Italia d'oltremare.
IPS	Istituto Poligrafico dello Stato.
JRS	Journal of Roman studies.
LA	Libya antiqua.
MAL	Monografie di archeologia libica.
MEJ	Middle East journal.
NA	Notiziario archeologico.
nd	No date.
np	No place.
OM	Oriente moderno.
PBSR	Papers of the British School at Rome.
PESL	Petroleum Exploration Society of Libya.
PGM	Petermanns geographische Mitteilungen.
RAST	Rivista di agricoltura subtropicale e tropicale.

RdC   Rivista delle colonie.
RdT   Rivista della Tripolitania.
REAI   Rassegna economica dell'Africa italiana.
Repr.   Reprint.
RIFP   Revue de l'Institut Français du Pétrole.
RIP   Rivista italiana di paleontologia.
RMDAT   Reports and monographs of the Dept. of Antiquities in
          Tripolitania.
RSAI   Rassegna sociale dell'Africa italiana.
RSO   Rivista degli studi orientali.
RSP   Rivista di scienze preistoriche.
sc   Selective cataloguing.
SCLNC   South-central Libya and northern Chad. Tripoli: PESL 1966.
SIFOG   Il Sahara italiano. P. 1. Fezzan e oasi di Gat. Roma 1937.
TIRS   Travaux de l'Institut de Recherches Sahariennes.
USGS   U.S. Geological Survey.
Wash.   Washington, D.C.
Zs   Zeitschrift.

Bibliography.

Baiou, M.A. 1
Al-muktar fi maraji' tarikh libya.
(Selected Libyan bibliography).
Benghazi: Dar Libya.
Vol. 1. 1967.

Bibliografia dell'impero 2
fascista (colonie e possedimenti).
Roma 1938.
Suppl. 1. 1939.
Suppl. 2. 1940.

Bibliografia dell'Istituto 3
Fascista dell'Africa Italiana.
Roma 1939.

Bibliografia dell'Italia 4
d'oltremare. Anno 1939.
Roma 1940.
(Bibliografie del ventennio. 2,1.)

Bibliografia generale del 5
fascismo.
Roma.
Vol. 1. Opere straniere. 1932.
Vol. 2. Opere italiane. 1933.
Vol. 3. I libri coloniali. A cura
di A.V. Pellegrineschi. 1934.

A bibliographical list of works 6
about Libya.
Cairo: National Library Press 1961.
(Bibliographical lists of the Arab
 world. 9.)

Bibliographie arabe. 7
(Transliterated).
AAN 4. 1965 (1966)-

Bibliographie Maghreb- 8
Sahara.
Anthropologie, préhistoire, ethno-
graphie.
Libyca 17. 1969-

Bibliographie systématique 9
suivie d'un index par noms
d'auteurs.
AAN 7. 1968-

Blaudin de Thé, B. 10
Essai de bibliographie du Sahara
français et des regions avoisinantes.
2nd ed.
Paris: Arts et Métiers Graphiques,
Klincksieck 1960.

Bono, F. 11
Bibliografie italiane della Libia.
Libia 1. 1953, n.1, p. 119-121.

Catalogue of the Colonial 12
Office Library London.
Boston, Mass.: Hall 1964.
Suppl. 1. 1963-1967. 1967.

Ceccherini, U. 13
Bibliografia della Libia.
Roma 1915.

Contributo italiano alla cono- 14
scenza dell'oriente: repertorio
bibliografico dal 1935 al 1958.
Firenze: Le Monnier 1962.

Crudgington, J.W. 15
Literature on Arab Libya.
MEJ 6. 1952, p. 247-251.

A current bibliography on   16
African affairs.
African Bibliographic Center.
Wash.: Greenwood.
1. 1968-

Gabrieli, G.   17

Bibliografia degli studi orientalistici in Italia dal 1912 al 1934.
Roma 1935.

Hill, R.W.   18

A bibliography of Libya.
University of Durham: Dept. of Geo-
graphy 1959.
(Research papers series. 1.)

Jemma, E.   19

Bibliografia degli scritti di Ettore
Rossi.
OM 35. 1955, p. 418-424.

Lewin, E.   20

Subject catalogue of the library of
the Royal Empire Society.
London 1930.
1. The British Empire generally, and
   Africa.

Library catalogue. School of   21
Oriental and African Studies,
University of London.
Boston, Mass.: Hall 1963.
Suppl. 1.1968.

Merighi, A.   22

Bibliografia (La Tripolitania antica).
Verbania 1940, vol. 2, p. 311-423.

Murabet, M.   23

A bibliography of Libya, with particular reference to sources available
in libraries and public archives in
Tripoli.
La Valetta: Progress Press 1959.

Pearson, J.D.   24

Index islamicus. 1906-55.
Cambridge: Heffer 1958.
Suppl. 1. 1956-60. 1962.
Suppl. 2. 1961-65. 1967.

Pubblicazioni islamistiche   25
in Italia. Mostra delle
pubblicazioni islamistiche in Italia,
Tripoli 1959.
Roma: Bardi 1959.

Rivlin, B.   26

A selective survey of the literature
in the social sciences and related
fields on modern North Africa.
American political science review
48. 1954, p. 826-848.

Valensin, G.   27

Per un archivio bibliografico coloniale.
ACSC 1. 1931, vol. 2, p. 203-210.

Ward, P.   28

What to read on Libya. 4th ed.
Tripoli: Oasis Oil Co. 1965.

Ward, P.   29

A survey of Libyan bibliographical
resources. 2nd ed.
Tripoli: Libyan Publishing House
1965.

Ward, P.   30

Libyan research library catalogue.
Tripoli: Oasis Oil Co. 1970.
(Publication. Library Services
 Division. 13.)

Willms, A.   31

Auswahlbibliographie des berberolo-
gischen Schrifttums.
Afrika und Übersee 50. 1967, p. 64-
128.

Zanutto, S. 32
Pubblicazioni edite dall'amministrazione coloniale o sotto i suoi
auspici 1882-1937.
Roma 1938.

Zanutto, S. 33
Bollettino bibliografico coloniale.
Suppl. alla RdC 1. 1940-
RdC 14. 1940-

Zoubi, A.H. 34
Libya (Bibliographical services
throughout the world).
Bibliography. Documentation. Termi-
nology 8. 1968, p. 197-198.

Current Information.
The Press.

Africa contemporary record. 35
Annual survey and documents.
London: Africa Research Ltd.
1968-1969 (1969).

Africa research bulletin. 36
Political, social and cultural
series.
Economic, financial and technical
series.
London: Africa Research Ltd.
6. 1969- ianc

Annuaire de l'Afrique du nord. 37
Centre d'études nord-africaines.
Paris: Centre National de la Recherche Scientifique.
1. 1962 (1964)-

Arid zone research. 38
Paris: UNESCO.
29. 1968-

sc

AUFS [American Universities 39
Field Staff] reports service.
North Africa series.
New York: American Universities
Field Staff, Inc.
13. 1967- ianc

Bulletin of the faculty of 40
arts. University of Libya.
Benghazi.
3. 1969- sc

Libyan news. 41
London: Press Counseller's
Office, Embassy of the Kingdom of
Libya.
1968, n. 1- ianc

Libyan review. 42
Tripoli: Dept. of Public Relations, Ministry of Information and
Culture.
4. 1969, n. 6- ianc

Libyca. 43
Ser. archéologie-épigraphie.
Ser. anthropologie-préhistoire-
ethnographie.
Alger: Direction de l'Intérieur et
des Beaux-Arts.
17. 1969- sc

Libyscher Brief. 44
Bonn: Presseabteilung, Botschaft
des Königreichs Libyen,
- 1969, n. 68, 15.7.
... der Arabischen Republik,
1969, n. 1, 15.11. - ianc

Maghreb. 45
La Fondation Nationale des
Sciences Politiques.
Paris: La Documentation Française.
1969, n. 31- sc

The Maghreb digest. 46
North African perspectives.
Los Angeles: University of Southern
California, School of International
Relations, Middle East and North
African program.
5. 1967- ianc

The Middle East journal.   47
Wash.: Middle East Institute.
23. 1969-

The Middle East and North   48
Africa.
London: Europa Publications Ltd.
16. 1969-70 (1969)-

News from Libya. Information   49
bulletin.
Wash.: Libyan Embassy.
5. 1969, n. 10-

                        ianc

Oriente moderno.   50
Roma: Istituto per l'Oriente.
49. 1969-

Realités libyennes.   51
Tripoli: Dépt. des Relations
Publiques du Ministère de l'Information et de la Culture.
2. 1969, n. 1-

                        ianc

Alman, M.   52
Ethiopia, Libya, ... (Periodicals
published in Africa, part 3.)
Library materials on Africa 3. 1966,
n. 3. Suppl.

Arabic press summary.   53
Benghazi: U.S. Embassy.
nd

Daily bulletin of domestic   54
news.
Tripoli: Libyan News Agency.
nd

Daily translation service.   55
Tripoli: Translation Office,
Ibrahim Hafez Ramadan.
1970, 28.8.-

Dollas, D.J.   56
Libya. Organization of a national
news agency.
Paris: UNESCO 1965.

Feuereisen, F. - Schmacke , E.   57
Die Presse in Afrika. Ein Handbuch
für Wirtschaft und Werbung.
München: Verlag Dokumentation 1968.

Micus, I.   58
Die Presse des italienischen Kolo-
nialreiches.
Würzburg 1941.
(Studien zur Geschichte der italie-
  nischen Presse. 3.)

Monthly translation service.   59
Tripoli: Translation Office,
Ibrahim Hafez Ramadan.
1970, n. 128-

Muddathir, A.   60
Die arabische Presse in den Maghreb-
Staaten.
Pfaffenhofen: Afrika-Verlag 1966.
(Hamburger Beiträge zur Afrika-
Kunde. 3.)

Periodicals in Libya.   61
A union list.
Tripoli: Oasis Oil Co. 1963.

Souriau, C.   62
L'opinion dans la presse maghrébine
arabe de 1966.
AAN 5. 1966, p. 823-853.

Souriau, C.   63

Mutuation culturelle et publications
maghrébines.
AAN 6. 1967, p. 197-264.

Souriau-Hoebrechts, C.   64

La presse maghrébine: Libye- Tunisie-
Maroc-Algerie.
Paris: Centre National de la Recher-
che Scientifique 1969.

General Works. Collective
Works. Handbooks.

Acanfora, M.O. - Fantoli, M. -   65
Staccioli, R.

Libia (Africa settentrionale).
Enciclopedia universale dell'arte.
Vol. 1. 1958, col. 80-92.

Afrika.   66
Handbuch der praktischen Kolonial-
wissenschaften. Ed. E. Obst. Vol. 1-
18.
Berlin 1941-43.

Afrika.   67
Enciklopediceskij spravocnik.
Red. I.I. Potechin.
Moskva: Sovetskaja Enciklopedija
1963.

Afrika-Handbuch fuer Wirt-   68
schaft und Reise. Ed. P. Col-
berg, M. Krämer.
Hamburg: Übersee-Verlag.
Vol. 1. Nord-West - und Zentral-
     Afrika. 1967.

Aneizi, A.   69

Libya today.
Pakistan horizon 20. 1967, n. 1,
p. 27-36.

Area handbook for Libya.   70
American University, Foreign
Area Studies, Stanford Research
Institute.
Wash.: GPO 1969.
(DA Pam 550 - 85.)

Arpea, M.   71

La Libia, oggi.
Italiani nel mondo 20. 1964, n. 11.

Askgaard, P.   72

Libyen.
København 1964.
(Mellemfolkeligt samvirke's små-
     skrifter. 4.)

Assan, G.   73

La Libia e il mondo arabo.
Roma: Editori Riuniti 1959.
(Nostro tempo.)

Atti del convegno nazionale   74
coloniale per il dopo guerra
delle colonie. Roma, 15-21 gennaio
1919. Relazioni, commissioni e reso-
conti delle sedute.Istituto Coloniale Italiano.
Roma 1920.

Background notes.   75
Kingdom of Libya. Rev. ed.
Libyan Arab Republic. Rev. ed.
Wash.: GPO 1968.
Wash.: GPO 1970.
(Dept. of State publication. 7815.)

Barbour, N.   76

Libya. Twentieth-century Africa. Ed.
P.J.M. MacEwan. New York 1968,
p. 107-160.

Barthel, G.   77

Libyen. Die arabischen Länder. Ed.
G. Nötzold. Gotha/Leipzig 1970,
p. 179-192.

Beguinot, F.   78

Al-Nafūsa. Al-Nafūsi.
EI.

Bersellini, M.   79

La Tripolitania: il presente e
l'avvenire.
Milano 1924.

Bethmann, E.W.   80

Basic facts on Libya.
Wash.: American Friends of the
Middle East 1966.

Blunsum, T.   81

Libya. The country and its people.
London: Queen Anne Press 1968.
(The world today series.)

Bodjanskij, V.L. - Šagal, V.E.   82

Sovremennaja Livija. Spravočnik.
Moskva: Nauka 1965.

Canard, M.   83

Les travaux de T. Lewicki concernant
le Maghrib et en particulier les
Ibâdites.
Revue africaine 103. 1959, p. 356-
371.

Canard, M.   84

Quelques articles recents de l'ara-
bisant polonais T. Lewicki.
Revue africaine 105. 1961, p. 186-
192.

Candole, E.A.V. de   85

Libya.
Africa. A handbook. Ed. C. Legum.
London 1965, p. 35-41.

La circonscription de   86
Ghadamès.
Notes et études documentaires 1948,
n. 939.

Colosimo, G.   87

Relazione al parlamento sulla
situazione politica, economica ed
amministrativa delle colonie italiane.
Roma 1918.

Copeland, P.W.   88

The land and people of Libya.
Philadelphia: Lippincott 1967.
(Portraits of the nations series.)

Corò, F.   89

Il Sahara nel passato, nel presente
e nel suo avvenire.
Libia 2. 1954, n. 2, p. 57-66, n. 3,
p. 39-45, n. 4, p. 33-44.

Dependents information on   90
Libya. U.S. Dept. of the Air
Force.
Wash.: GPO 1957.
(AFP 34-8-20.)

Despois, J.   91

Problèmes de Libye.
Paris: CHEAM 1946.
(Publication 945.)

Development of tribal lands   92
and settlements project.
Vol. 1-4.
Rome: FAO 1969.
(Funds-in-trust for Libya. 20.)

The encyclopaedia of Islam.   93
New ed. Ed. H.A.R. Gibb, ...
Leiden: Brill 1954-

Kabazi, F. - Siala, B. -   109
Goodchild, R.G. - Renson, J.

Libye. Libya.
Sabena Revue 29. 1964, n. 2.

Kingdom of Libya. General   110
information.
Review of Arab petroleum and economics 1968, Jan., p. 3-40.

Kraeling, C.H.   111

Now and then in Libya.
Journal of the American Oriental
Society 80. 1960, p. 104-111.

Leone, E. de   112

Le prime ricerche di una colonia e
la esplorazione geografica, politica ed economica.
Roma: IPS 1955.
(L'Italia in Africa. Serie storica.)

Libia.   113
Rassegna mensile illustrata.
Tripoli 1. 1937-6. 1942.

Libia. Il paese e i suoi   114
abitanti. Ordinamento politico
e amministrativo. Vita economica.
Milano 1937.
(Stati e colonie. 9.)

Libya.   115
London: Central Office of
Information, Reference Division
1960.
(Government overseas information
 sources. R. 4640.)

Libya.   116
British survey 1960, February.

Libya. From a mirage to a   117
miracle.
Islamic review 56. 1968, n. 8-9,
suppl., p. I-LVI.

Libya. A special report.   118
The Times 1969, 31. 1., p. 15-
19.

Libya today.   119
New York: Standard Oil Co.
1969.

La Libye.   120
Articles et documents 1959,
n. 0861.

Libye. La difficulte d'être   121
riche.
Continent 2.000 1970, n. 7, p. 28-
33.

Libyen. Land der Zukunft.   122
Delegation der Liga der Arabi-
schen Staaten.
Bonn 1963.
(Veröffentlichungen der Liga der
 Arabischen Staaten. 5.)

Libyen. Land der Zukunft.   123
Obst und Gemüse. Hamburg 1965,
n. 5, p. 27-28.

Lugani, V. - Mercatali, R.   124

Libia.
Milano: Aristea 1968.
(Tuttilmondo. Enciclopedia degli
 stati. Egitto.Libia.)

Magnis, F. von   125

Libyen - Tor nach Afrika.
Neues Afrika 6. 1964, p. 171-173.
Confrontation 4. 1964, 4. 10.,
p. 18-22.

Maitre-Devallon, C.   126

Quelques considérations sur la
Libye.
Paris: CHEAM 1951.
(Publication 5016.)

Maquart   127

La Libye.
Paris: CHEAM 1937.
(Publication 122 bis.)

Micheli, D. de   128

La nouvelle Libye et l'oeuvre
italienne.
Bulletin. Société belge d'études
et d'expansion 50. 1951, n. 147,
p. 651-656.

Modern Libya.   129
Publ. in cooperation with the
Permanent Mission of Libya to the
United Nations.
Afro-Mideast economic bulletin
1965, spring. Suppl.

Murabet, M.   130

Tripolitania - the land and its
people.
La Valetta: Progress Press 1959.

Murabet, M.   131

Facts about Libya.
La Valetta: Progress Press 1964.

North Africa.   132
1) Development in the Maghreb.
2) Libya.
British survey 1965, n. 198.

North Africa.   133
Ed. R. Steel.
New York: H.W. Wilson Co. 1967.
(The reference shelf. 38,5.)

Notes sur le Fezzân.   134
Paris: CHEAM 1945.
(Publication 649.)

Notizie generali sulla   135
Tripolitania, Cirenaica,
Eritrea e Somalia.
Milano 1925.

Nuovo digesto italiano.   136
A cura di M. d'Amelio.
Vol. 1-12.
Torino: UTET 1937-39.

                                  ianc

Paradisi, U.   137

Tripolitania d'oggi.
Vie del mondo 18. 1956, p. 931-946.

Pareja, F.M.   138

Islamologie.
Beyrouth: Impr. catholique 1957-63.

Per le nostre colonie.   139
Istituto Agricolo Coloniale
Italiano.
Firenze 1927.

Piccioli, A.   140

La nuova Italia d'oltremare.
Vol. 1.2.
Milano 1933.

Piccioli, A.   141
La rinascita della Libia sotto il
regime fascista.
L'impero coloniale fascista. Novara
1936, p. 461-496.

Pierrelat, F.   142
La culture française en Libye.
Culture française 17. 1968, n. 3,
p. 6-12.

A pocket guide to North Africa. 143
U.S. Dept. of Defense.
Wash.: GPO 1958.
(DOD Pam-2-17.)

Portrait of Libya.   144
Architects' journal 150.
1969, 15. 10., p. 958-962.

La région de Ghat et Serdeles.   145
Notes et études documentaires
1948, n. 937.

Regno di Libia.   146
Mondo afro-asiatico 2. 1964,
n. 5, numero speciale dedicato al
Regno di Libia.

A review of the natural   147
resources of the African
continent.
Paris: UNESCO 1963.
(Natural resources research. 1.)

Ronart, S. - Ronart, N.   148
Concise encyclopaedia of Arab
civilization.
Amsterdam: Djambatan.
Vol. 2. The Arab west. 1966.

Rondot, P.   149
La Libye d'aujourd'hui.
Études. Revue mensuelle 329. 1968,
p. 218-231.

Roselli Cecconi, M.   150
Scritti africani e coloniali.
Firenze 1943.

                                ianc

South-central Libya and   151
northern Chad. A guidebook
to the geology and prehistory.
Ed. J.J. Williams.
Tripoli: PESL 1966.
(Annual field conference. 8.)

Statistical abstract.   152
Tripoli: Census and Statistical
Dept.
1967.(1968).

Stefanini, G.   153
I possedimenti italiani in Africa
(Libia, Eritrea, Somalia).
Firenze 1923.

Steffan, E.B.   154
Libyen. Die Sandkiste Afrikas.
Echo der Welt. Ed. M.S. Metz. Zürich
1962, p. 304-310.

Stoeckl, K.   155
Die kulturelle Entwicklung Libyens
und die deutsch-libyschen Kulturbe-
ziehungen.
Aus der Schule der Diplomatie. Festschrift P. Pfeiffer. Düsseldorf   1.

Stoeckl, K.   155
1965, p. 651-659.

A survey of North West Africa 156
(the Maghrib). Ed. N. Barbour.
2nd ed.
London/New York: Oxford UP 1962.

Thomas, B.E. - Barbour, N. 157
Libya (Mamlakatu Libiya al-Mutta-
hida).
Collier's encyclopedia with bibliography and index. Vol. 8. 1964,
p. 642/643, vol. 14. 1964, p. 607-
612.

Tondeur, F. 158
Libye. Royaume des sables.
Paris: Nathan 1969.
(Pays et cités d'art.)

Vallilo, E. 159
La Cirenaica orientale.
Lecce 1923.

Ventimiglia, S.G. 160
Arabesca.
Palermo 1929.
(L'Africa nostra.)

Vernier, B. 161
Le Fezzân.
Alger 1944.

Vitali, F.A. 162
Das zweite Afrika - Libyen als Bei-
spiel.
Atlantis 32. 1960, p. 439-442.

Wandell, W. 163
Rivers to the sea: a profile of modern Libya.
Wiesbaden: You and Europe Publications 1960.

Weis, H. 164
Libyen - Land mit zwei Gesichtern.
Österreichische Volkshochschule
Wien 1956, n. 23.

Weis, H. 165
Schatzkammer Libyen.
Bustan 6. 1965, n. 2, p. 11-16.

Wellard, J. 166
The great Sahara.
London: Hutchinson 1964.

Wuelfing, W. 167
Libia.
Bologna 1943.
(Libri coloniali.)

Maps.
Aerial Photographs.

The British Museum catalogue 168
of printed maps, charts and
plans. Photolithographic ed. to the
end of 1964.
London: Trustees of the British
Museum 1967-68.

Europe and Africa map 169
catalog.
Wash.: AMS 1954-

Index to maps in books and 170
periodicals. American Geographical Society, Map Dept.
Boston, Mass.: Hall 1968.

Topographic map of United   187
Kingdom of Libya.

1:2 000 000.
Compiled by G.H. Goudarzi ...
Wash.: USGS 1962.
(Miscellaneous geologic investi-   1.

Topographic map of United   187

gations. Map I-350 B.)

                                    2.

Libya.   188

1:2 000 000.
London: War Office 1964.
(GSGS 4948. Sheet C 14.)

Africa.   189

1:2 000 000.
Wash.: AMS.
(AMS-series 2201.) [GSGS 2871.]
Sheet 3. Tunis. 1969. Sheet 4.
Banghāzī. 1969. Sheet 8. Sabhah.
1969. Sheet 9. Dâkhla Oasis. 1969.

Afrika.   190

1:2 000 000.
Generalstab des Heeres. Abteilung
für Kriegskarten und Vermessungswesen. Berlin 1941-   1.
3. Tunesien. 4. Cyrenaika. 8. Fessan.

Afrika.   190

9. Libysche Wüste.

                                    2.

Livija.   191

1:2 500 000.
(Gënin, J.A.: Livija).
Moskva: GUGK 1960.

Livija.   192

1:2 500 000.
(Dlin, N.A.: Livija).
Moskva: GUGK 1968.

Karta mira. World map.   193

1:2 500 000.
Bucharest: Military Topographical
Direction .
73. Tripoli (Tarābulus el-Gharb) 1968.
74. Cairo (Al Qāhira) 1968.   1.

Karta mira. World map.   193

93. Niamey 1968.
94. Khartoum 1968.

                                    2.

Aero Exploration.   194
Frankfurt a.M., Flughafen.
Flughafenstr. 316.
v. Völger n.254.

Ammann-International.   195
Base map and air photo
library.
San Antonio 78215.
223, Tenth Street.
v. Photogrammetric engineering 27.
    1961, p. 217.

Ente Italiano Rilievi Aero-   196
fotogrammetrici (E.I.R.A.).
Firenze.
Via S. Vito a Bellosguardo 4.
v. Bollettino della Associazione
    Italiana di Cartografia 1970,n.19.

Fairchild Aerial Surveys, Inc.   197
New York 20, New York.
9, Rockefeller Plaza.
v. Photogrammetric engineering 27.
    1961, p. 217.

Fairey Surveys Limited.   198
London W.1.
24, Bruton Street.
v. International yearbook of carto-
    graphy 9.1969, p. 191.

Hunting Aerosurveys Limited.   199
Boreham Wood, Herts.
6, Elstree Way.
v. Libya n. 3419.

Institut Géographique National. 200
Photothèque. Centre de Documentation de Photographies Aériennes.
94- Saint Mandé.
2, Avenue Pasteur.   (by letter)

Royal Air Force. 201
v. U.N. Regional Cartographic Conference for Africa 1. 1963, vol. 2, p. 170, 2. 1966, vol.2, p. 149, 152.

United States Air Force. 202
v. Goudarzi n. 3843.

Haffner, W. 203
Satelliten-Luftbild zentrale Sahara.
Erde 97. 1966, p. 81-83.

Klitzsch, E. - Jany, E. 204
Bemerkungen zu der Interpretation eines Satelliten-Luftbildes der Zentralsahara.
Erde 98. 1967, p. 298-300.

Luftgeographisches Einzelheft. 205
Ägypten und Cyrenaika. Vol. 1.2.
Generalstab der Luftwaffe.
Berlin 1942.

Pesce, A. 206
Gemini space photographs of Libya and Tibesti. A geological and geographical analysis. Ed. A.S. Campbell.
Tripoli: PESL 1968.

Smith, H.T.U. 207
Photo-interpretation studies of desert basins in northern Africa.
Bedford, Mass.: U.S. Air Force Cambridge Research Laboratories 1969.

Voelger, K. 208
Ermittlung sozio-ökonomischer Daten für die Stadt- und Regionalplanung durch Luftbild-Interpretation.
Bildmessung und Luftbildwesen 37. 1969, p. 141-161.

Cartography.
Historical Cartography.

Ade, L.P. 209
Mapping the Libyan Desert.
Army information digest 1962, p. 21-24.

Agostini, E. de 210
Il programma cartografico della Cirenaica. Condizioni attuali del suo sviluppo.
ACGI 11. 1930, vol. 3, p. 136-142.

Agostini, E. de 211
La cartografia nelle colonie libiche.
RdC 8. 1934, p. 445-462.

Agostini, E. de 212
Il riordinamento del programma cartografico per le colonie libiche. Condizioni attuali del suo sviluppo.
ACSC 2. 1934, vol. 3, p. 13-29.

Agostini, E. de 213
Cartografia.
SIFOG 1937, p. 645-658.

Agostini, E. de 214
La cartografia della Libia. Suo programma e suo sviluppo.
ACSC 3. 1937, vo. 5, p. 226-236.

Ball, J. 215

Note on the cartographical results
of Hassanein Bey's journey.
Geographical journal 64. 1924, p.
367-386.

Bartorelli, U. 216

Attività sperimentale e operativa
dell' IGM nel campo della triango-
lazione aerea.
Boll. geodetico 7. 1948, p. 82-89.

Belfiore, P. 217

Cartografia coloniale e impiego
della fotogrammetria.
Milano 1936.
(Pubblicazioni dell'Istituto di Topografia e Geodesia. 21.)

Bianchi, E. - Millosevich, E. 218

Determinazione delle coordinate
astronomiche di Tripoli d'Occidente.
AANL. Memorie della classe di scienze fisiche ... Ser. 5, vol. 6. 1906,
p. 205-266.

Bianchi d'Espinosa, R. 219

La cartografia della Libia.
ASIPS 25. 1936, vol. 4, p. 137-144.

Bianchi d'Espinosa, R. 220

Lavori fotogrammetrici in Libia.
ASIPS 25. 1936, vol. 4, p. 145-150.

Bracca, G. 221

I rilievi speditivi nell'Africa
italiana fra le due grandi guerre
mondiali.
Annali di ricerche e studi di geografia 1. 1945, p. 11-28.

Broughton, R.L. 222

Engineer desert rats.
Military engineer 56. 1964, p. 18-
19.

Caputo, E. 223

Cenno sui nostri lavori geodetico-
topografici nella Libia.
ASIPS 6. 1912, p. 333-351.

Caviglia, E. 224

Lavori eseguiti in Libia dall'IGM
nella primavera del 1913.
ASIPS 7. 1913, p. 81-89.

Corò, F. 225

La nuova carta della zona Zanzur-
Tripoli-Tagiura.
Oltremare 6. 1932, p. 476.

Corò, F. 226

Il servizio studi della Libia alla
VIII fiera di Tripoli.
Oltremare 8. 1934, p. 184-185.

Dardano, A. 227

Cartografia coloniale.
ACGI 10. 1927, vol. 2, p. 630-636.
RdC 1/2. 1927/28, p. 265-272.

Dardano, A. 228

Il servizio cartografico del
Ministero delle Colonie e le direttive per l'inquadramento generale dei lavori cartografici coloniali.
ACGI 11. 1930, vol. 3, p. 131-135.

Dardano, A. 229

Sviluppo e direttive della cartografia coloniale.
ACSC 1. 1931, vol. 3, p. 74-90.

Dore, P. 230

Sul rilevamento di carte topografiche coloniali.
Riv. geografica italiana 31. 1924,
p. 56-59.

Finsterwalder, R. - Hueber, E.   231

Vermessungswesen und Kartographie
in Afrika.
Berlin 1943.
(Afrika. 1.)

Franchi, N.   232

Cartografia italiana in Africa.
Africa. Roma 1951, p. 275-279,
p. 329-332.

Ghelardoni, L.   233

Relazione sui lavori di rilevamento
eseguiti per lo studio del piano
regolatore di Tripoli.
Universo 16. 1935, p. 61-67.

Hall, D.N.   234

Solitary map-maker in Libya.
Geographical magazine 39. 1966/67,
p. 861-866.

Hall, D.N.   235

A simple method of navigating in
deserts.
Geographical journal 133. 1967,
p. 192-205.

Libya survey. Army engineer   236
school notes.
Military engineer 51. 1959, p. 413.

Loperfido, A.   237

Notizie sui lavori astronomico-
geodetici eseguiti in Libia.
Riv. di artiglieria e genio 29.
1912, p. 278-298.

Loperfido, A.   238

I lavori geodetici e topografici
eseguiti dall'IGM in Asia Minore
e nelle colonie dal 1915 al 1920.
ACGI 8. 1922, vol. 2, p. 504-506.

Maio, R. di   239

Osservazioni altrimetriche.
Annali del museo libico di storia
naturale 3. 1941, p. 37-39.

Mapping in Libya. Army Map   240
Service.
Military engineer 54. 1962, p. 278.

Marinelli, O.   241

Le edizioni della carta al 50 000
della Cirenaica.
Universo 4. 1923, p. 483-490.

Masserano, G.   242

Lavori geotopografici nella Sirte.
Universo 12. 1931, p. 169-183.

Mininni, M.   243

La cartografia coloniale e l'opera
del Ministero dell'Africa Italiana.
ACGI 14. 1947, p. 213-221.

Palazzolo, F.   244

Orientamenti moderni della cartografia di tipo coloniale.
ACGI 14. 1947, p. 367-369.

Pillewizer, W. - Richter, N.   245

Beschreibung und Kartenaufnahme der
Krateroase Wau en-Namus in der zentralen Sahara.
PGM Ergänzungsheft 264. 1957, p.
303-320.

Romagna-Manoia, G.   246

Determinazioni astronomiche di coordinate geografiche in Libia ...
ACSC 1. 1931, vol. 3, p. 90-98.

Rumeau, A.   247

Topographic mapping of Africa.
A review of the natural resources
of the African continent. Paris
1963, p. 19-49.

Scalamandré, G.   248

I rilievi dell'IGM nelle colonie.
ACSC 1. 1931, vol. 3, p. 98-109.

Scarin, E.   249

Determinazioni altrimetriche rile-
vate durante un viaggio nel Fezzàn.
BSGI 72. 1935, p. 666-670.

Sheppard, T.H.   250

Desert navigation.
Geographical journal 136. 1970,
p. 235-239.

Sixtyfourth Engineer   251
Battalion (Base Topographic).
Military engineer 53. 1961, p. 380.

Tazzari, G.   252

I lavori fotogrammetrici eseguiti
dall'IGM in patria, nelle colonie
ed in Albania durante l'anno XVI
E.F.
ASIPS 27. 1938, vol. 2, p. 259-262.

Traversi, C.   253

Storia della cartografia coloniale
italiana.
Roma: IPS 1964.
(L'Italia in Africa. Serie scienti-
fico-culturale.)

Voelger, K.   254

Luftbilder und Regional-Planung in
Libyen.
Allgemeine Vermessungsnachrichten
74. 1967, p. 28-30.

Aurigemma, S.   255

A proposito di un'antica pianta di
Tripoli.
RdC 7. 1933, p. 54-57.

Aurigemma, S.   256

Vedute di Tripoli che si riferiscono
all'azione navale dei francesi nel
1685.
RdC 7. 1933, p. 537-546.

Fumagalli, G.   257

La più antica pianta di Tripoli.
Accademie e biblioteche d'Italia
1932/33, p. 28-40.

Kamal, Y.   258

Monumenta cartographica Africae et
Aegypti.
Leiden/Cairo 1926-

Monchicourt, C.   259

Essai bibliographique sur les plans
imprimés de Tripoli ... au XVIe
siècle.
Revue africaine 66. 1925, p. 385-
418.

Piri Reis kitabi bahriye.   260
Istanbul 1935.
(Türk tarihi araştırma kurumu yayın-
larından. 2.)

Der Seeatlas des Sejjid Nûh.   261
Ed. H.J. Kissling.
München: Trofenik.
1. Einleitung und Karten. 1966.

Place Names.

Agostini, E. de   262

La toponomastica nella cartografia
della Cirenaica.
ACGI 11. 1930, vol. 3, p. 239-242.

Beguinot, F.   263

Per la toponomastica coloniale.
AIn 34. 1915, p. 70.

Beguinot, F.   264

Per gli studi di toponomastica libi-
co-berbera.
ACGI 11. 1930, vol. 3, p. 243-247.

Buonomo, G.   265

I punti sugli i a proposito di toponomastica coloniale.
AIn 34. 1915, p. 71-76.

Buru, M.M.   266

"On geographical names in Libya".
United Nations conference on the
standardization of geographical names, Geneva 1967. New York 1968/69,
vol. 1.2.: passim.

Capot-Rey, R. - Cornet, A. -   267
Blaudin de Thé, B.

Glossaire des principaux termes géographiques et hydrogéologiques
sahariens.
Alger: Institut de Recherches Sahariennes 1963.

Collection and treatment of   268
geographic names in Libya.
Submitted by the government of the
U.S.A.
United Nations conference on the
standardization of geographical   1.

Collection and treatment of ... 268

names, Geneva 1967. Documents issued
during the conference.
New York: UN 1967.
(ECOSOC. Series E/Conf. 53/ L 32.)
                                    2.

Collection and treatment of   269
geographical names in Libya.
Paper presented by Libya.
United Nations conference on the
standardization of geographical names, Geneva 1967. Vol. 2. Proceedings. 1969, p. 127-128.

Directions for the treatment   270
of geographic names in Libya.
Wash.: AMS, Geographic Names Branch
1956.
(Stanag. 2208.)

Elenco dei nomi di località.   271
Fascicolo 1° annesso alla carta
della Tripolitania settentrionale
alla scala di 1:100 000.
Tripoli 1936.

Elenco di termini topografici   272
e di voci che entrano comune-
mente in uso nella toponomastica
della Cirenaica.
Bengasi 1929.

Galand, L.   273

Afrique du Nord et Sahara.
Revue internationale d'onomastique
12. 1960, p. 293-308.

Guglielmi, G.   274

Origine e remoto uso dei nomi Libia
ed Africa. 1. Libia.
Africa. Roma 25. 1970, p. 183-201.

Index gazetteer showing   275
place-names on 1:100 000 and
1:400 000 map series. Cyrenaica.
Survey Directorate, General Head-
quarters, Middle East.
Cairo 1941.

International cooperation in   276
cartography. (Standardization
of geographical names). Guatemala,
Libya, ...: draft resolution.
New York: UN 1968.
(ECOSOC. E/AC.6/L.375.)

Lewicki, T.   277
Szczątki języka romańskiego w pół-
nocno-zachodniej Afryce w epoce
arabskiej.
Biuletyn polskiego towarzystwa ję-
zykoznawczego 10. 1950, p. 158-159.

Lewicki, T.   278
Sur les vestiges d'une langue romane parlée dans l'Afrique du Nord-
ouest à l'époque arabe.
Bulletin. Centre polonais de recherches scientifiques de   1.

Lewicki, T.   278
Paris. Académie polonaise des sciences et des lettres 1951, n. 9,
p. 15.

                                   2.

Lewicki, T.   279
Une langue romane oubliée de l'Afrique du Nord.Observations d'un arabi-
sant.
Rocznik orientalistyczny 17. 1951/52,
p. 415-480.

Lewicki, T.   280
A propos du nom de l'oasis de Koufra
chez les géographes arabes du XIe
et du XIIe siècle.
Journal of African history 6. 1965,
p. 295-306.

Libya. Official standard   281
names approved by the U.S.
Board on Geographic Names.
Wash.: GPO 1958.
(U.S. Board on Geographic Names.
Gazetteer. 41.)

Mercier, G.   282
La langue libyenne et la toponymie
antique de l'Afrique du Nord.
Journal asiatique 205. 1924, p. 189-
320.

Mercier, G.   283
Quelques étymologies libyennes.
Revue africaine 84. 1940, p. 149-
153.

Moreno, M.M.   284
Toponomastica coloniale italiana.
ACGI 14. 1947, p. 473-476.

Murabet, M.   285
Sull'etimologia storica di "Libia".
Libia 1. 1953, n. 1, p. 109-112.

Nallino, C.A.   286
Norme per la trascrizione italiana e
la grafia araba dei nomi propri geo-
grafici della Tripolitania e della
Cirenaica. Ministero delle Colonie.
Roma 1915.

Pflaum, H.G.   287
Nomenclature des villes africaines
de "Lepcis magna" et "Lepti minus".
Bulletin de la societé nationale
des antiquaires de France 1959
(1961), p. 85-92.

Piel, J.M.   288
Tadeusz Lewicki: Une langue oubliée
de l'Afrique du Nord. Kraków 1953.
Romanische Forschungen 70. 1958,
p. 137-141.

Pottier, R.   289
Ghat. L'étymologie du nom de cette
oasis.
Géographie 68. 1937, p. 76-80.

Repertorio dei nomi di   290
località contenuti nella carta
dimostrativa della Cirenaica in 7
fogli alla scala 1:400 000.
Bengasi 1929.

Reyniers, F.   291
Toponymie et arpantage: un toponyme
caractéristique de l'ouest tunisien.
Revue internationale d'onomastique
12. 1960, p. 198-204.

Reyniers, F.   292

Signalisation et toponymie en Tunisie et Tripolitaine.
Revue internationale d'onomastique 13. 1961, p. 41-53, 100-102.

Romanelli, P.   293

Del nome delle due Leptis africane.
AANL. Classe di scienze morali...
Rendiconti ser. 5, vol. 33. 1924, p. 253-262.

Romanelli, P.   294

L'origine del nome "Tripolitania".
Atti della pontifica accademia romana di archeologia. Rendiconti ser. 3, vol. 9. 1933, p. 25-31.

Segert, S.   295

Some Phoenician etymologies of North African toponyms.
Oriens antiquus 5. 1966, p. 19-25.

Transliteration system for   296
Arabic geographic names, the
BGN/PCGN system. U.S. Board on Geographic Names.
Wash. 1957.

Trotter, A.   297

Le piante nella toponomastica libica.
RdT (Libya) 3. 1927, p. 237-243.

Una carta della Libia con   298
la toponomastica in lingua araba.
IdO 2. 1937, n. 14, p. 3.

Ward, P.   299

Place-names of Cyrenaica.
GANC 1968, p. 3-12.

Geography. General.

Rivista geografica italiana.   300
Firenze.
Indici del cinquantennio 1894-1943. 1952.
Indici del decennio 1944-1953. 1954.

Universo.   301
Firenze.
Indice generale, annate 1920-1960.
1965.

The Aberdeen university   302
expedition to Cyrenaica,
1951.
Scottish geographical magazine 68. 1952, p. 57-63, 110-119.
69. 1953, p. 22-32.

Agostini, E. de   303

Còmpiti ed attività dell'ufficio studi presso il governo della Cirenaica.
ACGI 10. 1927, p. 596-599.

Boxhall, P.   304

Way to the Murzuk sand sea. Geographical surveys in the Libyan desert.
Geographical magazine 41. 1968, p. 120-124.

Capot-Rey, R.   305

L'activité géographique d'une unité française au Fezzân.
BLS 2. 1951, n. 7, p. 6-9.

Cipriani, L.   306

Esplorazioni scientifiche nel Fezzan.
Universo 14. 1933, p. 761-778.

Cipriani, L.   307

Relazione preliminare delle ricerche
eseguite nel Fezzan dalla Società
Geografica Italiana.
BSGI 70. 1933, p. 398-410.

Cipriani, L.   308

Una missione scientifica italiana
nel Fezzan.
Vie d'Italia 39. 1933, p. 679-691.

Clarke, J.I.   309

Geographical studies of Libya.
Cahiers de Tunisie 7. 1959, p. 475-
480.

Cufra. Le esplorazioni ed i   310
viaggi.
Oltremare 5. 1931, p. 100-104.

Fantoli, A.   311

Il deserto.
Vie d'Italia 48. 1941, p. 482-487.

Galli, F.   312

Sulle finalità dei viaggi aerei di
esplorazione coloniale con particolare riguardo alle nostre colonie.
ACGI 10. 1927, p. 600-603.

Kanter, H.   313

Dreissig Jahre Forschungsreisen in
Libyen.
Deutsche Hochschullehrer-Zeitung
11. 1963, n. 1/2, p. 8-16, n. 3,
p. 23-28, n. 4, p. 14-19.

Meckelein, W.   314

Die Sahara-Forschungsfahrt 1954/55
der Gesellschaft für Erdkunde zu
Berlin. Vorläufiger Expeditionsbe-
richt.
Erde 7. 1955, p. 312-319.

Meckelein, W.   315

Eine Sahara-Expedition.
Afrika heute 1. 1957, p. 124-130.

Meckelein, W.   316

Une mission scientifique allemande
en Libye.
TIRS 16. 1957, p. 213-216.

Migliorini, E.   317

Nuovi contributi alla conoscenza
della Libia interna.
Riv. geografica italiana 66. 1959,
p. 173-177.

Migliorini, E.   318

L'esplorazione del Sahara.
Torino: UTET 1961.
(La conquista della terra. 6.)

Monod, T.   319

Orientation bibliographique sur le
sud-est du désert libyque (triangle
Uweinat-Erdis-Merga).
Fort Lamy: Institut National Tcha-
dien pour les Sciences Humaines 1967.

Monod, T.   320

Les bases d'une division géographique du domaine saharien.
Bulletin de l'IFAN sér.B, 30. 1968,
p. 269-288.

Monterin, U.   321

Relazione delle ricerche compiute
dalla missione della R. Società Geografica Italiana nel Sahara libico e
nel Tibesti (Febbr.-apr. 1934).
BSGI 72. 1935, p. 115-162.

Monterin, U.   322

L'esplorazione del Tibesti settentrionale e delle zone confinarie
del sud libico.
ASIPS 25. 1936, vol. 4, p. 113-130.

Mori, A.   323

Storia dell'esplorazione.
SIFOG 1937, p. 15-37.

Palieri, M. - Crema, C.   324

Esplorazioni in Libia.
Oltremare 7. 1933, p. 336-340, 452-
453.

Parona, C.F.   325

Il Gebel tripolitano e la sua fronte
sulla Gefara.
RdT 2. 1925/26, p. 307-320.

Perona, R.   326

I progressi nelle conoscenze del
deserto libico dall'occupazione italiana ad oggi.
AIr 1941-42, n. 37, p. 91-95.

Pesce, E.   327

Exploration of the Fezzan.
GAPSF 1969, p. 53-65.

Pesenti, G.   328

Alcune notizie sugli esploratori del
Fezzan e sulla sua storia fino ai
giorni nostri.
BSGI 54. 1917, p. 714-724.

Pfalz, R.   329

Landeskundliche Hauptprobleme Tripolitaniens.
PGM 75. 1929, p. 127-132.

Pfalz, R.   330

Zwei Jahrzehnte Libyen.
Geographischer Anzeiger 43. 1942,
p. 459-467.

Piccioli, A.   331

L'attività dell'ufficio studi e propaganda della Tripolitania.
ACGI 10. 1927, p. 604-608.

Rellini, G.   332

Con la spedizione Miani nel Fezzàn.
BSGI 64. 1927, p. 260-285, 383-412,
497-557.

Riccardi, R.   333

Il contributo degli italiani alla
conoscenza dell'Africa mediterranea.
Italia e Africa mediterranea. Firenze 1942, p. 45-84.

Richter, N.B.   334

Zum Beitrag der deutschen Wissenschaft an der Erforschung der zentralen Sahara.
Forschungen und Fortschritte 30.
1956, p. 353-360.

Richter, N.B.   335

Vorläufiger Bericht über Verlauf
und Ergebnisse der deutschen Sahara-Expedition 1958.
PGM 103. 1959, p. 100-106.

Richter, N.B.   336

Die vier Stadien der Wüstenforschun-
gen in Libyen.
Erde 91. 1960, p. 165-177.

Savoia, A. di   337

La Libia interna e le esplorazioni
della R. Società Geografica Italiana.
ASIPS 25. 1936, vol. 4, p. 101-111.

Scarin, E.   338

Esplorazioni e ricerche geografiche
e topografiche effettuate in Libia
nel secolo XX.
Annali di ricerche e studi di geografia 2. 1947, p. 45-61.

Schiffers, H.   339

Hundert Jahre Sahara-Forschung.
PGM 94. 1950, p. 41-42.

Schiffers, H.   340

Begriff, Grenze und Gliederung der
Sahara.
PGM 95. 1951, p. 239-246.

Schiffers, H.   341

Forschungsergebnisse aus der Sahara.
Geographische Rundschau 12. 1960,
p. 411-414.

Schiffers, H.   342

Neuere Feldforschung in der Sahara.
PGM 104. 1960, p. 1-22.

Schiffers, H.   343

Neuere Literatur aus Afrika.
Erdkunde 16. 1962, p. 132-146.

Schiffers, H.   344

Neuere Forschungen in der Sahara.
Naturwissenschaftliche Rundschau
21. 1968, p. 365-373.

Visintin, L.   345

La Libia: cenni geografici generali.
L'impero coloniale fascista. Novara
1936, p. 363-374.

Weis, H.   346

Libyen - Land mit zwei Gesichtern.
Neuere Feldforschung in der libyschen Sahara.
Österreichische Hochschulzeitung
15. 1963, n. 20, p. 9-10.

Weis, H.   347

Die Wüste erwacht - 100 Jahre Sahara-
forschung.
Bustan 9. 1968, p. 27-40.

Zoli, C.   348

L'esplorazione del Sahara.
AIn 52. 1934, p. 137-161.

Geography. Regional.

Aagesen, A.   349

Libyen.
Kulturgeografi 1963, n. 82, p. 265-
274.

Afrika.   350
Mannheim: Bibliographisches
Institut 1968.
(Meyers Kontinente und Meere.)

Agostini, E. de   351

Taluni principali caratteri geografici della zona di Cufra.
ACSC 1. 1931, vol. 3, p. 117-128.

Agostini, E. de   352

El-Auenât chiave del deserto libico.
RdC 8. 1934, p. 807-823.

Agostini, E. de   353

Aspetti geografici del Sahara libico.
AIr 2. 1939, n. 1, p. 5-11.

Ahlmann, H.W.   354

Norra Libia.
Ymer 49. 1929, p. 153-184.

Almagia, R.   355

La Cirenaica. Il paese ed i suoi
aspetti nel passato e nel presente.
BSGI 49. 1912, p. 479-504.

Almagia, R.   356

Nuove conoscenze intorno alla Cirenaica.
BSGI 52. 1915, p. 298-308.

Amato, A.   357

"Gebèl es-Soda".
Oltremare 6. 1932, p. 511-512.

Amato, A.   358

Nel Fezzan.
Oltermare 6. 1932, p. 351-353.

Aroca, A.   359

Uau el Chebir, l'oasi della reden-
zione.
Milano 1942.
(Collezione scientifica e documen-
 taria dell'Africa italiana. 7.)

Awad, H.   360

Le Gilf-el-Kébir et l'Ouénat.
Bulletin de la société de géographie
d'Egypte 22. 1947-48, p. 137-150.

Brehony, J.A.N.   361

A geographical study of the Jebel
Tarhuna, Tripolitania. Vol. 1.2.
Durham: Dept. of Geography 1961.
Diss.

Buru, M.M.   362

El-Marj plain (Libya). A geographi-
cal study.
Durham: Dept. of Geography 1965.
Diss.

Carnevale, S.   363

La Msellata.
Tripoli 1935.

Clarke, J.I.   364

The Sahara. Libya.
Africa and the islands. By R.J.H.
Church ... London 1965, p. 133-152.

Cauneille, A.   365

La Libye.
Géographie universelle Larousse.
Vol. 2. 1959, p. 49-52.

Clayton, P.A.   366

The western side of the Gilf Kebir.
Geographical journal 81. 1933,
p. 254-259.

Desio, A.   367

Uau en-Namus.
Vie d'Italia 42. 1936, p. 572-580.

Despois, J.   368

Géographie du Fezzân.
TIRS 3. 1945, p. 178-181.

Despois, J.   369

Le Fezzân.
Encyclopédie coloniale et maritime.
Algérie et Sahara. Vol. 2. 1948,
p. 355-364.

Despois, J.   370
Barka. Fazzān (Fezzān).
EIne.

Fisher, W.B.   371
The Aberdeen university expedition
to Cyrenaica, 1951. Part 1.
Scottish geographical magazine 68.
1952, p. 57-63.

Fisher, W.B. - Fraser, I.R. - 372
Ross, D.W.
The Aberdeen university expedition
to Cyrenaica, 1951. Part 3.
Scottish geographical magazine 69.
1953, p. 22-32.

Fisher, W.B.   373
The Middle East. 5th ed.
London: Methuen 1963.

Gotev, G.   374
Libija.
Sofia: Izdatelstvo na Natsionalniya
S'vet na Otechestveniya Front 1965.
(Poreditsa pred novata karta na
 sveta. 9.)

Grothe, H.   375
Libyen und die italienischen Kraft-
felder in Nordafrika.
Leipzig/Berlin 1941.

Hajjaji, S.A.   376
The new Libya. A geographical, social, economic and political study.
Tripoli: Government Printing Press
1967.

Hance, W.A.   377
The geography of modern Africa.
New York: Columbia UP 1965.

Heger, R.   378
Der Fezzan: ein Reisebericht.
Geographische Wochenschrift 1935,
p. 689-696.

Jany, E.   379
Salma Kebir, Kufra, Djabal al-Uwe-
nat: ein Reisebericht aus der östlichen Sahara.
Erde 94. 1963, p. 334-362.

Jongmans, D.G.   380
Libie, land van de dorst.
Meppel: Boom 1964.
(Terra-Bibliotheek.)

Kanter, H.   381
Libyen.
Westermann Lexikon der Geographie.
Braunschweig: Westermann 1968-

Karasapan, C.T.   382
Libya. Trablus-garb, Bingazi ve
Fizan.
Ankara 1960.

Khuga, M.A.   383
The Jebel Garian in Tripolitania.
Durham: Dept. of Geography 1960.
Diss.

Kiker, D.   384
Libya.
Atlantic monthly 225. 1970, n. 6,
p. 30-39.

Koegel, L.   385
Libyen, mit besonderer Beleuchtung
des tripolitanischen Djebel.
Zeitschrift für Erdkunde 1941,
p. 9-12, 278-297.

Lefranc, J.P. 386

De Zouila aux lacs de la Marzoukia.
TIRS 15. 1957, p. 89-109.

Le Houerou, H.N. - Martel, A. 387

De Ghadâmes à Ghât. Notes et im-
pressions de mission (mars 1964).
TIRS 24. 1965, p. 191-204.

MacLachlan, K.S. 388

A geographical study of the coastal
zone between Homs and Misurata, Tripolitania. Vol. 1-4.
Durham: Dept. of Geography 1961.
Diss.

Martel, A. 389

Les confins saharo-tripolitaine de
la Tunisie (1881-1911). Vol. 1.2.
Paris: PUF 1965.
(Publications de l'université de
 Tunis. Sér.4,5.)

Marthelot, P. 390

Libye 1965.
Acta geographica 1966, n. 64, p. 2-8.

Mazzarelli, G. 391

Il golfo di Bomba e le regioni adia-
centi.
Messina 1930.
(Memorie dell'istituto di geografia
 dell'università di Messina. 2.)

Meckelein, W. 392

Der Fezzan heute.
Stuttgarter geographische Studien
69. 1957, p. 325-336.

Meigs, P. 393

Outlook for arid North Africa: the
Sahara.
Focus 5. 1954, n. 4, p. 1-6.

Meigs, P. 394

Geography of coastal deserts.
Paris: UNESCO 1966.
(Arid zone research. 28.)

Mensching, H. 395

Nordafrika.
Die grosse illustrierte Länderkunde. Gütersloh: Bertelsmann.
Vol. 2. 1965,
col. 87-209.

Migliorini, E. 396

L'Africa.
Torino: UTET 1955.

Migliorini, E. 397

Il territorio (Libia).
Il territorio e le popolazioni.
Roma: IPS 1955, p. 77-116.

Mil-Geo Beschreibung von 398
Libyen.
Berlin 1941.

Monterin, U. 399

Attraverso il deserto libico fino
al Tibesti.
Universo 16. 1935, p. 803-843.

Pace, B. 400

Civiltà italiana nel Sahara.
AIr 2. 1939, n. 1, p. 1-4.

Peel, R.F. 401

The sands of Libya.
Scottish geographical magazine 57.
1941, p. 103-108.

Peel, R.F.   402

The landscape in aridity.
Transactions. Institute of British
geographers 1966, n. 38, p. 1-23.

Richter, N.B.   403

Wau en Namus - eine Vulkan-Oase im
Herzen der Sahara.
Naturwissenschaftliche Rundschau
3. 1950, p. 32-37.

Richter, N.B.   404

Haurudsch - Terra incognita.
Naturwissenschaftliche Rundschau
6. 1953, p. 111-115.

Richter, N.B.   405

Wau en Namus - die Mücken-Oase.
Wissenschaft und Fortschritt 8. 1958,
p. 265-267.

Savoia Aosta, A. di   406

Fezzan e Cufra.
ACSC 1. 1931, vol. 3, p. 7-12.

Scarin, E.   407

Un'escursione nel Fezzan meridionale
(Um-el-Araneb-Tummo).
Universo 14. 1933, p. 711-725.

Scarin, E.   408

Alcune osservazioni sulla Sirtica.
Universo 15. 1934, p. 316-318.

Scarin, E.   409

Il Fezzan.
Universo 16. 1935, p. 387-403.

Schiffers, H.   410

Die Sahara und die Syrtenländer.
Stuttgart: Franckh 1950.
(Kleine Länderkunden.)

Schiffers, H.   411

Die Sahara gestern und morgen. Rück-
blick, Gegenwarts-Analysen und Aus-
blick.
Geographische Rundschau 10. 1958,
p. 441-452.

Schiffers, H.   412

Libyen und die Sahara. 2nd ed.
Bonn: Schröder 1962.
(Die Länder Afrikas. 6.)

Schiffers, H. - Weis, H.   413

Nordafrika.(Afrika. 8th ed.)
München: List 1967.
(Harms Handbuch der Erdkunde. 5.)

Shaw, W.B.K.   414

The mountain of Uweinat.
Antiquity 8. 1934, p. 63-72.

Shaw, W.B.K.   415

An expedition in the southern
Libyan desert.
Geographical journal 87. 1936,
p. 193-221.

Voelger, K.   416

The geographic subregions of the
Jabal al Akhdar in aerial photo-
graphs.
GANC 1968, p. 173-181.

Walton, K.   417

The Aberdeen university expedition
to Cyrenaica, 1951. Part 2.
The oasis of Jalo.
Scottish geographical magazine 68.
1952, p. 110-119.

Weis, H.   418

Erwachtes Libyen. Land der Gegen-
sätze, Staat der Zukunft.
Universum - Natur und Technik 12.
1957, p. 609-615.

Weis, H.   419

Harudsch - Terra incognita.
Universum - Natur und Technik 12.
1957, p. 649-654.

Weis, H.   420

Einsame Wüsteninsel Wau el Kebir.
Universum - Natur und Technik 13.
1958, p. 65-70.

Weis, H.   421

Kundfahrt in die "Schwarzen Berge"
Libyens.
Österreichische Hochschulzeitung
10. 1958, 15. 4., p. 1, 4.

Weis, H.   422

Beitrag zur Kulturgeographie des
Fessan und der östlichen Zentralsahara.
Mitteilungen der österreichischen
geographischen Gesellschaft 103.
1961, p. 25-47.

Geography. Historical.

Astuto, R.   423

Congiungere Tripolitania e Cirenaica.
Oltremare 2. 1928, p. 11-14.

Barth, H.   424

Travels and discoveries in North and
Central Africa... Centenary ed.
London: Cass 1965. Repr.

Beguinot, F.   425

Sugli Atarantes di Erodoto e sul
nome berbero del Grande Atlante.
Mémorial Henri Basset. Vol. 1. 1928,
p. 29-42.

El-Bekri, A.O.A.   426

Description de l'Afrique septentrionale.
Paris: Maisonneuve 1965. Repr.

Boahen, A.A.   427

Britain, the Sahara, and the western
Sudan 1788-1861.
Oxford: Clarendon Press 1964.

Bono, S.   428

Il viaggio da Tripoli alla Cirenaica
del ligure Paolo della Cella.
Italiani nel mondo 23. 1967, 25.11.,
p. 15-17.

Bono, S.   429

La Libia nella descrizione di Paolo
della Cella.
Levante 16. 1969, n. 1-2, p. 31-40.

Borchardt, P.   430

Neue Erkundungen alter Strassen und
Oasen in der Libyschen Wüste.
Mitteilungen aus den deutschen
Schutzgebieten 29. 1916, p. 31-35.

Borchardt, P.   431

Die grossen Ost-West-Karawanen-
strassen durch die Libysche Wüste.
PGM 70. 1924, p. 219-223.

Borchardt, P.   432

Neue Beiträge zur alten Geographie
Nordafrikas und zur Atlantisfrage.
Zeitschrift der Gesellschaft für
Erdkunde zu Berlin 1927, p. 197-216.

Borchardt, P.   433
Platos Insel Atlantis.
PGM 73. 1927, p. 19-32.

Borchardt, P.   434
Oasen und Wege der südlichen Liby-
schen Wüste.
PGM 75. 1929, p. 302-306.

The Bornu mission 1822-   435
1825. Part 1-3.
Cambridge UP 1966.
(Missions to the Niger. 2.3.4.)

Bovill, E.W.   436
The Niger explored.
London: Oxford UP 1968.

Canard, M.   437
Une description de la côte barba-
resque au XVIIIe siècle par un
officier de marine russe.
Revue africaine 95. 1951, p. 121-
186.

Caracciolo, I.   438
La costa sirtica e cirenaica secon-
do gli antichi geografi.
Geopolitica 1. 1939, p. 437-439.

Cauneille, A.   439
Note sur l'assassin de Mlle Tinné.
BLS 4. 1953, n. 14, p. 50-53.

Denham, D. - Clapperton, H. -   440
Oudney, W.
Narrative of travels and discoveries
in Northern and Central Africa in
the years 1822, 1823 and 1824.
Cambridge UP 1966. Repr.

Despois, J. - Schiffers, H. -   441
Klein-Franke, F.
Souvenirs de H. Barth (1821-1865).
Acta geographica 1967, n. 69/70,
p. 1-41.

Eggink, C.   442
De merkwaardige reizen van Henriette
en Alexandrine Tinne.
Amsterdam: Meulenhoff 1960.

Ferri, S.   443
Testi geografici antichi relativi
alla Cirenaica.
Bengasi 1924.

Forbiger, A.   444
Handbuch der alten Geographie, aus
den Quellen bearbeitet.
Graz: Akademische Druck- und Ver-
lagsanstalt 1967. Repr.

Fruehe Wege zum Herzen   445
Afrikas. 7 Biographien.
Ed. K. Schleucher.
Darmstadt: Turris 1969.
(Deutsche unter anderen Völkern.)

Furon, R.   446
L'amitié de deux princes sahariens:
Henri Barth et Henri Duveyrier.
HBFA 1967, p. 184-193.

Gladstone, P.   447
Travels of A. Tinne, 1835-1869.
London: Murray 1970.

Grosso, M.   448
Una donna nel Fezzàn.
RdC 4. 1930, p. 61-67.

Hallett, R.   449

The penetration of Africa. Euro-
pean exploration in North and West
Africa to 1815.
New York: Praeger 1965.

Heinrich Barth. Ein Forscher   450
in Afrika. Leben-Werk-Leistung.
Ed. H. Schiffers.
Wiesbaden: Steiner 1967.

Hoenerbach, W.   451

Das nordafrikanische Itinerar des
'Abdari vom Jahre 688/1289.
Leipzig 1940.
(Abhandlungen für die Kunde des
Morgenlandes. 25,4.)

Ibn Hauqal   452

Configuration de la terre (Kitab
surat al-ard). Vol. 1.2.
Paris: Maisonneuve 1964. Repr.

The journal of Friedrich   453
Hornemann's travels from
Cairo to Murzuk in the years 1797-
1798.
Cambridge UP 1964. Repr.
(Missions to the Niger. 1.)

Leo Africanus   454

Description de l'Afrique.Vol. 1.2.
Paris: Maisonneuve 1956-57.

Leo Africanus   455

The history and description of Africa
and of the notable things therein
contained. Vol. 1-3.
New York: Franklin 1963. Repr.

The letters of major   456
Alexander Gordon Laing 1824-26.
Cambridge UP 1964. Repr.
(Missions to the Niger. 1.)

Leva, A.E.   457

Tripoli in una descrizione di cent'
anni fa.
Africa. Roma 22. 1967, p. 73-83.

Lewicki, T.   458

Sur l'oasis de Sbru (Dbr, Shbru) des
géographes arabes.
Revue africaine 83. 1939, p. 45-64.

Lyon, G.F.   459

A narrative of travels in Northern
Africa in the years 1818-1819 and
1820.
London: Cass 1966. Repr.

Mannert, K.   460

Geographie der Griechen und Römer.
Vol. 10, 1.2.: Afrika.
Nürnberg 1825.

Micacchi, R.   461

Le straordinarie avventure di Domin-
go Badia y Leblich e il suo soggior-
no a Tripoli di Barberia nell'inver-
no 1805-1806.
RdC 7. 1933, p. 617-642, 703-719.

Miller, K.   462

Itineraria romana. Römische Reise-
wege an der Hand der Tabula Peutin-
geriana dargestellt.
Roma: L'Erma di Bretschneider 1964.
Repr.

Missions to the Niger.   463
Ed. E.W. Bovill. Vol. 1-4.
Cambridge UP 1964-66.
(Works issued by the Hakluyt Society.
Ser. 2, 123. 128-130.)

Monchicourt, C. - Grand-   464
champ, P.

Lanfreducci et Bosio. Costa e discorsi di Barberia.
Revue africaine 66. 1925, p. 419-549.

Mueller, K.   465

Geographi graeci minores. Vol. 1-3.
Hildesheim: Olms 1965. Repr.

Nachtigal, G.   466

Sahara und Sudan: Ergebnisse sechs-
jähriger Reisen in Afrika. Vol. 1-
3.
Graz: Akademische Druck- und Ver-
lagsanstalt 1967. Repr.

Pareti, L.   467

Il giardino delle Esperidi e lo
Pseudo Scilace. Considerazioni.
Riv. geografica italiana 25. 1918,
p. 195-199.

Plott, A.   468

Literatur von und über Dr. Heinrich
Barth.
HBFA 1967, p. 491-499.

Proceedings of the association 469
for promoting the discovery
of the interior parts of Africa.
Introduction by R. Hallett. Vol.1.2.
London: Dawson 1967. Repr.

Prothero, R.M.   470

Barth and the British.
HBFA 1967, p. 164-183.

Rebuffat, R.   471

Routes d'Egypte de la Libye inté-
rieure.
Studi magrebini 3. 1970, p. 1-20.

Records of the African   472
association 1788-1831.
Ed. R. Hallett.
London: Nelson 1964.

Lord Rennell of Rodd   473

A memoir of Heinrich Barth.
HBFA 1967, p. 216-223.

Richardson, J.   474

Travels in the great desert of Saha-
ra in the years of 1845 to 1846.
Vol. 1.2.
London: Cass 1970. Repr.

Richardson, J.   475

Narrative of a mission to Central
Africa, performed in the years
1850-1851. Vol. 1.2.
London: Cass 1970. Repr.

Riese, A.   476

Geographi latini minores.
Hildesheim: Olms 1964.

Romanelli, P.   477

Strade della Libia romana.
AIr 2. 1939, n. 12, p. 25-28.

Ruggieri, R.   478

Manfredo Camperio.
RdC 6. 1932, p. 931-948.

Scarin, E.   479

Le comunicazioni dell'Africa settentrionale.
Universo 16. 1935, p. 323-326.

Schiffers, H.   480

Die deutsche Sahara-Sudan-Forschung
und die koloniale Aufteilung Nordafrikas.
Koloniale Rundschau 27. 1936, p.177-
186.

Schiffers, H.   481

Heinrich Barth-ein Forscher in Afrika. Gedanken zur Erinnerung an sei-
nen 100. Todestag.
Geographische Rundschau 17. 1965,
p. 435-443.

Schiffers, H.   482

"Heinrich Barth".
HBFA 1967, passim.

Schubarth, K.   483

Ethnographische Berichte über die
Sahara im Kitab al-masalik wa'l-ma-
malik des 'Abdallah Ibn-'Abd-al-
'Aziz al-Bakri.
Mitteilungen des Instituts für   1.

Schubarth, K.   483
Orientforschung 10. 1964, p. 109-122.

                                 2.

Schubarth-Engelschall, K.   484

Arabische Berichte muslimischer Rei-
sender und Geographen des Mittel-
alters über die Völker der Sahara.
Berlin: Akademie-Verlag 1967.

Soelken, H.   485

Wangara. Afrikanistische Betrachtun-
gen zur alten Geographie des Sudan.
Frankfurter geographische Hefte
37. 1961, p. 201-225.

Toschi, P.   486

Fonti inedite di storia della Tripolitania. Il "Voyage to the Straits"
di Augusto Holsteyn.
AION 2. 1930, p. 47-91, 3. 1931,
p. 3-49.

Miss Tully   487

Letters written during a ten year's
residence at the Court of Tripoli.
Ed. S. Dearden.
London: Barker 1957. Repr.

Weis, H.   488

Tripolis, das Tor zur Sahara.
Bustan 6. 1965, n. 4, p. 33-40.

Weis, H.   489

Die Bornustrasse - der Weg in das
Herz Afrikas.
HBFA 1967, p. 421-490.

Zur Atlantisfrage.   490

PGM 73. 1927, p. 143-152, 280-293,
326-343.

Travel.

Bargagli Petrucci, O.   491

Nel Fezzan (aprile-maggio 1932).
Firenze 1934.

Bary, E. de   492

Ghadames Ghadames.
München: Ehrenwirth 1961.

Bary, E. de   493

Struktur und Funktion der südwest-
libyschen Oasen.
Entwicklungsländer 3. 1961, p. 183-
187.

Bary, E. de   494

Im Oasenkreis.
München: Ehrenwirth 1963.

Berenson, B.   495

The passionate sightseer: from the
diaries, 1947-1956.
London: Thames and Hudson 1960.

Bittrich, F.O.   496

Ägypten und Libyen.
Berlin: Safari-Verlag 1953.

Bonneuil, M.E. de   497

Dans le désert de Libye. Du royaume
des Garamantes à Koufra.
La Géographie 61. 1934, p. 34-48.

Brandi, C.   498

Città del deserto.
Milano/Verona: Mondadori 1958.
(Le scie.)

Brodrick, A.H.   499

Mirage of Africa.
London: Hutchinson 1953.

Carrara, F.   500

Il Fezzan.
Tripoli 1929.

Castellanza, I. da   501

Orizzonti d'oltremare.
Torino 1940.

Cesari, C.   502

I nostri precursori coloniali.
Roma 1928.

Chistov, A.A.   503

Po Tunisu i Livii.
Moskva: Nauka 1966.

Corò, F.   504

La via del sud.
Tripoli 1930.

Cury, A.R.   505

Through Libya from border to border.
Cairo 1941.

Desana, D.   506

The White Squadron.
London: Hale 1961.

Diolé, P.   507

Le plus beau désert du monde.
The most beautiful desert of all.
Paris: Michel 1955.
London: Cape 1959.

Diolé, P.   508

Dans le Fezzan inconnu.
Paris: Michel 1956.

Esch, H.J. van der   509

Weenak - die Karawane ruft.
Leipzig 1941.

Fidel, C.   510

L'évolution du problème libyen. Im-
pressions du voyage.
Afrique française 32. 1922, p. 536-
542.

Furlonge, G.   511

The lands of Barbary.
London: Murray 1966.

Gabbrielli, D.   512

Sguardi sulla Libia dall'aeroplano.
Vol. 1. Tripolitania.
Tripoli 1939.

Gaudio, A.   513

La via del Sahara.
Universo 48. 1968, p. 29-68, 241-
266, 881-912.

Gerstner, H.   514

Mit Helge südwärts. Roman einer Reise. 3rd ed.
München 1942.

Gori, F.   515

Cammini del sud.
Milano 1939.

Hamilton, N.   516

Tripolitania the timeless.
African world 1964, June, p. 8-9.

Henze, A.   517

Deutsche Entwicklungshilfe im Maghreb. Eindrücke von einer Reise
durch Marokko, Algerien, Tunesien
und Libyen.
Herrenalb: Erdmann 1965.

Heseltine, N.   518

From Libyan sands to Chad.
London: Museum Press 1959.

Holmboe, K.   519

Ørkenen braender. Oplevelser blandt
Saharas og Libyens beduiner. 2nd ed.
København: Borgen 1956.

Loeben, W. von   520

Libyen, Entwicklungsland auf eige-
nen Füssen - Eindrücke einer Reise.
Afrika heute 1968, n. 6, p. 81-85.

Ludwig, H.   521

Moscheen, Zelte, Karawanen. Eindrücke einer Exkursion durch Tunesien und Libyen.
Giessen/Basel: Brunnen 1966.

Maffei, M.   522

Lo sbocco atlantico della Libia.
Dal "mare nostrum" al Golfo di
Guinea.
Vie del mondo 9. 1941, p. 219-227.

Magliocco, V.   523

Dall'Italia alle rive della Sirte.
Milano: Nuove edizioni d'Italia
1957.

Maugham, R.   524

North African notebook.
London: Chapman & Hall 1948.
New York: Harcourt, Brace 1949.

Monmarche, M.   525

Une semaine en Tripolitaine.
La Géographie 58. 1932, p. 121-142.

Mueller, J.H.   526

Libyen. Glut, Wind, Wüstensand.
Olten: Walter 1942.

Neher, K.   527

Nordafrika findet keinen Frieden.
Bericht einer Reise durch die ehe-
maligen Kampfgebiete des Deutschen
Afrikakorps.
München: Knorr und Hirth 1953.

Orlando, C.   528

In Tripolitania con il Touring.
Vie d'Italia 62. 1956, p. 189-196.

Petragnani, E.   529

Quatre ans de captivité au Fezzân.
Renseignements coloniaux 1922, p. 85-
94.

Pfalz, R.   530

Bei Faschisten und Senussi. Mussoli-
nis Kolonialpolitik in der Cyrenaika.
Leipzig 1933.

Pomeroy, M. - Collins, C.   531

The great Saharan mouse-hunt.
London: Hutchinson 1962.

Rava, C.E.   532

Viaggio a Tunin.
Bologna 1932.

Rava, C.E.   533

Ai margine del Sahara.
Bologna 1936.

Reisch, M.   534

Auf nach Afrika!
Wien: Ullstein 1957.
(Bunte leuchtende Welt.)

Reisch, M.   535

Mausefalle Afrika.
Neckargemünd: Vowinckel 1962.
(Im Blick zurück. 13.)

Richter, L.   536

Inseln der Sahara.
Islands of the Sahara.
Leipzig: Brockhaus 1957.
Leipzig: Edition Leipzig 1960.

Richter, N.B.   537

Auf dem Wege zur schwarzen Oase.
Leipzig: Brockhaus 1958.

Richter, N.B. - Richter, L.   538

Libyen. Libya.
Heidelberg: Keyser 1960.

Rossi, P. - Edelstein, S.   539

Libye.
Lausanne: Editions Rencontre 1965.
(Atlas des voyages. 35.)

Sahara.   540

Ed. C. Krüger.
Wien: Schroll 1967.

Sanz y Diaz, J.   541

Viaje a Libia.
Africa. Madrid 22. 1965, p. 247-
250.

Schiffers, H.   542

Die grosse Reise. Dr. Heinrich
Barths Forschungen und Abenteuer
1850-1855.
Minden: Köhler 1952.

Schiffers, H.   543

Wen die Wüste ruft. Abenteuer in
Afrika.
München: Ehrenwirth 1955.

Schiffers, H.   544

Wilder Erdteil Afrika.
Bonn: Athenäum 1962.

Schmidt, F.   545

Wie ich Libyen sah.
Zeitschrift für Veterinärkunde 1942,
p. 210-218.

Scortecci, G.   546

Sahara.
Milano: Hoepli 1945.

Siciliani, D.   547

Paesaggi libici.
Tripoli 1930.

Siciliani, D.   548

Il Fezzàn nella visione di coloro
che lo hanno occupato.
RdC 7. 1933, p. 371-379.

Slouschz, N.   549

Travels in North Africa.
Phliladelphia 1927.

Slouschz, N.   550

Masa'ai Be-Eretz Luv.
Tel Aviv 1937.

Stevens, J.   551

The Sahara is yours: a handbook for
desert travellers.
London: Constable 1969.

Tadema-Sporry, J.   552

Gelukkig Libië. Libia felix.
Amsterdam: Elsevier 1956.

Thwaite, A.   553

The deserts of Hesperides: an expe-
rience of Libya.
London: Secker and Warburg 1969.
New York: Roy Publ. 1969.

Toy, B.   554

A fool on wheels, Tangier to Baghdad
by land-rover.
London: Murray 1955.

Toy, B.   555

The way of the chariots, Niger river-
Sahara-Libya.
London: Murray 1964.

Tratz, E.P.   556

Quer durch Libyen und die Sahara.
Salzburg 1933.
(Die Welt. 11.)

Travel in the Libyan desert: 557
information and regulations.
Tripoli: Esso Standard Libya, Inc.
1958.

Tumiati, D.   558

Nell'Africa romana. Tripolitania.
Milano 1928.

Tuninetti, D.M.   559

Il mistero di Cufra.
Bengasi 1931.

Tuninetti, D.M.   560

Alla scoperta della Cirenaica.
Roma 1935.

Verdat, M.   561

Dans le désert tripolitain.
Géographie 57. 1932, p. 95-118,
183-206.

Vergani, O.   562

Riva africana.
Milano 1937.

Vietta, E.   563

Romantische Cyrenaika. Dichtung
einer Reise.
Hamburg 1941.

Ward, E.   564

Sahara story.
London: Hale 1962.

Weis, H.   565

Der Fezzan - das Vorfeld des Impe-
riums.
Österreichische Hochschulzeitung
8. 1956, n. 12, p. 1-2.

Wellard, J.   566

Desert rescue (Libya) R.A.F.
Geographical magazine 38. 1965/66,
p. 830-841.

Wellington, F.C.   567

The gateway to the Sahara. Observations and experiences in Tripoli.
London 1929.

Werner, B.E.   568

Zwischen den Kriegen. Abendländische
Reisen (Libyen).
Leipzig 1940.

Wian, G.   569

La Libia vista da un italiano di
Tunisi.
RdC 15. 1941, p. 57-65.

Wimmer, H.   570

Unvergessenes Nordafrika. Auf Rom-
mels Spuren. Ein Bildwerk.
Karlsruhe: Braun 1959.

Wohlfahrt, E.   571

Libyen - brennende Wüste.
Berlin: Safari 1970.

Prehistory.

Arkell, A.J.   572

Preliminary report on the archaeological results of the British Ennedi
expedition 1957.
Kush 7. 1959, p. 15-26.

Arkell, A.J. - Cornwall, J.W. - 573
Mori, F.

Analisi degli anelli componenti la
collana della mummia infantile di
Uan Muhuggiag.
Riv. di antropologia 48. 1961,
p. 161-166.

Arkell, A.J.   574

The petroglyphs of Wadi Zirmei in
north-eastern Tibesti.
Actes du congrès panafricain de préhistoire et de l'étude du quaternaire 4. 1962, sect. 3, p. 391-394.

Arkell, A.J.   575

Wanyanga and an archaeological reconnaissance of the south-west Libyan
Desert. The British Ennedi expedition, 1957.
London: Oxford UP 1964.

Baramki, D.C.   576

Rupestrian art of Libya.
American University of Beirut festi-
val book (Festschrift). Ed. F. Sar-
rûf and S. Tamim. Beirut 1967,
p. 19-32.

Battaglia, R.   577

Su qualche selce lavorata della
Gefára.
Atti della accademia scientifica ve-
neto-trentino-istriana ser. 3, vol.
16. 1925, p. 108-118.

Battaglia, R.   578

Iscrizioni e graffiti rupestri della
Libia.
RdC 1/2. 1927/28, p. 407-421.

Battaglia, R.   579

Selci preistoriche scoperte in Cirenaica.
RdC 4. 1930, p. 788-800.

Bellair, P. - Pauphilet, D.   580

L'âge des tombes préislamiques de
Tejerhi (Fezzân).
TIRS 18. 1959, p. 183-185.

Bellini, E. - Ariè, S.   581

Segnalazione di pitture rupestri in
località Carcur Dris nel Gebel
Áuenat (Libia).
RSP 17. 1962, p. 261-267.

Brentjes, B.   582

Fels- und Höhlenbilder Afrikas.
African rock art.
Leipzig: Koehler und Amelang 1965.
London: Dent 1969.

Breuil, H.   583

Gravures rupestres du désert libyque
identiques à celles des ancien
Bushmen.
Anthropologie 36. 1926, p. 125-127.

Breuil, H. - Pâques, V.   584

Gravures rupestres préhistoriques
du Fezzân.
Journal de la société des africanistes 28. 1958, p. 25-32.

Butzer, K.W.   585

Studien zum vor- und frühgeschicht-
lichen Landschaftswandel der Sahara.
1-3.
Abhandlungen. Akademie der Wissenschaften und der Literatur. Mainz.
1.
Butzer, K.W.   585

Mathem. - naturwissenschaftliche
Klasse 1958, n. 1, 1959, n. 2.

2.
Camps, G. - Delibrias, G. -   586
Thommeret, J.

Chronologie absolue et succession
des civilisations préhistoriques
dans le Nord de l'Afrique.
Libyca. Anthropologie-préhistoire-
ethnographie 16.1968, p. 9-28.

Caporiacco, L. di - Graziosi,P. 587

Le pitture rupestri di Ain Dôua
(El-Auenat).
Firenze 1934.

Cavazza, F.   588

Notizie preistoriche e storiche
sugli animali domestici della Libia.
RdC 10. 1936, p. 522-545.

Chamla, M.C. 589
Les populations anciennes du Sahara
et des régions limitrophes.
Paris: Arts et Métiers Graphiques
1968.

Corò, F. 590
La prima missione libica di ricerca
della preistoria del sud Tripolitano.
Africa. Roma 18. 1963, p. 297-301.

Desio, A. 591
Sculture rupestri di nuove località
del Tibesti settentrionale e del
deserto libico.
AAI 4. 1941, vol. 1, p. 203-206.

Fabbri, M. - Winorath- 592
Scott, A.
Stazione litica all'aperto nei pres-
si di Garian.
LA 2. 1965, p. 83-90.

Fantoli, A. 593
La scoperta di manufatti litici in
Libia.
RdC 3. 1929, p. 1029-1049, 1161-
1183, 4. 1930, p. 51-60.

Fantoli, A. 594
Sull'età della pietra in Libia.
ACSC 1. 1931, vol. 2, p. 7-18.
REAI 19. 1931, p. 1297-1305.

Frobenius, L. 595
Ekade Ektab. Die Felsbilder Fezzans.
Graz: Akademische Druck- und Ver-
lagsanstalt 1963. Repr.

Gautier, E.F. 596
The ancesters of the Tuaregs.
Geographical review 25. 1935, p. 12-
20.

Graziosi, P. 597
Escursione paletnologica nella Tri-
politania settentrionale.
AAE 63. 1933, p. 227-233.

Graziosi, P. 598
Graffiti rupestri del Gebèl Bu
Chnèba nel Fezzàn.
AIb 5. 1933, p. 188-197.

Graziosi, P. 599
Graffiti rupestri del Fezzan orien-
tale.
ACSC 2. 1934, vol. 3, p. 229-232.

Graziosi, P. 600
Recherches préhistoriques au Fezzân
et dans la Tripolitaine du nord.
Anthropologie 44. 1934, p. 33-43.

Graziosi, P. 601
Incisioni rupestri di carri dell'
uàdi nel Fezzan.
AIb 6. 1935-37, p. 54-60.

Graziosi, P. 602
Le incisioni rupestri dell'Uadi
Belheran nel Fezzan.
AAE 66. 1936, p. 41-47.

Graziosi, P. 603
Le pitture della grotta di In
Elegghi presso Gat.
BSGI 74. 1937, p. 408-411.

Graziosi, P. 604
Preistoria.
SIFOG 1937, p. 241-274.

Graziosi, P.   605

Graffiti e pitture sulle rocce del
Sahara italiano.
Emporium 88. 1938, p. 213-220.

Graziosi, P.   606

Graffiti rupestri e stazioni preistoriche del Fezzan.
AAI 1. 1938, vol. 3/4, p. 971-978.

Graziosi, P.   607

Missione preistorica nel Fezzan 1938.
AAE 68. 1938, p. 375-376.

Graziosi, P.   608

Nuovi graffiti rupestri scoperti
nella Libia orientale.
Riv. di antropologia 32. 1938, p. 47-
123.

Graziosi, P.   609

Nuove scoperte di arte rupestre in
Libia.
Libia 3. 1939, n. 1, p. 20-23.

Graziosi, P.   610

Preistoria della Libia.
ASIPS 28. 1939, vol. 4, p. 371-379.

Graziosi, P.   611

Su alcune pitture rupestri dell'
Uadi Takisset e su una incisione
dell'Uadi Arrechim a sud di Gat.
AAE 69. 1939, p. 85-90.

Graziosi, P.   612

Una stazione dell'età della pietra
presso Gadames.
Annali del museo libico di storia
naturale 1. 1939, p. 397-406.

Graziosi, P.   613

Graffiti rupestri a Sidi Ali nell'
Uadi el Agial (Fezzàn).
AAE 70. 1940, p. 75-80.

Graziosi, P.   614

La Libia preistorica.
Firenze/Roma 1943.
(La Libia nella scienze e nella
   storia.)

Graziosi, P.   615

Necropoli di Ghira presso Brach
(Fezzàn).
AAE 72. 1943, p. 212-218.

Graziosi, P.   616

The prehistoric animal artists of a
fertile Sahara.
Illustrated London news 1954, 26.6.,
p. 1096-1097.

Graziosi, P.   617

Le incisioni rupestri dell'Uadi-el-
Chel in Tripolitania.
RSP 11. 1956, p. 234-238.

Graziosi, P.   618

Arte rupestre del Sahara libico.
Firenze: Vallecchi 1962.

Graziosi, P.   619

Pitture e graffiti nel Sahara.
Vie del mondo 26. 1965, p. 758-769.

Graziosi, P.   620

Prehistory of southwestern Fezzan.
GAPSF 1969, p. 3-19.

Guerri, M. 621
Manufatti della "pebble culture" nel Fezzan.
RSP 18. 1963, p. 255-260.

Heekeren, H.R. van - Jawad, A.J. 622
An archaeological report on the stone implements from the Fezzan desert, Libya.
Anthropos 61. 1966, p. 767-775.

Hey, R.W. 623
Pleistocene screes in Cyrenaica (Libya).
Eiszeitalter und Gegenwart 14. 1963, p. 77-84.

Huard, P. 624
Gravures rupestres de la lisière nord-occidentale du Tibesti.
TIRS 10. 1953, p. 75-106.

Huard, P. 625
Recherches sur les traits culturels des chasseurs anciens du Sahara centre-oriental et du Nil.
Revue d'egyptologie 17. 1965, p. 21-80.

Huard, P. - Léonardi 626
Nouvelles gravures rupestres des chasseurs du Fezzan méridional, du Djado et du Tibesti.
RSP 21. 1966, p. 135-156.

Joleaud, L. 627
Gravures rupestres et rites de l'eau en Afrique du nord.
Journal de la société des africanistes 3. 1933, p. 197-282, 4. 1934, p. 285-302.

Klitzsch, E. - Pesce, A. 628
Remarks about prehistorical sites in southern Libya and Tibesti.
SCNLC 1966, p. 69-74.

Leva, A.E. 629
Le più recenti conclusioni di fondo sulla preistoria dell'Africa settentrionale.
Africa. Roma 23. 1968, p. 39-43.

Lhote, H. 630
La route des chars de guerre libyens Tripoli-Gao.
Archeologia 1966, n. 9, p. 28-36.

Mac Burney, C.B.M. - Trevor, J.C. - Wells, L.H. 631
A fossil human mandible from a Levalloiso-Mousterian horizon in Cyrenaica.
Nature 172. 1953, p. 889-891.

Mac Burney, C.B.M. 632
The Haua Fteah fossil jaw.
Journal of the Royal Anthropological Institute 83. 1953, part1, p. 71-85.

Mac Burney, C.B.M. 633
Evidence of a post-Würm II cold climate oscillation in eastern Libya with archaeological association.
Actes congrès d'INQUA 4. 1956, p. 931-936.

Mac Burney, C.B.M. 634
Evidence for the distribution in space and time of Neanderthaloids and allied strains in northern Africa. 1.
Hundert Jahre Neanderthaler. Nean-

Mac Burney, C.B.M. 634
derthal centenary 1856-1956. Köln 1958, p. 253-264.

Mac Burney, C.B.M. 635
The stone age in northern Africa.
Harmondsworth: Penguin Books 1960.

Mac Burney, C.B.M.   636

Absolute age of Pleistocene and Ho-
locene deposits in the Haua Fteah.
Nature 192. 1961, n. 4803, p. 685-
686.

Mac Burney, C.B.M.   637

Absolute chronology of the Palaeolithic in eastern Libya and the problem of upper Palaeolithic origins.
Advancement of science 18. 1962,
p. 494-497.

Mac Burney, C.B.M.   638

The Haua Fteah (Cyrenaica) and the
stone age of the South-east Mediterranean.
Cambridge UP 1967.

Mac Burney, C.B.M.   639

Pleistocene and early post-Pleisto-
cene archaeology of Libya.
GANC 1968, p. 13-21.

Massari, C.   640

L'arte rupestre della Libia (in una
recente pubblicazione italiana).
BSGI 80. 1943, p. 219-224.

Montet, A.   641

Grotte de Hagfet et-Tera (Cyrénaïque).
Bulletin de la société préhistorique française 52. 1955, p. 230.

Montet-White, A.   642

Industrie de lamelles de Hagfet et-
Tera (Cyrénaïque).
Quaternaria 5. 1962, p. 35-52.

Mori, F.   643

Ricerche paletnologiche nel Fezzan.
Relazione preliminare.
RSP 11. 1956, p. 211-229.

Mori, F.   644

Nuove scoperte d'arte rupestre nell'
Acacus.
RSP 12. 1957, p. 251-263.

Mori, F.   645

Sahara presente e passato: cenno
sulla civiltà preistorica e sui
Tuareg.
Africa. Roma 12. 1957, p. 137-140.

Mori, F.   646

Pitture rupestri del Fezzan.
Levante 5. 1958, n. 3-4, p. 29-42.

Mori, F. - Ascenzi, A.   647

La mummia infantile di Uan
Muhuggiag. Osservazioni antropologiche.
Riv. di antropologia 46. 1959,
p. 125-148.

Mori, F.   648

Arte preistorica del Sahara libico.
Roma: De Luca 1960.

Mori, F.   649

IV missione paletnologica nell'
Acacus (Sahara fezzanese).
Ricerca scientifica 30. 1960, p. 61-
72.

Mori, F.   650

Aspetti di cronologia sahariana
alla luce dei ritrovamenti della V
missione paletnologica nell'Acacus
(1960-61).   1.
Ricerca scientifica ser. 2, p.1,

Mori, F.   650

vol. 1. 1961, p. 204-215.

2.

Mori, F. 651

Un singolare esempio di scultura rupestre nell'Acacus: i "fori accoppiati".
RSP 16. 1961, p. 231-238.

Mori, F. 652

Some aspects of the rock-art of the Acacus (Fezzan Sahara) and data regarding it.
Viking fund publications in anthropology 39. 1964, p. 225-251.

Mori, F. 653

Contributions to the study of the prehistoric pastoral peoples of the Sahara.
Miscelánea en homenaje al abate Henri Breuil. Ed. E. Ripoll Perelló.
Barcelona 1965, vol. 2, p. 173-179.

Mori, F. 654

Sulle analogie e possibilità di contatti fra le culture sahariane connesse all'arte rupestre e quelle pre e protodinastiche egiziane.
Quaternaria 7. 1965, p. 301-302.

Mori, F. 655

Tadrart Acacus. Arte rupestre e culture del Sahara preistorico.
Torino: Einaudi 1965.

Mori, F. 656

Researches in the Tadrart Acacus.
LA 3/4. 1966/67, p. 221-227.

Mori, F. 657

Figure umane incise di tipo ittiomorfo scoperte nel Tadrart Acacus.
Origini. Preistoria e protostoria delle civiltà antiche 1. 1967, p. 37-52.

Mori, F. 658

Prehistoric cultures in Tadrart Acacus, Libyan Sahara.
GAPSF 1969, p. 21-30.

Neuville, P. 659

Prise de date pour le site d'Abiar Miggi (Tripolitaine).
Bulletin de la société préhistorique française 53. 1956, p. 24-25.

Neuville, P. - Bentor, Y. 660

Stratigraphie néolithique et gravures rupestres en Tripolitaine septentrionale (Abiar-Miggi).
Libyca 4. 1956, p. 61-123.

Paradisi, U. 661

Nuovi ritrovamenti preistorici scoperti nel Fezzan dalla missione italiana.
Libia 3. 1955, n. 1, p. 66.

Paradisi, U. 662

I recenti ritrovamenti d'arte preistorica nel margine orientale della Hamada el-Hamra (Sud tripolitano).
Libia 3. 1955, n. 1, p. 55-63.

Paradisi, U. 663

Le incisioni rupestri di Bir Ghan (Tripolitania).
AION 11. 1961, p. 1-15.

Paradisi, U. 664

La doppia protome di toro nell'arte rupestre sahariana e nella tavolozza predinastica egiziana della caccia al leone.
Aegyptus 43. 1963, p. 269-277.

Paradisi, U. 665

Incisioni rupestri nei pressi di Sinawen (Tripolitania).
AION 13. 1963, p. 259-278.

Paradisi, U. 666

Arte rupestre nel Harûǧ el-Aswed (Fezzân nord-orientale).
LA 1. 1964, p. 111-113.

Paradisi, U.   667

Incisioni rupestri preistoriche a
Tagnît (Tripolitania).
LA 1. 1964, p. 107-109.

Paradisi, U. - Mac Burney,   668
C.B.M.
Prehistoric art in the Gebel el-
Akhdar (Cyrenaica).
Antiquity 39. 1965, p. 95-101.

Paradisi, U. - Graziosi, P.   669
Arte rupestre preistorica nel Gebel
el-Akhdar in Cirenaica.
QAL 5. 1967, p. 5-18.

Pasa, A. - Pasa Durante, M.V.   670
Analisi paleoclimatiche nel deposito
di Uan Muhuggiag, nel massiccio dell'
Acacus (Fezzan meridionale).
Memorie del museo civico di storia
naturale di Verona 10. 1962, p. 251-
255.

Pauphilet, D.   671
Gravures rupestres de Maknusa
(Fezzân).
TIRS 10. 1953, p. 107-122.

Pesce, A.   672
Segnalazione di nuove stazioni d'ar-
te rupestre negli Uidian Telîssaghen
e Matrhandùsc (Messak Settafet,
Fezzan).
RSP 22. 1967, p. 393-416.

Petrocchi, C.   673
Relazione sui ritrovamenti di es-
Sahabi.
ACSC 2. 1934, vol. 3, p. 238-247.

Petrocchi, C.   674
Ricerche preistoriche in Cirenaica.
Relazione sui ritrovamenti in grotta
Hagfet et-Tera.
ACSC 2. 1934, vol. 3, p. 80-90.

Petrocchi, C.   675
I ritrovamenti faunistici di Es-Sa-
hâbi.
RdC 8. 1934, p. 733-742.

Petrocchi, C.   676
Nuovi contributi stratigrafici allo
studio del paleolitico della Libia.
ASIPS 25. 1936, vol. 4, p. 250-251.

Petrocchi, C.   677
Stratigrafia e industrie litiche sul
Gebel Cirenaico (Hagfet et-Tera).
ASIPS 26. 1937, vol. 1, p. 434-439.

Petrocchi, C.   678
Sahabi: una nuova pagina nella sto-
ria della terra.
AAI 5. 1942, vol. 3, p. 745-751.

Pfalz, R.   679
Problematische Wegmarken in Tripoli-
tanien.
Anthropos 25. 1930, p. 321-323.

Puccioni, N.   680
Di alcuni manufatti litici raccolti
in Cirenaica.
CGEP 1923, p. 263-266.

Quincey, A.B. de   681
Notes on a palaeolithic factory site
at Temenhint, Sebha Oasis, and of
other surface finds from the Libyan
desert.
London: Army and Navy Club 1963.

Resch, W.F.E.   682
Gedanken zur stilistischen Gliederung der Tier-Darstellungen in der
nordafrikanischen Felsbildkunst.
Paideuma 11. 1965, p. 105-113.

Resch, W.F.E. 683

Die kleinafrikanischen Felsbilder
im Lichte der neueren Forschung.
Frobenius, L.: Hadschra maktuba.
Graz 1965, p. 69-89.

Resch, W.F.E. 684

Das Rind in den Felsbilddarstellun-
gen Nordafrikas.
Wiesbaden: Steiner 1967.
(Studien zur Kulturkunde. 20.)

Rhotert, H. 685

Forschungsreise nach Südwest-Libyen.
Tribus 12. 1963, p. 12-31.

Rhotert, H. 686

Neue Felsbilderfunde im Wadi Tar-
hoscht (Südwest-Libyen).
Festschrift für A.E. Jensen. Ed. E.
Haberland. München 1964, p. 501-512.

Sattin, F. 687

Arte rupestre fezzanese.
RSP 14. 1959, p. 295-305.

Sattin, F. 688

Le incisioni rupestri di Kuleba e
dello Zinkekra.
LA 2. 1965, p. 73-81.

Sattin, F. 689

Le incisioni rupestri di Gasr Mimûn.
LA 3/4. 1966/67, p. 161-177.

Sattin, F. - Gusmano, G. 690

La cosidetta "mummia" infantile dell'
Acacus nel quadro delle costumanze
funebri preistoriche mediterranee e
sahariane.
Tripoli: Directorate-general of 1.

Sattin, F. - Gusmano, G. 690

Antiquities, Museums and Archives
1968.
(LA. Suppl. 1.)

Scarin, E. 691

Distribuzione topografica delle incisione rupestri nel Fezzan.
Vie d'Italia e del mondo 2. 1934,
p. 1429-1448.

Serra, L. 692

Umberto Paradisi.
AION 15. 1965, p. 357.

Valori, B. 693

Osservazioni sui rapporti preistorici fra l'Egitto e la Libia.
AAE 58. 1928, p. 291-295.

Vita, A. di 694

In memoriam: Umberto Paradisi
(27.3.1925 - 14.4.1965).
LA 2. 1965, p. 147-148.

Vita-Finzi, C. - Kennedy, R.A. 695

"Seven Saharan sites".
Journal of the Royal Anthropological
Institute 95. 1965, p. 195-213.

Vita-Finzi, C. - Fabbri, M. 696

Nuove stazioni litiche di Libia.
LA 3/4. 1966/67, p. 229-231.

Watson, W. 697

The surface implements of Cyrenaica.
Man 44. 1945, p. 100-104.

Winorath-Scott, A. - Fabbri, M.   698

The horn in Libyan prehistoric art
and its traces in other cultures.
LA 3/4. 1966/67, p. 233-239.

Zanon, V.   699

Appunti di paletnologia bengasina.
Memorie della pontificia accademia
delle scienze nuovi Lincei   ser. 2,
vol. 9. 1926, p. 137-171.

Zanon, V.   700

Materiali paletnologici bengasini.
AAE 58. 1928, p. 315-331.

Ziegert, H.   701

Neue Ergebnisse für die Klima- und
Besiedlungs-Geschichte der zentralen
Sahara.
Umschau 64. 1964, n. 23, p. 712-715.

Ziegert, H.   702

Climatic changes and palaeolithic
industries in East Fezzan, Libya.
Current anthropology 6. 1965,
p. 104-105.

Ziegert, H.   703

Climatic changes and paleolithic industries in eastern Fezzan, Libya.
SCLNC 1966, p. 65-67.

Ziegert, H. - Klitzsch, E.   704

Dor el Gussa und Gebel ben Ghnema.
Zur nachpluvialen Besiedlungsge-
schichte des Ostfezzan.
Wiesbaden: Steiner 1967.

Ziegert, H.   705

Gebel ben Ghnema und Nord-Tibesti.
Pleistozäne Klima- und Kulturenfolge
in der zentralen Sahara.
Wiesbaden: Steiner 1969.

Ziegert, H.   706

Pleistocene climatic changes and human industries in the central Sahara (eastern Fezzan and northern
Tibesti).
Bulletin de liaison. Association 1.

Ziegert, H.   706

sénégalaise pour l'étude du quaternaire de l'ouest africain 1969,
n. 22, p. 38-46.

Zoli, G.   707

Scolture libiche del Fezzàn.
RdC 1/2. 1927/28, p. 7-13.

Archaeology.
Bibliography.
Current Information.

Bono, F.   708

Bibliografia dell'archeologia tripolitana del dopo guerra.
Italia che scrive 34. 1951, p. 32.

Gasperini, L. - Romanelli, P.   709

Bibliografia archeologica della
Libia.
A) Cirenaica.
B) Tripolitania.
QAL 4. 1961, p. 141-146.

Gasperini, L. - Romanelli, P.   710

Bibliografia archeologica della
Libia 1962-1966.
A) Cirenaica.
B) Tripolitania.
QAL 5. 1967, p. 153-159.

Romanelli, P.   711

Bibliografia archeologica ed artisti-
ca della Tripolitania.
Boll. del reale istituto di archeologia e storia dell'arte 1. 1927,
p. 113-130.

Sichtermann, H. 712

Archäologische Funde und Forschungen in der Kyrenaika 1942/58.
Archäologischer Anzeiger 1959 (1960), p. 239-348.

Sichtermann, H. 713

Archäologische Funde und Forschungen in Libyen. Kyrenaika 1959/1961, Tripolitanien 1942/1961.
Archäologischer Anzeiger 1962 (1962/63), p. 417-535.

Archaeologische Bibliographie. 714
(Beilage zum Jahrbuch des Deutschen Archäologischen Instituts) Berlin: de Gruyter.
1968 (1970)-

Fasti archeologici. 715
Annual bulletin of classical archaeology.
Firenze: Sansoni.
21. 1966 (1970)-

Libya antiqua. 716
Tripoli: Directorate-general of Antiquities, Museums and Archives.
4. 1967-

Quaderni di archeologia 717
della Libia.
Roma: L'Erma di Bretschneider.
5. 1967-

Inscriptions.

Alvarez Delgado, J. 718

Inscripciónes líbicas de Canarias: ensayo de interpretación libica.
Tenerife: Universidad de la Laguna 1964.

Applebaum, S. 719

Three Greek epitaphs from Teuchira, Cyrenaica.
Bulletin of the Israel exploration society 22. 1958, p. 74.

Applebaum, S. 720

A Jewish inscription from Bereniki in Cyrenaica.
Bulletin of the Israel exploration society 25. 1961, p. 167-174.

Aurigemma, S. 721

Iscrizioni latino-neopuniche scoperte presso il Forte del Faro in Tripoli.
NA 2. 1916 (1918), p. 381-393.

Aurigemma, S. 722

Iscrizioni lepitane.
AIb 3. 1930, p. 76-92.

Aurigemma, S. 723

Due iscrizioni tripolitane.
AIb 7. 1940, p. 132-140.

Bartoccini, R. 724

Dolabella e Tacfarinas in una iscrizione di Leptis Magna.
Epigraphica 20. 1958, p. 3-13.

Beguinot, F. 725

Appunti di epigrafia libica.
AIn 46. 1927, p. 79-81.

Beguinot, F. 726

Note e appunti di epigrafia libica.
AION 1. 1928-29, p. 15-33, 7. 1935, p. 5-13.

Beguinot, F.   727
Le iscrizioni rupestri in caratteri
"Tifînagh".
ACSC 2. 1934, vol. 4, p. 104-112.

Beguinot, F.   728
Le iscrizioni berbere del Sahara.
Riv. d'oriente 3. 1935, p. 59-62.

Beguinot, F.   729
Saggi di iscrizioni rupestri sahariane.
Atti del congresso internazionale
degli orientalisti 19. 1935 (1938),
p. 116-124.

Beguinot, F.   730
Di alcune iscrizioni in caratteri
latini e in lingua sconosciuta tro-
vate in Tripolitania.
RSO 24. 1949, p. 14-19.

Beguinot, F.   731
Gli studi sull'epigrafia e sulle
iscrizioni tuâregh fatti in Italia
nell'ultimo quarantennio.
Libia 1. 1953, n. 1, p. 82-90.

Benario, H.W.   732
C. Paccius Africanus at Sabratha.
Epigraphica 28. 1966, p. 135-139.

Bonelli, L. - Nallino, C.A.   733
Iscrizioni turco-arabe delle porte
di Tripoli.
NA 2. 1916 (1918), appendice 1,
p. 395-399.

Bottiglieri, R.   734
Studi italiani sull'epigrafia libi-
ca e sulle iscrizioni "tifînagh".
AIn 54. 1936, p. 367-377.

Brogan, O. - Reynolds, J.   735
Seven new inscriptions from Tripoli-
tania.
PBSR 28. 1960, p. 51-54.

Brogan, O. - Reynolds, J.M.   736
Inscriptions from the Tripolitanian
hinterland.
LA 1. 1964, p. 43-46.

Caputo, G.   737
Note di epigrafia della Tripolita-
nia.
Epigraphica 2. 1940, p. 196-200.

Caputo, G. - Goodchild, R.G.   738
Diocletian's price-edict at Ptole-
mais (Cyrenaica).
JRS 45. 1955, p. 106-115.

Cerbella, G.   739
Un'epigrafe cufica del 326 eg.
(937-938 d.C.) rinvenuta in Tripolitania.
Libia 1. 1953, n. 4, p. 45-52.

Chabot, J.B.   740
Recueil des inscriptions libyques.
Paris 1940/41.

Chamoux, F.   741
Epigramme de Cyrène en l'honneur du
roi Magas.
Bulletin de correspondance helléni-
que 82. 1958, p. 571-587.

Daux, G.   742
Note sur une inscription de Cyrène.
Bulletin de correspondance helléni-
que 87. 1963, p. 388-390.

Février, J.G. - Levi della Vida, G. 743

La ligne néopunique de l'inscription bilingue: I.R.T. 305.
Revue des études anciennes 55. 1953, p. 358-360.

Février, J.G. 744

Les découvertes épigraphiques puniques et néopuniques depuis la guerre.
Studi orientalistici in onore di Giorgio Levi della Vida. Roma.
Vol. 1. 1956, p. 274-286.

Février, J.G. 745

Remarques sur l'épigraphie néopunique.
Oriens antiquus 2. 1963, p. 257-267.

Forbes, K. 746

Some Cyrenean dedications.
Philologus 100. 1956, p. 235-252.

Fraser, P.M. 747

An inscription from Euesperides.
Bulletin. Société d'archéologie d'Alexandrie 39. 1951, p. 132-143.

Fraser, P.M. 748

Inscriptions from Cyrene.
Berytus 12. 1956-58(1959), p. 101-128.

Fraser, P.M. 749

Two dedications from Cyrenaica.
Annual of the British school at Athens 57. 1962, p. 24-27.

Galand, L. 750

Inscriptions libyques.
Paris: Centre National de la Recherche Scientifique 1966.

Gallavotti, C. 751

Due epitafi cirenaici.
Riv. di filologia e di istruzione classica 90. 1962, p. 416-418.

Gallavotti, C. 752

Una "defiscio" dorica e altri nuovi epigrammi cirenaici.
Maia 15. 1963, p. 450-463.

Gasperini, L. 753

Due nuovi apporti epigrafici alla storia di Cirene romana.
QAL 5. 1967, p. 53-64.

Goodchild, R.G. 754

Some inscriptions from Tripolitania.
RMDAT 2. 1949, p. 29-35.

Goodchild, R.G. 755

The decline of Cyrene and rise of Ptolemais: two new inscriptions.
QAL 4. 1961, p. 83-95.

Goodchild, R.G. - Reynolds, J.M. 756

Some military inscriptions from Cyrenaica.
PBSR 30. 1962, p. 37-46.

Lavagnini, B. 757

Il centurione di Bu Ngem.
Riv. di filologia e di istruzione classica NS 6. 1928, p. 416-422.

Lefranc, J.P. 758

Inscriptions antiques au Fezzân.
TIRS 10. 1953, p. 191-192.

Levi della Vida, G.   759

Le iscrizioni neopuniche della Tripolitania.
RdT (Libya) 3. 1927, p. 91-116.

Levi della Vida, G.   760

Due iscrizioni imperiali neopuniche
di Leptis Magna.
AIb 6. 1935-37, p. 1-29.

Levi della Vida, G.   761

Iscrizione araba di Ras el-Hammâm.
AION NS 3. 1949, p. 77-81.

Levi della Vida, G.   762

Iscrizioni neopuniche di Tripolitania.
AANL. Rendiconti. Classe di scienze
morali ... ser. 8, vol. 4. 1949,
p. 399-412.

Levi della Vida, G.   763

The neo-Punic dedication of the
Ammonium at Ras el-Haddagia.
PBSR 19. 1951, p. 65-68.

Levi della Vida, G.   764

Iscrizione punica di Lepcis.
AANL. Rendiconti. Classe di scienze
morali ... ser. 8, vol. 10. 1955,
p. 550-561.

Levi della Vida, G.   765

Tracce di credenze e culti fenici
nelle iscrizioni neopuniche della
Tripolitania.
Festschrift Johannes Friedrich.
Heidelberg 1959, p. 299-314.

Levi della Vida, G.   766

Frustuli neopunici tripolitani.
AANL. Rendiconti. Classe di scienze
morali ... ser. 8, vol. 18. 1963,
p. 463-482.

Levi della Vida, G.   767

Sulle iscrizioni "latino-libiche"
della Tripolitania.
Oriens antiquus 2. 1963, p. 65-94.

Levi della Vida, G.   768

Le iscrizioni neopuniche di Wadi
El-Amud.
LA 1. 1964, p. 57-63.

Levi della Vida, G.   769

Ostracon neopunico della Tripolitania.
Orientalia 33. 1964, p. 1-14.

Levi della Vida, G.   770

"Parerga neopunica".
Oriens antiquus 4. 1965, p. 59-70.

Levi della Vida, G.   771

Iscrizione punica da Sabratha.
LA 3/4. 1966/67, p. 9-11.

Lidzbarski, M.   772

Handbuch der nordsemitischen Epigra-
phik nebst ausgewählten Inschriften.
Hildesheim: Olms 1962. Repr.

Meinhof, K.   773

Die libyschen Inschriften.
Nendeln: Kraus Repr. 1966.
(Abhandlungen für die Kunde des
 Morgenlandes. 19,1.)

Mordini, A.   774

Les inscriptions rupestres tifinagh
du Sahara et leur signification
ethnologique.
Ethnos 2. 1937, p. 333-337.

Morelli, G.   775
Una glossa di Esechio e due nuovi
epitafi cirenaici.
Maia 15. 1963, p. 168-183.

Moretti, L.   776
Tiberio Claudio Giasone Magno di
Cirene.
Epigraphica 31. 1969, p. 139-143.

Oliver, J.H.   777
On edict III from Cyrene.
Hesperia 29. 1960, p. 324-325.

Oliverio, G.   778
Cirene-Bengasi. Iscrizioni inedite.
NA 2. 1916 (1918), p. 179-191.

Oliverio, G.   779
Documenti epigrafici del santuario
di Apollo.
AIb 1. 1927-28, p. 156-158.

Oliverio, G.   780
I principali documenti epigrafici
(Cirene).
AIb 1. 1927-28, p. 317-336.

Oliverio, G.   781
Indice dei nomi propri e dei termi-
ni ricorrenti nelle iscrizioni ...
(Cirene).
AIb 3. 1930, p. 230-236.

Oliverio, G. - Pugliese Carra- 782
telli, G.

Iscrizioni cirenaiche.
QAL 4. 1961, p. 3-54.

Oliverio, G. - Pugliese Carra- 783
telli, G. - Morelli, D.

Supplemento epigrafico cirenaico.
Annuario della scuola archeologica
di Atene 39/40. 1961/62, p. 219-375.

Pflaum, H.G. - Picard, G.C.   784
Notes d'épigraphie latine. 3. L'occu-
pation romaine de Ghadamès.
Karthago 2. 1951, p. 105-106.

Pugliese Carratelli, G.   785
Nuovi documenti del culto privato
ellenistico.
Miscellanea di studi alessandrini in
memoriam di A. Rostagni. Torino
1963, p. 162-165.

Pugliese Carratelli, G.   786
Praxidika a Cirene.
AANL. Rendiconti. Classe di scienze
morali ... ser. 8, vol. 18. 1963,
p. 340-344.

Reynolds, J.M.   787
Three inscriptions from Ghadames in
Tripolitania.
PBSR NS 13. 1958, p. 135-136.

Reynolds, J.M.   788
Four inscriptions from Roman Cyrene.
JRS 49. 1959, p. 95-101.

Reynolds, J.M.   789
Cyrenaica, Pompey and Cn. Cornelius
Lentulus Marcellinus.
JRS 52. 1962, p. 97-103.

Reynolds, J.M.   790
Vota pro salute principis.
PBSR 30. 1962, p. 33-36.

Reynolds, J.M.   791

S.E.G. IX 63.
Proceedings of the Cambridge philological society 189. 1963, p. 2-4.

Reynolds, J.M.   792

Notes on Cyrenaican inscriptions.
PBSR 33. 1965, p. 52-54.

Reynolds, J.M. - Simpson, W.G.   793

Some inscriptions from el-Auenia
near Yefren in Tripolitania.
LA 3/4. 1966/67, p. 45-47.

Romanelli, P.   794

Iscrizione tripolitana che ricorda
un'offerta di denti d'avorio.
AANL. Rendiconti. Classe di scienze
morali ... ser. 5, vol. 29. 1920,
p. 376-383.

Romanelli, P.   795

Tre iscrizioni tripolitane di interesse storico.
Epigraphica 1. 1939, p. 99-118.

Romanelli, P.   796

Iscrizione inedita di Leptis Magna
con nuovi contributi ai fasti della
provincia d'Africa.
QAL 2. 1951, p. 71-79.

Rossi, E.   797

Le epigrafi musulmane del Museo di
Tripoli.
Libia 1. 1953, n. 1, p. 103-107.

Rossi, E.   798

Le iscrizioni arabe e turche del
Museo di Tripoli (Libia).
RMDAT 3. 1953.

Salama, P.   799

Déchiffrement d'un milliaire de
Lepcis Magna.
LA 2. 1965, p. 39-45.

Servais, J.   800

Les suppliants dans la "loi sacrée"
de Cyrène.
Bulletin de correspondance helléni-
que 84. 1960, p. 112-147.

Supplementum epigraphicum   801
graecum. Ed. A.G. Woodhead.
Lugduni Batavorum.
18. 1962, p. 228-242 Cirenaica.
20. 1964, p. 174-212 Cirenaica.

Sznycer, M.   802

Sur l'inscription neopunique "Tripolitaine 27".
Semitica 12. 1962, p. 45-50.

Sznycer, M.   803

Les inscriptions dites "latino-liby-
ques".
CR des séances. Groupe linguistique
d'études chamito-semitiques 10. 1965,
p. 97-104.

Vattioni, F.   804

Appunti sulle iscrizioni puniche tripolitane.
AION 16. 1966, p. 37-55.

Vattioni, F.   805

Note fenicie.
AION 18. 1968, p. 71-73.

Vita-Evrard, G. di   806

La dédicace du temple d'Isis à Sabratha: une nouvelle inscription
africaine à l'actif de C. Paccius
Africanus.
LA 3/4. 1966/67, p. 13-20.

Vitucci, G. 807

Nuova iscrizione da Leptis Magna.
Atti del congresso internazionale
di epigrafia 3. 1957 (1959), p. 271-
275.

Volterra, E. 808

L'adozione testamentaria e un'iscrizione latina e neopunica della Tripolitania.
AANL. Rendiconti. Classe di scienze
morali ... ser.8, vol.7.1952,p. 175-
188.

Zanon, V. 809

L'iscrizione di er-Règima.
Atti della pontificia accademia
delle scienze nuovi Lincei 80. 1927,
p. 261-263.

Numismatics.

Bond, R.C. - Swales, J.M. 810

Surface finds of coins from the city of Euesperides.
LA 2. 1965, p. 91-101.

Borelli, N. 811

Fauna e flora nella tipologia mone-
tale libica.
IdO 2. 1937, n. 16, p. 16-17.

Bousquet, J. 812

Un statère d'or de Cyrène sur la
côte du Finistère.
CR. Académie des inscriptions et
belles-lettres 1960 (1961), p. 317-
323.

Chamoux, F. 813

Hermès Parammon.
Études d'archéologie classique. Ed.
F. Chamoux. Paris 1959, p. 31-40.

Cimino, G. 814

La zecca di Tripoli d'Occidente nell'
opera di Mr. Valentine.
Riv. italiana di numismatica 29.
1916, p. 251-260.

Cimino, G. 815

La zecca di Tripoli d'Occidente sotto il dominio dei Caramanli.
Riv. italiana di numismatica 29.
1916, p. 527-540.

Cimino, G. 816

La zecca di Tripoli d'Occidente sotto il dominio degli ottomani.
NA 1922, fasc. 3, p. 113-143.

Cimino, G. 817

Storia e numismatica dell'Africa
del nord.
RdT (Libya) 3. 1927, p. 202-227.

Colbert de Beaulieu, J.B. 818

Un statère d'or de Cyrène trouvé
sur la côte du Finistère.
Bulletin de la société française de
numismatique 15. 1960, p. 407.

Colbert de Beaulieu, J.B. - 819
Giot, P.R.

Un statère d'or de Cyrénaïque dé-
couvert sur une plage bretonne ...
Bulletin. Société préhistorique
française 58. 1961, p. 324-331.

Falbe, C.T. - Lindberg, J.C. 820
Mueller, L.

Numismatique de l'ancienne Afrique.
Vol. 1-3.
Bologna: Forni 1964. Repr.

Farrugia de Candia, J. 821

Monnaies frappées à Tripoli et à
Gafsa par Dragut.
Revue tunisienne 1936, p. 85-92.

Ferri, S.   822

Manualetto numismatico per la Cirenaica.
Bengasi 1924.

Goodchild, R.G.   823

A coin-hoard from "Balagrae" (El
Beida), and the earthquake of A.D.
365.
LA 3/4. 1966/67, p. 203-211.

Hazard, H.W.   824

The numismatic history of the late
medievalNorth Africa.
New York: American Numismatic
Society 1952.
(Numismatic studies. 8.)

Johnson, M.   825

The nineteenth-century gold
"mithqal" in West and North Africa.
Journal of African history 9. 1968,
p. 547-569.

Meliu, A.   826

Bronzi rari della Cirenaica.
Numismatica 5. 1939, p. 120-121.

Meliu, A.   827

Roma e l'Africa nel campo numismatico.
Libia 4. 1940, n. 1, p. 13-15.

Ricci, S.   828

La stato odierno della numismatica
coloniale e relative proposte.
ACSC 1. 1931, vol. 2, p. 116-133.

Robinson, E.S.G.   829

The Libyan hoard (1952): addenda,
and the Libyan coinage in general.
Numismatic chronicle 1956, p. 9-14.

Welz, K.   830

Le monete greche di Cirene.
Italia numismatica 13. 1962, p. 50.

Zambaur, E. de   831

Münzprägungen des Islam. Zeitlich
und örtlich geordnet.
Wiesbaden: Steiner.
1. Der Westen und Osten ... 1968.

Archaeology.
General.

Abdussaid, A.   832

Early Islamic monuments at Ajdabi-
yah.
LA 1. 1964, p. 115-119.

Abdussaid, A.   833

An early mosque at Medina Sultan.
LA 3/4. 1966/67, p. 155-160.

Alcock, L.   834

A seaside villa in Tripolitania.
PBSR 18. 1950, p. 92-100.

Apollonj, B.M.   835

Note sulla copertura e il corona-
mento dell'arco di Traiano a Leptis
Magna.
AIb 7. 1940, p. 106-111.

Applebaum, S.   836

A lamp and other remains of the
Jewish community of Cyrene.
Israel exploration journal 7. 1957,
p. 154-162.

Aswed, A.S. el   837

Tomba e camera di Lamaia (Tripolitania).
LA 3/4. 1966/67, p. 263-264.

Atti del congresso di studi   838
romani.
Roma.
1. 1929.
2. 1931.
3. 1933.   ianc
4. 1935.

Aurigemma, S.   839

Pietre miliari tripolitane.
RdT 2. 1925/26, p. 3-21, 135-150.

Aurigemma, S.   840

L'arco di Marco Aurelio in Tripoli.
Boll. d'arte 6. 1926/27, p. 554-570.

Aurigemma, S.   841

Mosaici di Leptis Magna tra l'Uádi
Lébda e il circo.
AIb 2. 1928-29, p. 246-261.

Aurigemma, S.   842

Note al programma per l'esplorazione
archeologica della Tripolitania.
ACSC 1. 1931, vol. 2, p. 27-37.

Aurigemma, S.   843

Tipi architettonici di mausolei tripolitani e loro analogia coi tipi
architettonici di monumenti similari
italiani.
ACSC 2. 1934, vol. 2, p. 64-65.

Aurigemma, S.   844

L'arco di Marco Aurelio in Tripoli.
Libia 1. 1937, n. 3, p. 8-16.

Aurigemma, S.   845

Sculture del foro vecchio di Leptis
Magna raffiguranti la dea Roma e
principi della casa dei Giulio-
Claudi.
AIb 8. 1941, p. 1-94.

Aurigemma, S.   846

L'avo paterno, una zia ed altri
congiunti dell'imperatore Severo.
QAL 1. 1950, p. 59-77.

Aurigemma, S.   847

Il mausoleo di Gasr Dóga in territorio di Tarhúna.
QAL 3. 1954, p. 13-31.

Aurigemma, S.   848

Sopraluogo alle antichità libiche.
Vie d'Italia 63. 1957, p. 1559-
1569.

Aurigemma, S.   849

Un sepolcreto punico-romano sotto
il "Forte della Vite" o "Forte
nord-ovest" in Tripoli (Libia).
RMDAT 4. 1958.

Aurigemma, S.   850

Le scoperte archeologiche (1911/
1943). Tripolitania. Vol. 1. I monumenti d'arte decorativa.
Roma: IPS 1960-62.

Ayoub, M.S.   851

Excavation at Germa, the capital of
the Garamants. Preliminary report.
Tripoli 1962.

Ayoub, M.S.   852

The royal cemetary at Germa.
LA 3/4. 1966/67, p. 213-219.

Ayoub, M.S.   853

Excavations in Germa between 1962
and 1966.
Tripoli 1967.

Bakir, T. - Sa'dawiyah, A. al -   854
Ayoub, M.S.

Archaeological news. 1965-1967.
Tripolitania. Cyrenaica. Fezzan.
LA 3/4. 1966/67, p. 241-255.

Bakir, T.   855

Historical and archaeological guide
to Leptis Magna.
Tripoli: Ministry of Tourism and
Antiquities 1968.

Balty, J.   856

Un nouveau portrait romain de Septime Sévère.
Hommages à Albert Grenier. Collection Latomus 58. 1962, p. 187-196.

Barringer, B. - Carter, T.H.   857

Finding a Phoenician colony.
Expedition 3. 1960/61, n. 1, p. 2-
10.

Bartoccini, R.   858

I recenti scavi di Sabratha e di
Leptis.
RdT 1. 1924/25, p. 281-322.

Bartoccini, R.   859

Le ricerche archeologiche in Tripolitania.
RdT 1. 1924/25, p. 59-73.

Bartoccini, R.   860

Il recinto giustinianeo di Leptis
Magna.
RdT 2. 1925/26, p. 63-73.

Bartoccini, R.   861

Asâbaa - Tripoli - Gurgi - En-Ngila
- Henscir Suffit.
AIb 2. 1928/29, p. 77-110.

Bartoccini, R.   862

La fortezza romana di Bu Ngem.
AIb 2. 1928/29, p. 50-58.

Bartoccini, R.   863

La necropoli punica di Sabratha e
il culto delle divinità egiziane in
Tripolitania.
AION 3. 1949, p. 35-54.

Bartoccini, R.   864

La curia di Sabratha.
QAL 1. 1950, p. 29-58.

Bartoccini, R.   865

Relazione della prima campagna di
scavo della missione archeologica
italiana in Libia.
QAL 3. 1954, p. 67-89.

Bartoccini, R. - Zanelli, A. -   866
Blanc. A.C.

Il porto romano di Leptis Magna.
Roma: Abete 1960.
(Boll. del centro studi per la sto-
 ria dell'architettura.13.Suppl.)

Bartoccini, R.   867

Il foro severiano di Leptis Magna.
Campagna di scavo 1958.
QAL 4. 1961, p. 105-126.

Bartoccini, R.   868

La missione archeologica italiana
nel porto di Leptis Magna.
Atti del congresso internazionale
di archeologia classica 7. 1961,
vol. 3, p. 231-241.

Bartoccini, R.   869

Archeologi in Tripolitania.
Quadrivio 2. 1962, p. 37-48.

Bartoccini, R.   870

Il porto di Leptis Magna nella sua
vita economica e sociale.
Hommages à Albert Grenier. Collection Latomus 58. 1962, p. 228-243.

Bartoccini, R.   871

Il tempio antoniniano di Sabratha.
LA 1. 1964, p. 21-42.

Bauer, G.   872

Le due necropoli di Ghîrza.
Oltremare 8. 1934, p. 219-221.
AIb 6. 1935/37, p. 61-78.

Bellwood, P.S.   873

A Roman dam in the Wadi Caam, Tripolitania.
LA 3/4. 1966/67, p. 41-44.

Bertocci, F.   874

Sculture greche e romane di Cirene.
Pubblicazioni della facoltà di lettere e filosofia. Università di Padova 33. 1959, p. 149-168.

Bisi, A.M.   875

Scavo di una tomba punica a Mellita
(Sabratha).
Archeologia 7. 1968, p. 290-292.
Oriens antiquus 8. 1969, p. 221-222.

Boardman, J.   876

Evidence for the dating of Greek
settlements in Cyrenaica.
Annual of the British school at
Athens 61. 1966, p. 149-156.

Boardman, J. - Hayes, J.   877

Excavations at Tocra 1963-65: the
archaic deposits. Vol. 1.
London: Thames and Hudson 1966.

Bonacasa, N.   878

Una testa marmorea dal porto di
Leptis.
Annuario della scuola archeologica
di Atene 37/38. 1959/60, p. 381-
388.

Bonacasa, N.   879

Nota allo Zeus 14138 di Cirene.
Archeologia classica 13. 1961,
p. 132-140.

Bono, S.   880

Dieci anni di lavoro degli archeologi italiani a Cirene.
Italiani nel mondo 24. 1968, 10.5.,
p. 17-19.

Bordenache, G.   881

Scavi italiani a Leptis.
Studii clasice 8. 1966, p. 277-280.

Brogan, O. - Smith, D.   882

The Roman frontier settlement at
Ghirza: an interim report.
JRS 47. 1957, p. 173-184.

Brogan, O. - Vita-Finzi, C.   883

Ancient systems for making the desert blossom as a rose: water conservation in Roman Tripolitania.
Illustrated London news 239. 1961,
p. 1058-1061.

Brogan, O.   884

A Tripolitanian centenarian.
Hommages à Albert Grenier. Collection Latomus 58. 1962, p. 368-373.

Brogan, O.   885

The Roman remains in the Wadi el-
Amud. An interim note.
LA 1. 1964, p. 47-56.

Caputo, G.   893

Scavi archeologici nel Sahara.
AION 3. 1949, p. 11-33.

Brogan, O.   886

Henscir el-Ausâf by Tigi (Tripolita-
nia) and some related tombs in the
Tunisian Gefara.
LA 2. 1965, p. 47-56.

Caputo, G.   894

Sculture dallo scavo a sud del foro
di Sabratha (1940-1942).
QAL 1. 1950, p. 7-28.

Brogan, O.   887

Notes on the wadis Neina and Bei-el-
Kebir and on some predesert tracks.
LA 2. 1965, p. 57-64.

Caputo, G.   895

Trent'anni di scavi greco-romani in
Tripolitania e Cirenaica.
Libia 1. 1953, n. 4, p. 39-44.

Brogan, O. - Smith, D.   888

Notes from the Tripolitanian predesert, 1967.
LA 3/4. 1966/67, p. 139-144.

Caputo, G.   896

La protezione dei monumenti di Tolemaide negli anni 1935-1942.
QAL 3. 1954, p. 33-66.

Cagiano de Azevedo, M.   889

La data dei mosaici di Zliten.
Hommages à Albert Grenier. Collection
Latomus 58. 1962, p. 374-380.

Caputo, G.   897

Note sugli edifici teatrali della
Cirenaica.
Anthemon. Scritti di archeologia e
di antichità classiche in onore di
C. Anti. Firenze 1955, p. 281-291.

Caputo, G. - Levi della Vida, G. 890

Il Teatro Augusteo di Leptis Magna
secondo le ultime scoperte e un'
iscrizione bilingue in latino e in
neo-punico.
AIb 6. 1935-37, p. 92-109.

Caputo, G.   898

La sinagoga di Berenice in Cirenaica in una iscrizione greca inedita.
Parola del passato 12. 1957, p. 132-
134.

Caputo, G.   891

Archeologia.
SIFOG 1937, p. 301-330.

Caputo, G.   899

Nuovi ritratti colossali di Marco
Aurelio e Lucio Vero.
Archeologia classica 10. 1958, p.64-
68.

Caputo, G.   892

Principali restauri monumentali e
lavori vari di protezione nel
triennio 1946-48 in Sabratha e Leptis Magna.
RMDAT 2. 1949, p. 15-19.

Caputo, G.   900

Il teatro di Sabratha e l'architet-
tura teatrale africana.
Roma: L'Erma di Bretschneider 1959.
(MAL 6.)

Caputo, G. 901

Leptis Magna e l'industria artisti-
ca campana in Africa.
Rendiconti della accademia di Napoli 35. 1960-61, p. 11-27.

Caputo, G. 902

Ritratto leptitano di Settimio Seve-
ro-Ercole.
Hommages à Albert Grenier. Collection Latomus 58. 1962, p. 381-385.

Caputo, G. 903

L'Artemide-Sabina del teatro di
Leptis Magna.
Studi in onore di Luisa Banti. Roma
1965, p. 125-131.

Caputo, G. 904

Spigolature architettoniche lepitane.
LA 2. 1965, p. 9-14, 3/4. 1966/67,
p. 29-39.

Caputo, G. 905

Frontescena, palcoscenico e sipario
nel teatro romano di Leptis Magna.
Dioniso 41. 1967, p. 175-183.

Carter, T.H. 906

Reconnaissance in Cyrenaica.
Expedition 5. 1962-63, p. 18-27.

Carter, T.H. 907

Western Phoenicians at Leptis Magna.
American journal of archaeology
69. 1965, p. 123-132.

Chiesa, C. 908

Sui materiali da costruzione di pro-
venienza locale usati dagli antichi
in Tripolitania.
RMDAT 2. 1949, p. 25-28.

Comfort, H. 909

Notes on sigillata from Sabratha
and Ampurias and at Vienna.
Rei cretariae fautorum acta. Asua-
tucae Tungrorum 7. 1965, p. 15-24.

Corò, F. 910

Il mausoleo di Khascem El Ruman.
Oltremare 4. 1930, p. 288-289.

Corò, F. 911

La strada romana da Tabunacti a
Cydamus.
ACSC 1. 1931, vol. 2, p. 45-52.

Corò, F. 912

I "miliari" romani della carovaniera
Zintan-Mizda.
ACSC 2. 1934, vol. 2, p. 69-75.

Corò, F. 913

Leptis Magna amò Roma.
IdO 2. 1937, n. 17, p. 20-22.

Corò, F. 914

Gadames archeologica.
Libia 4. 1956, n. 3-4, p. 3-26.

Crova, B. 915

Opere idrauliche romane all'uadi
Caàm, il Cinyps della Tripolitania
romana.
QAL 5. 1967, p. 99-120.

Crownover, D. 916

Discoveries at Cyrene.
Expedition 5. 1962-63, p. 28-31.

Cumont, F.   917

Les antiquités de la Tripolitaine au
XVIIe siècle.
RdT 2. 1925/26, p. 151-167.

Cumont, F.   918

Les fouilles de Tripolitaine.
Bulletin de la classe des lettres et
des sciences morales et politiques
de l'académie royale de Belgique
ser. 5, vol. 11. 1925, p. 285-300.

Daniels, C.   919

The Garamantes of Fezzan: excavations on Zinchecra 1965-67.
The antiquaries journal 50. 1970,
p. 37-66.

Degrassi, N.   920

L'ordinamento di Leptis Magna nel
primo secolo dell'impero e la sua
costituzione a municipio romano.
Epigraphica 7. 1945 (1946).

Degrassi, N.   921

L'attività archeologica in Libia dal
1939 ad oggi.
Atti del convegno di studi africani
3. 1948, p. 67-71.

Degrassi, N.   922

Il mercato romano di Leptis Magna.
QAL 2. 1951, p. 27-70.

Dupree, L.   923

Archaeological reconnaissance in
southern Tripolitania and northern
Fezzan, Libya.
Man 65. 1965, p. 147-149.

Ferri, S.   924

Tre anni di lavoro archeologico a
Cirene (1919-1922).
Aegyptus 4. 1923, p. 163-182.

Ferri, S.   925

Firme di legionari della Siria nella Gran Sirte.
RdT 2. 1925/26, p. 363-386.

Ferri, S.   926

L'Iside basilissa di Tolmetta
(Cirenaica).
RdT (Libya) 3. 1927, p. 38-49.

Ferri, S.   927

Statuetta di Afrodite Urania nel
museo di Bengasi.
RdT (Libya) 3. 1927, p. 117-123.

Ferri, S.   928

Il telesterio isiaco di Cirene.
Studi class. e orient. 12. 1963,
p. 5-15.

Flemming, N.   929

Underwater adventure in Apollonia.
Geographical magazine 31. 1958/59,
p. 497-508.

Flemming, N.   930

Apollonia revisited.
Geographical magazine 33. 1960/61,
p. 522-530.

Floriani-Squarciapino, M.   931

Problemi di gigantomachia di Leptis
Magna.
Atti della pontificia accademia
romana di archeologia. Rendiconti
28. 1955-56, p. 169-179.

Floriani-Squarciapino, M.   932

Un rilievo lepcitano.
QAL 4. 1961, p. 127-132.

Floriani-Squarciapino, M. - 933
Ward-Perkins, J.B.

Le sculture severiane di Leptis
Magna.
Congrès international d'archéologie
classique 8. 1963(Texte),p. 229-235.

Floriani-Squarciapino, M. 934
Leptis Magna.
Basel: Raggi 1966.
(Ruinenstädte Nordafrikas. 2.)

Floriani-Squarciapino, M. 935
Fortuna o Astarte-Genius coloniae?
QAL 5. 1967, p. 79-87.

Foucher, L. 936
Sur les mosaïques de Zliten.
LA 1. 1964, p. 9-20.

Gentilucci, I. 937
Resti di antichi edifici lungo
l'Uàdi Sofeggìn.
AIb 5. 1933, p. 172-187.

Giampietro, M. 938
Roma antica in Africa.
Milano: Gastaldi 1961.

Gismondi, I. 939
Il restauro dello strategheion di
Cirene.
QAL 2. 1951, p. 7-25.

Goodchild, R.G. 940
The organisation and work of the An-
tiquities Department, 1943-1948.
RMDAT 2. 1949, p. 9-14.

Goodchild, R.G. 941
Euesperides, a devastated city site.
Antiquity 26. 1952, p. 208-212.

Goodchild, R.G. 942
La necropoli romano-libica di Bir
ed-Dréder.
QAL 3. 1954, p. 91-107.

Goodchild, R.G. 943
The discovery of a huge imperial
frieze, unseen since A.D. 365, at
Cyrene.
Illustrated London news 230. 1957,
p. 303-305.

Goodchild, R.G. - Reynolds, J.- 944
Herington, C.J.

The temple of Zeus at Cyrene. Studies and discoveries in 1954/57.
PBSR 26. 1958, p. 30-62.

Goodchild, R.G. 945
Cyrene and Apollonia. An historical
guide.
Tripoli 1959 (1963).

Goodchild, R.G. 946
A Byzantine palace at Apollonia
(Cyrenaica).
Antiquity 34. 1960, p. 246-258.

Goodchild, R.G. 947
Benghazi (Euesperides-Berenice-Mar-
sa ibn Ghazi): the story of a city.
Shahhat: Department of Antiquities
of Cyrenaica 1962.

Goodchild, R.G. 948
The fountain of the Maenads at Pto-
lemais.
LA 1. 1964, p. 121-125.

Goodchild, R.G.   949

Medina Sultan (Charax-Iscina-Sort).
LA 1. 1964, p. 99-106.

Goodchild, R.G.   950

The unfinished "imperial" baths of
Leptis Magna.
LA 2. 1965, p. 15-27.

Goodchild, R.G.   951

Chiese e battisteri bizantini della
Cirenaica.
Corsi Ravenna 13. 1966, p. 205-223.

Goodchild, R.G.   952

Fortificazioni e palazzi bizantini
in Tripolitania e in Cirenaica.
Corsi Ravenna 13. 1966, p. 225-250.

Goodchild, R.G. - Pedley, J.G. - 953
White, D.

Recent discoveries of archaic sculpture at Cyrene. Preliminary report.
LA 3/4. 1966/67, p. 179-198.

Goodchild, R.G.   954

The forum of Ptolemais (Cyrenaica).
QAL 5. 1967, p. 48-51.

Guey, J.   955

Lepcitana Septimiana VI.
Revue africaine 94. 1950, p.51-84,
96. 1952, p. 25-63, 275-310,
97. 1953, p. 273-313.

Guidi, G   956

I recenti scavi di Leptis Magna e
di Sabratha e l'ordinamento dei
musei archeologici in Tripolitania.
ACSC 1. 1931, vol. 2, p. 37-45.

Hammond, N.   957

The lost Roman road of Tunis and
Libya.
Illustrated London news 247. 1965,
n. 6571, p. 27-29.

Hammond, N.   958

The Limes Tripolitanus: a Roman
road in North Africa.
Journal of the British archaeological association ser. 3, vol. 30.
1967, p. 1-18.

Harrison, R.M. - Reynolds, J.   959
Stern, S.M.

A sixth-century church at Ras el-
Hilal in Cyrenaica.
PBSR NS 19. 1964, p. 1-20.

Haynes, D.E.L.   960

An archaeological and historical
guide to the pre-Islamic antiquities of Tripolitania.
Tripoli: Antiquities Dept. of Tripolitania 1956.

Hopkins, C.   961

Excavations at Apollonia, Libya.
Archaeology 19. 1966, p. 56-57.

Ioppolo, G.   962

La tavola delle unità di misura nel
mercato augusteo di Leptis Magna.
QAL 5. 1967, p. 89-98.

Kachler, K.G.   963

Römische Theater in Tunesien und
Libyen.
Atlantis 34. 1962, p. 253-266.

Kirsten, E.   964

Nordafrikanische Stadtbilder. Anti-
ke und Mittelalter in Libyen und
Tunesien.
Heidelberg: Winter 1966.

Kraeling, C.H. 965
Ptolemais, city of the Libyan Penta-
polis.
University of Chicago Press 1962.
(University of Chicago Oriental
 Institute publications. 90.)

Lauer, J.P. 966
L'enceinte d'Apollonia a Mersa-Souza
(Cyrénaïque).
Revue archéologique 1963, p. 129-153.

Laurenzi, L. 967
I grandi complessi architettonici
della Tripolitania e della Cirenaica.
Corsi Ravenna 13. 1966, p. 251-274.

Maddoli, G. 968
Le cretule del nomophylakion di Cirene.
Annuario della scuola archeologica
di Atene 41/42. 1963/64, p. 39-145.

Magi, F. - Scichilone, G. - 969
Fiandra, E.
Missione archeologica della univer-
sità di Perugia a Leptis Magna.
Annali. Facoltà di lettere e filoso-
fia della università di Perugia 1.

Magi, F. - Scichilone, G. - 969
Fiandra, E.
3. 1965-66, p. 669-688.

                                    2.

Maioletti, B. 970
Le fonti dell'architettura romana in
Cirenaica.
RdC 4. 1930, p. 568-588.

Marchiori, G. 971
Pitture romane in Libia. Gli affre-
schi della tomba di Gargaresh.
Libia 4. 1940, n. 3, p. 18-22.

Matthews, K.D. - Cook, A.W. 972
Cities in the sand: Leptis Magna
and Sabratha in Roman Africa.
Philadelphia: Pennsylvania UP 1957.

Mingazzini, P. 973
Sulla vera denominazione del cosi-
detto Capitolium di Cirene.
QAL 4. 1961, p. 101-103.

Mingazzini, P. - Fiandra, E. 974
L'insula di Giasone Magno a Cirene.
Roma: L'Erma di Bretschneider 1966.
(MAL. 8.)

Mostafa, M. 975
Excavations in Medinet Sultan.
LA 3/4. 1966/67, p. 145-154.

Nicolet, C. 976
Somptueuse Leptis-Magna.
Archeologia 1965, n. 4, p. 40-49.

Oliverio, G. 977
La stele di Tolemeo Neóteros, re di
Cirene.
Bergamo/Roma 1932.
(Documenti antichi dell'Africa
 italiana. 1,1.)

Oliverio, G. 978
I conti dei demiurgi.
Bergamo/Roma 1933.
(Documenti antichi dell'Africa
 italiana. 1,2.)

Oliverio, G. 979
La stele dei nuovi comandamenti e
dei cereali.
Bergamo/Roma 1933.
(Documenti antichi dell'Africa
 italiana. 2,1.)

Oliverio, G.   980

Il decreto di Anastasio Io su l'or-
dinamento politico-militare della
Cirenaica.
Bergamo/Roma 1936.
(Documenti antichi ... 2,2.)

Pace, B.   981

Ritratto Giulio-Claudio di Lepcis
Magna.
QAL 3. 1954, p. 5-12.

Paribeni, E.   982

Catalogo delle sculture di Cirene,
statue e rilievi di carattere reli-
gioso.
Roma: L'Erma di Bretschneider 1959.
(MAL. 5.)

Pedley, J.G.   983

Apollonia excavations.
Archaeology 20. 1967, p. 219-220.

Pedley, J.G.   984

Excavations at Apollonia, Cyrenaica.
Second preliminary report.
American journal of archaeology 71.
1967, p. 141-147.

Penel, M.C.   985

Le Uadi el Adjal.
Archeologia 1970, n. 33, p. 64-68.

Pernier, L.   986

Il tempio e l'altare di Apollo a
Cirene.
Bergamo 1935.
(Africa italiana. Serie di monogra-
fie. Ministero delle Colonie. 5.)

Picard, G.   987

Bas-relief romain de Tigi (Tripolitaine).
Bulletin archéologique du comité
des travaux historiques et scientifiques 1959/60 (1962), p. 35-40.

Pietrogrande, A.L.   988

La fontana presso i propilei nel
santuario di Apollo a Cirene.
AIb 7. 1940, p. 112-131.

Rainey, F.   989

In search of Egi Zuma.
Expedition 11. 1969, n. 4, p. 2-11.

Rebuffat, R. - Deneauve, J. -   990
Hallier, G.

Bu Njem 1967.
LA 3/4. 1966/67, p. 49-137.

Rebuffat, R.   991

Deux ans de recherches dans le sud
de la Tripolitaine.
CR des séances de l'académie des
inscriptions et belles lettres
1969, p. 189-212.

Reynolds, J.M. - Goodchild, R.G.992

The city lands of Apollonia in Cyrenaica.
LA 2. 1965, p. 103-107.

Romanelli, P.   993

Dieci anni di esplorazione archeologica in Tripolitania.
Aegyptus 3. 1922, p. 295-314.

Romanelli, P.   994

Gli archi di Tiberio e di Traiano
in Leptis Magna.
AIb 7. 1940, p. 87-105.

Romanelli, P.   995

Topografia e archeologia dell'Africa romana.
Torino: Società Editrice Internazionale 1970.
(Enciclopedia classica. Sez.3,10,7.)

Rosenbaum, E.   996
A catalogue of Cyrenaican portrait
sculpture.
London: Oxford UP 1960.

Rowe, A. - Buttle, D. -   997
Gray, J. - Healy, J.F.
Cyrenaican expeditions of the Uni-
versity of Manchester. Vol. 1.2.
Manchester UP 1956-60.

Rowe, A.   998
New light on Aegypto-Cyrenaean relations.
Annales du service des antiquités de
l'Egypte 12. 1958. Suppl.

Sabratha.   999
Architectural review 136. 1964,
p. 339-441.

Salama, P.   1000
Les trésors maxentiens de Tripoli-
taine: rapport préliminaire.
LA 3/4. 1966/67, p. 21-27.

Stucchi, S.   1001
Un nuovo frammento di tridacna inci-
sa.
Boll. d'arte 44. 1959, p. 158-166.

Stucchi, S.   1002
Il "Portico delle Erme" di Cirene.
Boll. d'arte 44. 1959, p. 57-61.

Stucchi, S.   1003
La statua dello strategheion di Cirene.
Archeologia classica 12. 1960, p. 71-
90.

Stucchi, S.   1004
Le fasi costruttive dell'Apollonion
di Cirene.
QAL 4. 1961, p. 55-81.

Stucchi, S.   1005
I lavori della missione archeologica italiana a Cirene dal 1957 al
1960.
QAL 4. 1961, p. 133-139.

Stucchi, S.   1006
Il restauro del portico detto
"delle Cariatidi" a Cirene.
Atti del congresso internazionale
di archeologia classica 7. 1961,
vol. 1, p. 443-448.

Stucchi, S.   1007
Attività della missione archeologica italiana a Cirene.
Annuario della scuola archeologica
di Atene 39/40. 1961/62, p. 659-
664.

Stucchi, S.   1008
La tomba a tumulo presso Messa in
Cirenaica.
LA 1. 1964, p. 127-131.

Stucchi, S. - Gasperini, L. -   1009
Pandolfi, L.
L'agorà di Cirene.
Roma: L'Erma di Bretschneider 1965.
(MAL. 7.)

Stucchi, S.   1010
I lavori di restauro eseguiti dalla
missione archeologica italiana a Cirene dal 1957 al '65.
LA 2. 1965, p. 109-122.

Stucchi, S.   1011
La ripresa dei lavori nel temenos
di Zeus a Cirene.
LA 3/4. 1966/67, p. 199-201.

Stucchi, S. 1012

Cirene, 1957-1966: un decennio di attività della missione archeologica italiana a Cirene.
Tripoli: Istituto Italiano di Cultura 1967.

Stucchi, S. 1013

Prime tracce tardo-minoiche a Cirene: i rapporti della Libia con il mondo egeo.
QAL 5. 1967, p. 19-45.

Tomlinson, R.A. 1014

False-façade tombs at Cyrene.
Annual of the British School at Athens 62. 1967, p. 241-256.

Traversari, G. 1015

L'altorilievo di Afrodite a Cirene.
Roma: L'Erma di Bretschneider 1959.

Traversari, G. 1016

Statue iconiche femminili cirenaiche.
Roma: L'Erma di Bretschneider 1960.

Turba, L. 1017

Graffiti con figure di navi nelle pareti di un fornice del teatro di Sabratha.
QAL 3. 1954, p. 109-112.

Vergara-Caffarelli, E. 1018

Le antichità della Tripolitania negli ultimo due anni.
Libia 2. 1954, n. 1, p. 77-81.

Vergara-Caffarelli, E. - Caputo, G. - Bianchi Bandinelli, R.- 1019
Clerici, F.

Leptis Magna.
The buried city. Excavations at Leptis Magna. 1.

Vergara Caffarelli, E. ... 1019

Milano/Verona: Mondadori 1964.
London: Weidenfeld & Nicholson 1966.

2.

Vilimková, M. - Wimmer, H. 1020

Roman art in Africa.
London: Hamlyn 1964.

Ville, G. 1021

Essai de datation de la mosaïque des gladiateurs de Zliten.
La mosaique gréco-romaine. Paris 1965, p. 147-155.

Vita, A. di - Goodchild, R.G. - 1022
Ayoub, M.S.

Archaeological news 1962-1963. Tripolitania. Cyrenaica. Fezzan.
LA 1. 1964, p. 133-147.

Vita, A. di 1023

Il "limes" romano di Tripolitania nella sua concretezza archeologica e nella sua realtà storica.
LA 1. 1964, p. 65-98.

Vita, A. di 1024

Ricordo di Ernesto Vergara Caffarelli (1907-1961).
LA 1. 1964, p. 149-150.

Vita, A di - Goodchild, R.G. 1025

Archaeological news 1963-1964.
Tripolitania. Cyrenaica.
LA 2. 1965, p. 129-139.

Vita, A. di 1026

La villa della "Gara delle Nereide" presso Tagiura.
Tripoli: Directorate-general of Antiquities, Museums and Archives 1966.
(LA. Suppl. 2.)

Vita, A. di   1027

Influences grecques et tradition orientale dans l'art punique en Tripolitaine.
Mélanges d'archéologie et d'histoire 80. 1968, p. 7-44.

Vita, A. di   1028

Shadrapa e Milk'achtart dèi patri di Leptis ed i templi del lato nord-ovest del foro vecchio lepitano.
Orientalia NS 37. 1968, p. 201-211.

Vita, A. di   1029

Le date di fondazione di Leptis e di Sabratha.
Hommages à Marcel Renard. Collection Latomus 103. 1969, vol. 3, p. 196-202.

Vita-Evrard, G. di   1030

Les dédicaces de l'amphithéâtre et du cirque de Leptis.
LA 2. 1965, p. 29-37.

Vita-Finzi, C.   1031

Post-Roman changes in Wadi Lebda.
FSL 1960, p. 46-51.

Vita-Finzi, C.   1032

Roman dams in Tripolitania.
Antiquity 35. 1961, p. 14-20.

Vita-Finzi, C.   1033

Water conservation in Roman Tripolitania.
Illustrated London news 1961, December, p. 1058-1061.

Vita-Finzi, C. - Brogan, O.   1034

Roman dams on the Wadi Megenin.
LA 2. 1965, p. 65-71.

Ward Perkins, J.B.   1035

Interim report on excavations at Sabratha in 1948.
RMDAT 2. 1949, p. 21-24.

Ward Perkins, J.B.   1036

The art of the Severan age in the light of Tripolitanian discoveries.
Proceedings of the British academy 37. 1951, p. 269-304.

Ward Perkins, J.B. - Ballance, M.H. - Reynolds, J.M.   1037

The caesareum at Cyrene and the basilica at Cremna.
PBSR 26. 1958, p. 137-194.

Ward Perkins, J.B.   1038

A new group of sixth-century mosaics from Cyrenaica.
Riv. di archeologia cristiana 34. 1958, p. 183-192.

Ward Perkins, J.B.   1039

Apollonia.
Reallexikon zur byzantinischen Kunst 1963, fasc. 2, p. 218-227.

Warmington, B.H.   1040

The municipal patrons of Roman North Africa.
PBSR 22. 1954, p. 39-55.

Weis, H.   1041

Der antike Fezzan - das Glacis des Limes Tripolitanus.
Jahreshefte des österreichischen archäologischen Instituts 44. 1959, Beiblatt, p. 167-208.

Wheeler, R.E.M. - Wood, R.   1042

Roman Africa in colour.
Römisches Afrika in Farben.
London: Thames & Hudson 1966.
München: Droemer-Knaur 1968.

White, D.   1043

Excavations at Apollonia, Cyrenaica.
American journal of archaeology 70.
1966, p. 259-265.

Widrig, W.M. - Goodchild, R.G.   1044

The west church at Apollonia in Cyrenaica.
PBSR 28. 1960, p. 70-90.

Wright, G.R.H.   1045

Cyrene: a survey of certain rock-cut
features to the south of the sanc-
tuary of Apollo.
Journal of Hellenic studies 77. 1957,
p. 300-310.

Wright, G.R.H.   1046

Excavations at Tocra incorporating
archaeological evidence of a community of the diaspora.
Palestine exploration quarterly 95.
1963, p. 22-64.

Ximenes, E.   1047

Leptis Magna.
Emporium 42. 1915, p. 341-355.

Zoehrer, L.G.H.   1048

Prehistoric and historic cultural
monuments in the Fezzan (Libya).
Antiquity and survival 2. 1957/58,
p. 321-348.

History. General.

Arista, G.B.   1049

La Libia nella sua storia dalle origini alle ultime vicende (Sintesi
politico-militare).
Rassegna cult. milit. 9. 1943,
p. 1119-1140.

Aumeunier, V. - Miège, J.L.   1050

Sources italiennes sur l'Afrique du
Nord.
AAN 3. 1964, p. 713-726, 5. 1966,
p. 793-811.

Bono, S.   1051

Fonti inedite di storia della Tripolitania.
Libia 1. 1953, n. 2, p. 117-122.

Bono, S.   1052

La situazione attuale dell'archivio
storico della Tripolitania.
OM 47. 1967, p. 825-827.

Bovill, E.W.   1053

Caravans of the old Sahara.
London: Oxford UP 1933.

Bovill, E.W.   1054

The golden trade of the Moors ...
with additional material by
R. Hallett. 2nd ed.
London: Oxford UP 1968.

Caputo, G.   1055

Nuovi elementi della storicità del
Sahara.
Libia 5. 1941, n. 1-2, p. 13-15.

Carcione, A.   1056

Le cause della decadenza dell'Africa
romana e la rinascita della Libia.
RdC 4. 1930, p. 603-614.

Compendio storico della   1057
Tripolitania.
Tripoli 1961.

Filesi, T.   1058

Evoluzione storico-politica dell'
Africa. Lineamenti fondamentali.
Como: Cairoli 1967.

Fushaika, M. ben M.   1059

A short history of Libya, from the
remotest times up to date.
Tripoli: Government Printing Press
1962.

Lefèvre, R.   1060

Fonti per la storia coloniale: l'archivio storico dell'Africa italiana.
Rassegna storica del risorgimento
1940, febbr., p. 173-176.

Murabet, M.   1061

A brief history of Tripolitania.
Tripoli 1965.

Nickerson, J.S.   1062

A short history of North Africa,
from pre-Roman times to the present:
Libya, Tunisia, Algeria, Morocco.
New York: Devin-Adair Co. 1961.

Paribeni, R.   1063

L'influenza dell'Italia nell'Africa
mediterranea dalla romanità all'età
di mezzo.
Italia e Africa mediterranea. Firenze 1942, p. 3-41.

Piccioli, A.   1064

La collezione sulla storia della
Libia.
ASIPS 25. 1936, vol. 3, p. 195-199.

Romanelli, P.   1065

La Libia dalle origini alla conquista
italiana: storia e monumenti.
L'impero coloniale fascista. Novara
1936, p. 401-438.

Thiry, J.   1066

Le Fezzân. Notes historiques et so-
cio-économiques.
Correspondance d'orient. Études
3. 1963, p. 36-65.

Toschi, P.   1067

Per la raccolta delle fonti storiche della Libia.
RdC 5. 1931, p. 878-879.

Toschi, P.   1068

Rerum libycarum scriptores.
ACSC 1. 1931, vol. 2, p. 210-216.

Valori, F.   1069

Storia della Cirenaica.
Firenze: Sansoni 1961.
(Le piccole storie illustrate. 62.)

Vernier, B.   1070

Histoire d'un pays saharien: le
Fezzân.
Orient 14. 1960, p. 57-72.

Wright, J.   1071

Libya.
London: Benn 1969.
New York: Praeger 1969.
(Nations of the modern world.)

History.
- 645.

Afrika und Rom in der Antike.   1072
Ed. H.J. Diesner.
Halle(Saale) 1968.
(Wissenschaftliche Beiträge der Mar-
tin-Luther-Universität Halle-Witten-
berg 1968/6, C 8.)

ianc

Anderson, J.K.   1073

Homeric, British and Cyrenaic chariots.
American journal of archaeology 69.
1965, p. 349-352.

Applebaum, S.   1074

The Jewish revolt in Cyrene in 115-
117, and the subsequent recolonisa-
tion.
Journal of Jewish studies 2. 1950/51,
p. 177-186.

Applebaum, S.   1075

The rebellion of the Jews of Cyrenaica in the time of Trajanus.
Zion 19. 1954, p. 23-56, 22. 1957,
p. 81-85.

Applebaum, S.   1076

A possible Jewish military settlement in Cyrenaica.
Bulletin of the Israel exploration
society 19. 1955, p. 188-197.

Applebaum, S.   1077

The Jewish community of Hellenistic
and Roman Teucheira in Cyrenaica.
Scripta hierosolymitana 7. 1961,
p. 27-52.

Arangio-Ruiz, V.   1078

Epigrafia cirenaica e il diritto
pubblico dell'antichità.
ACSC 1. 1931, vol. 2, p. 68-84.

Aurigemma, S.   1079

In a Roman villa at Zliten.
Art and archaeology 23. 1927, p. 161-
169.

Aurigemma, S.   1080

L'elefante di Leptis Magna.
AIb 7. 1940, p. 67-86.

Aurigemma, S.   1081

Il culto della casa di Augusto in
Leptis Magna.
AAI 4. 1941, vol. 2, p. 587-590.

Balty, J.   1082

Un prototype officiel dans l'icono-
graphie de Septime Sévère.
Bulletin de l'institute historique
belge de Rome 33. 1961, p. 101-113.

Barnes, T.D.   1083

The family and career of Septimius
Severus.
Historia 16. 1967, p. 87-107.

Bates, O.   1084

The eastern Libyans.
London: Cass 1970. Repr.

Blessich, A.   1085

Geografia storica delle dipendenze
continentali. Il disegno dell'Africa
romana.
AIn 35. 1916, p. 81-101.

Boardman, J.   1086

Bronze age Greece and Libya.
Annual of the British school at
Athens 63. 1968, p. 41-44.

Bonacelli, B.   1087

L'agro bengasino nell'antichità.
RdC 1/2. 1927/28, p. 581-588.

Bonacelli, B.   1088

Olivicoltura e civiltà nel Nord
Africa.
RdC 6. 1932, p. 675-688.

Borrelli, N. 1089

Della politica monetaria dei romani
nelle colonie e nelle province con
particolare riguardo alla Cirenaica.
ACSC 1. 1931, vol. 2, p. 88-94.

Boruchovič, V.G. 1090

Die Achäer in der Überlieferung von
der Gründung Kyrenes.
Učenije zapiski gorkovskogo gosud.
universiteta 67. 1965, p. 52-73.

Bovill, E.W. 1091

The camel and the Garamantes.
Antiquity 30. 1956, p. 19-21.

Brunel, J. 1092

Les anténorides à Cyrène et l'inter-
prétation littérale de Pindare,
"Pythique V", v. 82-88.
Revue des études anciennes 66. 1964,
p. 5-21.

Burian, J. 1093

Die einheimische Bevölkerung Nordafrikas von den punischen Kriegen
bis zum Ausgang des Prinzipats.
Altheim, F.: Die Araber in der alten
Welt. 1.

Burian, J. 1093

Berlin: de Gruyter.
Vol. 1. 1964, p. 420-549.

2.

Burian, J. 1094

Nordafrika und die Spätantike.
Helikon 7. 1967 (1968), p. 549-554.

Burian, F. 1095

Die einheimische Bevölkerung Nord-
afrikas in der Spätantike bis zur
Einwanderung der Wandalen.
Altheim, F.: Die Araber in der alten
Welt. 1.

Burian, F. 1095

Berlin: de Gruyter.
Vol. 5,1. 1968, p. 170-304.

2.

Camps, G. 1096

Du nouveau sur l'archéologie du
Fezzân.
TIRS 13. 1955, p. 189-198.

Capovilla, G. 1097

Callimachea et Libyca.
Aegyptus 42. 1962, p. 27-97.

Capovilla, G. 1098

Callimaco e Cirene storica e mitica.
Aegyptus 43. 1963, p. 141-191, 356-
383.

Caputo, G. 1099

Storia e arte della Libia antica.
Emporium 88. 1938, p. 319-329.

Caputo, G. 1100

La campagna della missione di archeologia e paleantropologia.
Oltremare 8. 1934, p. 105-107.

Caputo, G. 1101

Il tempio oeense al genio della colonia.
AIb 7. 1940, p. 35-45.

Caputo, G. 1102

Corrente preistorica dell'artigianato della Tripolitania in prodotti
coevi ai vasi ellenistici e romani.
Atti del congresso internazionale di
preistoria e protostoria mediterranea 1. 1950 (1952), p. 325-329.

Caputo, G.   1103

Sculture di Leptis Magna.
Parola del passato 10. 1955, p. 306-
310, 11. 1956, p. 139-144, 12. 1957,
p. 378-383.

Caputo, G.   1104

Fezzan.
Enciclopedia dell'arte antica, classica e orientale vol. 3. 1960,
p. 636-638.

Carpenter, R.   1105

A trans-Saharan caravan route in He-
rodotus.
American journal of archaeology 60.
1956, p. 231-242.

Castagnoli, F.   1106

Euesperides.
Enciclopedia dell'arte antica, classica e orientale vol. 3. 1960,
p. 520.

Cauvet, G.   1107

Que sont devenus les Libyens des
anciens ?
Actes du congrès de la federation
des soc. savantes de l'Afrique du
Nord. Alger 2. 1936, vol. 2, p. 387-
400.

Chamoux, F.   1108

L'hellénisme en Cyrénaïque.
Phoibos 3/4. 1948/50, p. 5-19.

Chamoux, F.   1109

Cyrène sous la monarchie des Battia-
des.
Paris: Boccard 1953.
(Bibliothèque des écoles françaises
d'Athènes et de Rome. 177.)

Chastagnol, A.   1110

Les gouverneurs de Byzacène et de
Tripolitaine.
Antiquités africaines 1. 1967, p.119-
134.

Ciaceri, E.   1111

I più antichi coloni siciliani a
Tripoli.
ACSC 1. 1931, vol. 2, p. 52-59.

Corò, F.   1112

L'Africa settentrionale nell'antichità. Condizioni climatiche e idriche.
Oltremare 6. 1932, p. 328-330.

Corò, F.   1113

Le grandi proprietà romane nella
provincia d'Africa.
Oltremare 6. 1932, p. 26-27.

Corò, F.   1114

Fulgori di Leptis Magna nel mondo.
Ricordi di un colloquio con Giacomo
Guidi.
IdO 2. 1937, n. 4, p. 18-20.

Coster, C.H.   1115

The economic position of Cyrenaica
in classical times.
Studies in Roman economic and social
history in honour of A.C. Johnson.
Princeton 1951, p. 3-26.

Daniels, C.M.   1116

The Garamantes.
GAPSF 1969, p. 31-52.

Daniels, C.M.   1117

Garamantes of southern Libya.
Stoughton/Wisc.: Oleander Press 1970.

Dart, R.A.   1118

The Garamantes of Central Sahara.
African studies 11. 1952, p. 29-34.

Désanges, J. 1119

A propos du triomphe de Cornélius
Balbus.
TIRS 14. 1956, p. 213-215.

Désanges, J. 1120

Le triomphe de Cornélius Balbus (19
av. J.C.).
Revue africaine 101. 1957, p. 5-43.

Despréaux, J. 1121

Cités garamantiques au pays de Ghadamès.
Bulletin économique de Tunisie 1950,
n. 39, p. 63-68.

Diringer, D. 1122

La grande sommossa giudaica nell'antica Cirenaica e le sue cause.
ACSC 1. 1931, vol. 2, p. 94-104.

Dulière, C. 1123

Les autels de Philènes dans le fond
de la Grande Syrte.
Correspondance d'orient. Etudes
1965/66, n. 8/9, p. 17-26.

Ferri, S. 1124

La "lex cathartica" di Cirene.
NA 1927, fasc. 4, p. 91-145.

Ferri, S. 1125

Osservazioni al testo della "lex
cathartica" di Cirene.
ACSC 2. 1934, vol. 2, p. 68-69.

Ferri, S. 1126

Sulla acconciatura "libica".
ACSC 3. 1937, vol. 4, p. 162-168.

Ferri, S. 1127

Paestum e la lex cathartica di Cirene.
Parola del passato 10. 1955, p. 195-
196.

Fuks, A. 1128

Aspects of the Jewish revolt in A.D.
115-117.
JRS 51. 1961, p. 98-104.

Galassi, G. 1129

Tehenu e le origini mediterranee
della civiltà egizia.
Roma 1942.

Galassi, G. 1130

Tehenu.
AAI 6. 1943, vol. 2, p. 321-326.

Gasparrini, T. 1131

Il silfio, preziosa pianta dell'
antica Cirenaica.
REAI 29. 1941, p. 436-443.

Gerola, G. 1132

Che cosa potrebbero insegnare i si-
gilli dei vescovi titolari di Tripoli.
AIb 1. 1927/28, p. 286-295.

Gigli, G. 1133

Orme di Roma in Tripolitania.
RdC 4. 1930, p. 900-903.

Goodchild, R.G. 1134

Helios on the Pharos.
The antiquaries journal 41. 1961,
p. 218-223.

Goodchild, R.G. 1135

Graeco-roman Cyrenaica.
GANC 1968, p. 23-40.

Hammamy, A. el 1136

Roman North Africa.
Le Caire: Imprimerie Sociale 1948.

Harrison, R.M. 1137

An Orpheus mosaic at Ptolemais in
Cyrenaica.
JRS 52. 1962, p. 13-18.

Haywood, R.M. 1138

A further note on the African policy
of Septimius Severus.
Hommages à Albert Grenier. Collection Latomus 58. 1962, p. 786-790.

Hoelscher, W. 1139

Libyer und Ägypter. Beiträge zur Ethnologie und Geschichte libyscher
Völkerschaften nach den altägypti-
schen Quellen.   Repr.
Glückstadt-Hamburg: Augustin 1955.

Honigmann, E. 1140

Libye/Libya.
Paulys Real-Encyclopaedie der classi-
schen Altertumswissenschaft vol.13,1.
1926, p. 149-202.

Jefferey, L.H. 1141

The pact of the first settlers at
Cyrene.
Historia 10. 1961, p. 139-147.

Kwapong, A. 1142

Citizenship and democracy in fourth
century Cyrene.
Nigeria and the classics. Ed. J. Fer-
guson. Ibadan 1958, p. 80-91.

Lallemand, J. 1143

L'administration civile de l'Égypte
de l'avènement de Dioclétien à la
création du diocèse (284-382).
Mémoire de l'académie royale de Belgique. Classe des lettres 57,2.1964.

Law, R.C.C. 1144

Garamantes and trans-Saharan enterprise in classical times.
Journal of African history 8. 1967,
p. 181-200.

Lenger, M.T. 1145

Corpus des ordonnances des Ptolé-
mées.
Mémoire de l'académie royale de Belgique. Classe des lettres 57,1.1964.

Levi, M.A. 1146

I politeumata e la evoluzione della
società ellenica nel IV sec. a.C.
Parola del passato 18. 1963, p. 321-
336.

Lhote, H. 1147

L'expédition de Cornelius Balbus au
Sahara (en 19 av. J.C. d'après le
texte de Pline).
Revue africaine 98. 1954, p. 41-81.

Mac Michael, H.M.A. 1148

A history of the Arabs in the Sudan
and some account of the people who
preceded them ... Vol. 1.2.
London: Cass 1967. Repr.

Machu, J. 1149

Cyrène: la cité et le souverain à
l'époque hellénistique.
Revue historique 75. 1951, p. 41-55.

Massano, G. 1150

Tripoli centro turistico e stazione
di sverno nell'antica Roma.
RdC 1/2. 1927/28, p. 297-305.

Meliu, A. 1151

Albori della dominazione romana in
Cirenaica.
RdC 11. 1937, p. 1587-1591.

Meliu, A. 1152

La Cirenaica sotto i Lagidi. Alessan-
dro il Macedone e Tolomeo I Soter.
Libia 2. 1938, n. 6, p. 17-23.

Micacchi, R. 1153

La missione antropologica ed archeologica nel Fezzan. La scoperta dei
Garamanti.
Riv. di antropologia 30. 1933/34,
p. 499-506.

Millar, F. 1154

Local cultures in the Roman empire:
Libyan, Punic and Latin in Roman
Africa.
JRS 58. 1968, p. 126-134.

Mitchell, B.M. 1155

Cyrene and Persia.
Journal of Hellenic studies 86. 1966,
p. 99-113.

Moeller, G. 1156

Die Ägypter und ihre libyschen Nach-
barn.
Zeitschrift für Ethnologie 53. 1921,
p. 427-430.

Montet, P. 1157

Mission en Égypte et en Cyrénaïque.
CR des séances. Académie des inscriptions et belles-lettres 1955, p.327-
331.

Morton, J.A. 1158

Notes on visits to the ancient cities
of Cyrenaica.
Proceedings. Society of Antiquaries
of Newcastle upon Tyne ser. 4, vol.
10. 1942/46, p. 358-366.

Morton, J.A. 1159

The Roman cities of Tripolitania.
Proceedings. Society of Antiquaries
of Newcastle upon Tyne ser. 4, vol.
10. 1942/46, p. 282-294.

Newbold, D. 1160

The history and archaeology of the
Libyan Desert.
Sudan notes and records 26. 1945,
p. 229-239.

Oost, S.I. 1161

Cyrene, 96-74 B.C.
Classical philology 58. 1963, p. 11-
25.

Pace, B. 1162

Roma nel Sahara.
Nuova antologia 69. 1934, fasc. 1489,
p. 374-385.

Pace, B. 1163

La romanizzazione del Sahara.
AIn 52. 1934, p. 206-224.

Pace, B. 1164

Scavi sahariani.
AANL. Rendiconti. Classe di scienze
morali ... ser. 6, vol. 10. 1934,
p. 164-173.

Pace, B. 1165

Relazione preliminare delle ricerche
compiute nel Fezzàn dalla missione
di archeologia e paleoantropologia
della R. Società Geografica Italiana.
BSGI 72. 1935, p. 163-179.

Pace, B. 1166

Storia antica.
SIFOG 1937, p. 275-299.

Pallottino, M.   1167

Note sulla stele di Gadàmes.
RdC 7. 1933, p. 547-553.

Pallottino, M.   1168

L'impero di Roma di fronte ai problemi sociali e politici della Cirenaica.
RSAI 5. 1942, p. 294-301.

Pallottino, M.   1169

Politica sociale dei romani in Cirenaica.
RSAI 5. 1942, p. 169-175.

Pallottino, M.   1170

Il volto romano della Cirenaica:
monumenti d'interesse pubblico e
sociale.
RSAI 5. 1942, p. 545-549.

Parri, W.   1171

Relitti di manifatture di porpora
a Tobruk.
RdC 6. 1932, p. 720-723.

Pesce, G. - Paribeni, E.   1172

Cirene.
Enciclopedia dell'arte antica, classica e orientale vol. 2. 1959,
p. 655-692.

Pesce, G.   1173

Tolemaide.
Enciclopedia dell'arte antica, classica e orientale vol. 7. 1966,
p. 896-898.

Picard, G.C.   1174

Influences étrangères et originali-
té dans l'art de l'Afrique romaine
sous les Antonines et les Sévères.
Antike Kunst 5. 1962, p. 30-41.

Polacco, L.   1175

Un ritratto da Cirene e l'espressio-
ne ellenistico.
Atti dell'istituto veneto di scienze,
lettere ed arti. Classe di scienze
morali 113. 1954-55, p. 223-247.

Polacco, L.   1176

Il volto di Tiberio. Saggio di critica iconografica.
Memorie della accademia patavina di
scienze, lettere e arti 67. 1954-
55, p. 1-207.

Polacco, L.   1177

L'atleta Cirene-Perinto.
Roma: L'Erma di Bretschneider 1955.

Polacco, L.   1178

Genius Tiberi.
Arte antica e moderna 1. 1958, n. 1,
p. 13-17.

Premerstein, A. von   1179

Die fünf neugefundenen Edikte des
Augustus aus Kyrene.
Zeitschrift der Savigny-Stiftung
für Rechtsgeschichte. Romanistische
Abteilung 48. 1928, p. 419-531.

Pugliese Carratelli, G.   1180

Cari in Libia.
Parola del passato 3. 1948, p. 15-
19.

Read, E.   1181

Leptis Magna - pushing back the
sands of time.
Contemporary review 209. 1966, p.73-
77.

Rellini, U.   1182

I garamanti.
Boll. di paleontologia italiana
NS 1. 1936-37, p. 148-153.

Reynolds, J.M. 1183
The Jewish revolt of A.D. 115 in Cyrenaica.
Proceedings of the Cambridge Philological Society NS 5. 1958-59,
p. 24-28.

Romanelli, P. 1184
Antichità della regione di Gurgi (Tripoli).
NA 1922, fasc. 3, p. 35-38.

Romanelli, P. 1185
Tomba romana con affreschi del IV secolo dopo Cristo nella regione di Gargàresh (Tripoli).
NA 1922, fasc. 3, p. 21-32.

Romanelli, P. 1186
La politica romana delle acque in Tripolitania.
La rinascita della Tripolitania.
Milano 1926, p. 569-576.

Romanelli, P. 1187
L'unità storica geografica della Tripolitania antica.
ACSC 2. 1934, vol. 2, p. 7-13.

Romanelli, P. 1188
Problemi di storia e di archeologia dell'Africa libico-romana (dalla Grande Sirte all'Atlantico) sulla base degli scavi più recenti.
ACSC 3. 1937, vol. 4, p. 114-132.

Romanelli, P. 1189
Il confine orientale della provincia romana di Cirene.
Atti della pontificia accademia romana di archeologia. Rendiconti.
Ser. 3, vol. 16. 1940, p. 215-223.

Romanelli, P. 1190
I libi di fronte alla romanità e all'ellenismo.
AION NS 3. 1949, p. 237-243.

Romanelli, P. 1191
Note storico-geografiche relative all'Africa al tempo di Augusto. 1-3.
AANL. Rendiconti. Classe di scienze morali ... ser. 8, vol. 5. 1950,
p. 472-492.

Romanelli, P. 1192
Apollonia di Cirenaica. Leptis Magna. Sabratha. Tripoli.
Enciclopedia dell'arte antica, classica e orientale vol. 1. 1958,
p. 482-483, 4. 1961, p. 572- 1.

Romanelli, P. 1192
594, 6. 1965, p. 1050-1060, 7. 1966,
p. 986-987.

2.

Romanelli, P. 1193
"Fulvii Lepcitani".
Archeologia classica 10. 1958,
p. 258-261.

Romanelli, P. 1194
Storia delle province romane dell'Africa.
Roma: L'Erma di Bretschneider 1959.
(Studi pubbl. dall'Istituto Italiano per la Storia Antica. 14.)

Romanelli, P. 1195
Un nuovo governatore della provincia di Creta e Cirene: P. Pomponio Secondo.
QAL 4. 1961, p. 97-100.

Romanelli, P. 1196
Roma e i libi durante le guerre puniche.
Annuario accad. etrusca Cortona
12. 1961-64, p. 153-165.

Rossi, M. 1197
Una leggenda libica in Sallustio e le Arae Philaenorum nella Sirtica.
ASIPS 7. 1913, p. 1031.

Schaefer, H. 1198

Die verfassungsgeschichtliche Entwicklung Kyrenes im 1. Jahrhundert nach seiner Begründung.
Rheinisches Museum für Philologie,
NS 95. 1952, p. 135-170.

Seibert, J. 1199

Metropolis und Apoikie.
Würzburg 1963. Diss.

Seibert, J. 1200

Untersuchungen zur Geschichte Ptolemaios'I.
München: Beck 1969.   56.
(Münchner Beiträge zur Papyrusforschung und antiken Rechtsgeschichte.)

Sergi, S. 1201

Le reliquie dei garamanti.
BSGI 70. 1936, p. 1-12.

Sergi, S. 1202

I garamanti della Libia.
Atti del congresso nazionale di studi romani 4. 1935 (1938), vol. 2,
p. 67-76.

Teutsch, L. 1203

Das Städtewesen in Nordafrika in der Zeit von C. Gracchus bis zum Tode des Kaisers Augustus.
Berlin: de Gruyter 1962.

Thieling, W. 1204

Der Hellenismus in Kleinafrika.
Roma: L'Erma di Bretschneider 1964.
Repr.

Thomasson, B.E. 1205

Die Statthalter der römischen Provinzen Nordafrikas von Augustus bis Diocletianus. Vol. 1.
Lund: Gleerup 1960.

Valgimigli, M. 1206

Sulle orme di Callemaco a Cirene.
Inno ad Apollo e Inno a Demètra di Callimaco. Versione metrica.
AIb 2. 1928-29, p. 211-217.

Varriale, V. 1207

Romani in Tripolitania.
Napoli 1940.

Vergara Caffarelli, E. 1208

Ghirza.
Enciclopedia dell'arte antica, classica e orientale vol. 3. 1960,
p. 864-869.

Veyne, P. 1209

Ordo et populus, génies et chefs de file.
Mélanges d'archéologie et d'histoire 73. 1961, p. 229-274.

Visscher, F. de 1210

La justice romaine et cyrénaïque.
Revue internationale des droits de l'antiquité ser. 3, vol. 11. 1964,
p. 321-333.

Vita-Evrard, G. di 1211

Un "nouveau" proconsul d'Afrique, parent de Septime-Sévère: Caius Septimius Severus.
Mélanges d'archéologie et d'histoire 75. 1963, p. 389-414.

Vita-Evrard, G. di 1212

Nouvelles précisions sur la famille de Septime-Sévère.
Cahiers de Tunisie 12. 1964, p. 69-72.

Vitali, L. 1213

Una divinità della Cirenaica: Aristeo.
AIb 2. 1928-29, p. 17-29.

Vycichl, W.   1214

Three problems of North African
chronology. The Canary Islands - the
Hoggar in the central Sahara - old
Egypt.   1.
Actes du congrès international des

Vycichl, W.   1214

sciences anthropologiques et ethnologiques 4. 1952, vol. 3, p. 5-8.

Vycichl, W.   1215

Die Fürsten von Libyen. Zur 3000-
jährigen Geschichte eines Berber-
stammes.
AION NS 6. 1954-56, p. 43-48.

Vycichl, W.   1216

Atlanten, Isebeten, Ihaggaren. Ein
Beitrag zur Geschichte der Sahara
in der Antike.
RSO 31. 1956, p. 211-220.

Vycichl, W.   1217

L'allaitement du pharaon expliqué
par une coutume africaine.
Genève-Afrique 5. 1966, p. 261-265.

Wainwright, G.A.   1218

The Meshwesh.
Journal of Egyptian archaeology,
48. 1962, p. 89-99.

Waisglass, A.A.I.   1219

An historical study of Cyrene from
the fall of the Battiad monarchy to
the close of the fourth century B.C.
Ann Arbor, Mich.: University Micro-
films 1955. Diss.

Wellard, J.   1220

Lost worlds of Africa.
London: Hutchinson 1967.

Wheeler, R.E.M.   1221

Rome beyond the Imperial frontiers.
Harmondsworth: Penguin Books 1955.
(Pelican books. A 335.)

Woelfel, D.J.   1222

Weissafrika (Nordafrika).
Geographische Rundschau 6. 1954,
p. 405-409.

Woelfel, D.J.   1223

Weissafrika von den Anfängen bis zur
Eroberung durch die Araber.
Abriss der Geschichte antiker Rand-
kulturen. Ed. W.D. Barloewen. München vol. 1,C Ergänzungsbd.   1.

Woelfel, D.J.   1223

1961, p. 193-236.

2.

History.
645 - 1911.

Agostini, E. de   1224

Una spedizione americana in Cirenaica nel 1805.
RdC 1/2. 1927/28, p. 721-732, 3.1929,
p. 41-56.

Allen, G.W.   1225

Our navy and the Barbary corsairs.
Hamden, Conn.: Archon Books 1965.

Anderson, M.S.   1226

Great Britain and the Barbary states
(Morocco, Algiers, Tunis and Tripoli)
in the 18th century.
Bulletin of the Institute of Historical Research 29. 1956, p. 87-107.

Aurigemma, S.   1227

Murâd Aghâ.
RdC 4. 1930, p. 853-873.

Aurigemma, S.   1228

Mohàmmed Abdàlla di Chio.
AAI 5. 1942, vol. 3, p. 703-744.

Ausiello, A.   1229

Un tentativo di protettorato americano in Libia (1805).
RdC 17. 1943, p. 31-34.

Bergna, C.   1230

I primi italiani in Tripolitania.
Oltremare 3. 1929, p. 166-169.

Bergna, C.   1231

Il bagno di S. Michele (Tripoli).
Libia 1. 1937, n. 3, p. 34-35.

Bergna, C.   1232

I Caramanli.
Libia 1. 1953, n. 2, p. 5-59.

Bernard, A.   1233

Un mémoire inédit de Pellissier de
Reynaud.
Mémorial Henri Basset. Paris 1928,
p. 69-82.

Bodin, M.   1234

Le bombardement de Tripoli de Barbarie par le maréchal d'Estrées en
1685.
Revue tunisienne 1918, p. 204-209.

Bono, S.   1235

La pirateria nel Mediterraneo. Bolognesi schiavi a Tripoli nei sec. XVII
e XVIII.
Libia 2. 1954, n. 3, p. 25-37.

Bono, S.   1236

I corsari barbareschi.
Torino: ERI 1964.
(Saggi. 39.)

Bottini Massa, E.   1237

Tripoli di un secolo fa.
RdC 3. 1929, p. 984-991.

Bovill, E.W.   1238

Colonel Warrington.
Geographical journal 131. 1965,
p. 161-166.

Brett, M.   1239

Ifriqiya as a market for Saharan
trade from the tenth to the twelfth
century A.D.
Journal of African history 10. 1969,
p. 347-364.

Briggs, B.N.   1240

To the shores of Tripoli. A story
of the United States marines.
Philadelphia: Winston 1955.

Brunschvig, R.   1241

Le sac de Tripoli de Barbarie en
756/1355.
Arabica 2. 1955, p. 228.

Brunschvig, R.   1242

La Berberie orientale sous les Haf-
sides des origines à la fin du XVe
siècle. Vol. 1.2.
Alger/Paris 1940-47. Diss.

Brunschvig, R. 1243

Une texte arabe du IXe siècle in-
térressant le Fezzân.
Revue africaine 89. 1945, p. 21-25.

Cauneille, A. 1244

Le Fezzân sous Bey Khalifa.
BIS 9. 1958, n. 32, p. 298-300.

Cerbella, G. 1245

I colori della bandiera libica nella
storia e nella letteratura arabo musulmana.
Libia 2. 1954, n. 1, p. 45-76.

Charles-Roux, F. 1246

Bonaparte et la Tripolitaine.
Renseignements coloniaux 1925, p. 397-
398, 1926, p. 474-476.

Charles-Roux, F. 1247

Un horloger diplomate: Naudi et les
rétablissements des relations entre
la France et Tripoli en 1802.
Revue d'histoire des colonies françaises 17. 1929, p. 1-44.

Corò, F. 1248

Una relazione veneta su Tripoli nel
settecento.
RdC 4. 1930, p. 1092-1102.

Corò, F. 1249

Un incidente veneto-tripolino.
RdC 6. 1932, p. 451-460.

Corò, F. 1250

Ristabilimento del consolato veneto
a Tripoli nel 1683.
RdC 6. 1932, p. 949-958.

Corò, F. 1251

Il consolato americano di Tripoli
nei secoli XVIII, XIX e XX.
RdC 10. 1936, p. 1104-1111.

Corò, F. 1252

Che cos'era la Libia dal punto di
vista civile ed economico prima dell'
occupazione italiana.
Tripoli: Maggi 1937.

Corò, F. 1253

Cinque anni di storia tripolina.
AAI 2. 1939, vol. 2, p. 619-630.

Corò, F. 1254

Il consolato della repubblica di Venezia a Tripoli dal 1764 al 1797.
Libia 3. 1955, n. 3, p. 49-59.

Corso, R. 1255

Echi legendari delle incursioni barbaresche sopra Nicotera.
Libia 3. 1955, n. 2, p. 35-41.

Crocetta, A. 1256

Ibaditi.
ACSC 2. 1934, vol. 4, p. 169-184.

Djaït, H. 1257

La wilâya d'Ifrîqiya au IIe/VIIIe
siècle: étude institutionelle.
Studia islamica 27. 1967, p. 77-
121, 28. 1968, p. 79-107.

Ducati, B. 1258

La Libia musulmana dalla conquista
araba alla conquista turca.
Roma 1932.

Ducati, B.   1259

I berberi.
3. Dopo l'invasione beduina.
RdC 16. 1942, p. 755-768.

Eck, O.   1260

Seeräuberei im Mittelmeer.
München/Berlin 1940.

Eickhoff, E.   1261

Seekrieg und Seepolitik zwischen
Islam und Abendland (650-1040).
Berlin: de Gruyter 1966.

Fantoli, A.   1262

Una tragedia d'amore a Tripoli sullo sfondo di un contrasto politico.
Levante 13. 1966, p. 3-52.

Filesi, T.   1263

La reggenza di Tripoli secondo alcuni documenti dell'archivio di stato di Napoli relativi al 1790.
Africa. Roma 23. 1968, p. 233-244.

Frend, W.H.C.   1264

North Africa and Europe in the early Middle Ages.
Transactions. Royal Historical Society. London ser. 5, vol. 5. 1955,
p. 61-80.

Gaster, M.   1265

A mahdi in Tripoli in the year 1589.
Islamica 2. 1926, p. 193-199.

Godechot, J.   1266

La course maltaise le long des côtes barbaresques à la fin du XVIIIe
siècle.
Revue africaine 96. 1952, p. 105-
113.

Goodchild, R.G.   1267

Byzantines, Berbers and Arabs in
7th-century Libya.
Antiquity 41. 1967, p. 114-124.

Guidi, M.   1268

Ettore Rossi: La cronaca araba tripolina di Ibn Ġalbūn (sec. XVIII).
RSO 17. 1937, p. 287-292.

Hafkemeyer, G.B.   1269

Kaiserliche Lehnsurkunde über di Be-
lehnung des Ordens des Hl. Johannes
von Jerusalem mit dem Gebiet und den
Inseln von Tripolis, Malta und Gozzo.
Annales de l'ordre souverain   1.

Hafkemeyer, G.B.   1269

militaire de Malte 18. 1960, n. 2,
p. 10-15.

                                    2.

Herre, P.   1270

Nordafrika als Objekt der europäischen Kolonialpolitik.
Welt als Geschichte 2. 1936, p.169-
185, 259-278.

Ibn Khaldoun   1271

Histoire des berbères et des dy-
nasties musulmanes de l'Afrique
septentrionale. Vol. 1-4.
Paris: Geuthner 1925-56.

Icenhower, J.B.   1272

Mr. midshipman Murdock and the Barbary pirates.
Philadelphia: Winston 1956.

Idris, H.R.   1273

La Berbérie orientale sous les Zīrī-
des, Xe-XIIe siècles.
Paris: Maisonneuve 1962.
(Publications de l'Institut d'Études
Orientales d'Alger. 22.)

Idris, H.R.   1274

De la réalité de la catastrope hilâ-
lienne.
Annales. Economies. Societés. Civilisations 23. 1968, p. 390-396.

Irwin, R.W.   1275

The diplomatic relations of the
United States with the Barbary
powers 1776-1816.
Chapel Hill 1931.

Kemali   1276

Documenti inediti sulla caduta dei
Caramanli.
RdC 4. 1930, p. 1-24, 178-216.

Laperrousaz, A.   1277

Comment Ghadamès est devenue libyenne.
Paris: CHEAM 1956.
(Publication 2581.)

Lee, H.I.   1278

The supervising of the Barbary con-
suls during the years 1756-1836.
Bulletin of the Institute of Historical Research 23. 1950, p. 191-199.

Lefèvre, R.   1279

Tripoli sotto i Cavalieri di Malta.
Carlo V e la cessione di Tripoli all'
Ordine Gerosolimitano.
Mediterranea 1935, luglio, p. 39-44.

Lewicki, T. - Motylinski, A. de 1280

Abū Hātim al-Malzūzī. Abū'l Khattāb
al Ma'āfirī. Abū Mansūr al-Nafūsī.
Abū Zakariyyā' al-Djanāwunī. Abū Zakariyyā' al-Wardjlānī. Al Bughtūrī.
Al-Dardjīnī. Al-Djanāwanī.   1.

Lewicki, T.   1280

Al-Djaytālī. Al'Irdjanī.
EIne.

                              2.

Lewicki, T.   1281

Une chronique ibādite. "Kitāb as-
Sijar" d'Abū'l-'Abbās Ahmad aš-Šam-
māhi.
Revue des études islamiques 8. 1934,
p. 59-78.

Lewicki, T. - Basset, A.   1282

De quelques textes inédits en vieux
berbère provenant d'une chronique
ibādite anonyme.
Revue des études islamiques 8. 1934,
p. 275-305.

Lewicki, T. - Basset, A.   1283

Mélanges berbères-ibādites.
Revue des études islamiques 10. 1936,
p. 267-296.

Lewicki, T.   1284

Études ibādites nord-africaines.
Warszawa: Państwowe Wydawnictwo
Naukowe 1955.
(Prace orientalistyczne. 4.)

Lewicki, T.   1285

Les commerçants ibādites nord-africains dans le Soudan au moyen âge.
Trudy meždunarodnogo kongressa vosto-
kovedov 25. 1960 (1963), vol. 2,
p. 35-38.

Lewicki, T.   1286

Quelques extraits inédits relatifs
aux voyages des commerçants et des
missionaires ibādites nord-africains
au pays du Soudan occidental et central au moyen âge.   1.

Lewicki, T.   1286

Folia orientalia 2. 1960, p. 1-27.

                                 2.

Lewicki, T.   1287

Z dziejów handlu transsaharyjskiego:
Kupcy i misjonarze ibādyccy w zachod-
nim i środkowym Sudanie w VIII-XII w.
Przeglad orientalistyczny 37. 1961,
p. 3-18.

Lewicki, T.   1288

Les historiens, biographes et tradi-
tionnistes ibāḍites-wahbites de
l'Afrique du Nord du VIIIe au
XVIe siècle.
Folia orientalia 3. 1961, p. 1-134.

Lewicki, T.   1289

Ibāḍitica.
Rocznik orientalistyczny 25. 1961,
p. 87- 120, 26. 1962, p. 97-123.

Lewicki, T.   1290

Data nawrócenia Berberów na islam.
Sprawozdania z posiedzeń komisji.
Oddzial w Krakowie 7/12. 1964(1965),
p. 386-388.

Lewicki, T.   1291

Traits d'histoire du commerce trans-
saharien. Marchands et missionaires
ibāḍites en Soudan occidental et
central au cours des VIIIe-XIIe
siècles.   1.

Lewicki, T.   1291

Etnografia polska 8. 1964, p. 291-
311.

     2.

Lo Celso, M.T.   1292

Approci del Regno delle Due Cicilie
per allacciare rapporti commerciali
con Tripoli di Barberia verso la metà del XIX secolo.
Africa. Roma 22. 1967, p. 406-412.

Longhena, M.   1293

La spedizione contro Tripoli del
1510. (Da documenti bolognesi).
Archiginnasio 1936, luglio-dicembre,
p. 242-270.

Longhena, M.   1294

Le imprese contro Tripoli e l'isola
di Gerba dal 1284 al 1560.
Atti e memorie dell'accademia di
agricoltura, scienze e lettere di
Verona ser. 6, vol. 9. 1957-58,
p. 25-124.

Manfroni, C.   1295

Il maresciallo d'Estrées a Tripoli.
RdC 7. 1933, p. 533-536.

Mantran, R.   1296

Le statut del'Algérie, de la Tunisie
e de la Tripolitaine dans l'Empire
ottoman.
Atti del congresso internazionale di
studi nord-africani 1.1965,p.205-216.

Mantran, R.   1297

Rossi, E.: Storia di Tripoli e della
Tripolitania della conquista araba
al 1911.
AAN 7. 1968, p. 930-931.

Martin, B.G.   1298

Five letters from the Tripoli archives.
Journal of the Historical Society
of Nigeria 2. 1962, p. 350-372.

Martin, B.G.   1299

Kanem, Bornu and the Fazzān: notes
on the political history of a trade
route.
Journal of African history 10. 1969,
p. 15-27.

Martin, B.G.   1300

Mai Idris of Bornu and the Ottoman
Turks, 1576-78.
Documents from Islamic chanceriesII.
Ed. S.M. Stern. Oxford 1969.

Mas-Latrie, J.M.J.L. de   1301

Traités de paix et de commerce et
documents divers concernant les relations des chrétiens avec les Arabes de l'Afrique septentrionale au
moyen âge. Vol. 2.
New York: Franklin 1960. Repr.

Micacchi, R.   1302

Tripoli e la Tripolitania anterior-
mente all'occupazione italiana.
La rinascita della Tripolitania.
Milano 1926, p. 69-113.

Micacchi, R. 1303

Le ultime gesta dei corsari tripolini e la reazione degli stati italiani.
RdC 7. 1933, p. 201-222.

Micacchi, R. 1304

I rapporti tra il Regno di Francia e
la Reggenza di Tripoli di Barberia
nella prima metà del secolo XVIII.
RdC 8. 1934, p. 65-81, 159-182,
247-276.

Micacchi, R. 1305

La Tripolitania dal 1835 al 1858.
RdC 11. 1937, p. 816-832, 974-990.

Micacchi, R. 1306

Aspirazioni franco-russe sulla rada
di Bomba alla fine del'700.
RdC 12. 1938, p. 1595-1603.

Monterisi, M. 1307

L'Ordine a Malta, Tripoli e in Italia.
Milano 1940.

Naldoni, N. 1308

La dominazione spagnola a Tripoli.
ACSC 1. 1931, vo. 2, p. 274-296.

Nallino, C.A. 1309

Rossi, E.: La cronaca araba tripolina di Ibn Galbun (sec.XVIII) tradot-
ta e annotata.
OM 17. 1937, p. 60.

Orlandi, A. 1310

Vicende storico-sociali a Tripoli
dal dominio spagnolo alla caduta dei
Caramanli (sec XVI-XIX).
RSAI 3. 1940, p. 862-870.

Paladino, G. 1311

La spedizione della marina napoleta-
na a Tripoli nel 1828.
RdC 3. 1929, p. 909-924, 1003-1014.

Paternò Castello di Carcaci, F. 1312

Una battaglia nelle acque di Tripoli.
Riv. del sovrano militare ordine di
Malta 3. 1939, fasc. 7, p. 28-29.

Pedrazzi, O. 1313

Tripoli pattuglia di punta.
Riv. del sovrano militare ordine di
Malta 3. 1939, fasc. 4, p. 15-21.

Poncet, J. 1314

Le mythe dela "catastrope" hilalien-
ne.
Annales. Economies. Sociétés. Civilisations 22. 1967, p. 1099-1120.

Poncet, J. 1315

Encore a propos des Hilaliens. La
"mise au point" de R. Idris.
Annales. Economies. Sociétés. Civilisations 23. 1968, p. 660-662.

Rava, M. 1316

I Cavalieri di Malta a Tripoli.
Oltremare 3. 1929, p. 253-257.

Roncière, C. de 1317

Une histoire de Bornou au XVIIe siè-
le. Par un chirurgien français captif
à Tripoli.
Revue d'histoire des colonies françaises 7. 1919, n. 27, p. 78-88.

Rossi, E. 1318

Corrispondenza tra i Gran Maestri
dell'Ordine di S. Giovanni a Malta e
i Bey di Tripoli dal 1714 al 1778.
RSO 10. 1923-25, p. 414-432.

Rossi, E.　　　　　　　　　　1319

Una missione di redentoristi a Tri-
poli di Barberia nel 1730 sotto
Aḥmad (Io) Caramanli.
RSO 10. 1923-25, p. 140-144, 413.

Rossi, E.　　　　　　　　　　1320

Il dominio dei Cavalieri di Malta a
Tripoli (1530-1551) e i rapporti
dell'Ordine con Tripoli nei secoli
seguenti (1551-1798).
Archivum melitense 7. 1924, n. 2.

Rossi, E.　　　　　　　　　　1321

Il secondo periodo del dominio otto-
mano a Tripoli (1835-1911).
Riv. coloniale 22. 1927, p. 292-
300, 343-353.

Rossi, E.　　　　　　　　　　1322

La colonia italiana a Tripoli nel
secolo XIX.
RdC 4. 1930, p. 1053-1068.

Rossi, E.　　　　　　　　　　1323

Considerazioni generali sulla storia della Libia durante il dominio
degli arabo-berberi e dei turchi.
ACSC 1. 1931, vol. 2, p. 297-306.

Rossi, E.　　　　　　　　　　1324

Una "rassegna africanista" manoscrit-
ta a Tripoli un secolo fa. I consoli
Gråberg e Rousseau.
OM 12. 1932, p. 256-260.

Rossi, E.　　　　　　　　　　1325

Gli studi intorno alla storia della
Tripolitania nell'età musulmana.
ASIPS 25. 1936, vol. 3, p. 200-206.

Rossi, E.　　　　　　　　　　1326

Storia del medio evo e dell'età
moderna.
SIFOG 1937, p. 333-351.

Rossi, E.　　　　　　　　　　1327

Storia della Libia dalla conquista
araba al 1911.
Libia 2. 1954, n. 1, p. 3-44.

Rossi, E.　　　　　　　　　　1328

Carta di affrancamento di uno schia-
vo maltese.
Jean Deny Armağani. Mélanges Jean
Deny. Ankara 1958, p. 209-211.

Rossi, E.　　　　　　　　　　1329

Storia di Tripoli e della Tripolita-
nia dalla conquista araba al 1911.
Ed. M. Nallino.
Roma: Istituto per l'Oriente 1968.

Rubinacci, R.　　　　　　　　1330

Notizia di alcuni manoscritti ibaditi esistenti presso l'Istituto Uni-
versitario Orientale di Napoli.
AION NS 3. 1949, p. 431-438.

Rubinacci, R.　　　　　　　　1331

Orientamenti nelle ricerche sugli
ibaditi dell'Africa settentrionale.
Atti del congresso internazionale
di studi nord-africani 1. 1965,
p. 217-223.

Sacerdoti, A.　　　　　　　　1332

Venise et les régences d'Alger, Tunis et Tripoli (1699-1764).
Revue africaine 101. 1957, p. 273-
297.

Savage, M.A.　　　　　　　　1333

American diplomacy in North Africa,
1776-1817.
Wash. 1948.

Serres, J.　　　　　　　　　1334

La politique turque en Afrique du
Nord sous la Monarchie du Juillet.
Paris 1925.

Strothmann, R. 1335

Lewicki, T.: Études ibāḍites nord-
africaines.
Orientalistische Literaturzeitung
54. 1959, col. 48-50.

Toschi, P. 1336

Le condizioni degli schiavi a Tripoli nei passati secoli.
RSAI 5. 1942, p. 666-669.

Tucker, G. 1337

Dawn like thunder, the Barbary wars
and the birth of the U.S. Navy.
Indianapolis: Bobbs-Merrill 1963.

Vadala, R. 1338

Essais sur l'histoire des Karamanlis,
pachas de Tripolitaine de 1714 à
1835.
Revue d'histoire des colonies françaises 7. 1919, n. 1, p. 177-288.

Valori, F. 1339

L'abolizione della schiavitù in
Cirenaica.
RdC 14. 1940, p. 1263-1268.

Valori, F. 1340

Risorgimento italiano sulla quarta
sponda. Il carteggio del V. consolato di Toscana a Bengasi nel 1848-49.
Azione coloniale 1940, 16.4., p. 3.

Valori, F. 1341

L'espansione politica e commerciale
dell'Italia meridionale e della Sicilia nell'Africa del Nord.
AAI 6. 1943, vol. 2, p. 393-406.

Veccia Vaglieri, L. 1342

La santa sede e i barbareschi al
principio del secolo scorso.
ACSC 1. 1931, vol. 2, p. 307-317.

Veccia Vaglieri, L. 1343

Una controversia a Tripoli di Barberia nel 1825 fra i consoli inglese
e francese.
RdC 6. 1932, p. 371-378.

Veccia Vaglieri, L. 1344

Santa sede e barbareschi dal 1814
al 1819.
OM 12. 1932, p. 465-484.

Woolbert, R.G. 1345

Un tentativo di protettorato americano in Libia nel 1801.
Oltremare 7. 1933, p. 378-379.

History.
1911 -

A la frontière tuniso-tripo-   1346
litaine. Un peu d'histoire.
Afrique française 34. 1924, p. 493-
494, p. 555-556.

Agostini, E. de 1347

La prima occupazione del Gebel (1913).
RdC 9. 1935, p. 666-680, 800-818.

Albrecht-Carrié, R. 1348

Italian colonial problems in 1919.
Political science quarterly 58.
1943, p. 562-580.

Almagià, G. 1349

Le operazioni navali in Libia dopo
la pace italo-turca.
ACSC 2. 1934, vol. 2, p. 246-271.

Almagià, G.   1350

Le operazioni navali nella guerra
italo-turca (1911-1912).
ASIPS 25. 1936, vol. 3, p. 153-173.

Annane, M.   1351

Libya of Idris - el Senoussi.
Beirut: Systeco 1968.

Bernasconi, P.   1352

Vent'anni di azione italiana in
Cirenaica.
RdC 7. 1933, p. 796-807.

Bettanini, A.M.   1353

La conquista libica e i problemi
del Mediterraneo.(Studi di storia
dei trattati e politica internazionale).
Padova 1939, p. 53-95.

Biani, V.   1354

Ali italiane sul deserto. 3rd ed.
Firenze 1936.

Blanchi, G.   1355

Nel cinquantesimo anniversario dello
sbarco a Tripoli.
Riv. marittima 94. 1961, n. 2,
p. 5-23.

Bondarevskij, G.L.   1356

Boŕba za Tripolitaniju i Kirenaiku
na rubeže XIX-XX vv.(1899-1904).
Kolonializm včera i segodnja. Ed.
G.L. Bondarevskij. Moskva 1964,
p. 35-102.

Bondarevskij, G.L.   1357

Struggle for Tripolitania and Cyrenaica at the turn of the century.
Colonialism, old and modern. Ed.
G.L. Bondarevskij. Moscow 1966,
p. 56-130.

Buggelli, G.   1358

La riconquista di Misurata e l'azione di G. Girardini.
Udine 1939.

Cabiati, A.   1359

La conquista della Libia (1911-1931).
ASIPS 25. 1936, vol. 3, p. 135-152.

Campagna di Libia.   1360
Ministero della Guerra. Stato
Maggiore Centrale. Ufficio
Storico. Vol. 1-5.
Roma 1922-1927.

Casetti, F.   1361

Restauratio libyca.
Roma 1935.

Castagna, L.   1362

La Regia Marina in Libia nel 1917.
RdC 1/2. 1927/28, p. 385-406.

Castagnetti, A.   1363

I recenti avvenimenti in Tripolitania e la questione berbera.
AIn 36. 1917, p. 5-10.

Cesari, C.   1364

Manuale di storia coloniale.
Bologna 1937.

Chierici, A.   1365

Italiani e arabi in Libia.
Roma nd (1919).

Ciasca, R. 1366

La moderna espansione coloniale nella storiografia.
ACSC 3. 1937, vol. 4, p. 168-211.

Ciasca, R. 1367

Storia coloniale dell'Italia contemporanea.
Milano 1940.

La conquista della Tripolitania. (R.A. di Lucchesi - O. Pedrazzi). 1368
La rinascita della Tripolitania.
Milano 1926, p. 117-185.

Corò, F. 1369

La relazione ufficiale dell'occupazione di Cufra.
RdC 5. 1931, p. 507-526.

Corò, F. 1370

Suleiman el Baruni, il sogno di un principato berbero e la battaglia di Asàaba (1913).
AAI 1. 1938, vol. 3/4, p. 957-969.

Corò, F. 1371

Tunisia e Tripolitania attraverso il secolo nelle loro relazioni politiche e economiche.
Africa. Roma 1963, n. 2, p. 89-91.

Costa, G.B. 1372

Le operazioni nel sud tripolitano.
Oltremare 4. 1930, p. 22-26.

Cunsolo, R.S. 1373

Libya, Italian nationalism, and the revolt against Giolitti.
Journal of modern history 37. 1965, p. 186-207.

Cutry, F. 1374

L'aeronautica italiana nella guerra di Libia.
ASIPS 25. 1936, vol. 3, p. 174-187.

La Cyrénaïque pacifiée. 1375
Afrique française 43. 1933, p. 358-362.

Drago, F. 1376

Passi e voli sul deserto.
Torino 1929.

Dresler, A. 1377

Das italienische Kolonialreich.
Reichskolonialbund.
Berlin 1939.

Felici, O. 1378

Terra nostra di Cirenaica.
Roma 1932.

Fioravanzo, G. - Viti, G. 1379

L'opera della marina (1868-1943).
Roma: IPS 1959.
(L'Italia in Africa. Serie storico-militare. 2.)

Forlani, R. 1380

Quel che si dovrà fare nella Libia.
Torino 1922.

La formazione dell'impero coloniale italiano. Vol. 1-3. 1381
Milano 1938-39.

Fornari, G. 1382

Gli italiani nel sud libico. Le co-
lonne Miani (1913-1915).
Roma 1941.
(Collezione scientifica e documenta-
ria dell'Africa italiana. 2.)

Die Franzosen im Fezzan. 1383
Zeitschrift für Geopolitik
26. 1955, p. 221-222.

Gaibi, A. 1384
Cronologia della Libia.
Roma 1928.

Galli, C. 1385
Diari e lettere. Tripoli 1911 -
Trieste 1918.
Firenze: Sansoni 1951.

Gaslini, M. dei 1386
Col generale Cantore alla caccia del
Gran Senusso.
Milano 1927.

Gawad, A. - Schumacher, D. 1387
Eine türkische Ehe in Briefen. Tri-
polis 1911-12.
Berlin 1913.

Gherardi, P. 1388
La reconquête de la Tripolitaine vue
du camp des rebelles.
Renseignements coloniaux 1925,
p. 292-322.

Giaccardi, A. - Verdat, M. 1389
La réoccupation de la Tripolitaine
par les italiens.
Revue d'histoire des colonies françaises 20. 1932, p. 113-152.

Giglio, V. - Ravenni, A. 1390
Le guerre coloniali d'Italia.
Milano 1935.

Grosso, M. 1391
Cronologia delle colonie italiane.
Roma 1934.

Guerra italo-turca 1911-12. 1392
Atti della R. Commissione
delle Prede. Raccolta eseguita a
cura della Direzione Generale della
Marina Mercantile. Vol. 1-5.
Roma 1912-15.

Hérelle, S. 1393
Le nouveau régime des musulmans en
Libye.
Renseignements coloniaux 1939,
p. 142-147.

L'impresa del Fezzan. Memoria 1394
confidenziale. Ministero delle
Colonie.
Roma 1915.

In memoria di due eroi italiani 1395
in Libia. Maria e Costantino
Brighenti. (Tarhuna - Beni Ulid
1915). Ministero delle Colonie.
Roma 1918.

Invrea, A. 1396
La cavalleria libica in Cirenaica.
Bengasi 1939.

Italy in Africa. 1397
World today 4. 1948,
p. 62-73.

Lalla, A. de   1398
L'ammiraglio Favarelli e l'occupa-
zione di Tripoli.
Riv. militare 17. 1961, p. 1411-1416.

Lefèvre, R.   1399
Fonti per la storia coloniale: l'archivio storico dell'Africa italiana.
Rassegna storica del risorgimento
1940, p. 173-176.

Lessona, A.   1400
Il fascismo per le colonie. Le colo-
nie italiane nel quadro europeo.
Roma 1932.

Lessona, A.   1401
Scritti e discorsi coloniali.
Milano 1935.

Libya. The military treaties   1402
with the U.K. and the U.S.A.
Africa institute international bulletin 2. 1964, p. 205-208.

Lioy, V.   1403
L'opera dell'aeronautica. Vol. 1.
Eritrea-Libia (1888-1932).
Roma: IPS 1964.
(L'Italia in Africa. Serie storico-
  militare. 3,1.)

Lischi, D.   1404
Viaggio d'un cronista fascista in
Cirenaica.
Pisa 1934.

Lo Bello, F.   1405
Le vicende politico-militari dei
primi dodici anni di occupazione
italiana in Cirenaica.
Bengasi 1925.

Longrigg, S.H.   1406
Disposal of Italian Africa.
International affairs 21. 1945,
p. 363-369.

Maltese, P.   1407
La terra promessa. La guerra italo-
turca e la conquista della Libia
1911-12.
Milano: Sugar 1968.
(Nuova biblioteca storica. 2.)

Malvezzi, A.   1408
Italian colonies and colonial poli-
cy.
International affairs 6. 1927,
p. 233-245.

Martel, A.   1409
Etat des recherches historiques
françaises sur le Maghreb contempo-
rain.
Atti del congresso di studi arabi
e islamici 3. 1966 (1967), p. 493-
509.

Martel, A.   1410
Histoire contemporaine de la Libye,
dimensions et recherches.
AAN 5. 1966, p. 781-792.

Martel, A.   1411
Question libyenne et fascisme (1919-
1939).
La Méditerranée de 1919 à 1939.
Paris 1969, p. 58-66.

Masi, C.   1412
Italia e Tripolitania.
AIr 1941-42, n. 37, p. 14-20.

Mazzucconi, R.   1413
Storia della conquista dell'Africa.
Milano 1938.

Meriano, F.   1414
La riconquista della Tripolitania.
Milano 1923.

Messal, R.   1415
L'Italia en Libye.
Renseignements coloniaux 1923, p.413-
424.

Miège, J.L.   1416
L'impérialisme colonial italien de
1870 à nos jours.
Paris: SEDES 1968.

Mira, G.   1417
In Libia.
Roma 1924.

Monaco, A.   1418
Morti in Libia. (Cronache dei battag-
lioni d'Africa).
Milano 1930.

Mondaini, M.G.   1419
La politique coloniale italienne par
rapport aux us et coutumes indigènes.
CR des séances ... Institut Colonial
International 19. 1924, vol. 2,
p. 113-161.

Mori, G.   1420
L'industria toscana fra gli inizi
del secolo e la guerra di Libia.
La Toscana nell'Italia unita. Firenze 1962, p. 219-331.

Mori, R.   1421
La penetrazione pacifica italiana in
Libia dal 1907 al 1911 e il Banco di
Roma.
Riv. di studi politici internazionali
24. 1957, p. 102-118.

Muzio, C.   1422
Libia.
Milano 1924.

Nobili Massuero, F.   1423
Ombre e luci di due continenti. Due
anni di politica coloniale e mediterranea, 1923-24.
Milano 1926.

L'occupazione di Cufra.   1424
Governo della Tripolitania.
Tripoli 1931.

L'occupazione del Fezzan.   1425
Comando Regio Corpo Truppe
Coloniali.
Tripoli 1930.

Le operazioni militari in   1426
Tripolitania dall'ottobre
1911 al dicembre 1924. Governo della
Tripolitania.
Tripoli 1925.

Pace, B.   1427
Il completamento della occupazione
libica.
RdC 4. 1930, p. 452-463.

Palumbo, A.   1428
Studio organico per un corpo di
truppe coloniali indigene della
Libia.
Roma 1919.

Palumbo, A.   1429
Le organizzazioni militari nei
territori sahariani.
AIn 39. 1920, p. 164-185.

Palumbo, A.   1430

Ufficiali indigeni e metropolitani
per le truppe libiche.
AIn 41. 1922, p. 126-132.

Papi, G.   1431

Come fu conquistato il Fezzan.
Riv. militare 19. 1963, p. 929-939.

Parent, G.   1432

Camicie nere in Libia.
Oltremare 8. 1934, p. 74-77.

Passamonti, E.   1433

Negoziati mediterranei anglo-franco-
italiani dalla guerra di Libia al
conflitto mondiale.
Verbania 1941.
(Storia della Libia.)

Perticone, G. - Guglielmi, G.   1434

La politica coloniale dell'Italia
negli atti, documenti e discussioni
parlamentari.
Roma: IPS 1965.
(L'Italia in Africa. Serie storica.)

Pesenti, G.   1435

Le guerre coloniali dell'Italia.
Bologna: Zanichelli 1947.

Peteani, L.   1436

La questione libica nella diplomazia
europea.
Firenze 1939.
(Biblioteca di studi coloniali. 4.)

Petragnani, H.   1437

Turcs et senoussistes au Fezzan pen-
dant la Grande Guerre.
Renseignements coloniaux 1925,
p. 508-526.

Piccioli, A.   1438

Il re imperatore in Libia.
RdC 12. 1938, p. 685-691.

Pisani, V.   1439

Libia colonizzata - Libia pacifica-
ta.
Roma 1929.

Pistolese, G.E.   1440

La Libia nel sistema mediterraneo.
REAI 26. 1938, p. 204-209.

Prigionia di un soldato   1441
a Cufra.
RdC 1/2. 1927/28, p. 15-24, 129-145.

I primi voli di guerra nel   1442
mondo. Libia 1911.
Ufficio Storico dell'Aeronautica
Militare.
Roma 1951.

Rainero, R.   1443

I socialisti genovesi e la spedizione di Tripoli.
Misc. stor. ligure 4. 1966, p. 437-
480.

Ravagli, F.   1444

Tripolitania nostra.
Tripoli 1929.

Ravagli, F.   1445

Il viaggio del sovrano in Libia.
AAI 1. 1938, vol. 2, p. 425-435.

La ribellione in Tripolitania   1446
nell'anno 1915.
Ministero delle Colonie.
Roma 1916.

Roncagli, G. - Manfroni, C.   1447
Guerra italo-turca: cronistoria del-
le operazioni navali. Vol. 1.2.
Ufficio Storico della Marina.
Milano/Roma 1918-26.

Rossi, G.   1448
La mancata instaurazione del Senus-
so a Bengasi nel 1941.
Continenti 3. 1948, n. 1, p. 20-22.

Russo, M.   1449
L'assetto della Cirenaica.
AIn 38. 1919, p. 93-101.

Salvemini, G.   1450
Come siamo andati in Libia e altri
scritti dal 1900 al 1915. A cura di
A. Torre.
Milano: Feltrinelli 1963.
(Scritti di politica estera. 1.)

Sandri, S.   1451
Il generale Rodolfo Graziani.
Roma 1933.
(Le grandi figure coloniali. 1.)

Sandri, S.   1452
Il principe sahariano. Amadeo di
Savoia Duca d'Aosta.
Roma 1933.
(Le grandi figure coloniali. 2.)

Sani, M.   1453
Storia politica e militare della
Libia dalla guerra italo-turca sino
alla fine del 1921.
L'impero coloniale fascista. Nova-
ra 1936, p. 439-458.

Sansone, L.   1454
I dominii libici.
AIn 47. 1928, p. 10-19.

Scaglione, E.   1455
Tripoli e la guerra.
Napoli 1918.

Scala, E.   1456
Le fanterie italiane nelle conquiste
coloniali.
Roma: Tipografia Regionale 1952.
(Storia delle fanterie italiane. 4.)

Schanzer, C.   1457
Italian colonial policy in North
Africa.
Foreign affairs 2. 1923/24, p. 446-
456.

Serra, F.   1458
La pacificazione di Derna nel 1915.
Oltremare 3. 1929, p. 139-143.

Sertoli Salis, R.   1459
Storia e politica coloniale italiana
(1869-1937).
Messina 1938.
(Biblioteca di cultura politica.2,2.)

Silvestri, U.   1460
Il fascismo e il problema coloniale.
La riconquista della Libia e la sua
rinascita.
RdC 14. 1940, p. 137-143.

La situazione in Cirenaica.   1461
Oltremare 2. 1928, p. 474-
475.

Susani, L. 1462

Pagine di gloria di cinquant'anni
fa.
Riv. militare 18. 1962, p. 470-480.

Terrier, A. 1463

Les aspirations italiennes vers le
Lac Tchad.
Afrique française 37. 1927, p. 128-
130, 38. 1928, p. 159-162, 213-216,
417-419, 496-503.

Terruzzi, A. 1464

Politica fascista in Libia.
AIn 52. 1934, p. 199-205, 53. 1935,
p. 113-121.

Tondo, F. di 1465

Campagne coloniali italiane.
Torino: Loescher 1967.
(La ricerca. Serie storica C,39.)

Turati, F. - Kuliscioff, A. 1466

Dal carteggio inedito Turati-Kuli-
scioff. L'annessione della Libia
(1912).
Critica sociale 46. 1954, p. 139-
141.

"Umar al-Mukhtar". A hero of 1467
Libya who resisted the Italian
occupation of his country from 1911
to 1931.
Islamic review 54. 1966, December,
p. 36-37, 40.

Vailati, V. 1468

Campagne d'Africa: Eritrea 1896 e
Tripolitania 1911.(Badoglio raccon-
ta).
Torino 1955, p. 65-98.

Vecchia Vaglieri, L. 1469

La partecipazione di Suleimàn el-
Barùni alla guerra di Libia.
Oltremare 8. 1934, p. 70-73.

Vernè, V. 1470

Le camicie nere in Libia.
Ministero delle Colonie. Ufficio
Propaganda.
Roma 1927.

Vitale, M.A. 1471

Il cammello e i reparti cammellati.
Roma nd (1931).
(Collezione di opere e monografie
a cura del Ministero delle Colonie.
11.)

Vitale, M.A. 1472

Africa settentrionale (1911-1943).
Avvenimenti militari e impiego.
Roma: IPS 1964.
(L'Italia in Africa. Serie storico-
militare. 1,3.)

Volpe, G. 1473

L'impresa di Tripoli 1911-12.
Roma: Sograro 1946.
(Studi storici e politici. 11.)

Le voyage de M. Mussolini 1474
en Tripolitaine et les aspirations italiennes.
Afrique française 36. 1926, p. 211-
215.

Zanon, F. 1475

Come la Francia occupò le zone a
nord del Tchad.
Oltremare 3. 1929, p. 247-248.

Zanon, F. 1476

Come la Francia ha occupato ai
nostri danni l'estremo Sahara tripolitano.
AIn 56. 1938, p. 497-505.

Zoli, C. 1477

La completa conquista e l'occupazione definitiva della Libia.
RdC 6. 1932, p. 9-24, 85-100, 168-
177.

Second World War.

Jahresbibliographie.   1478
Bibliothek für Zeitgeschichte.
Weltkriegsbücherei Stuttgart.
Frankfurt a.M.: Bernard und Graefe.
39. 1967-

Second world war military   1479
operations. African theatre.
Part 1. Libya and Egypt.
London: Imperial War Museum, Library
1954.

The North African campaign.   1480
Second world war military
operations.
London: Imperial War Museum, Library
1961.

Allmayer-Beck, J.C.   1481

Die internationale amtliche Kriegs-
geschichtsschreibung über den zwei-
ten Weltkrieg.
Jahresbibliographie. Weltkriegsbücherei 34. 1962, p. 507-540.

Seeger, W.   1482

Der zweite Weltkrieg im Mittelmeer-
raum. Bericht über die italienische
Literatur.
Jahresbibliographie. Weltkriegsbücherei 30. 1958, p. 306-321, 31.
1959, p.413-421, 34.1962, p.554-572.

Susani, L. - Longo, V.   1483

Saggio bibliografico sulla seconda
guerra mondiale. 2nd ed.
Roma: Stato Maggiore Esercito 1955.

Rivista aeronautica.   1484
Roma 45. 1969-

Rivista marittima.
Roma 102. 1969-   sc

Rivista militare.
Roma 1969-

Addington, L.H.   1485

Operation Sunflower: Rommel versus
the general staff.
Military affairs 31. 1967, p. 120-
130.

In Africa settentrionale.   1486
La preparazione al conflitto.
L'avanzata su Sidi el Barrani (ottob-
re 1935 - novembre 1940).
Roma: Stato Maggiore Esercito 1955.

Agar-Hamilton, J.A.I. -   1487
Turner, L.C.F.

Crisis in the desert, May-July 1942.
Oxford UP 1952.

Agar-Hamilton, J.A.I. -   1488
Turner, L.C.F.

The Sidi Rezeg battles 1941. Union
of South Africa. War Histories
Section.
Oxford UP 1957.

Alexander, H.R.   1489

D'El-Alamein à Tunis et à la Sicile
(1942-1943). Rapport off. du comman-
dant en chef ...
Paris: Lavauzelle 1949.

André   1490

Tobrouk.
Revue historique de l'armée 7. 1951,
n. 2, p. 49-71.

Australia in the war of 1939-   1491
1945.Australian War Memorial.
Canberra.
Ser. 1. Army.   Ser. 4. Civil.
Ser. 2. Navy.   Ser. 5. Medical.
Ser. 3. Air.

Balkenkreuz ueber Wuesten-   1492
sand. Farbbilderwerk vom
deutschen Afrikakorps. Luftwaffen-
Kriegsberichter-Kompanie.
Oldenburg 1943.

Barnett, C. 1493

The desert generals.
Wüstengenerale.
London: Kimber 1960.
Hannover: Verlag für Literatur und
Zeitgeschehen 1961.

Bauer, E. 1494

La guerre des blindés. Les opérations
de la 2e guerre mondiale sur les
fronts d'Europe et d'Afrique. 2nd ed.
Lausanne: Payot 1962.

Bernotti, R. 1495

La marina nella perdita della Libia.
Riv. marittima 92. 1960, n. 3, p. 5-
26.

Bernotti, R. 1496

Storia della guerra nel Mediterraneo
(1940-43).2nd ed.
Roma: Bianco 1960.
(I libri del tempo. 10.)

Bharucha, P.C. 1497

The North African campaign 1940-
1943. Ed. B. Prasad.
London: Longmans, Green & Co. 1956.

Bingham, J.K.W. - Haupt, W. 1498

North African campaign, 1940-1943.
London: Macdonald 1969.

Bollati, A. 1499

Guerra in Africa.
RdC 14. 1940 ⎫
   15. 1941 ⎬ passim.
   16. 1942 ⎭

Braddock, D.W. 1500

The campaigns in Egypt and Libya,
1940-1942.
Aldershot: Gale & Polden 1964.

Bragadin, M.A. 1501

La marina italiana nella seconda
guerra mondiale (1940-43).
Roma: Lega Navale Italiana 1945.

I britanni in Cirenaica. 1502
Documenti da ricordare.
(24.12.1941 - 29.1.1942).
AAI 5. 1942, vol. 1, p. 37-59.

The British capture of Bardia. 1503
(December 1941 - January 1942).
Military Intelligence Service.
Wash.: GPO 1942.
(Information bulletin. 21.)

Brod, T. 1504

Tobrucké krysy.
Praha: NV/SPB 1967.

Bueschleb, H. 1505

Feldherrn und Panzer im Wüsten-
krieg. Die Herbstschlacht "Crusader"
im Vorfeld von Tobruk, 1941.
Neckargemünd 1966.
(Die Wehrmacht im Kampf. 40.)

Campagnes d'Afrique. 1506
1940-1943.
Paris: Flammarion 1947.

Canevari, E. 1507

La guerra italiana. Retroscena della
disfatta. Vol. 1.2.
Roma: Tosi 1948-49.

Caracciolo di Feroleto, M. 1508

La campagna 1940-42 in Libia.
Riv. militare 3. 1947, p. 1051-
1069, 1181-1200.

Carell, P.   1509

Die Wüstenfüchse.
The foxes of the desert.
Hamburg: Nannen 1961.
New York: Bantam Books Inc. 1962.

Carver, M.   1510

Tobruk.
London: Batsford 1964.

Carver, R.M.P.   1511

Desert dilemmas.
Royal armoured corps journal
2. 1948, n. 4, 3. 1949, n. 1,
5. 1951, n. 2-4, 6. 1952, n.1.2.

Castagna, S.   1512

La difesa di Giarabub.
Milano: Longanesi 1950.

Catroux, G.   1513

Dans la bataille de Méditerranée.
Egypte - Levante - Afrique du Nord
1940-1944.
Paris: Juillard 1949.

Clarke, D.   1514

The Eleventh at war.
London 1952.

Clifford, A.G.   1515

The conquest of North Africa, 1940-
1943.
Boston 1943.

The conquest of North Africa.   1516
The first complete authorita-
tive account of the entire three
years North African campaign from
Egypt to Tunisia.
London 1943.

Crew, F.A.E.   1517

The army medical services. Vol.1.
London: HMSO 1956-
(U.K. medical series.)

Crisp, R.   1518

Brazen chariots. An account of tank
warfare in the western desert,
Nov. - Dec. 1941.
London: Muller 1959.

Le cronache dell'Africa   1519
italiana.
AAI 3. 1940, vol. 3 - 6. 1943,
vol. 2: passim.

Cumpston, J.S.   1520

The rats remain. Tobruk siege 1941.
Melbourne: Grayflower Productions
1966.

Cunningham, H.F.   1521

Sahara victory. The fighting
French march to Tripoli.
Infantry journal 53. 1943, n. 4.

Dawson, W.D.   1522

18 battalion and armoured regiment.
Wellington, N.Z. 1961.

Debyser   1523

La deuxième guerre mondiale en
Afrique. Essai bibliographique.
Cahiers d'histoire de la guerre
1949, n. 2, p. 56-77.

The development of German   1524
defensive tactics in Cyre-
naica - 1941.
Military Intelligence Service.
Wash.: GPO 1942.
(Special series. 5.)

Devine, J.   1525

The rats of Tobruk.
Sydney: Angus and Robertson 1943.

Douglas, K.   1526

Alamein to Zem Zem.
London: Faber 1966.

Dronne, R.   1527

Le serment de Koufra.
Paris: Editions du Temps 1965.

The eighth army, September   1528
1941 to January 1943.
War Office.
London: HMSO 1944.
(The army at war.)

Engely, G.   1529

Gli inglesi in Cirenaica.
AAI 4. 1941, vol. 2, p. 371-401.

Esebeck, H.G.   1530

Afrikanische Schicksalsjahre. Geschichte des deutschen Afrika-Korps
unter Rommel.
Wiesbaden: Limes 1950.

Fazi, L.   1531

Bersaglieri e Panzerjäger in Africa
settentrionale.
Roma: Volpe 1965.

Ferrara, A.   1532

Lo sforzo dell'Italia in Africa durante l'attuale conflitto.
AAI 4. 1941, vol. 4, p. 1105-1132.

Ferrara, A.   1533

La guerra in Africa settentrionale.
AAI 5. 1942, vol. 2 - 6. 1943,
vol. 1: passim.

Ferrara, A.   1534

La quarta offensiva britannica contro la Libia.
AAI 5. 1942, vol. 1, p. 49-59.

Francis, C.   1535

The cave dwellers (Australians at
Tobruk).
Reveille 31. 1957, n. 3.

Gause, A.   1536

Der Feldzug in Nordafrika im Jahre
1941.
Wehrwissenschaftliche Rundschau 12.
1962, p. 594-618, 652-680, 720-
728.

German methods of warfare   1537
in the Libyan desert.
Military Intelligence Service.
Wash.: GPO 1942.
(Information bulletin. 20.)

Giamberardino, O. di   1538

Operazioni navali relative alla
campagna 1940-42 in Libia.
Riv. militare 4. 1948, p. 104-114.

Gicca Palli, E.   1539

Viaggio di piacere.
Roma: Edizioni Italiane Abruzzini
1963.

Goutard, A.   1540

La réalité de la "menace" allemande
sur l'Afrique du Nord en 1940.
Revue d'histoire de la deuxième
guerre mondiale 11. 1961, n. 44,
p. 1-20.

Graziani, R.   1541

Africa settentrionale (1940-1941).
Roma: Danesi 1948.

Graziani, R.   1542

La campagna in Africa settentrionale
1940-1941.
Milano 1951.

Hafiz   1543

The offensive in Libya: December
1940 - February 1941.
Journal of the Royal United Service
Institution 101. 1956, p. 206-216.

Hart, B.H.L.   1544

The tanks.
Vol. 2. North Africa.
London: Cassell 1959.

Haupt, W. - Bingham, J.K.W.   1545

Der Afrika - Feldzug 1941-1943.
Dorheim/H.: Podzun-Verlag 1968.

Heckstall-Smith, A.   1546

Tobruk.
London: Blond 1959.
New York: Norton 1960.

Herington, J.   1547

Air war against Germany and Italy
1939-1943.
Canberra 1954.
(Australia in the war of 1939 -
 1945. 3,3.)

History of the second   1548
world war.
London: HMSO.
United Kingdom military series.
United Kingdom civil series.
United Kingdom medical series.

Iachino, A.   1549

Le due Sirti. Guerra ai convogli in
Mediterraneo.
Milano: Mondadori 1953.

Ingold, F.   1550

Soldats du Tchad, campagnes sahariennes 1940-1943.
Alger 1944.

Ingold, F.   1551

L'épopée Leclerc au Sahara 1940-
1943.
Paris: Berger-Levrault 1948.

Jars, R.   1552

Les campagnes d'Afrique. Libye-
Égypte-Tunisie 1940-1943.
Paris: Payot 1957.

Joly, C.   1553

Take these men. The campaign of the
desert rats 1940-43.
Harmondsworth: Penguin Books 1956.
(Penguin books. 1207.)

Kay, R.L.   1554

Long Range Desert Group in Libya,
1940-41.
Wellington, N.Z. 1949.
(Episodes and studies. 10.)

Kidson, A.L.   1555

Petrol company.
Wellington, N.Z. 1961.

Kippenberger, H.   1556

Infantry brigadier.
London 1951.

Kurz, H.R.   1557
Tobruk.
Schweizerische Militärzeitschrift
117. 1951, p. 617-632.

Lapie, P.O.   1558
Mes tournées au Tchad. 2nd ed.
Alger: Office Français d'Editions
1945.

Lapie, P.O.   1559
Les déserts de l'action.
Paris: Flammarion 1946.

Laude, J.   1560
Die Eroberung Nordafrikas durch Mont-
gomery.
Wehrwissenschaftliche Rundschau 15.
1965, p. 697-712.

The Libyan campaign.   1561
November 1941 to January
1942. Military Intelligence Service.
Wash.: GPO 1942.
(Campaign study. 1.)

The Libyan campaign.   1562
May 27 to July 27, 1942.
Military Intelligence Service.
Wash.: GPO 1942.
(Campaign study. 4.)

Long, G.   1563
To Benghazi.
Canberra 1952.
(Australia in the war of 1939-1945.
 1,1.)

Mac Intyre, D.   1564
The battle for the Mediterranean.
London: Batsford 1964.

Macksey, K.J.   1565
Afrika Korps.
New York: Ballentine Books 1968.
(Ballentine's illustrated history
 of world war II. Campaign book. 1.)

Mannerini, A.   1566
Il "Sahara libico" nell'ultima fase
della guerra in Libia.
Riv. militare 4. 1948, p. 508-539.

Manzetti, F.   1567
Seconda offensiva britannica in Africa settentrionale e ripiegamento
italo-tedesco nella Sirtica orientale (18.11.1941 - 17.1.1942).
Roma: Ministero della Difesa 1949.

Maravigna, P.   1568
Come abbiamo perduto la guerra in
Africa (1940-43).
Roma: Tosi 1949.

La marina in Libia 1940-   1569
1943.
Riv. marittima 91. 1957, n. 3,
p. 495-522.

La marina italiana nella   1570
seconda guerra mondiale.
Vol. 1-17.
Roma: Ufficio Storico della Marina
Militare 1950-63.

Martinelli, M.   1571
La divisione "Savona" nella seconda
offensiva britannica in Cirenaica
(18.11.1941 - 17.1.1942).
Riv. militare 3. 1947, p. 946-962.

Maughan, B.   1572
Tobruk and El Alamein.
Canberra 1966.
(Australia in the war of 1939-1945.
 1,3.)

The Mediterranean fleet. 1573
Greece to Tripoli. The
Admiralty account of naval operations
April 1941 to January 1943.
London: HMSO 1944.

Mellenthin, F.W. von 1574

Panzer battles 1939-45.
Ed. L.C.F. Turner. 2nd ed.
London: Cassell 1956.

Moorehead, A. 1575

African trilogy: the North African
campaign 1940-43.
London: Hamilton 1965.

Moorehead, A. 1576

The desert war: the North African
campaign 1940/1943.
London: Hamilton 1965.

Moynet, P. 1577

L'épopée du Fezzân.
Alger: Office Français d'Edition
1945.

Muraise, E. 1578

La campagne de Libye (1940-1943).
Revue militaire générale 1969,
p. 451-470.

Murphy, W.E. 1579

The relief of Tobruk.
Wellington, N.Z. 1961.

Nicolson, N. 1580

The Mediterranean campaigns (1942-
1945).
Aldershot: Gale & Polden 1949.

Official history of New 1581
Zealand in the second world
war 1939 - 1945. Dept. of Internal
Affairs. War History Branch.
Wellington, N.Z.

Owen, D.L. 1582

The desert my dwelling place.
London: Cassell 1957.

Owen, R. 1583

The Desert Air Force.
London: Hutchinson 1948.

Pedoja, G. 1584

La disfatta nel deserto.
Roma: O.E.T. 1946.

Pitman, S. 1585

Second Royal Gloucestershire Hussars.
Libya-Egypt 1941-42.
London: St. Catherine Press 1950.

Playfair, I.S.O. - Stitt, G.S.- 1586
Flynn, F.C.

The Mediterranean and Middle East.
Vol. 1-4.
London: HMSO 1954-66.
(United Kingdom military series.)

Rainier, P.W. 1587

Pipeline to battle. The battles in
North Africa, 1940-1943.
London: Heinemann 1944.

Raymond, J. 1588

Libye et Afrique du Nord française.
Revue de défense nationale NS 7.
1951, p. 143-150.

Rexford-Welch, S.C.   1589
Libya and Tunisia 1940-43.
The Royal Air Force medical services. London 1958, vol. 3, p. 71-
140.

Rodger, G.   1590
Desert journey.
London 1944.

Rommel, E.   1591
Krieg ohne Hass. 3rd ed.
Guerra senza odio.
Heidenheim/Brenz: Verlag Heidenhei-
mer Zeitung 1956.
Milano: Garzanti 1952.

Rosenthal, E.   1592
Fortress on sand. An account of the
siege of Tobruk.
London 1943.

Saint Pereuse   de   1593
Supériorité aérienne dans la campagne de Libye.
Forces aériennes françaises 1951,
n. 62, p. 172-191.

Salter, J.C.   1594
A padre with the rats of Tobruk.
Hobart: Walch 1946.

Santoro, G.   1595
L'aeronautica italiana nella seconda
guerra mondiale. Vol. 1.2.
Milano/Roma: Esse 1958.

Scala, E.   1596
Le fanterie nella seconda guerra
mondiale.
Roma: Tipografia Regionale 1956.
(Storia delle fanterie italiane.10.)

Scalfaro, G.   1597
56 giorni di "civiltà" inglese a
Bengasi.
Roma 1941.

Schicksal Nordafrika.   1598
Verband ehemaliger Angehöri-
ger deutsches Afrika-Korps.
Böblingen 1954.

Schmidt, H.W.   1599
With Rommel in the desert.
London: Harrap 1953.

Sears, S.W.   1600
Desert war in North Africa.
New York: American Heritage Publ.
Co, Inc. 1967.

Seconda controffensiva   1601
italo-tedesca in Africa settentrionale da El Agheila a El Alamein
(gennaio-settembre 1942).
Roma: Stato Maggiore Esercito 1951.

Shores, C. - Ring, H.   1602
Fighters over the desert.
Luftkampf zwischen Sand und Sonne.
London: Spearman 1969.
Stuttgart: Motorbuch Verlag 1970.

Silvester, C.   1603
Journal d'un soldat de l'Afrika-
Korps.
Paris: Editions de la Pensée Moderne
1962.

Stark, W.   1604
German Afrika Corps.
Military review 45. 1965, n. 7,
p. 91-97.

Stevens, W.G.   1605

Bardia to Enfidaville (1942/43).
Wellington, N.Z. 1962.

Strawson, J.   1606

The battle for North Africa.
London: Batsford 1969.

Stubbe, C.   1607

Zoeklicht op Rommel's Nederlaag.
Antwerpen: Van Ravenstijn 1954.

Tedde, A.   1608

Fiamme nel deserto. Da Tobruk ad
El Alamein.
Milano: Istituto Editoriale Cisalpi-
no 1962.

Terza offensiva britannica   1609
in Africa settentrionale.
La battaglia di El Alamein e il ripiegamento in Tunisia (6.9.1942-
4.2.1943). Vol. 1.2.
Roma: Stato Maggiore Esercito 1961.

Terzi, O.   1610

Warwàrowka. Alzo zero.
Brescia: Vannini 1963.

Thompson, H.L.   1611

Mediterranean and Middle East,
South-East Asia.
Wellington, N.Z. 1959.

Tosti, A.   1612

La prima fase delle operazioni italiane in Africa settentrionale.
AAI 3. 1940, vol. 4, p. 179-188.

Tosti, A.   1613

Vicende della lotta in Libia ed in
Africa orientale.
AAI 4. 1941, vol. 2, p. 359-367.

Il traffico di rifornimento   1614
delle armate italiane e tedeschi operanti in Libia nella campagna 1940-42.
Riv. marittima 81. 1948, p. 18-33,
204-218, 436-450.

Trizzino, A.   1615

Die verratene Flotte. Tragödie der
Afrikakämpfer.
Bonn: Athenäum 1957.

Tucker, E.N.   1616

Per noctem per diem, the story of
24 Squadron, South African Air Force.
Pretoria: 24 Squadron Album Committee 1962.

Tuker, F.   1617

Approach to battle. A commentary.
Eighth army, Nov. 1941 to May 1943.
London: Cassell 1963.

Valori, F.   1618

L'occupazione inglese di Bengasi.
RdC 15. 1941, p. 1009-1027.

Verney, G.L.   1619

The desert rats. The history of the
7th armoured division 1938 to 1945.
London: Hutchinson 1954.

Weichold, E.   1620

Tobruk, sacrario anche per gli
uomini di mare caduti nel Mediterraneo.
Riv. marittima 90. 1956, p. 245-250.

Westphal, S.   1621

Notes on campaign in North Africa, 1941-1943.
Journal of the Royal United Service Institution 55. 1960, n. 617, p. 70-81.

Wilmot, C.   1622

Tobruk 1941. Capture - siege - relief.
Sydney/London: Angus and Robertson 1945.

Woolcombe, R.   1623

The campaigns of Wavell, 1939-1943.
London: Cassell 1959.

Yindrich, J.   1624

Fortress Tobruk.
London: Benn 1951.

Politics. Current History. Military Affairs.

Bibliographie courante   1625
d'articles de périodiques
postérieurs à 1944 sur les problemes
politiques ... Fondation Nationale
des Sciences Politiques, Paris.
Boston, Mass.: Hall 1968

Index to periodical articles   1626
1950-1964 in the library of
the Royal Institute of International
Affairs.
Boston, Mass.: Hall 1964.

United Nations documents   1627
index.
New York: United Nations.
20. 1969-

Afrikanische Koepfe.   1628
Deutsche Afrika-Gesellschaft.
Bonn: Deutscher Wirtschaftsdienst
1962-

Annuario di politica inter-   1629
nazionale.
Milano: Istituto per gli Studi di
Politica Internazionale.
23. 1966-

The statesman's year-book.   1630
Statistical and historical
annual of the states of the world.
London: MacMillan.
103. 1966-1967 (1966)-

Acquaviva, S.   1631

Il problema libico ed il senussis-
mo.
Roma 1917.

Ambrosini, G.   1632

Il valore politico della Libia nell'
impero italiano.
ACSC 3. 1937, vol. 2, p. 85-98.

Andel, H.J.   1634

Libyen: Staatsstreich oder Revolution ?
Aussenpolitik 21. 1970, p. 44-53.

Ansprenger, F.   1635

Afrika. Eine politische Länderkunde.
6th ed.
Berlin: Colloqium Verlag 1968.
(Zur Politik und Zeitgeschichte.
8/9.)

Asal, M.S.   1636

Die Entstehung Libyens als souve-
räner Staat.
Berlin 1965. Diss.

Ausiello, A.   1637

La politica italiana in Libia.
Roma 1939.

Badday, M.   1638

Libye: les suites du coup de Tripoli.
Revue française d'études politiques
africaines 1969, déc., p. 10-12.

Baker, C.L.   1639

The U.S. and Libya meeting mutual
needs.
Carlisle, Pa.: Army War College
1968. Diss.

Baker, C.L.   1640

The United States and Libya.
Military review 49. 1969, n. 4,
p. 83-91.

Balbo, I.   1641

Italia e Islam.
AIr 2. 1939, n. 3-4, p. 5-10.

Becker, G.H.   1642

The disposition of the Italian colonies, 1941-1951.
Annemasse 1952. Diss.

Ben Yahmed, B.   1643

La Libye entre en révolution.
Jeune Afrique 1969, 16-22.9.,
p. 22-29.

Benedetti, L. de   1644

Il nostro programma coloniale per
la Libia e la pregiudiziale della
"costituzione" già consentita.
AIn 39. 1920, p. 316-320.

Berreby, J.J.   1645

La Libye à la recherche d'un diffi-
cile équilibre.
Confluent. France et Maghreb 1960,
p. 452-460.

Berreby, J.J.   1646

La Libye face a sa fortune.
Etudes méditerranéennes 7. 1960,
p. 99-107.

Biays, J.   1647

Le sort des anciennes colonies ita-
liennes.
Ann. Fac. Droit. Univ. St. Joseph
Beyrouth 1956, p. 31-101.

Bibes, G.   1648

Les italiens de Libye et les relations italo-libyennes.
Maghreb 1970, n. 42, p. 34-38.

Boltho, A. von   1649

Libyen: Idealismus und Strategie.
Aussenpolitik 5. 1954, p. 188-191.

Booth, R.   1650

The armed forces of African states,
1970.
London: Institute for Strategic
Studies 1970.
(Adelphi papers. 67.)

Brinton, J.Y.   1651

Federations in the Middle East. A
documentary survey.
Cairo: Egyptian Society of International Law 1964.

Brown, C.E.   1652

The Libyan revolution sorts itself
out.
Africa report 14. 1969, Dec.,
p. 12-15.

Carey, J.P.C. - Carey, A.G.   1653
Libya. From colony to nation.
Foreign policy bulletin 40. 1961,
p. 109-111.

Carey, J.P.C. - Carey, A.G.   1654
Libya - no longer "arid nurse of
lions".
Political science quarterly 76.
1961, p. 47-68.

Caroselli, F.S.   1655
Gli accordi anglo-libici (Bengasi
29 luglio 1953).
Riv. di studi politici internazionali 20. 1953, p. 345-358, 459-478.

Carrà, A.   1656
Correnti di opinione in Sicilia
sull'impresa libica.
Storia e politica 5. 1966, p. 248-
281.

Cavazza, F.   1657
Precedenti storici ed economici della
unità e indipendenza libica.
Riv. di studi politici internazionali
19. 1952, p. 47-76.

Cecil, C.O.   1658
The determinants of Libyan foreign
policy.
MEJ 19. 1965, p. 20-34.

Chronologie 1963.   1659
Libye.
AAN 2. 1963, p. 779-793.

Ciamarra, G.   1660
Posizioni coloniali italiane in
cinquant'anni di espansione africana.
ACSC 1. 1931, vol. 5, p. 111-138.

Colliard, C.A.   1661
Les anciennes colonies italiennes.
Revue juridique et politique de
l'union française 6. 1952, p. 246-
286.

Commaire, J.   1662
Soudan-Libye: en marge de deux ré-
volutions.
France Eurafrique 1969, oct., p. 3-
6.

Cooley, J.K.   1663
U.S. Air Base in Libya one of
busiest abroad.
Christian science monitor 1966,
14. February.

Couland, J.   1664
La Libye, le pétrole et les bases.
Démocratie nouvelle 1964, 6.6.,
p. 45-47.

Couland, J.   1665
La Libye: un nouveau renfort.
Cahiers du communisme 1969, oct.,
p. 99-104.

Cresta, M.   1666
Die Staatswerdung Libyens. Hoffnun-
gen der europäischen Auswanderung.
Aussenpolitik 2. 1951, p. 110-117.

Cumming, D.C.   1667
British stewardship of the Italian
colonies: an account rendered.
International affairs 29. 1953,
p. 11-21.

Deambrosis, D.   1668
Importanza del Mediterraneo centrale
nell'espansione coloniale italiana.
BSGI 73. 1936, p. 226-232.

Dethan, G.   1669

Le rapprochement franco-italien
après la chute de Crispi jusqu'aux
accords Barrère-Visconti-Venosta
sur le Maroc et la Tripolitaine 1.

Dethan, G.   1669

(1896-1900) d'après les archives
du Quai d'Orsay.
Revue d'histoire diplomatique 70.
1956, p. 323-339.
                              2.

Discours du trône.   1670
Libye.
AAN 5. 1966, p. 689-695.

I documenti diplomatici   1671
italiani. Ministero degli
Affari Esteri.
Roma: IPS 1952-
Ser. 4. 1908-1914 ... - ser.9.
1939-1943.

Documenti relativi alla siste- 1672
mazione delle ex colonie
italiane.
OM 31. 1951, p. 116-124.

Elections du 8 mai 1965:   1673
liste des députés de la
Ve législature.
AAN 4. 1965, p. 661-666.

Etienne, B.   1674

Chronique diplomatique.
AAN 6. 1967, p. 319-375, 8. 1969,
p. 399-424.

Evans, T.   1675

The new Libya: coming to terms with
revolution in the Arab world.
The round table 1970, n. 239,
p. 265-273.

Fawzi, R.N.   1676

Trends in independent Libya.
Wash.: Georgetown University 1962.
Diss.

Fekini, M.   1677

Le règlement de la question libyen-
ne par l'organisation des Nations-
Unies.
Paris 1952. Diss.

Fidel, C.   1678

L'accord anglo-italien et la position de l'Italie en Afrique.
Renseignements coloniaux 1920,
p. 132-135.

France woos Libyans with arms 1679
and aid.
Africa report 15. 1970, n. 6, p.20-
21.

García, L.R.   1680

Libia y los intereses franceses: el
Fezzan.
Cuadernos de estudios africanos y
orientales 1952, n. 17, p. 19-36.

Gil Benumeya, R.   1681

Efectos externos y realidades in-
ternas en la nueva República de
Libia.
Revista de política internacional
1969, n. 105, p. 75-82.

Golino, F.R.   1682

Patterns of Libyan national identi-
ty.
MEJ 24. 1970, p. 338-352.

Golino, P.L.   1683

Colpo di stato dei militari in Libia.
Relazioni internazionali 33. 1969,
p. 762-763.

Gomez Tello, J.L.   1684
Bases y petrolio en Libia.
Africa. Madrid 1970, n. 338, p. 7-
10.

Grossbritannien und die Unab-   1685
haengigkeit Libyens.
Wahn/Rhld 1953.
(British information. 126.)

Haines, C.G.   1686
The problem of the Italian colonies.
MEJ 1. 1947, p. 417-431.

Heim, P.   1687
La Libye, nouvelle puissance arabe.
Articles et documents 1967,n. 01858.

Herreman, P.   1688
Maghreb, Libye, R.A.U.
L'année politique africaine 1967,
p. 1-24.

Hinterhoff, E.   1689
Implications of the coup in Libya.
Contemporary review 216. 1970,
n. 1248, p. 15-18.

Hottinger, A.   1690
10 mal Nahost.
München: Piper 1970.

Idriss Senussi I,   1691
King of Libya.
Current biography yearbook 1956,
p. 297-299.

The independence of Libya   1692
(December 1951).
Yearbook of the United Nations
5. 1951, p. 266-277.

Indipendenza libica: linee   1693
giuriche e politiche del suo
assetto costituzionale.
Comunità internazionale 6. 1951,
p. 587-600.

Ingrassia, F. - Manfrè, G.   1694
Il Regno Unito di Libia.
Palermo: Ediz. Andò 1961.

Italiaander, R.   1695
Italo Balbo. Der Mensch, der Politi-
ker, der Flieger, der Kolonisator.
München 1942.

Italiaander, R.   1696
Die neuen Männer Afrikas. Ihr Leben-
ihre Taten - ihre Ziele.
Düsseldorf: Econ 1960.

Ivanov, D.   1697
Gosudarstvennyj stroj Livii.
Moskva 1957.

Italy, Libya and others.   1698
Africa confidential 11. 1970,
n. 16, p. 3-4.

Khadduri, M.   1699
Modern Libya. A study in political
development.
Baltimore: Johns Hopkins Press 1963.

Khalil, M.   1700

The Arab states and the Arab League.
Vol. 1.2.
Beirut: Khayats 1962.

Khamiri, T.   1701

The Libyan question.
London: Arab Office 1948.
(Pamphlets on Arab affairs. 7.)

Kirkbride, A.   1702

Libya - which way facing ?
African affairs 56. 1957, p. 49-55.

Klopfer, H.   1703

Aspekte der Bewegung des Muhammad
Ben Ali As-Sanusi.
Kairo 1967.

Langella, V.   1704

Un debole organismo statale: il
giovane Regno Unito di Libia.
Universo 34. 1954, p. 71-80.

Lavenir, H.   1705

Au royaume d'Idriss de Libye.
Revue militaire d'information 1960,
n. 319, p. 56-67.

Lentin, A.P.   1706

Libye: la C.I.A. ridiculisée.
Politique aujourd'hui 1969, nov.,
p. 27-37.

Lessona, A.   1707

L'Africa settentrionale nella poli-
tica mediterranea.
Roma 1941.
(Collezione dell'Istituto di Studi
 Coloniali. Università di Roma.)

Lewis, W.H.   1708

Libya: an experiment.
Current history 29. 1955, p. 103-
109.

Lewis, W.H.   1709

North Africa in ferment.
Year book of world affairs 14. 1960,
p. 114-141.

Lewis, W.H.   1710

Libya: the end of monarchy.
Current history 58. 1970, p. 34-38.

Libya.   1711
(Newly independent nations).
Wash.: GPO 1961.
(U.S. Dept. of State. Publication
 7270.)

Libya: arms and the men.   1712
Africa confidential 11. 1970,
n. 3, p. 6-8.

Libya, a new constitutional   1713
monarchy in the making.
British survey 1951, p. 21-27.

Libya: Qathafi's vision.   1714
Africa confidential 11. 1970,
n. 15, p. 5-7.

Libya: seven years of inde-   1715
pendence.
The world today 15. 1959, February,
p. 59-68.

Libya and the colonialist   1716
treaties.
Libyen und die kolonialistischen
Verträge.
Scribe/Der Schreiber 1964, n. 9,
p. 25-29.

Libya today. Its widening   1717
horizons. Based upon an address
by A.N. Aneizi before the Council
of Islamic Affairs, in New York,
27.7.1954. Rev. March 1956.
Tripoli: Government Printing Press
1956.

The Libyan flag.   1718
Tripoli: Ministry of Information and Guidance 1964.
(Bulletin. Dept. of Public Relations. 1.)

Libyan reshuffle.   1719
Africa report 15. 1970,
n. 3, p. 4-6.

The Libyan revolution in   1720
the words of its leaders.
MEJ 24. 1970, p. 203-219.

La Libye.   1721
Chronique de politique
étrangère 11. 1958, p. 135-148.

Libye.   1722
AAN 2. 1963, p. 927-949,
3. 1964, p. 591-596, 4. 1965, p.661-
666.

Libye.   1723
1. Remaniements ministériels
   et nouveaux gouvernements.
2. Discours du trone, 17.11.1968.
AAN 7. 1968, p. 715-720.

La Libye et le Maghreb.   1724
Maghreb 1965, n. 12, p. 3-11.

Macartney, M.H.H. - Cremona, P. 1725
Italy's foreign and colonial policy
1914-1937.
London: Oxford UP 1938.

Le Maghreb et la Libye devant   1726
la mort de Nasser.
Maghreb 1970, n. 42, p. 13-16.

Malley, S.   1727
Tripoli à l'heure du choix.
Africasia 1970, n. 12, p. 6-8.

Mantran, R.   1728
Chronique libyenne.
AAN 2. 1963, p. 771-793, 3. 1964,
p. 325-333, 4. 1965, p. 381-393.

Martel, A.   1729
Aux origines du Royaume de Libye.
Atti del congresso internazionale di
studi nord-africani 1. 1965, p. 289-
302.

Memoirs of King Idris: 1730
a definitive clarification
of the political history of Libya
(January 1955).
Khalil, M.: The Arab states and the
Arab League. Beirut 1962, p.207-214.

Micheli, D. de   1731
La valorizzazione della Libia nei
suoi riflessi politici mediterranei.
ACSC 3. 1937, vol. 2, p. 98-102.

Military agreement between 1732
the United Kingdom and Libya.
Benghazi 29.7.1953.
British and foreign state papers
160. 1962, p. 315-334.

Moessner, J.M. 1733

Die Völkerrechtspersönlichkeit der
Barbareskenstaaten (Algier, Tripo-
lis, Tunis 1518-1830).
Berlin: de Gruyter 1968.

Molinelli, R. 1734

Il nazionalismo italiano e l'impresa di Libia.
Rassegna storica del risorgimento
53. 1966, p. 285-318.

Mondaini, G. 1735

Contribution financière des indigènes aux dépenses d'organisation et
d'administration des colonies d'Italie.
CR des séances ... Institut Colonial
International 24. 1939, p.419-455.

Mondaini, G. 1736

Il problema politico-giuridico.
Comunicazione orale.
Atti del convegno di studi colo-
niali 2. 1947(1948), p. 114-120.

Mondaini, G. 1737

L'attività delle imprese italiane,
elemento indispensabile per il be-
nessere della Libia, Eritrea ...
Atti del convegno di studi africani 3. 1948, p. 175-177.

Natan, N. 1738

Libyen zwischen Kairo und Tunis.
Aussenpolitik 12. 1961, p. 356-
359.

The national anthem. 1739
Tripoli: Ministry of Infor-
mation and Guidance 1964.
(Bulletin. Department of Public
Relations. 2.)

The national anthem of Libya. 1740
Islamic review 54. 1966,
September, p. 23.

Neher, K. 1741

Bericht aus Libyen.
Zeitschrift für Geopolitik 23. 1952,
p. 741-743.

O'Ballance, E. 1742

Libya as a base.
Army quarterly and defense journal
78. 1959, p. 64-70.

Owen, R. 1743

Libya. A brief political and economic survey.
London: Royal Institute of International Affairs 1961.
(Chatham House memoranda.)

Pace, B. 1744

La Libia nella politica fascista
(1922-1935). La riconquista, la definizione dei confini, l'ordinamento.
Messina 1935.

Pelt, A. 1745

The United Kingdom of Libya - from
colony to independent state.
United Nations bulletin 1952, 15.2.,
p. 176-177, 204.

Pelt, A. 1746

Libyan independence and the United
Nations. A case of planned decolo-
nization.
New Haven/London: Yale UP 1970.

Pentzlin, H. 1747

Libyen im politische Spannungsfeld.
Zeitschrift für Geopolitik 25. 1954,
p. 21-26.

Perspectives de l'independence 1748
libyenne.
L'Afrique et l'Asie 1950, n. 11,
p. 51-59.

Pontecorvo, V.   1749
Gli istituendi organi rappresenta-
tivi in Libia e gli statuti del '19.
Atti del convegno di studi coloniali 2. 1947(1948), p. 109-111.

Power, T.F.   1750
Libya and the U.N.
United Nations review 1. 1954/55,
n. 11, p. 51-56.

Proclamation of Libyan   1751
independence.
International survey 10. 1952, p.3-
7.

Quintano Ripollés, A.   1752
Libia, nuevo estado africano.
Cuadernos de estudios africanos 14.
1951, p. 27-37.

Rapport annuel du gouverne-   1753
ment français à l'assemblée
générale des Nations Unies sur l'administration du Fezzân.
Paris: CHEAM 1950.
(Publication 1606.)

Rashid, R.   1754
Libyen zwischen Reaktion und Revolution.
Blätter für deutsche und internationale Politik 14. 1969, p. 1099-
1110.

Rassat, J.   1755
Die Integrationsbemühungen im
Maghreb.
Afrika Spektrum 1968, n. 2, p. 81-
86.

Rassat, J.   1756
Einigungsbestrebungen in Nordafrika.
Afrika heute 1969, n. 1, p. 1-4.

Il regno di Libia fra passato   1757
e presente.
Relazioni internazionali 1964, n.9,
p. 278-280.

Relations et échanges   1758
entre la Libye et des voisins
maghrebins.
Maghreb 1969, n. 35, p. 30-33.

Renseignements constituant   1759
une mise au point de l'oeuvre
française au Fezzân.
Paris: CHEAM 1948.
(Publication 1431.)

Résultats des élections à   1760
la chambre des députés
10 octobre 1964.
AAN 3. 1964, p. 591-596.

Rifai, N.   1761
Libya. A study of national and international factors leading to its
unity and independence.
Ann Arbor, Mich.: University Micro-
films 1959. Diss.

Rondot, P.   1762
La Libye entre l'Afrique, le monde
arabe et l'occident.
Etudes 1956, juillet-août, p. 104-
115. Problèmes économiques 1957,
n. 475, p. 18-22.

Rondot, P.   1763
Die neuen Staaten Nordafrikas und
ihre Stellung in der Welt.
Europa-Archiv 18. 1963, p. 521-532.

Rondot, P.   1764

La Libye accède au premier rang par-
mi les états arabes.
Revue de défense nationale 23. 1967,
p. 1824-1831.

Rondot, P.   1765

La Libye sur l'échiquier méditerranéen.
Revue militaire générale 1969, nov.,
p. 457-485.

Rondot, P.   1766

Perspectives nouvelles en Libye.
Revue de défense nationale 25. 1969,
p. 1807-1820.

Rossi, E.   1767

Il Regno Unito della Libia.
OM 31. 1951, p. 157-177.

Rouleau, E.   1768

Oil and monarchies don't mix.
Africa report 14. 1969, November,
p. 24-27.

Le Royaume de Libye.   1769
Afrique actualité 1966,
mai, p. 16-50.

Le Royaume-Uni de Libye.   1770
Les cahiers français. Docu-
ments d'actualité 1963, déc., p. I-
IV.

Rubinacci, R.   1771

La società degli stati arabi e la
Libia.
Atti del convegno di studi colonia-
li 2. 1947(1948), p. 89-94.

Sabki, H.M.   1772

International authority and the
emergence of modern Libya.
Indiana University 1967. Diss.

Serra, F.   1773

L'azione politica in Cirenaica e
l'accordo con la Senussia.
ACGI 8. 1922(1923), vol. 2, p. 493-
500.

Sharabi, H.B.   1774

Libya's pattern of growth.
Current history 44. 1963, p. 41-45.

Silva, L.   1775

L'organizzazione politica della
Libia.
ACSC 3. 1937, vol. 2, p. 81-85.

Silvestri, U.   1776

Il fascismo e il problema coloniale.
La riconquista della Libia e la sua
rinascita.
RdC 14. 1940, p. 137-143.

Slonim, S.   1777

Egypt, Algeria and the Libyan revolution.
The world today 26. 1970, n. 3,
p. 125-130.

Smith, A.   1778

North African arms race.
The Atlantic 223. 1969, n. 2, p.20-
28.

Spotlight on the United   1779
Kingdom of Libya. Ed. R.A.E.
Hefter.
London: Diplomatist Publications
1959.

United States interests   1796
in the Middle East.
Ed. G. Lenczowski.
Wash.: American Enterprise Institute
for Public Policy Research 1968.

Valentinow, V.   1797

Libyen: Menschen und Probleme.
Neue Zeit. Moskau 1959, n. 33,
p. 25-27.

Vedovati, G.   1798

Conclusione riassuntiva sul problema politico-giuridico.
Atti del convegno di studi coloniali
2. 1947(1948), p. 121-129.

Villard, H.S.   1799

Libya: experiment in independence.
Current history 37. 1959, July,
p. 7-12.

Villard, H.S.   1800

Das Vereinigte Königreich Libyen.
Bustan 4. 1963, n. 2, p. 11-15.

Vitale, M.A.   1801

Organi, ordinamenti e impiego delle
forze armate. L'opera dell'esercito
(1885-1943).
Roma: IPS 1960.

Vitale, M.A. - Cepollaro, A.   1802

Le medaglie d'oro d'Africa (1887-
1945).
Roma: IPS 1961.
(L'Italia in Africa. Serie storico-
militare. 5.)

Wilhelmy, H.   1803

Die staatliche Neugestaltung der
islamischen Welt. Pakistan, Indone-
sien, Senussi-Staat.
Saeculum 1. 1950, p. 535-554.

Yofdat, A.   1804

The U.S.S.R. and Libya.
New outlook 13. 1970, n. 6, p. 37-
40.

Zartman, I. W.   1805

Government and politics in northern
Africa.
London: Methuen 1964.

Libyen - neue arabische Repu-   1806
blik.
Zastrow, R.: Entwicklungsländerprob-
leme in sowjetischen Periodika.
Vierteljahresberichte. Hannover
1970, n. 39, p. 90-91.

Zoli, C.   1807

Accordi coloniali italo-francesi.
BSGI 72. 1935, p. 3-14.

Zoli, C.   1808

L'espansione coloniale italiana
(1922-37).
Roma: L'Arnia 1949.

Constitucion del Reino de   1809
Libia.
Informacion juridica 1966, n.282-
283, p. 27-46.

Constitution du 7 octobre   1810
1951, 8 décembre 1962: révi-
sion constitutionelle, 25 avril
1963: amendement à la constitution.
AAN 2. 1963, p. 927-944, 946-949.

Constitution du Royaume de   1811
Libye (adoptée le 7 octobre
1951 - révisée en 1963).
Informations constitutionelles et
parlementaires ser.3, vol. 17. 1966,
juillet, p. 112-135.

Constitution of the Kingdom 1812
of Libya, (adopted on Oct.7,
1951 - amended in 1963).
Constitutional and parliamentary
information ser. 3, vol. 17. 1966,
p. 112-136.

Constitution of the Kingdom 1813
of Libya, as modified by law
no. 1 of 1963.
Benghazi: National Press 1964.

Costituzione del Regno 1814
Unito di Libia (7 ottobre
1951).
Riv. di studi politici internazionali 19. 1952, p. 269-288.

Dustur. 1815
A survey of the constitutions
of the Arab and Muslim states.
Leiden: Brill 1966.

Giannini, A. 1816
Nuove costituzioni di stati arabi
(Siria, Libia, Giordania).
OM 32. 1952, p. 273-284.

Godchot, J.E. 1817
Les constitutions du Proche et du
Moyen-Orient.
Paris: Sirey 1957.

L'indépendance de la Libye et 1818
la constitution libyenne.
Notes et études documentaires 1952,
n. 1606.

Khalidi, I.R. 1819
Constitution of the United Kingdom
of Libya. Background and summary.
MEJ 6. 1952, p. 221-228.

Khalidi, I.R. 1820
The origins of the constitution of
the United Kingdom of Libya.
Revue de droit international pour
le Moyen-Orient 5. 1956, p. 57-63,
178-183.

Loi organique de la province 1821
du Fezzân 1954.
Gazette officielle du Fezzân 1954,
1er nov., numéro spécial.

Peaslee, A.J. 1822
Constitutions of Nations.
Vol. 1. Africa. 3rd ed.
The Hague: Nijhoff 1965.

Recent constitutional 1823
changes in Libya.
Inter-parliamentary bulletin 1963,
n. 2, p. 70-73.

Stramacci, M. 1824
Le costituzioni degli stati africa-
ni.
Milano: Giuffre 1963.

United Kingdom of Libya 1825
law amending certain provisions of the constitution.
MEJ 17. 1963, p. 162-164.

Law. Administration. Boundaries.

Bertola, A. 1826
Gli studi di diritto coloniale in
Italia nel ventennio fascista.
Roma 1941.
(Bibliografie del ventennio. 1,3.)

Cucinotta, E.   1827

Rassegna di diritto coloniale.
AAI 3. 1940, vol. 3, p. 181-195,
4. 1941, vol. 1, p. 229-273, vol.3,
p. 935-945.

Mininni Caracciolo, M.   1828

Bibliografia giuridica coloniale.
Roma 1943.

Parpagliolo, A.   1829

Notiziario legislativo.
RdC 12. 1938 - 16. 1942: passim.
AAI 6. 1943, vol. 1, p. 243-250,
vol. 2, p. 503-507.

Ambrosini, G.   1830

La condizione giuridica dei libici
dall'occupazione all'avvento del
fascismo.
RdC 13. 1939, p. 75-90, 169-195.

Ambrosini, G.   1831

Lo statuto dei nativi dell'Algeria
e della Libia.
Scritti giuridici in onore di Santi
Romano. Padova 1940, vol. 3, p. 289-
344.

Ansell, M.O. - Arif, I.M. al   1832

The Libyan civil code. An English
translation and comparison with the
Egyptian civil code.
Stoughton/Wisc.: Oleander Press 1970.

Aroca, A.   1833

Die Organisation der Rechtspflege in
Libyen.
Koloniale Rundschau 33. 1942/43,
p. 327-338.

Bassi, U.   1834

I parlamenti libici: sulla partecipazione degli indigeni al governo
della Libia.
Modena 1924.
(Raccolta di monografie giuridiche.1.)

Bertola, A.   1835

Sulla efficacia del diritto otto-
mano in Libia in materia di waqf
igiaretein.
Città di Castello 1919.

Bertola, A.   1836

Corso di diritto coloniale.
Torino 1944.

Bollettino ufficiale.   1837
Ministero delle Colonie -
(Ministero dell'Africa Italiana)
Roma.
1. 1913-

                                     ianc

Caffarel, W.   1838

Giurisprudenza coloniale della corte
di appello per la Libia, 1915-1919.
Tripoli 1920.

Calendario giudiziario.   1839
Corte d'Appello della Libia.
Tripoli.
1940-1941(1940)-

Capotorti, F.   1840

Sulla sorte dei beni degli enti
pubblici italiani in Libia.
Riv. di diritto internazionale
40. 1957, p. 362-383.

Cardinale, N.   1841

Il retratto nel diritto e nella
giurisprudenza coloniali.
ACSC 2. 1934, vol. 5, p. 275-295.

Carusi, E.   1842

Usucapione e interversione del
possesso nel diritto musulmano di
Libia.
Corte di cassazione. Raccolta completa della giurisprudenza... 1. 1924.

Casoni, G. 1843

Prontuario di legislazione coloniale.
Roma 1938.

Cattaneo, S. 1844

Discorso per l'inaugurazione dell'
anno giudiziario 1932.
Tripoli 1932.

Chiofalo, A. 1845

La nuova colonia penitenziaria agricola di Ain Zara.
RdC 6. 1932, p. 717-719.

Cibelli, E. 1846

Sudditanza coloniale e cittadinanza
italiana libica.
Napoli 1930.

Civil and commercial 1847
procedure code.
Benghazi 1954.

Colucci, M. 1848

Rapporti e coincidenze fra alcune
consuetudini cirenaiche e gli antichi diritti mediterranei.
Atti del congresso nazionale delle
tradizioni popolari 1. 1930, p. 150-
155.

Colucci, M. 1849

Il diritto consuetudinario della
Cirenaica.
Roma 1931.

Colucci, M. 1850

Il diritto consuetudinario della
Cirenaica.
Riv. giuridica del medio ed estremo
oriente e giustizia coloniale 1932,
sett.-ott., col. 37-50, nov.-dic.,
1.

Colucci, M. 1850

col. 197-206, 1937, maggio-giugno,
col. 41-58.

2.

Colucci, M. 1851

Estensione e limiti di applicazione
dei diritti consuetudinari indigeni
nelle colonie.
ACSC 2. 1934, vol. 5, p. 241-251.

Cucinotta, E. 1852

Istituzioni di diritto coloniale
italiano.
Roma 1930.
(Biblioteca scientifica coloniali.1.)

Cucinotta, E. 1853

Problemi ed aspetti dell'ordinamento
giuridico della Libia.
RdC 5. 1931, p. 43-51.

Cucinotta, E. 1854

Gli studi giuridici coloniali in
Italia.
Oltremare 5. 1931, p. 197-203.

Cucinotta, E. 1855

Diritto coloniale italiano. 3rd ed.
Roma 1938.

Ebner, G. 1856

La giustizia in Tripolitania nel
1927.
Roma 1940.

Emilia, A. de 1857

La giurisprudenza del tribunale superiore sciaraitico della Libia in materia di fidanzamento, matrimonio e
divorzio (1929-1941).
RSO 21. 1945/46, p. 15-50.

Emilia, A. de   1858

Per il nuovo diritto libico delle
obbligazioni.
Atti del convegno di studi africani
3. 1948, p. 156-172.

Ferrara, F.   1859

Il diritto islamico vigente in Tripolitania e Cirenaica.
ASIPS 7. 1913, p. 199-225.

Ghersi, E.   1860

Diritto coloniali.
Milano 1942.
(Manuali CETIM.)

Gianturco, V.   1861

La corte suprema del Regno Unito di
Libia.
Libia 2. 1954, n. 2, p. 15-50.

Kruse, H. - Oppermann, T. -   1862
Yousry, A.

Das Staatsangehörigkeitsrecht der
arabischen Staaten. Vol. 1.2.
Frankfurt a.M.: Metzner 1955-64.

Leone, E. de   1863

Il "waqf" nel diritto coloniale italiano.
RdC 4. 1930, p. 651-670, 770-787.

Leone, E. de   1864

Il concetto di ordine pubblico coloniale.
RdC 5. 1931, p. 261-274, 463-472,
546-558.

Leone, E. de   1865

Alcuni istituti giuridici consuetudinari nel territorio di Homs.
ACSC 2. 1934, vol. 5, p. 261-269.

The Libyan civil code.   1866
English translation based
upon the English translation of the
Egyptian civil code ...
Benghazi nd.

Libyan civil service law   1867
no. 36 for the year 1956.
Wash.: U.S. Joint Publications Research Service 1962.

The Libyan criminal procedure   1868
code. Royal decree amending
certain provisions of the code of
penal procedure.
Tripoli 1955.

The Libyan penal code.   1869
Tripoli 1953.

Lombardi, L.   1870

Discorso per l'inaugurazione dell'
anno giudiziario 1929.
Tripoli 1929.

Lo Verde, G.   1871

Die Rasse im italienischen Kolonial-
recht.
Zeitschrift für vergleichende Rechts-
wissenschaft 54. 1941, p. 1-7, 109-
113.

Marchi, G.   1872

Seduta inaugurale della commissione
per lo studio della riforma della
legislazione penale libica.
Roma 1924.

Martina, G. - Valenzi, F.   1873

Giurisprudenza della corte d'appello
della Libia 1920-25.
Tripoli 1926.

Massart, E. 1874
L'ordinamento amministrativo e
giudiziario della Libia.
Pisa 1936.

Minnini, M. - Ongaro, G. 1875
Codice tributario dell'Africa italia-
na. Vol. 1.2.
Roma 1939-40.

Mirza, C. 1876
Cenni sull'istituto dei beni auqaf
in Libia.
Riv. di diritto coloniale 1. 1938,
p. 465-475.

Mondaini, G. 1877
Il problema della cittadinanza ai
sudditi coloniali.
RdC 13. 1939, p. 51-73.

Mondaini, G. 1878
La legislazione coloniale italiana
nel suo sviluppo storico e nel suo
stato attuale (1881-1940). 2nd ed.
Milano 1941.

Ordinamento di polizia per 1879
la Tripolitania e la Cirenaica. Ministero delle Colonie.
Roma 1933.

Panetta, E. 1880
Una waqfiyyah ḥanifita del secolo
XVIII.
AION NS 3. 1949, p. 315-332.

Panetta, E. 1881
Un contratto tripolino di permuta
del XVIII secolo.
AION NS 5. 1953, p. 141-144.

Parpagliolo, A. 1882
Raccolta dei principali ordinamenti
legislativi delle colonie italiane.
Vol. 1.2.
Roma 1930-31.

Parpagliolo, A. 1883
La tecnica legislativa per le colo-
nie italiane.
ACSC 2. 1934, vol. 5, p. 208-218.

Porcelli, N.S. 1884
Il diritto penale italiano in Libia.
Torino 1933.

Qasem, A.M. 1885
A judicial experiment in Libya: uni-
fication of civil and Shariat courts.
International and comparative law
quarterly ser. 4, vol. 3. 1954,
p. 134-137.

Queirolo, E. 1886
Il muchtár nella legislazione otto-
mana. Governo della Tripolitania.
Tripoli 1918.

Ravizza, A. 1887
Il codice penale italiano nella
Libia.
Città di Castello 1925.

Ravizza, A. 1888
La giustizia.
La rinascita della Tripolitania.
Milano 1926, p. 321-335.

Ravizza, A. 1889
Per l'inaugurazione dell'anno
giudiziario 1927.
Tripoli 1927.

Ravizza, A.   1890

Aspetti della giurisprudenza coloniale italiana.
ACSC 1. 1931, vol. 5, p. 196-215.

Rivista di diritto coloniale.   1891
Bologna/Roma.
1. 1938 - 4. 1941.

sc

Royal decree for a law   1892
for the organization of the
courts.
Tripoli 1958.

Scandura, A.   1893

La recente giurisprudenza musulmana
e i beni auqâf in Tripolitania.
ACSC 2. 1934, vol. 5, p. 251-261.

Scandura, A.   1894

L'istituto della "tauliya" nel
Maghreb e nella recente giurisprudenza libica.
Riv. di diritto coloniale 3. 1940,
p. 60-69.

Scandura, A.   1895

Esegesi storica e natura giuridica
dei contratti agrari delle popolazioni indigene della Libia.
RdC 15. 1941, p. 655-670. Riv. di
diritto agrario 20. 1941, p.27-42.

Sergio, R.   1896

Massime penali ricavate dalle sentenze della corte d'appello per la
Libia pronunziate dal 1913 a tutto
il 1924.
Tripoli 1925.

Sertoli Salis, R.   1897

La giustizia indigena nelle colo-
nie.
Padova 1933.
(Studi coloniali. 8.)

Sertoli Salis, R.   1898

Gli ordinamenti giudiziari delle
colonie italiane (Libia-Eritrea-
Somalia).
RdC 10. 1936, p. 748-764.

Sertoli Salis, R.   1899

Nozioni di diritto coloniale.
Vol. 1.2.
Milano 1938-39.

Sisti, F. de   1900

Gli istituti di prevenzione e di
pena in Libia.
AAI 1. 1938, vol. 3/4, p. 943-953.

Tallarigo, C.   1901

Il lavoro negli istituti di prevenzione e di pena della Libia.
ACSC 3. 1937, vol. 3, p. 182-195.

Tambaro, I.   1902

Il nuovo statuto libico.
AIn 46. 1927, p. 218-230.

Tambaro, I.   1903

L'ordinamento giudiziario delle
nostre colonie.
ACSC 2. 1934, vol. 5, p. 164-174.

Vaccari, U.   1904

Discorso per l'inaugurazione dell'
anno giudiziario 1922.
Tripoli 1923.

Valenzi, F.   1905

Il contratto di "enzel" nel diritto
musulmano.
RdC 5. 1931, p. 83-91.

Valenzi, F. - Nigro, G. -   1906
Casoli, C.
Giurisprudenza della corte d'appello
della Libia 1926-1932.
Tripoli 1933

Valenzi, F.   1907
La legislazione ed organizzazione
giudiziaria della Libia.
ACSC 3. 1937, vol. 3, p. 152-182.

Valenzi, F.   1908
La giustizia sciaraitica in Libia.
Riv. di diritto coloniale 3. 1940,
p. 8-18.

Villari, S.   1909
La condizione giuridica delle popolazioni coloniali. La cittadinanza
adiectitia.
Roma 1939.

Vuoli, R.   1910
La condizione giuridica del territorio libico.
Foro italiano 1939, fasc. 17, n.4,
col. 218-235.

Ward, P.   1911
Establishing a law library in Libya.
Bulletin. International Association
of Law Libraries 1966, n. 16,
p. 10-14.

Ziliotto, G.   1912
Proprietà immobiliare e libri fon-
diari nelle colonie.
Roma 1939.
(Studi giuridici coloniali. 1.)

L'accordo italo-anglo-   1913
egiziano per la frontiera
sud-orientale della Libia.
Oltremare 8. 1934, p. 233-234.

Ademollo, U.   1914
I confini della Libia e dell'Eritrea.
Vie d'Italia 41. 1935, p. 241-256.

Administrative survey of the   1915
federal government and the
province administration of Libya.
New York: United Nations 1957.

Agostini, E. de   1916
La definizione del confine fra la
Cirenaica e l'Egitto.
ACGI 10. 1927, p. 580-588.

Agostini, E. de   1917
La nuova frontiera fra la Libia ed
il Sudàn anglo-egiziano.
ACSC 2. 1934, vol. 3, p. 30-36.

Agostini, E. de   1918
Sulle frontiere meridionali della
Libia.
RdC 9. 1935, p. 1179-1186.

Agostini, E. de   1919
Organizzazione amministrativa.
SIFOG 1937, p. 659-668.

Algeria-Libya boundary.   1920
Wash.: U.S. Dept. of State.
The Geographer 1961.
(International boundary study. 1.)

Allegrini, A.   1921
Le nuove frontiere sud-occidentali
della Tripolitania.
AIn 42. 1923, p. 66-67.

Ambrosini, G.   1922

Il diritto dell'Italia alla rettifica
del confine meridionale libico.
ACSC 2. 1934, vol. 5, p. 201-208.

Amministrazione fiduciaria   1923
all'Italia in Africa.
Firenze 1948.
(Università degli Studi di Firenze.
 Centro di Studi Coloniali. 36.)

Au Sahara. Sur les confins   1924
algéro-tripolitains.
Renseignements coloniaux 1915, p. 43-
47.

Bondoni, G.   1925

Il R.D.L. 9 gennaio 1939, n. 70 e la
natura giuridica del territorio
libico.
Riv. giuridica del medio ed estremo
oriente 4. 1940, col. 23-26.

Chad-Libya boundary.   1926
Wash.: U.S. Dept. of State.
The Geographer 1961.
(International boundary study. 3.)

Corò, F.   1927

La delimitazione della frontiera
tra la Libia ed il Sudan.
Oltremare 8. 1934, p. 324.

Corò, F.   1928

La frontiera fra la Tripolitania e
la Tunisia.
IdO 7. 1942, 5.12., p. 255-256,
264-266.

Crocetta, A.   1929

Il commissario regionale e la sua
funzione di governo tra le popolazioni musulmane con speciale riguardo a quelle della Tripolitania.
ACSC 2. 1934, vol. 5, p. 231-240.

Fallot, E.   1930

La délimitation entre les territoires français et italiens du
Sahara.
Afrique française 34. 1924, p. 246-
248.

Folchi, A.E.   1931

L'ordinamento amministrativo dell'
Africa italiana.
Milano 1936.

Franchini, F.   1932

Gli organi consultativi dell'
amministrazione coloniale.
Riv. di diritto coloniale 4. 1941,
p. 108-124.

Gasparini, J.   1933

L'accordo italo-egiziano per la
delimitazione dei confini tra la
Cirenaica e l'Egitto.
RdC 7. 1933, p. 1-10.

Giannini, A.   1934

L'accordo italo-egiziano per le
frontiere della Cirenaica.
OM 6. 1926, p. 1-6.

Gorini, P.M.   1935

L'amministrazione locale in regime di amministrazione fiduciaria.
Atti del convegno di studi coloniali 2. 1947(1948), p. 96-101.

Hopkins, J.F.P.   1936

Medieval Muslim government in Barba-
ry until the sixth century of the
Hijra.
London: Luzac 1958.

Libya-Niger boundary.   1937
Wash.: U.S. Dept. of State.
The Geographer 1961.
(International boundary study. 4.)

Libya-Sudan boundary. 1938
Wash.: U.S. Dept. of State.
The Geographer 1961.
(International boundary study. 10.)

Libya-United Arab Republic 1939
boundary.
Wash.: U.S. Dept. of State.
The Geographer 1966.
(International boundary study. 61.)

Libycus 1940
La frontiera meridionale della Libia
non è ancora fissata.
Oltremare 2. 1928, p. 50-53.

Marinucci, C. - Columbano, T. 1941
Il governo dei territori oltremare
(1869-1955).
Roma: IPS 1963.
(L'Italia in Africa. Serie giuridico-
amministrativa. 1.)

Marinucci, C. 1942
Repertorio delle disposizioni legis-
lative e regolamenti vigenti nelle
colonie italiane (1880-1943).
Roma: IPS 1969. 1.
(L'Italia in Africa. Serie giuridico-

Marinucci, C. 1942

  amministrativa. 3.)

2.

Masi, C. 1943
La frontière méridionale de la
Libye.
Afrique française 38. 1927, p. 251-
252.

Masi, C. 1944
I confini libici ...
Oltremare 2. 1928, p. 375, 3. 1929,
p. 80-82, 315, 4. 1930, p. 315-316,
5. 1931, p. 96, 241-242, 469-470,
8. 1934, p. 292.

Monheim, C. 1945
Les frontières libyennes.
Bulletin. Société de Géographie
d'Anvers 1935, p. 51-56.

Mori, A. 1946
I confini e l'area della Libia e
delle sue grandi circoscrizioni
amministrative.
Riv. geografica italiana 41. 1934,
p. 187-190.

Narducci, G. 1947
Le elezioni amministrative a Bengasi.
AIn 39. 1920, p. 283.

Nava, S. 1948
La contestata zona sud occidentale
della Tripolitania.
ACSC 1. 1931, vol. 2, p. 325-338.

New administrative division: 1949
10 provinces.
Cartactual 1965, n. 1/12.

The new administrative 1950
divisions in Libya.
Geographical digest 4. 1966, p. 8.

La nuova ripartizione 1951
politico-amministrativa
della Libia.
AIn 53. 1935, p. 328-329.

Nuovo ordinamento amministra- 1952
tivo - Libia.
OM 43. 1963, p. 502-503, 44. 1964,
p. 608-612.

Pellegrineschi, A.V.   1953
La barriera orientale della Cire-
naica.
Oltremare 7. 1933, p. 146-148.

Pfalz, R.   1954
Die neuen Grenzen von Italienisch-
Libyen und Eritrea.
PGM 81. 1935, p. 225-228.

Queirolo, E.   1955
Gli enti autonomi dell'amministra-
zione locale.
La rinascita della Tripolitania.
Milano 1926, p. 399-408.

Règlement organique pour   1956
l'administration de la Libye.
Renseignements coloniaux 1935,
p. 78-80, 94-96.

Il reticolato confinario.   1957
Governo della Cirenaica.
Bengasi 1932.

Rossi, E.   1958
Per la storia della penetrazione
turca nell'interno della Libia e
per la questione dei suoi confini.
OM 9. 1929, p. 153-167.

Sandford, K.S.   1959
Western frontiers of Libya.
Geographical journal 99. 1942,
p. 29-40.

Scarin, E.   1960
I confini della Libia.
Riv. geografica italiana 42. 1935,
p. 77-102.

Serra, F.   1961
Ordinamento politico-amministrativo
della Cirenaica prima della occupazione italiana ed attualmente.
CGEP 1923, p. 181-192.

Sertoli Salis, R.   1962
L'amministrazione locale delle colo-
nie libiche.
Milano 1933.
Oltremare 7. 1933, p. 308-310.

Suddivisione politica e   1963
amministrativa della Libia.
Governo della Libia.
Tripoli 1936.

Tummo è francese ?   1964
(Il confine libico a sud).
Oltremare 2. 1928, p. 111-114.

Tummo e Maurice Muret.   1965
Oltremare 4. 1930, p. 167-
168.

Vitale, A.M. - Antico, A.   1966
Longo, A. - Mezza, E.

I corpi armati con funzioni civili.
Roma: IPS 1962.
(L'Italia in Africa. Serie storico-
militare. 4.)

Religion. Cultural History.

Adams, C.C.   1967
The Sanusis.
Muslim world 36. 1946, p. 21-45.

Agostini, E. de   1968

La senussia e le nostre colonie libiche.
ACSC 1. 1931, vol. 2, p. 317-325.

Atiyah, A.S.   1969

Cyrenaica: Christian and mediaeval.
Cairo 1944.
(Handbook on Cyrenaica. 4.)

Aurigemma, S.   1970

L'"area" cemeteriale cristiana di
Áin Zára presso Tripoli di Barberia.
Roma 1932.
(Studi di antichità cristiana. 5.)

Balil Illana, A.   1971

Construcciones paleocristianas en
Tripolitania.
Zephyrus 5. 1954, p. 41-48.

Bartoccini, R.   1972

Sirte - Ipogeo cristiano del IV secolo.
AIb 2. 1928-29, p. 187-200.

Bartoccini, R.   1973

Una chiesa cristiana nel vecchio
foro di Lepcis.
Riv. di archeologia cristiana
8. 1931, p. 23-52.

Beguinot, F.   1974

Qualche traccia di cristianità nel
berbero sahariano.
ACSC 3. 1937, vol. 6, p. 18-21.

Beguinot, F.   1975

L'Islām nell'Africa del Nord.
Aspetti e problemi attuali del mondo musulmano. Roma 1941, p. 125-152.

Bergna, C.   1976

Missionari francescani in Libia e in
Somalia.
ACSC 1. 1931, vol. 2, p. 249-264,
vol. 4, p. 298-302.

Bergna, C.   1977

Le relazioni dei prefetti apostolici
della Libia nei sec. XVII-XVIII.
ACSC 2. 1934, vol. 2, p. 239-246.

Bergna, C.   1978

L'origine della missione francescana
in Libia.
Libia 4. 1956, p. 33-39.

Bernasconi, P.   1979

Le oasi di Cufra e la Senussia.
Oltremare 5. 1931, p. 47-52.

Bernasconi, P.   1980

Italia e Senussia.
Oltremare 7. 1933, p. 138-140.

Bertola, A.   1981

Sugli acquisti dei corpi morali in
Libia.
Milano 1918.

Bertola, A.   1982

Confessione religiosa e statuto personale dei cittadini italiani nell'
Egeo e libici.
OM 14. 1934, p. 105-111.

Bertola, A. - Jemolo, A.C.   1983

Codice ecclesiastico. Parte 10a: i
culti nelle colonie e nei possedimenti.
Padova 1937.

Bertola, A.   1984

Il regime dei culti nell'Africa italiana.
Bologna 1939.
(Manuali coloniali. 4.)

Bisi, A.M.   1985

Le influenze puniche sulla religione libica: la gorfa di Kef el-Blida.
Studi mater. stor. relig. 37. 1966, p. 85-112.

Bono, S.   1986

I primi missionari francescani a Tripoli. (Nel terzo centenario di un martirio).
L'Italia francescana NS 28. 1953, p. 377-380.

Brandl, L.   1987

Frühes Christentum in der Sahara und im Sudan.
Afrika heute 1966, Sonderbeilage, n. 24, 15.12.

Brown, P.   1988

Christianity and local culture in late Roman Africa.
JRS 58. 1968, p. 85-95.

Caputo, G.   1989

Schema di fonti e monumenti del primo cristianesimo in Tripolitania.
Tripoli 1947.

Casini, A.   1990

Io in Cirenaica.
Milano: Gastaldi 1969.

Casini, A.   1991

Sinesio di Cirene.
Milano: Gastaldi 1969.

Castaldo, A.   1992

Le fondazioni pie mussulmane. Manomorta islamica (waquf - auqaf - hubus).
Roma 1940.

Cauneille, A.   1993

Un ornement du sanctuaire de Sidi Abdesselam el Asmar (Tripolitaine).
BLS 2. 1951, n. 3, p. 40.

Cerbella, G.   1994

"El-id el-chebir" ovvero "la grande festa".
IdO 5. 1940, n. 7, p. 109-110.

Cerbella, G.   1995

El-id es-seghìr. La festa piccola dell'Islam.
Libia 4. 1940, n. 10, p. 25-29.

Cerbella, G.   1996

Ramadàn. Mese di penitenza per i musulmani.
Libia 4. 1940 n. 9, p. 28-30.

Cerbella, G.   1997

Il ritorno dei pellegrini dalla Mecca.
IdO 5. 1940, n. 6, p. 93.

Cerbella, G.   1998

Interpretazione storico-etnologica d'un rito islamo-cristiano.
Libia 1. 1953, n. 2, p. 61-108.

Ciompi, M.   1999

Relazioni di missionari sul nord-Africa durante il periodo barbaresco.
ACSC 2. 1934, vol. 4, p. 95-103.

Cirenaica cristiana.   2000
A ricordo della solenne con-
sacrazione della nuova cattedrale de-
dicata al SS. nome di Gesù.
Bengasi 1939.

Colin, G.S.   2001
Sayyidî Aḥmed Zarruq. Un saint maro-
cain enterré en Tripolitaine.
RdT 2. 1925/26, p. 23-34.

Corò, F.   2002
Edifici, memorie e tradizioni cristiane nel Gebel Nefusa.
Famiglia cristiana 1934, ottobre,
p. 201-203, 1936,giugno, p. 11-12,
luglio, p. 29-30, ottobre, p. 99-
102.

Corò, F.   2003
Un missionario a Tripoli informatore
degli inquisitori di Venezia.
RdC 8. 1934, p. 485-495.

Corò, F.   2004
Sopravivenze del culto di Tanit a
Gadames.
Riv. di etnografia 8/9. 1954/55,
p. 31-42.

Coster, C.H.   2005
Christianity and the invasions:
Synesius of Cyrene.
Classical journal 55. 1960, p. 290-
312.

Duepow, O.K.   2006
The Sanusi movement and the Islam
renaissance.
Islamic review 45. 1957, n. 4, p.30-
34.

Facchinetti, V.   2007
L'opera delle missioni cattoliche in
Libia.
L'impero coloniale fascista. Novara
1936, p. 527-532.

Ferri, S.   2008
Il santuario di Budrasc.
NA 1922, fasc. 3, p. 93-99.

Ferri, S.   2009
Le dee ignote di Cirene.
RdC 3. 1929, p. 710-717.

Ferri, S.   2010
Sulle antiche religioni della Libia.
ACSC 1. 1931, vol. 4, p. 210-213.

Ferri, S.   2011
Le dee ignote di Cirene.
Opuscula. Firenze 1962, p. 397-402.

Fornari, G.   2012
La senussia in Cirenaica (sec.XIX-
XX).
Riv. di studi politici internaziona-
li 15. 1948, p. 53-76.

Fornari, G.   2013
La senussia e la Tripolitania.
Rassegna italiana 27. 1950, p. 169-
177.

Gamba, M.   2014
Furono cristianizzati i Tuareg ?
Oltremare 7. 1933, p. 451-452.

Graefe, E.   2015
Der Aufruf des Scheichs der Senusi-
ja zum Heiligen Kriege.
Islam 3. 1912, p. 141-150, 312-313.

Grandchamp, P.   2016

La fin de la Senoussiya d'après les
sources italiennes.
Revue tunisienne 1935, p. 365-407.

Insabato, E.   2017

Gli abaditi del Gebel Nefusa e la
politica islamica in Tripolitania.
Istituto Coloniale Italiano.
Roma 1918.

Italia e Senussia.   2018
Oltremare 4. 1930, p. 317-
326.

Jannaccone, C.   2019

Corso di diritto ecclesiastico coloniale italiano. 2nd ed.
Milano 1939.

Kirwan, L.P.   2020

Christianity and the Ḳura'án.
Journal of Egyptian archaeology 20.
1934, p. 201-203.

Leva, A.E.   2021

Miti greci e scenari africani.
Roma: Istituto Italiano per l'Africa
1963.

Lewicki, T.   2022

Historyczne źródla sekty ibadyckiej.
Przegląd orientalistyczny 1964,
p. 273-283.

Lewicki, T.   2023

Przeżytki starych kultów i wierzeń
pogańskich u średniowiecznych berberów doby muzułmańskiej.
Lud 50. 1964/65, p. 230-295.

Lewicki, T.   2024

Prophètes, devins et magiciens chez
les berbères médiévaux.
Folia orientalia 7. 1965, p. 3-27.

Lewicki, T.   2025

Prophètes antimusulmans chez les
berbères médiévaux.
Atti del congresso di studi arabi
e islamici 3. 1966(1967), p.461-466.

Lewicki, T.   2026

Sur le nom de Dieu chez les berbères médiévaux.
Folia orientalia 8. 1966, p. 227-
229.

Lewicki, T.   2027

Survivances chez les berbères médiévaux d'ère musulmane de cultes
anciens et de croyances païennes.
Folia orientalia 8. 1966, p. 5-40.

Maioletti, B.   2028

La basilica cristiana di Apollonia
in Cirenaica.
RdC 4. 1930, p. 976-988.

Meynier, O.   2029

La guerre sainte de la Senoussiya.
Cahiers Charles de Foucauld 7.1947,
4e trim., p. 93-106, 11. 1948, 4e
trim., p. 54-78, 13. 1949, p. 169-
192, 15. 1949, 3e trim., p. 73-   1.

Meynier, O.   2029

92, 16. 1949, 4e trim., p. 71-97.

2.

Moreno, M.M.   2030

Lineamenti di istituzioni islamiche.
Bengasi 1925.

Mostafa, M. 2031
Islamic objects of art.
LA 2. 1965, p. 123-127.

Nallino, C.A. 2032
Rapporto fra la dogmatica mu'tazili-
ta e quella degli ibāditi dell'
Africa settentrionale.
RSO 7. 1916-18, p. 455-460.

Nallino, C.A. 2033
A proposito del viaggio di un pellegrino attraverso la Libia nel secolo XVIII.
RdT 1. 1924/25, p. 375-384.

Nallino, C.A. 2034
Ibaditi. Senussi.
Enciclopedia italiana vol. 18. 1933,
p. 663, vol. 31. 1936, p. 395-397.

Nallino, C.A. 2035
Cesàro, A.: Santuari islamici nel
secolo XVII in Tripolitania.
RSO 14. 1934, p. 323-328.

Paribeni, R. 2036
Sepolcreto cristiano di Engila pres-
so Suani Beni Adem.
AIb 1. 1927-28, p. 75-82.

Pettazzoni, R. 2037
Miti e leggende.
1. Africa, Australia.
Torino: UTET 1963.

Porrini, R. 2038
Il vicariato apostolico in Cirenaica.
Oltremare 2. 1928, p. 32.

Pugliese Carratelli, G. 2039
Legge sacra di Cirene.
Parola del passato 15. 1960, p. 294-
297.

Pugliese Carratelli, G. 2040
Un documento del culto di Ecate a
Cirene.
Parola del passato 16. 1961, p. 456-
457.

Pugliese Carratelli, G. 2041
Appunti per la storia dei culti ci-
renaici.
Maia 16. 1964, p. 99-111.

Religione, usi e consuetu- 2042
dini delle popolazioni dell'
Africa italiana. Vol. 1.2.
Ministero dell'Africa Italiana.
Roma 1941.

Reynolds, J. 2043
The Christian inscriptions of Cyrenaica.
Journal of theological studies NS 11.
1960, p. 284-294.

Reynolds, J. 2044
A Christian funerary curse at Tocra
in Cyrenaica.
Journal of theological studies NS 16.
1965, p. 462-463.

Romanelli, P. 2045
Monumenti cristiani del museo di Tripoli.
Nuovo boll. di archeologia cristiana
24/25. 1918, p. 27-49.

Romanelli, P. 2046
Le sedi episcopali della Tripolitania antica.
Atti della pontificia accademia romana di archeologia. Rendiconti
ser. 3, vol. 4. 1925-26, p. 155-166.

Rossi, E.   2047

Appunti su feste e costumanze reli-
giose dei musulmani di Tripoli.
AION NS 3. 1949, p. 179-186.

Ruggiero, R.   2048

Memorie cristiane nel Gebel Nefusa
in Tripolitania.
IdO 5. 1940, n. 8, p. 128.

Russo, M.   2049

Il senusso a Bengasi dopo le nostre
delusioni coloniali.
AIn 38. 1919, p. 248-250.

Sanità, G.   2050

La Barberia e la Sacra Congregazione
"De Propaganda Fide" (1622-1668) con
particolare riguardo all'origine e
allo sviluppo della Missione
Francescana in Libia (1668-1711). 1.

Sanità, G.   2050

Studia orientalia christiana. Collec-
tanea 8. 1963, p. 91-262.

                              2.

Sanità, G.   2051

Rapporti e decretali sulle missioni
di Barberia.
Studia orientalia christiana. Collec-
tanea 8. 1963, p. 265-348.

Strothmann, R.   2052

Berber und Ibāḍiten.
Islam 17. 1928, p. 258-279.

Testini, P.   2053

Archeologia cristiana.
Roma: Desclée &C., Editori Pontifici
1958.

Todesco, A.   2054

Frammenti di iscrizioni funerarie
cristiane.
AIb 6. 1935-37, p. 79-81.

Tragella, G.B.   2055

Le missioni della Libia italiana.
Pensiero missionario 11. 1939,
p. 111-120.

Tragella, G.B.   2056

Le missioni cattoliche della Libia.
RSAI 5. 1942, p. 287-293, 480-494.

Trimingham, J.S.   2057

The influence of Islam upon Africa.
London: Longmans 1968.
New York: Praeger 1968.
(Arab background series.)

Turchi, F.   2058

La cattedrale di Tripoli.
Oltremare 2. 1928, p. 31-32.

Valori, F.   2059

Una grande figure della storia della
Cirenaica. Sinesio, vescovo di Tole-
maide.
RdC 17. 1943, p. 204-208.

Vecchia Vaglieri, L.   2060

Viaggio di un pellegrino attraverso
la Libia nel secolo XVIII.
RdT 1. 1924/25, p. 133-142.

Ventimiglia, S.G.   2061

Il "Meilùd" a Bengasi.
RdC 6. 1932, p. 959-967.

Vita, A. di   2062

La diffusione del cristianesimo nell'interno della Tripolitania attraverso i monumenti e sue sopravivenze nella Tripolitania araba. QAL 5. 1967, p. 121-142.

Vycichl, W.   2063

Iusch, der berberische Himmelsgott. Orientalistische Literaturzeitung 42. 1939, col. 721-724.

Vycichl, W.   2064

Berberische Mythologie. Genève 1968.Typescript.

Ward-Perkins, J.B.   2065

The Christian antiquities of Libya since 1938. Actes du congrès international d'archéologie chrétienne 5. 1954 (1957), p. 159-162.

Ward-Perkins, J.B.   2066

L'archeologia cristiana in Cirenaica 1953-1962. Atti del congresso internazionale di archeologia cristiana 6. 1962 (1965), p. 641-657.

Zanon, F.   2067

I tuàregh e la loro mancata islamizzazione. RdC 9. 1935, p. 490-493.

Záuie ed ichuán senussiti   2068
della Tripolitania. Governo della Tripolitania. Tripoli 1917.

Ziadeh, N.A.   2069

Sanūsīyah. A study of a revivalist movement in Islam. Leiden: Brill 1958.

Ziadeh, N.A.   2070

The Sanusi movement, the first of its kind that set itself the task of reforming the Muslim world. Islamic review 56. 1968, n. 8-9, suppl., p. XIX-XXIV, XVIII.

Language. Literature.

Abdelkafi, M. - Brehony, N.   2071

Learn Arabic: ta'allam al-'arabiya. Tripoli 1966.

Agostini, E. de   2072

Indagini onomastiche ed etniche in Libia. AION NS 3. 1949, p. 167-178.

Basset, A.   2073

Ecritures libyque et touarègue. André Basset. Articles de dialectologie berbère. Paris 1959, p. 167-175.

Basset, H.   2074

Sur quelques termes berbères concernant la basse-cour. Mémorial Henri Basset. Paris vol. 1. 1928, p. 5-28.

Basset, R.   2075

A propos du parler berbère de Ghadamès. TIRS 3. 1945, p. 137-140.

Beguinot, F.   2076

Il gergo dei berberi della Tripolitania. Annuario dell'Istituto Orientale di Napoli 1917-18, p. 107-112.

Beguinot, F.   2077

A proposito di una voce libica citata da Erodoto.
AIn 43. 1924, p. 187-191.

Beguinot, F.   2078

Sul trattamento delle consonanti
3, V, F in berbero.
AANL. Rendiconti ser. 5, vol. 33.
1924, p. 186-199.

Beguinot, F.   2079

Saggio di fonetica del berbero Nefûsi di Fassâṭo.
AANL. Rendiconti. Classe di scienze
morali ... ser. 6, vol. 1. 1925,
p. 304-330.

Beguinot, F.   2080

Proposta di compilazione di un lessi-
co berbero comparato.
Actes congrès Institut International
de Langues et Civilisations Africaines 1931, p. 41-46.

Beguinot, F.   2081

Gli studi di linguistica berbera.
ACSC 1. 1931, vol. 4, p. 137-147.

Beguinot, F.   2082

Berberistica e manuali di berbero.
AIn 50/51. 1932/33, p. 34-48.

Beguinot, F.   2083

Gli studi di linguistica berbera.
Riv. d'oriente 2. 1934, fasc. 7,
p. 145-147.

Beguinot, F.   2084

I linguaggi.
SIFOG 1937, p. 493-513.

Beguinot, F.   2085

Di alcune parole di linguaggi nord-
africani derivate dal latino.
Roma 16. 1938, p. 460-463.

Beguinot, F.   2086

Funzione sociale e politica dei
linguaggi indigeni nella vita delle
popolazioni africane e suoi riflessi nella colonizzazione.
Atti dei convegni "Volta"   1.

Beguinot, F.   2086

8. 1938 "Africa", p. 939-948.

                               2.

Bradburne, C.P.   2087

Basic Tripolitanian Arabic: a course
for beginners in the spoken Arabic
of north-western Libya. Vol. 1.2.
New York: Mobil International Oil
Co. 1962.

Cerbella, G.   2088

L'italiano lingua franca nel Nord
Africa.
Atti del convegno di studi colonia-
li 2. 1947, p. 186-192.

Cerbella, G.   2089

Ricordo di Francesco Beguinot.
Libia 1. 1953, n. 2, p. 123-132.

Cesàro, A.   2090

Le caratteristiche fonetiche dei
linguaggi arabi e berberi della Libia nei riguardi della trascrizione
e della cartografia.
ACSC 2. 1934, vol. 4, p. 164-169.

Cesàro, F.   2091

Bibliografia degli scritti di Francesco Beguinot.
AION NS 3. 1949, p. IX-XII.

Chabot, J.B. 2092

Sur quelques signes de l'alphabet libyque.
Journal asiatique 231. 1939, p.117-124.

Ducati, B. 2093

L'arabo della Libia.
Oltremare 4. 1930, p. 419-420.

Ducati, B. 2094

Il berbero.
Oltremare 5. 1931, p. 220-221.

Ducati, B. 2095

Grammatica pratica della lingua araba parlata in Tripolitania e compresa dovunque si parli arabo.
Bologna 1933.

Essing, D. 2096

Die afrikanisch-linguistische Hinterlassenschaft von H. Barth.
HBFA 1967, p. 371-396.

Fevrier, J.G. 2097

Que savons-nous du libyque ?
Revue africaine 100. 1956, p. 263-273.

"Francesco Beguinot". 2098
AION NS 5. 1953, p. VII-XV.

Galand, L. 2099

Les études de linguistique berbère.
4. 1965, p. 743-765, 5. 1966, p. 813-822, 6. 1967, p. 1035-1043, 7. 1968, p. 865-873 , 8. 1969, p. 1073-1082.

Garbini, G. 2100

Note libiche.
Studi magrebini 1. 1966, p. 81-90, 2. 1968, p. 113-122.

Hamp, E.P. 2101

Zuara Berber personals.
Bulletin of the School of Oriental and African Studies 22. 1959, p. 140-141.

Lanfry, J. 2102

Deux notes grammaticales sur le berbère de Ghadamès.
Mémorial André Basset (1895-1956) Paris 1957, p. 57-60.

Lanfry, J. - Dallet, P.J.M. 2103

Ghadamès. Etude linguistique et ethnographique. Vol. 1. Texte.
Fort-National 1968.

Leva, A.E. 2104

Il contributo italiano alla conoscenza delle lingue parlate in Africa.
Roma: IPS 1969.
(L'Italia in Africa. Serie scientifico culturale.)

Lukas, J. 2105

Die Sprache der Tubu in der zentralen Sahara.
Berlin: Akademie-Verlag 1953.
(Veröffentlichungen des Instituts für Orientforschung. 14.)

Marquardt, D.E. 2106

Uniform procedure for Arabic transliteration. Preliminary comments.
Tripoli 1963.

Misallem, M.D. 2107

Libya: Tripolitanian phrase book.
Tripoli: Poligrafico Libico 1962.

Mitchell, T.F.   2108

The active participle in an Arabic
dialect of Cyrenaica.
Bulletin of the School of Oriental
and African Studies 14. 1952,
p. 11-33.

Mitchell, T.F.   2109

Particle-noun complexes in a Berber
dialect (Zuara).
Bulletin of the School of Oriental
and African studies 15. 1953,
p. 374-390.

Mitchell, T.F.   2110

Le language of buying and selling
in Cyrenaica: a situational statement.
Hésperis 44. 1957, p. 31-71.

Mitchell, T.F.   2111

Long consonants in phonology and
phonetics. A. Gemination in the Bedouin Arabic of the Cyrenaican
Jebel. B. Tense and lax articula-
tion in the Berber dialect   1.

Mitchell, T.F.   2111

of Zuara.
Studies in linguistic analysis
(special volume of the Philological
Society) 1957, p. 182-198.

                                2.

Mitchell, T.F.   2112

Some properties of Zuara nouns,
with special reference to those
with consonant initial.
Mémorial André Basset (1895-1956).
Paris 1957, p. 83-96.

Mukarovsky, H.G.   2113

Über den Grundwortschatz des Euro-
saharanischen.
Paideuma 12. 1966, p. 135-149.

Nallino, C.A.   2114

Indice dei nomi arabo-turchi citati
nelle relazioni riguardanti la
città di Tripoli.
NA 2. 1916 (1918) appendice 2,
p. 400-408.

Nomenclatura elementare   2115
ed espressioni nelle lingue
amharica, galla, araba(dialetto
tripolino).
Roma 1936.

Panetta, E.   2116

Francesco Beguinot (1879-1953).
OM 33. 1953, p. 523-527.

Panetta, E.   2117

Vocabolario e fraseologia di Bengasi.
Annali lateranensi 22. 1958, p. 318-
369, 26. 1962, p. 257-290.

Panetta, E.   2118

Vocabolario e fraseologia dell'ara-
bo parlato a Bengasi.
Studi orientali pubbl. a cura della
Scuola Orientale. Università di
Roma 5. 1964, p. 195-216.

Paradisi, U.   2119

El-Fógǎha, oasi berberofona del
Fezzân.
RSO 36. 1961, p. 293-302.

Paradisi, U.   2120

Il linguaggio berbero di El-Fógǎha
(Fezzân). Testi e materiale lessica.
AION NS 13. 1963, p. 93-126.

Paradisi, U.   2121

Sul nome del "topo" nel berbero di
Augila e una voce libica citata da
Erodoto.
RSO 38. 1963, p. 61-65. Parola del
passato 17. 1962, p. 201-205.

Roessler, O.   2122

Libyca.
Wiener Zeitschrift für die Kunde
des Morgenlandes 49. 1942, p. 282-
311.

Roessler, O. 2123

Verbalbau und Verbalflexion in den
semitohamitischen Sprachen.
Zeitschrift der deutschen morgenländischen Gesellschaft 100. 1950,
p. 461-514.

Roessler, O. 2124

Akkadisches und libysches Verbum.
Orientalia NS 20. 1951, p. 101-107,
366-373.

Roessler, O. 2125

Der semitische Charakter der libyschen Sprache.
Zeitschrift für Assyriologie 50.
1952, p. 121-150.

Roessler, O. 2126

Die lateinischen Reliktwörter im
Berberischen und die Frage des Vokal-
systems der afrikanischen Latinität.
Beiträge zur Namenforschung 13. 1962,
p. 258-262.

Roessler, O. 2127

Libysch - hamitisch - semitisch.
Oriens 17. 1964, p. 199-216.

Rossi, E. 2128

Esplicazione dei vocaboli tripolini
contenuti in P. Ricard: les arts
tripolitains.
RdT 2. 1925/26, p. 292-293.

Rossi, E. 2129

La lingua franca in Barberia.
RdC 1/2. 1927/28, p. 143-151.

Rossi, E. 2130

Vocaboli stranieri nel dialetto arabo della città di Tripoli.
Atti del congresso internazionale
dei linguisti 3. 1933, p. 186-193.

Sarnelli, T. 2131

Di alcuni gerghi arabi della Tripolitania.
AIn 43. 1924, p. 192-197.

Sarnelli, T. 2132

Il dialetto di Sokna.
AIn 43. 1924, suppl.

Sarnelli, T. 2133

Il dialetto ignorato di Sokna.
AIn 43. 1924, p. 34-37.

Sarnelli, T. 2134

Sull'origine del nome "silfio".
AION NS 3. 1949, p. 383-394.

Sarnelli, T. 2135

Sull'origine del nome Imāzîgen.
Mémorial André Basset (1895-1956).
Paris 1957, p. 131-138.

Scialhub, G. 2136

Grammatica italo-araba, con i rapporti e le differenze tra l'arabo
letterario e il dialetto libico.
Milano 1923.

Serra, L. 2137

Ricordo di Antonio Cesàro.
AION 18. 1968, p. 469-470.

Serra, L. 2138

L'ittionimia e la terminologia mari-
naresca nel dialetto berbero di
Zuara (Tripolitania).
Studi magrebini 3. 1970, p. 21-53.

Significato di taluni   2139
nomi arabi più comuni in
uso nella Libia. Ministero delle
Colonie.
Roma 1917.

Stumme, H.   2140
Zu den von K.M. v. Beurmann in ZDMG
16, 564 erwähnten Partikeln buk und
ḥot des Tripolitanischen.
Zs der deutschen morgenländischen
Gesellschaft 68. 1914, p. 457-458.

Torrisi, M.   2141
At-targumânu-t-tarâbulusîyu. Inter-
prete tripolino.
Catania 1915.

Turbet-Delof, G.   2142
Notes lexicologiques sur la désigna-
tion de certaines collectivités
ethniques ou géographiques d'Afrique
du Nord.
Français moderne 38. 1970, p.151-154.

Vaccari, P.   2143
L'arabo scritto e l'arabo parlato in
Tripolitania. Grammatica elementare
pratica.
Torino 1921.

Vycichl, W.   2144
L'histoire de la langue berbère.
Actes du congrès international des
orientalistes 21. 1948(1949), p.319-
320.

Vycichl, W.   2145
Das berberische Ziffernsystem von
Ghadames und sein Ursprung.
RSO 27. 1952, p. 81-83.

Vycichl, W.   2146
Die Nisbe-Formationen im Berberi-
schen.
AION NS 4. 1952, p. 111-117.

Vycichl, W.   2147
Punischer Spracheinfluss im Berberischen.
Journal of Near Eastern studies 11.
1952, p. 198-204.

Vycichl, W.   2148
Der Umlaut im Berberischen des
Djebel Nefusa in Tripolitanien.
AION NS 5. 1953, p. 145-152.

Vycichl, W.   2149
Der Umlaut in den Berbersprachen
Nordafrikas.
Wiener Zs für die Kunde des Morgen-
landes 52. 1953, p. 304-325.

Vycichl, W.   2150
Der Teufel in der Staubwolke.
Muséon 69. 1956, p. 341-346.

Vycichl, W.   2151
L'article défini du berbère.
Mémorial André Basset (1895-1956).
Paris 1957, p. 139-146.

Vycichl, W.   2152
Amĕsmir und Aẓarif.
Aegyptus 38. 1958, p. 147-150.

Vycichl, W.   2153
Diminutiv und Augmentativ im Berbe-
rischen.
Zs der deutschen morgenländischen
Gesellschaft 111. 1961, p. 243-253.

Vycichl, W.   2154
Berberisch Z-M-R "können, potere".
RSO 37. 1962, p. 77-78.

Vycichl, W. 2155

Tuareg "takuba", hausa "takobi",
"Schwert, Spada".
AION 15. 1965, p. 279-283.

Vycichl, W. 2156

Etude sur la langue de Ghadâmés
(Sahara).
Genève-Afrique 5. 1966, p. 248-260.

Vycichl, W. 2157

Sprachliche Beziehungen zwischen
Ägypten und Afrika.
Hamburger Beiträge zur Afrika-Kunde
5. 1966, p. 265-272.

Vycichl, W. 2158

Das hamitosemitische Nomen agentis
QATTĀL in den Berbersprachen.
Muséon 83. 1970, p. 541-545.

Ward, P. 2159

Uniform procedure for Arabic transliteration.
Journal of documentation 21. 1965,
p. 199-200.

Woelfel, D.J. 2160

Sprachenkarte von Weissafrika.
Beiträge zur Kolonialforschung 6.
1944, p. 196-202.

Woelfel, D.J. 2161

Die Gottesnamen der Libyer und der
Berber.
Sprache 2. 1950-52, p. 171-181.

Zanon, F. 2162

Contributo alla conoscenza linguisti-
co-etnografico dell'oasi di Augila.
AIn 50/51. 1932/33, p. 259-276.

Zanon, F. 2163

Una prima missione esplorativa nel
Deserto Libico organizzata dal R.
Istituto Orientale di Napoli.
Oltremare 7. 1933, p. 244-245.

Abdelkafi, M. 2164

One hundred Arabic proverbs from
Libya.
London: Vernon and Yates Ltd 1968.

Abel, A. 2165

Un grand poète libyen: Ahmad ash
Shârif.
Correspondance d'orient. Études
1965/66, n. 8/9, p. 5-15.

Beguinot, F. 2166

Recenti studi italiani sulla letteratura popolare cirenaica.
OM 27. 1947, p. 117-123.

Brulard, M. 2167

Contes merveilleux de Ghât (Libye
du Sud).
BLS 11. 1960, n. 39, p. 260-265,
n. 40, p. 339-346.

Buselli, G. 2168

Testi berberi del Gebel Nefûsa
(dialetto di Gemmâri).
AIn 40. 1921, p. 26-34.

Buselli, G. 2169

Berber texts from Jebel Nefûsi
(Žemmâri dialect).
Journal of the African society 23.
1923/24, p. 285-293.

Cerbella, G. 2170

I berberi e la novellistica berbera.
AIn 46. 1927, p. 267-277.

Cerbella, G.   2171

Canti di marinai tripolini.
Libia 2. 1954, n. 3, p. 21-24.

Corso, R. - Beguinot, F.   2179

Varianti arabo-berbere delle dodici
parole della verità.
AION 3. 1930, p. 3-15.

Cerbella, G.   2172

Gûma, poeta e patriota libico, nella
storia e nella leggenda.
Libia 3. 1955, n. 4, p. 3-23.

Cozzani, E.   2180

D'Annunzio e l'Africa italiana.
AIr 1941-42, n. 37, p. 43-51.

Cerbella, G.   2173

Poesie e canti popolari arabi.
Libia 4. 1956, n. 3-4, p. 27-40.

Giaccardi, A.   2181

Letteratura coloniale italiana.
RdC 9. 1935, p. 138-148.

Cesàro, A.   2174

Due racconti berberi in linguaggio
nefûsi.
AION NS 3. 1949, p. 395-404.

Giovannetti, E.   2182

"Alba d'impero".
AAI 1. 1938, vol. 3/4, p. 1255-1258.

Cesàro, A.   2175

Racconti in dialetto tripolino.
AION NS 6. 1954-56, p. 49-59.

Giovannetti, E.   2183

D'Annunzio e le colonie.
RdC 12. 1938, p. 169-172.

Corò, F.   2176

Il miracolo di Nanna Tala.
Bologna 1933.

Guida, O.   2184

Questa lettaratura coloniale.
Oltremare 3. 1929, p. 358-360.

Corò, F.   2177

La quadriga dei garamanti.
Milano 1934.

Jahn, Samia al Azharia   2185

Neue Sammlungen arabischer Volks-
märchen in Tunis, Libyen und der
V.A.R., die von den Arabern selbst
aufgezeichnet wurden.
Fabula 8. 1966, p. 251-259.

Corò, F.   2178

La cieca del "gusbet". Racconto berbero.
AIr 1. 1938, n. 2, p. XII-XIII.

Jaritz, K.   2186

Göttersagen vom Berge Idinen in der
Sahara.
Wiener völkerkundliche Mitteilungen
8. 1960, p. 41-50.

Lauro, R. di 2187
Tripolitania. Saggi e sensazioni.
Napoli 1932.

Il libro coloniale del 2188
tempo fascista.Catalogo.
Sindicato Romano degli Autori e
Scrittori. VII mostra-vendita ...
Roma 1936.

Libyan winter. 2189
Poems by a corporal in the
First Division.
Johannesburg: Central News Agency
1943.

Miganti, P. 2190
Una poesia di Ma'rūf ar-Ruṣāfī sulla
conquista italiana di Tripoli (1911).
AION 18. 1968, p. 335-337.

Narducci, G. 2191
Massime, sentenze e proverbi libici.
Riv. di etnografia 3. 1949, p. 103-
108.

Palieri, M. 2192
Letteratura coloniale.
Oltremare 8. 1934, p. 406-407.

Panetta, E. 2193
Racconti, proverbi e canti della
Cirenaica.
ACSC 2. 1934, vol. 4, p. 130-155.

Panetta, E. 2194
Proverbi, modi di dire e indovinelli
arabi di Bengasi.
RSO 19. 1941, p. 249-281.

Panetta, E. 2195
At-Tanūḫī: al-faraǧ ba'da aš-šidda.
Libia 1. 1953, n. 2, p. 109-116.

Panetta, E. 2196
Poesie e canti popolari arabi.
Parma: Guanda 1956.
(Collezione fenice. 30.)

Panetta, E. 2197
Note sulla novellistica dell'Africa
settentrionale.
Levante 6. 1959, n. 2, p. 32.

Panetta, E. 2198
Motivi fiabeschi del Maghrib.
Levante 7. 1960, n. 4, p. 3-12.

Paradisi, U. 2199
Testi berberi di Augila (Cirenaica).
AION 10 1961, p. 79-90.

Pozzi, M. 2200
Arte e propaganda nella letteratura
coloniale.
Oltremare 3. 1929, p. 210-212.

Raccah, G.V. 2201
Dizionaretto degli autori ebrei
della Libia.
ACSC 2. 1934, vol. 4, p. 267-272.

Rossi, E. 2202
Canti popolari della Tripolitania.
Tribuna coloniale 1923, 10 marzo.

Rossi, E.   2203

Poesia popolare della Tripolitania.
RdT 1. 1924/25, p. 229-243, 2.1925/
26, p. 91-97, 169-176, 237-247, 292-
293, 387-401.

Rossi, E.   2204

La poesia popolare araba della Tripolitania.
ACSC 1. 1931, vol. 4, p. 191-202.

Sacchetti, R.   2205

Premessa all'arte e alla letteratura
per la quarta sponda.
RdC 3. 1929, p. 244-247.

Serra, L.   2206

Testi berberi in dialetto di Zuara.
AION 14. 1964, p. 715-726.

Serra, L.   2207

Due racconti in dialetto berbero di
Zuara (Tripolitania).
Studi magrebini 2. 1968, p. 123-128.

Serra, L.   2208

Quelques remarques comme suite aux
premiers textes en dialecte berbère
de Zouara (Tripolitaine).
AION 18. 1968, p. 444-447.

Tobino, M.   2209

The deserts of Libya.
The lost legions.
London: Mac Gibbon and Kee 1967.

Toschi, P.   2210

Letteratura popolare libica.
Osservatore romano 1944, 28.-29.2.,
p. 3.

Ward, P.   2211

Poems for participants. A work book.
Tripoli 1967.
(Labyrinth series. 15.)

Ward, P.   2212

Seldom rains.
Stoughton/Wisc.: Oleander Press
1967.

Ward, P.   2213

At the best of times: Libyan poems.
Stoughton/Wisc.: Oleander Press
1968.

Ward, P.   2214

The poet and the microscope.
Tripoli 1968.

Ward, P.   2215

Grace and labour. A writer in Libya.
Books and bookmen 15. 1970, n. 8,
p. 11-12.

Ward, P.   2216

Maps on the ceiling: Libyan poems.
Stoughton/Wisc.: Oleander Press
1970.

Zanon, F.   2217

Le canzoni d'amore del popolo di
Cirenaica.
AIn 50/51. 1932/33, p. 277-289.

Zanon, F.   2218

Dai canti sahariani de l'ahâl.
Libia 4. 1940, n. 10, p. 30-31.

Education.

Hanson, J.W. - Gibson, G.W. 2219
African education and development
since 1960. A select and annotated
bibliography.
East Lansing: Michigan State University 1966.

Le Seelleur, T.N. 2220
Libya: educational statistics,
September-December 1962.
Paris: UNESCO 1963.

Le Seelleur, T.N. 2221
Libya: reorganization of educational
statistics.
Paris: UNESCO 1963.

Le Seelleur, T.N. 2222
Report on forecasts of school enrolment in Libya.
Paris: UNESCO 1963.

Le Seelleur, T.N. 2223
Libya: statistics for educational
planning.
Paris: UNESCO 1964.

Literacy in Libya. 2224
Population census 1964.
Paper no. 1.
Tripoli: Census and Statistical Dept.
1964.

Morrison, C.R. 2225
Education in Libya. A statistical
survey and end of tour report.
Tripoli: U.S. Operations Mission to
Libya 1959.

Mugribi, M. al 2226
Statistiques de l'enseignement primaire.
Tripoli 1967.

Report on educational 2227
development ... presented
to the international conference on
public education.
Geneva.
1963/64 (1964). 1966.

Report on educational 2228
development.
Ministry of Education.
Tripoli.
1963-64. 1964-65. 1965-66.

Report on educational 2229
progress.
Ministry of Education.
Tripoli 1961-

Young, T.C.J. 2230
Libya: education statistics. January
1968-August 1969.
Paris: UNESCO 1969.

Abdel-Aziz, A.H.F. 2231
Libya: adult education. 20 June 1965-
30 June 1968.
Paris: UNESCO 1968.

Annuario del R. Istituto 2232
Tecnico e della R. Scuola
Complementare di Tripoli d'Africa
per il 1927.
Roma nd.

Annuario del R. Liceo 2233
Ginnasio "Dante Alighieri"
di Tripoli per l'anno scolastico
1924-25 e 1925-26.
Tripoli nd.

Annuario delle scuole   2234
coloniali (della Cirenaica
e della Tripolitania). Ministero
delle Colonie.
Roma.
1924-25 (1926) - 1933-34 (1935).

Argo, A.C.   2235
Summary report (education).
Tripoli 1957.

Barton, L.C.   2236
Libya: English teaching. 27 August
1965-30 June 1968.
Paris: UNESCO 1968.

Becker, H.T.   2237
Das Schulwesen in Afrika.
Berlin 1943.
(Afrika. 13,2.)

Benton, I.R.   2238
Libya: a study of existing school
buildings.
Khartoum: Regional Educational
Building Institute for Africa 1969.

Boehne, J.   2239
Das italienische Kolonialschulwesen.
Hamburg 1942. Diss.

Cerbella, G.   2240
Idee e pareri sugli studi africani
e orientali e sui problemi scolasti-
ci coloniali in Italia.
Tripoli 1933.

Cerbella, G.   2241
Nuhab. Letture scelte ad uso delle
scuole medie coloniali.
Tripoli 1936.

Cerbella, G.   2242
I giuochi dei fanciulli tripolini
nelle scuole coraniche.
IdO 2. 1937, n. 8, p. 16-17.

Cerbella, G.   2243
Le scuole coraniche in Tripoli.
IdO 2. 1937, n. 6, p. 22-23.

Cerbella, G.   2244
L'arifa, secolare scuola delle
fanciulle tripoline.
IdO 4. 1939, p. 415-416.

Cerbella, G.   2245
Come si svolgono gli esami nelle
scuole coraniche di Tripoli.
IdO 5. 1940, n. 1, p. 15.

Cerbella, G.   2246
Le scuole coraniche della Libia.
Contributo alla conoscenza delle
tradizioni popolari libiche.
AION NS 2. 1943, p. 303-350.

La conferenza del duca   2247
delle Puglie.
Oltremare 5. 1931, p. 179-194.

Contini, F.   2248
Storia delle istituzioni scolastiche
della Libia.
Libia 1. 1953, n. 3, p. 7-103.

Corò, F.   2249
Il museo libico di storia naturale
di Tripoli.
AAI 2. 1939, vol. 1, p. 277-298.

Desio, A.   2250

Il museo libico di storia naturale.
ACSC 3. 1937, vol. 5, p. 264-269.

The development of education   2251
in Libya.
Tripoli: Ministry of Education 1966.
(Document 1.)

Development of educational   2252
planning and its machinery
in Libya.
Tripoli: Ministry of Education 1966.
(Document 2.)

Directory of teacher-   2253
training colleges.
Paris: UNESCO 1970.

Education and the first   2254
economic and social
development plan.
Tripoli: Ministry of Education 1966.
(Document 3.)

Education in Libya.   2255
Oversea quarterly 1965,
December, p. 239-240.

Eradication of illiteracy   2256
and adult education.
Tripoli: Ministry of Education 1966.
(Document 8.)

Festa, A.   2257

L'opera della scuola in colonia e la
politica scolastica del governo
fascista.
ACSC 1. 1931, vol. 4, p. 258-277.

Festa, A.   2258

Scuole per indigeni in Tripolitania.
Tripoli 1931.

Festa, A.   2259

La scuola italiana e l'opera di conquista morale della Libia.
Tripoli 1932.

Gabrieli, F.   2260

Per un centro scientifico di studi
arabo-islamici in Libia.
ACSC 3. 1937, vol. 6, p. 146-149.

Gulick, B.F.   2261

Libya.
The educated African. Ed. H. Kit-
chen. New York 1962, p. 54-66.

Gusbi, M.   2262

English for Libya.
Pupils'books 1-3.
Teacher's books 1-3.
London: University of London Press
1965-66.

Hoenerbach, W.   2263

Erziehungswesen im Fezzan. Seine
Entwicklung bis 1955.
Welt des Islam NS 8. 1962, p. 3-15.

Husain, M.M.   2264

Erwachsenenbildung in Libyen.
Afrika heute 3. 1962, p. 179-193.

Kerwin, H.   2265

An overview of the vocational education program in Benghazi, Cyrenaica.
np 1955.

Lancellotti, A.   2266
Il museo coloniale.
Oltremare 6. 1932, p. 246-248.

Ornato, G.Z.   2274
La scuola in Libia.
IdO 5. 1940, n. 5, p. 70-71.

Lingren, V.C.   2267
Teacher training in Libya.
School and society 1959, n. 2162,
p. 485-486.

Panorama sur la situation   2275
de l'enseignement en Libye.
Beirut: Regional Center for the
Advanced Training of Educational
Personnel in the Arab States 1962.

Malvezzi de Medici, A.   2268
Native education in the Italian
colonies.
Educational Yearbook of the Interna-
tional Institute of Teachers College,
Columbia University 1931,p.645-677.

Piccioli, A.   2276
La scuola.
La rinascita della Tripolitania.
Milano 1926, p. 285-319.

Micacchi, R.   2269
L'istruzione primaria in Libia.
Annali dell'istruzione elementare 5.
1930 , n. 3-4, p. 54-80.

Provision of school buildings 2277
in Libya to meet educational
expansion.
Tripoli: Ministry of Education 1966.
(Document 11.)

Micacchi, R.   2270
L'insegnamento agli indigeni nelle
colonie italiane di diretto dominio.
ACSC 1. 1931, vol. 4, p. 226-258.

Public and school libraries   2278
in Libya.
Tripoli: Ministry of Education 1966.
(Document 10.)

Micacchi, R.   2271
L'edilizia scolastica in Tripolitania.
Annali dell'istruzione elementare 9.
1934 , p. 129-157.

Qubain, F.I.   2279
Education and science in the Arab
world.
Baltimore: Johns Hopkins Press 1966.

Minnini Caracciolo, M.   2272
Le scuole nelle colonie italiane di
dominio diretto.
Riv. pedagogica 23. 1930, p. 183-
207, 273-298.

Religious education in   2280
Libya.
Tripoli: Ministry of Education 1966.
(Document 4.)

Organisation de l'enseignement 2273
dans les pays arabes. Libye.
Notes et études documentaires 1955,
n. 2106.

Report of the educational   2281
planning mission. Libya,
March-May 1964.
Paris: UNESCO 1964.

Riordinamento. Scuola arti   2282
e mestieri di Tripoli.
Statuto, regolamento, programma della fondazione musulmana e dell'
annessa scuola industriale.
Tripoli 1929.

Ritchie, H.S.   2283
Summary report (education).
np 1956.

Rummel, J.F.   2284
Development of education in Cyrenaica. U.S. Operations Mission to Libya.
Benghazi: Nazirate of Education
1957.

Rummel, J.F.   2285
Need for expansion and modification
of the teacher training program in
Tripolitania in the next five years.
np 1957.

Sakka, H.O. el   2286
Libya: adult education. September
1956-June 1964.
Paris: UNESCO 1965.

Sasnett, M. - Sepmeyer, I.   2287
Educational systems of Africa.
Berkeley: University of California
Press 1966.

Sassani, A.H.K.   2288
Educational data: Libya.
Wash.: U.S. Dept. of Health 1961.
(Information on education around
the world. 52.)

School health, hygiene   2289
and nutrition.
Tripoli: Ministry of Education 1966.
(Document 9.)

Shammas, Y.E.   2290
Education in Libya.
Muslim world 52. 1962, p. 137-140.

Soliman, S.M.   2291
Libya: audio-visual aids at the
Fuehat Center. December 1960-July
1964.
Paris: UNESCO 1965.

Teacher training in Libya.   2292
Tripoli: Ministry of
Education 1966.
(Document 7.)

Technical and vocational   2293
education in Libya.
Tripoli: Ministry of Education 1966.
(Document 5.)

Towfique, M.K.   2294
Libya: establishment of audio-visual aids center. October-November
1966.
Paris: UNESCO 1967.

University of Libya.   2295
Architects' journal
150. 1969, p. 956-957.

Vallardi, P.   2296
Il problema scolastico in Cirenaica.
CGEP 1923, p. 193-214.

Vietmeyer, W.F.   2297
Libya: primary teacher training.
July 1965-15 November 1969.
Paris: UNESCO 1970.

Waardenburg, J.J.   2298

Les universites dans le monde arabe
actuel. Documentation et essai d'interpretation. Vol. 1.2.
Paris: Mouton 1966.

Weis, H.   2299

Volksbildung in der Sahara.
Universum. Wien 17. 1962, p. 367-
373.

Wimbs, J.   2300

Libya: educational buildings. December 1968-June 1969.
Paris: UNESCO 1969.

Women's education in Libya.   2301
Tripoli: Ministry of Educa-
tion 1966.
(Document 6.)

Wood, W.R. - Bertrand, J.F.   2302

Higher education in Libya.
np 1955.
(Report to UNESCO.)

The world of learning.   2303
London: Europa Publications.
19. 1968/69-

World survey of education.   2304
Vol. 1-4.
Paris: UNESCO 1955-66.

Zoehrer, L.G.A.   2305

Problems of adult-education in the
Fezzan.
Wiener völkerkundliche Mitteilungen
2. 1954, p. 6-12.

Zoehrer, L.G.A.   2306

Bericht über meine Tätigkeit für
die UNESCO.
Bustan 1961, n. 4, p. 41-47.

Population.
General. Demography.

Censimento generale della   2307
popolazione. 1.12. 1921.
Roma 1930.
6. 1921, vol. 20. Colonie e possedimenti di diretto dominio.

Censimento generale della   2308
popolazione. 21.4. 1931.
Roma 1935.
7. 1931, vol. 5. Colonie e possedimenti.

Censimento generale della   2309
popolazione. 21.4. 1936.
Roma 1939.
8. 1936, vol. 5. Libia - isole italiane dell'Egeo - Tientsin.

Preliminary report of   2310
population census. 1954.
Tripoli: Census and Statistical
Dept. 1954.

General population census   2311
of Libya. 1954.
Report and tables.
Tripoli: Census and Statistical
Dept. 1959.

General population census.   2312
1964.
a) Instructions and lectures. b) Co-
ding instructions. c) Code for classification of economic activities.
d) Code for occupational   1.

General population census. 2312
classification. e) Code for geographical classification.
Tripoli: Census and Statistical Dept. 1964.
2.

Preliminary results of the 2313
general population census.
1964.
Tripoli: Census and Statistical Dept. 1964.

General population census. 2314
1964.
Tripoli: Census and Statistical Dept. 1966.

Abd-Esc-Scech 2315
Terre e genti di Cirenaica.
RdC 1/2. 1927/28, p. 91-101.

Agostini, E. de 2316
Indagini sulle popolazioni della Cirenaica.
ACGI 9. 1925, p. 137-139.

Agostini, E. de 2317
Il territorio di Gat e le sue popolazioni.
ACSC 2. 1934, vol. 4, p. 7-29.

Agostini, E. de 2318
Sulle popolazioni della Libia.
Libia 2. 1954, n. 2, p. 3-13.

Agostini, E. de. 2319
Le popolazioni della Libia.
Il territorio e le popolazioni.
Roma 1955, p. 307-348.

Andreozzi, L. 2320
Appunti demografici sulla popolazione di El-Gedid.
Atti della riunione scientifica.
Società italiana di statistica
19. 1959, p. 73-96.

Applebaum, S. 2321
Jewish status at Cyrene in the Roman period.
Parola del passato 19. 1964, p. 291-303.

Artom, E.S. 2322
L'importanza dell'elemento ebraico nella popolazione della Tripolitania.
ACSC 1. 1931, vol. 4, p. 116-123.

Attal, R. 2323
Pirsumin al yahadut Luv. (A bibliography of publications concerning Libyan jewry).
Sefunot 1965, p. 383-398.

Aymo, J. 2324
Les clans d'une cité berbère saharienne: Ghadamès.
Paris: CHEAM 1957.
(Publication 2663.)

Aymo, J. 2325
Notes de sociologie et de linguistique sur Ghadamès.
BLS 1959, n. 34, p. 129.

Balbo, I. 2326
La politica sociale fascista verso gli arabi della Libia.
Atti dei convegni "Volta". 8. 1938
"Africa", p. 733-749.

Basset, R. - Galand, L. - 2327
Pellat, C. - Yver, G.
Berbers.
EIne.

Battaglia, R.   2328
Africa. Genti e culture.
Roma: Istituto Italiano per l'Africa
1954.

Battara, P.   2329
Il movimento demografico della Tripolitania in rapporto allo sviluppo
agrario.
ACSC 1. 1931, vol. 4, p. 77-82.

Beguinot, F.   2330
Chi sono i berberi.
OM 1. 1921/22, p. 240-247, 303-311.

Beguinot, F.   2331
Frammenti di psicologia arabo-berbe-
ra.
La terra e la vita 1. 1922, p. 180-
186.

Beguinot, F.   2332
Note sulla popolazione della Cire-
naica.
CGEP 1923, p. 75-85.

Beguinot, F.   2333
I berberi e le recenti scoperte del
Fezzan.
AIn 50/51. 1932/33, p. 197-208.

Beguinot, F.   2334
A proposito di arabi e berberi della
Libia.
AIn 52. 1934, p. 40-43.

Beguinot, F.   2335
Le genti libiche: razze, vita, religione, usi e costumi, lingua e letteratura.
L'impero coloniale fascista. Novara
1936, p. 375-400.

Beguinot, F.   2336
I berberi tripolitani dal punto di
vista politico e sociale.
Atti del convegno di studi coloniali 2. 1947, p. 184-186.

Biasutti, R.   2337
L'italianità nell'Africa mediterranea.
Italia e Africa mediterranea. Firenze 1942, p. 87-143.

Bouvat, L.   2338
Les habitants de la Cyrénaïque.
Revue du monde musulman 35. 1917-18,
p. 273-284.

Bruggmann, M.   2339
Zwischen den Sandbergen des liby-
schen Fezzan eingeschlossen: die
Dauada.
Familienfreund. Luzern 1966, n. 35,
p. 8-11, 46.

Bulugma, H.M.R.   2340
Ethnic elements in the western
coastal zone of Tripolitania.
FSL 1960, p. 111-119.

Bulugma, H.M.R.   2341
The western coastal zone of Tripo-
litania. A human geography.
Durham: Dept. of Geography 1960.
Diss.

Calò, G.   2342
L'attività dell'elemento israelitico
in Cirenaica nel 1919.
ACSC 1. 1931, vol. 4, p. 123-127.

Camavitto, D.   2343
Le inchieste del comitato italiano
per lo studio della popolazione sulle genti della Tripolitania e in
particolare del Fezzàn.
ASIPS 25. 1936, vol. 4, p. 236-250.

Carpi, L.   2344
La condizione giuridica degli ebrei
nel Regno Unito di Libia.
Riv. di studi politici internazionali 30. 1963, p. 87-92.

Chillemi, A.   2345
La condition juridique des étrangers
en Libye.
Civilisations 7. 1957, p. 327-342.

Clarke, J.I.   2346
Some observations on Libyans in Tunisia.
Cahiers de Tunisie 6. 1958, p. 89-
100.

Corso, R.   2347
Le popolazioni della Libia.
IdO 2. 1937, n. 8, p. 6-8, n. 11,
p. 12-13, n. 15, p. 6-7.

Corso, R.   2348
Popolazioni del nostro Sahara.
AIr 2. 1939, n. 1, p. 19-22.

Corso, R.   2349
Africa italiana. Genti e costumi.
Napoli 1940.

Corso, R.   2350
Studi africani.
Napoli: Pironti 1950.

Les désordres anti-juifs   2351
de Tripoli des 12 et 13 juin
1948.
Cahiers de l'Alliance Israélite
Universelle 1948, n. 24-25, p. 12-
13, n. 26, p. 8-9.

Despois, J.   2352
Les populations de la Libye ita-
lienne.
Paris: CHEAM 1958.
(Publication 401.)

Ducati, A.   2353
A proposito di arabi e berberi del-
la Cirenaica.
Oltremare 7. 1933, p. 193-195.

Ducati, B.   2354
Prima dei berberi.
Oltremare 8. 1934, p. 297-299.

Ducati, B.   2355
I berberi arabizzati.
RSAI 5. 1942, p. 523-532.

Dupree, L.   2356
The Arabs of modern Libya.
Muslim world 48. 1958, p. 113-124.

Dupree, L.   2357
The non-Arab ethnic groups of Libya.
MEJ 12. 1958, p. 33-44.

Fanter, E.   2358
Libia. Der Amazonenstaat der Tebbu.
Berlin 1933.

Federici, N.   2359
Le più recenti spedizioni scientifi-
che del C.I.S.P.
Genus 5. 1942, n. 3/4, p. 119-132.

Felletti, L.   2360

La Libia e gli italiani.
Italiani nel mondo 1970, 10.4.,
p. 1-4.

Francolini, B.   2361

Alcuni dati sulla emigrazione e il
lavoro italiano in Africa.
ACGI 14. 1947, p. 444-446.

Francolini, B.   2362

L'emigrazione italiana in Africa.
Riv. geografica italiana 56. 1949,
p. 2-22.

Gallo, R.   2363

Le popolazioni delle colonie e possedimenti italiani secondo il censimento del 1931-IX.
ACSC 2. 1934, vol. 4, p. 273-290.

Gaslini, M. dei   2364

Gli arabi di Cirene e del Barca, come
vivono, pensano e credono.
RdC 3. 1929, p. 238-243.

Gaslini, M. dei   2365

L'anima e il volto degli arabi libici.
Oltremare 7. 1933, p. 287-290.

Gini, C.   2366

Relazione della missione demografica
del comitato italiano per lo studio
dei problemi della popolazione in
Tripolitania (23 febbraio-16 marzo
                                1.

Gini, C.   2366

1933).
BSGI 70. 1933, p. 681-686, Genus 1.
1934, n. 1/2, p. 109-116.

                                2.

Gini, C.   2367

Relazione su l'inchiesta demografica, antropologica e medico-biologica
sopra i Dauada ... (gennaio-febbraio
1935).
Genus 2. 1936, n. 1/2, p. 57-75.

Gini, C.   2368

Appunti sulle spedizioni scientifiche del comitato italiano per lo
studio dei problemi della popolazione febbr. 1933-febbr. 1935.
Genus 2. 1937, n. 3/4, p. 225-257.

Gini, C.   2369

Condizione demografiche.
SIFOG 1937, p. 401-449.

Glauert, G.   2370

Zur Bevölkerungs und Kulturland-
schaftsentwicklung der nördlichen
Sahara.
PGM 101. 1957, p. 252-259.

Goldberg, H.   2371

Patronymic groups in a Tripolitanian
Jewish village: reconstruction and
interpretation.
Jewish journal of sociology 9. 1967,
p. 209-225.

Harrison, R.S.   2372

Migration as a factor in the geography of western Libya, 1900-1964.
University of Cambridge 1965. Diss.

Hartley, R.G.   2373

Recent population changes in Libya.
Economic relationships and geogra-
phical patterns.
Durham: Dept. of Geography 1968.
Diss.

Hartley, R.G. - Norris, J.M.   2374

Demographic regions in Libya. A
principal components analysis of
economics and demographic variables.
Tijdschrift voor economische en sociale geografie 60. 1969, p.221-227.

Herzog, R.   2375
Ethnische und soziale Differenzie-
rung unter den Bewohnern der Oasen
des Wādī eš-Šaṭī'im Fezzan.
Afrika und Übersee 49. 1966, p. 136–
144.

Idris, H.R.   2376
Hilāl.
EIne.

Keith, A.N.   2377
Children of Allah.
London: Joseph 1966.
Boston, Mass.: Little Brown 1966

Lamaude, M.   2378
La géographie humaine du Fezzân,
d'après J. Despois.
Annales de géographie 56. 1947,
p. 297–300.

Leone, E. de   2379
Origini e speciali attribuzioni del-
la cabila "coroghlia" nel Sahel el
Ahamed (Homs).
ACSC 2. 1934, vol. 4, p. 66–72.

Lethielleux, J.   2380
Le Fezzân. 3. La population.
IBLA 1946, n. 36, p. 371.

Lewicki, T.   2381
Al-Ibāḍiya.
Handwörterbuch des Islam. Leiden
1941.

Lewicki, T.   2382
Ibâdiye.
Islâm Ansiklopedisi. Istanbul 1950.

Lewicki, T.   2383
Ibāḍiya.
Shorter encyclopedia of Islam. Lei-
den 1953.

Lewicki, T.   2384
Al-Ibāḍiyya.
EIne.

Lewicki, T.   2385
Banū Īfran. Hawwāra.
EIne.

Lewicki, T.   2386
On some Libyan ethnics in Johannis
of Corippus.
Rocznik orientalistyczny 15. 1939–
49, p. 114–128.

Lewicki, T.   2387
La répartition géographique des
groupements ibāḍites dans l'Afrique
du Nord au moyen âge, 1re partie.
Rocznik orientalistyczny 21. 1957,
p. 301–343.

Lewicki, T.   2388
Les subdivisions de l'Ibāḍiyya.
Studia islamica 9. 1958, p. 72–82.

Lewicki, T.   2389
À propos d'une liste de tribus ber-
bères d'Ibn Ḥawkal.
Folia orientalia 1. 1959, p. 128–135.

Lewicki, T.   2390
Un document ibāḍite inédit sur l'émi-
gration des Nafūsa du Ǧabal dans le
Ṣāḥil tunisien au VIIIe/IXe siècle.
Folia orientalia 1. 1959, p. 175–
191.

Lewicki, T.   2391

Un document ibādite inédit sur l'émi-
gration des Nafūsa du Ǧabal. Note
supplémentaire.
Folia orientalia 2. 1960, p. 214-
216.

Libya.   2392
Reports on the foreign scene
(American Jewish Committee Institute
of Human Relations) 1962, n. 2,
p. 1-4.

Macaluso Aleo, G.   2393

Popolamento europeo dell'Africa
settentrionale.
ACSC 1. 1931, vol. 4, p. 82-104.

Macchia, A.   2394

L'emigrazione italiana in Libia.
ACGI 14. 1947, p. 478-481.

Menasse, L.   2395

La vita nella Gefàra.
Oltremare 8. 1934, p. 264-267.

Migliorini, E.   2396

Intorno alla conoscenza attuale degli abitanti e dell'economia del Tibesti.
ASIPS 25. 1936, vol. 4, p. 202-206.

Montanari, R.   2397

Il concetto di autarchia ed i municipi libici (17.6.1938).
Riv. giuridica del medio ed estremo
oriente NS 2. 1938, col. 347-354.

Moreno, M.M.   2398

La politica indigena dell'Italia.
AAI 6. 1943, vol. 2, p. 305-320.

Mori, A.   2399

Sull'opportunità di precisare la
consistenza numerica della popolazione delle colonie italiane.
ACGI 11. 1930, vol. 3, p. 185-187.

Mori, A.   2400

La popolazione delle colonie e dei
possedimenti italiani.
Riv. geografica italiana 42. 1935,
p. 103-112.

Murdock, G.P.   2401

Africa. Its peoples and their
culture history.
New York: MacGraw-Hill 1959.

Nallino, C.A.   2402

Enrico de Agostini: Le popolazioni
della Cirenaica.
RdT 2. 1925/26, p. 331-343.

Nallino, C.A.   2403

A proposito di arabi e berberi della Cirenaica.
Oltremare 7. 1933, p. 169-171.

Narducci, G.   2404

I mangiatori di vermi dei laghetti
del Fezzan.
IdO 2. 1937, n. 13, p. 24-25.

Negrotto-Cambiaso, A.   2405

Indagini sui residuati e sulle forme superstiti di schiavitù esisten-
ti-nascoste o dissimulate-fra le popolazioni della Tripolitania; loro
portata giuridica.
                                        1.

Negrotto-Cambiaso, A.   2405
ACSC 2. 1934, vol. 5, p. 158-164.

                                        2.

Nicolicchia, P.E. 2406

Caratteristiche demografiche, economiche e sociali di Semmu (Fezzan).
Atti della riunione scientifica. Società italiana di statistica 22.
1962 (1963), p. 213-276.

Paradisi, U. 2407

I sudanesi di Tauórga.
Vie del mondo 18. 1956, p. 179-188.
Libia 4. 1956, n. 1.2.

Paradisi, U. 2408

I pescatori berberi della penisola
di Fàrwa (Tripolitania).
Universo 42. 1962, p. 293-300.

Paradisi, U. 2409

I tre giorni di Awússu a Zuara
(Tripolitania).
AION 14. 1964, p. 415-419.

Pazzi, M. 2410

Caratteri fondamentali delle popolazioni libiche.
RSAI 3. 1940, p. 36-42.

Peters, H. 2411

Vorläufiger Bericht über die Ergebnisse einer Studienreise nach Libyen.
Forschungen und Fortschritte 14.
1938, p. 304-306.

Pisani, V. 2412

Emigrazione a forma cooperativa all'
estero e nelle nostre colonie.
Roma 1922.

Puccioni, N. 2413

I sudanesi del campo di es-Sàbri
(Bengasi).
RdC 5. 1931, p. 201-204.

Quadrotta, G. 2414

Che cosa è la politica indigena
dell'Italia.
IdO 2. 1937, n. 5, p. 4-9.

Rossi, E. 2415

Il contributo della scienza italiana alla conoscenza delle popolazioni della Libia.
Atti del convegno di studi africani
3. 1948, p. 45-72.

Sarnelli, T. 2416

Le genti berbere e la nostra penetrazione in Tripolitania.
Idea nazionale 13. 1923, n. 60,11.3.,
p. 5, n. 62,14.3., p. 5.

Sarnelli, T. 2417

Il "buri" dei negri tripolini.
AIn 43. 1924, p. 229-237, 44. 1925,
p. 163-170, 204-224.

Sarnelli, T. 2418

Un vessillo berbero in Tripolitania.
AIn 46. 1927, p. 206-217.

Scarin, E. 2419

Sopra una prima rilevazione sta-
tistica di carattere etnografico in
Cirenaica.
ACSC 2. 1934, vol. 4, p. 249-254.

Seklani, M. 2420

Croissance démographique comparée
des pays du Maghreb 1950-1990.
Revue tunisienne de sciences sociales
6. 1969, n. 17-18, p. 29-51.

Stechman, S. 2421

Map of population distribution in
Libya.
Africana bulletin 3. 1965, p. 49-56.

Strothmann, R.   2422

Berber und Ibāḍiten.
Islam 17. 1928, p. 258-279.

Thomas, F.C.   2423

The Dawwādah of the Fezzan.
MEJ 22. 1968, p. 193-202.

Tibalducci, G.   2424

Inchiesta sul lavoro italiano in Libia.
Concretezza 1959, 1.1., p. 8-12.

Toni, Y.T.   2425

The social geography of Cyrenaica.
Durham: Dept. of Geography 1956.Diss.

Toni, Y.T.   2426

The population of Cyrenaica: a geographical interpretation of population data in the eastern province of
the United Kingdom of Libya.
Tijschrift voor economische en   1.

Toni, Y.T.   2426

sociale geografie 49. 1958, p. 1-11.

2.

Toschi, P.   2427

Le condizioni degli schiavi a Tripo-
li nei passati secoli (secc. XVI-
XVII).
RSAI 5. 1942, p. 666-669.

Treydte, K.P.   2428

Zur Sozialstruktur Libyens.
Vierteljahresberichte. Hannover
1969, n. 37, p. 271-288.

Valensi, L.   2429

Esclaves chrétiens et esclaves
noirs à Tunis au XVIIIe siècle.
Annales. Économies. Sociétés. Civilisations 22. 1967, p. 1267-1288.

Vergottini, M. de   2430

La popolazione nativa del regno presente nelle nostre colonie e possedimenti secondo il luogo di nascita.
(1921 e 1931).
ACSC 3. 1937, vol. 7, p. 133-139.

Virgilii, F.   2431

Dall'emigrazione alla colonizzazione.
ACSC 1. 1931, vol. 6, p. 184-193.

Wian, G.   2432

I nostri cittadini libici in Tunisia.
IdO 4. 1939, n. 21, p. 527.

Zanon, F.   2433

I berberi e la politica coloniale.
ACSC 2. 1934, vol. 4, p. 59-65.

Anthropology.

Catalogue of the library   2434
of the Peabody Museum of
Archaeology and Ethnology, Harvard
University.
Boston, Mass.: Hall 1963.

Bartoccini, R.   2435

Quali erano i caratteri somatici
degli antichi libi ?
Aegyptus 3. 1922, p. 156-167.

Beguinot, F. 2436

Bianchi mediterranei in zone sahariane.
Atti dell'accademia Leonardo da Vin-
ci 1934-35 (1936), p. 121-137.

Berque, J. 2437

The north of Africa (recent research
on racial relations).
International social science journal
13. 1961, p. 177-196.

Biasutti, R. 2438

I tebu secondo recenti indagini italiane.
AAE 63. 1933, p. 168-201.

Biasutti, R. 2439

Residui umani arcaici esistenti nelle oasi sahariane.
ACSC 2. 1934, vol. 3, p. 58-66.

Biasutti, R. 2440

Reste alter Rassenelemente in den
Oasen der Sahara.
Zs für Rassenkunde 1. 1935, p. 68-
74.

Biasutti, R. 2441

La posizione antropologica dei ber-
beri e gli elementi razziali della
Libia.
AION NS 3. 1949, p. 127-141.

Blundo, M.L. 2442

Caratteri antropometrici dei berberi
di Giado.
Atti della riunione scientifica. Società italiana di statistica 22.
1962 (1963), p. 105-212.

Briggs, L.C. 2443

Living tribes of the Sahara and the
problem of their prehistoric origins.
Pan African congress on prehistory
3. 1955 (1957), p. 195-199.

Briggs, L.C. 2444

A review of the physical anthropology of the Sahara and its prehistoric
implication.
Man 57. 1957, p. 20-23.

Briggs, L.C. 2445

The living races of the Sahara desert.
Cambridge, Mass.: Harvard UP 1958.
(Papers of the Peabody Museum ...
28,2.)

Briggs, L.C. 2446

Tribes of the Sahara.
Cambridge, Mass.: Harvard UP 1960.

Castelli, G. 2447

Sguardo generale alla composizione
razziale della Libia.
RdC 13. 1939, p. 1233-1242.

Charles, R.P. 2448

Recherches sur l'unité de structure
et d'origine du peuplement de l'Afrique méditerranéenne.
Bulletin. Société de géographie
d'Egypte 36. 1963, p. 41-86.

Charles, R.P. 2449

Recherches sur l'origine du peuplement de la Cyrénaïque d'après
l'étude de la structure céphalique.
Bulletin. Société de géographie
d'Egypte 38. 1965, p. 97-128.

Cipriani, L. 2450

Abitanti. Caratteri antropologici.
SIFOG 1937, p. 353-383.

Corso, R. 2451

Africa. Cenni razziali.
Roma 1941.

Demel, H.   2452

Bemerkungen zur Libyerfrage.
Mitteilungen der anthropologischen
Gesellschaft Wien 60. 1930, p. 285-
292.

Eickstedt, E. von   2453

Völkerbiologische Probleme der Saha-
ra.
Beiträge zur Kolonialforschung,
Tagungsband 1. 1943, p. 169-240.

Eickstedt, E. von   2454

Das Hamitenproblem.
Homo 1. 1949, p. 105-123.

Falco, G.   2455

Sulle figure papillari dei polpa-
strelli delle dita nei libici.
Riv. di antropologia 22. 1917-18,
p. 91-148.

Federici, N.   2456

Su talune caratteristiche bio-fisio-
logiche e demografiche di una popolazione primitiva (Dauada).
Genus 5. 1942, n. 3/4, p. 45-101.

Fleischhacker, H.   2457

Zur Rassen- und Bevölkerungsge-
schichte Nordafrikas unter besonderer Berücksichtigung der Äthiopiden,
der Libyer und der Garamanten.
Paideuma 15. 1969, p. 12-53.

Genna, G.   2458

Metabolismo basale e razza. Contributo all'antropologia fisiologica
degli indigeni della Libia.
Riv. di biologia coloniale 1. 1938,
p. 29-42.

Gerhardt, K.   2459

Paläanthropologische Probleme der
alten Mediterraneis und Weissafrikas.
Bericht über die Tagung der deutschen Gesellschaft für Anthropologie 5. 1957, p. 84-96.

Giuffrida-Ruggeri, V.   2460

L'Afrodite di Cirene, considerazioni antropologiche.
AAE 51. 1921, p. 97-115.

Keiter, F.   2461

Gesichtszüge in Italien und Libyen.
Homo 7. 1956, p. 122-142, 8. 1957,
p. 223-239.

Landra, G.   2462

Sulla morfologia del capello presso
alcune popolazioni africane.
ASIPS 25. 1936, vol. 4, p. 207-219.
Riv. di antropologia 31. 1935-37,
p. 299-337.

Mehlis, C.   2463

Die Berberfrage.
Archiv für Anthropologie NS 8. 1909,
p. 249-286.

Mueller, G.   2464

Juden in Tripolis.
Zs für Ethnologie 68. 1936, p. 373-
379.

Mueller, G.   2465

Rassebilder aus Tripolitanien.
Zs für Ethnologie 68. 1936, p. 141-
150.

Nicolas, F.   2466

Texte ethnographiques de la "Tamâ-
jeq" des Iullemmeden de l'est.
Anthropos 46. 1951, p. 754-800, 48.
1953, p. 458-484, 50. 1955, p. 635-
658.

Palmer, H.R.   2467

The white races of North Africa.
Sudan notes and records 9. 1926,
p. 69-74.

Parenti, R.   2468
Contributo alla conoscenza della
craniologia del Fezzan.
AAE 75. 1945, p. 5-116.

Patroni, G.   2469
Ancora dei pretesi libi biondi.
Aegyptus 3. 1922, p. 59-65.

Peters, E.L.   2470
The proliferation of segments in the
lineage of the Bedouin of Cyrenaica.
Journal of the Royal Anthropological
Institute 90. 1960, p. 29-53.

Peters, E.L.   2471
The tied and the free.
Contributions to Mediterranean sociology. Ed. J.G. Peristiany. Paris
1968, p. 167-188.

Peters, H.   2472
Beitrag zur Rassenanalyse der nordafrikanischen Bevölkerung.
Verhandlungen der deutschen Gesellschaft für Rassenforschung 10. 1940,
p. 44-47.

Prosdocimo, G. - Beltrame, G.   2473
Sulla antropologia delle popolazioni
di Augila e Gicherra.
Riv. di biologia coloniale 6. 1943,
p. 139-148.

Puccioni, N.   2474
Antropologia cirenaica (dati preven-
tivi della prima missione antropologica in Cirenaica).
RdC 3. 1929, p. 340-345.

Puccioni, N.   2475
Le esplorazione antropologica delle
colonie italiane.
ACSC 1. 1931, vol. 3, p. 309-326.

Puccioni, N.   2476
Le genti della Cirenaica.
ACSC 1. 1931, vol. 3, p. 246-252.

Puccioni, N.   2477
Sull'antropologia della Cirenaica.
OM 13. 1933, p. 391-395.

Puccioni, N.   2478
Berberi e arabi nell'Africa mediterranea.
Biasutti, R.: Le razze e i popoli
della terra. Torino vol. 3. 1955,
p. 131-147.

Puccioni, N.   2479
I nomadi del Sahara.
Biasutti, R.: Le razze e i popoli
della terra. Torino vol. 3. 1955,
p. 148-176.

Ricci, E.   2480
Sulla distribuzione etnica della
popolazione nella Tripolitania di
nord-ovest.
ACGI 11. 1930, p. 190-195.

Ricci, E.   2481
Il lavoro antico nella Libia.
ACSC 2. 1934, vol. 4, p. 254-267.

Ricci, E.   2482
Ricerche sui gruppi sanguigni nei
tebu.
ACSC 2. 1934, vol. 7, p. 555-572.

Sabatini, A.   2483
Le popolazioni delle oasi di Gialo
e di Cufra.
Giornale di medicina militare 1933,
fasc. 12.

Sabatini, A.   2484

Nuovi dati antropologici sui Tebu.
ASIPS 23. 1934, vol. 3, p. 384-385.

Sabatini, A.   2485

Antropologia delle popolazioni di
Cufra (gli zuéia, i tébu, i sudanesi).
Riv. di antropologia 31. 1935-37,
p. 161-186.

Sabatini, A.   2486

Cufra e le sue genti.
Bologna 1935.

Sabatini, A.   2487

I tipi di costituzione dominanti in
alcuni gruppi di popolazioni libiche.
ASIPS 26. 1937, vol. 1, p. 440-443.

Sabatini, A.   2488

Alcuni rilievi metrici cranio-faccia-
li su popolazioni delle oasi di Cufra
e di Gialo.
Riv. di antropologia 32. 1938/39,
p. 337-340.

Sergi, S.   2489

L'Afrodite di Cirene.
Riv. di antropologia 23. 1919, p.101-
126. Arte antica e moderna 1960,
n. 9, p. 3-15.

Sergi, S.   2490

Les caractères physiques des Garamantes de la Libye.
Actes. Congrès international d'anthropologie et d'archéologie préhistorique 16. 1935 (1936), p. 101-113.

Sergi, S.   2491

The eye of the Berbers. A particular
characteristic of the upperlid of the
Tuareg.
CR. Congrès international des sciences anthropologiques et ethnographiques 3. 1948(1960), p. 221-223.

Sergi, S.   2492

L'occhio berbero. Un particolare
carattere della palpebra superiore
nell'occhio dei tuaregh.
AION NS 3. 1949, p. 143-150.

Vaufry, R.   2493

Les "émeraudes" des Garamantes.
Anthropologie 59. 1955, p. 576.

Woelfel, D.J.   2494

Die Hauptprobleme Weissafrikas.
Archiv für Anthropologie NS 27.
1942, p. 89-140.

Ethnology. Folklore.

Abdelkafi, M.   2495

Les mariages en Tripolitaine.
Weddings in Tripolitania.
Tripoli: Libyan Publishing House
1964, Ministry of Information and
Culture 1966.

Abd-Esc-Scech   2496

Riti e costumanze nuziali degli
ebrei in Libia.
RdC 3. 1929, p. 273-280.

Agostini, E. de   2497

Profilo etnografico delle popolazioni della Libia.
Per le nostre colonie. Firenze 1927,
p. 27-50.

Agostini, E. de   2498

Etnografia delle popolazioni libiche.
ACSC 1. 1931, vol. 4, p. 7-24.

Beguinot, F. 2499

Libyen.
Afrika. Handbuch der angewandten
Völkerkunde. Ed. H.A. Bernatzik.
München: Bruckmann 1951.

Bellucci, G. 2500

Amuleti ed ornamenti con simboli ma-
gici della Libia.
Lares. Bullettino della società
di etnografia italiana 4. 1915,
p. 1-34.

Biordi, R. 2501

La Libia nell'arte dello xilografo
Francesco dal Pozzo.
Oltermare 5. 1931, p. 265-266.

Brulard, M. 2502

La hadhra des Senoussiya à Ghât.
BLS 8. 1957, n. 27, p. 157-158.

Brulard, M. 2503

N'tchisent. La fête du sel à Ghât
au 27 ramdhan.
BLS 8. 1957, n. 25, p. 12-17.

Brulard, M. 2504

La Sebbiba de 'Achoura à Ghât.
BLS 8. 1957, n. 26, p. 89-93.

Brulard, M. 2505

A travers le qsar et les jardins de
Ghât.
BLS 8. 1958, n. 28, p. 282-288.

Brulard, M. 2506

La culture à Ghât.
BLS 9. 1958, n. 32, p. 325-333.

Brulard, M. 2507

La musique et la danse à Ghât.
BLS 9. 1958, n. 29, p. 37-48.

Castaldi, A. 2508

Argentieri ed orafi tripolini.
Oltremare 6. 1932, p. 418.

Castaldi, A. 2509

La stuoia, tappeto del deserto.
Oltremare 8. 1934, p. 411.

Cauneille, A. 2510

Préparation culinaire des peaux au
Fezzân.
BLS 2. 1951, n. 5, p. 27-29.

Cerbella, G. 2511

Il "cuttàb" tripolino e il suo
folklore.
ACSC 2. 1934, vol. 4, p. 52-59.

Cerbella, G. 2512

I giuochi dei fanciulli nelle scuole
coraniche di Tripoli.
ACSC 3. 1937, vol. 6, p. 83-89.

Cerbella, G. 2513

Ramadân nelle tradizioni popolari
tripoline.
IdO 2. 1937, n. 24, p. 22-23.

Cerbella, G. 2514

Tradizioni popolari libiche. Il tè
nei canti tripolini.
IdO 2. 1937, n. 12, p. 14-15.

Cerbella, G.   2515

Scech er-Ràcchib e il pellegrinaggio alla Mecca.
IdO 5. 1940, n. 4, p. 64.

Cerbella, G.   2516

Caratteristiche della società musulmana libica.
Libia 1. 1953, n. 1, p. 7-81.

Cerbella, G.   2517

Il te nella vita, nella poesia e nelle tradizioni del popolo libico.
Libia 1. 1953, n. 4, p. 53-62, 2.
1954, n. 1, p. 83-94, n. 2, p. 67-72, n. 3, p. 57-76, n. 4, p. 51-71.

Cerbella, G.   2518

Il natale del profeta. La "himêsa" libica e il "ceppo" toscano.
Il capo dei pellegrini.
Libia 2. 1954, n. 4, p. 21-31.

Cerbella, G.   2519

Mare e marinai in Libia.
Libia 3. 1955, n. 1, p. 3-54, n. 2, p. 3-34.

Cerbella, G.   2520

Il Ramadàn nelle tradizioni popolari libiche. Il Gārāgûz in Libia e nell' oriente.
Libia 3. 1955, n. 3, p. 3-43.

Cerbella, G.   2521

Il capodanno in Libia e nell'oriente.
Libia 4. 1956, p. 21-25.

Coccioli, C.   2522

Costituzione e scioglimento del vincolo matrimoniale in Libia.
RdC 13. 1939, p. 1359-1367.

Coccioli, C.   2523

Su alcune costumanze libiche relative alla nascita ed alla morte.
RdC 16. 1942, p. 480-491.

Corò, F.   2524

A caccia con gli slughi in Tripolitania.
Oltremare 4. 1930, p. 510-513.

Corò, F.   2525

Danze, pantomime e fantasie delle gaie donne di Murzuch.
Libia 4. 1940, n. 9, p. 22-24.

Corò, F.   2526

Antichi artistici piatti di oricalco nelle caratteristiche dimore di Gadames.
Libia 5. 1941, n. 1-2, p. 10-12.

Corò, F.   2527

Folklore africano. Astronomia e scienze occulte presso i tuaregh.
Rassegna mediterranea 1951, dicembre, p. 19.

Corrain, C. - Fabbri, M. -   2528
Zampini, P.

Segni incisi o dipinti rilevati sulla ceramica, conservata nel museo archeologico di Sebha.
Riv. di etnografia 21. 1967, p. 67-70.

Corrain, C. - Fabbri, M. -   2529
Zampini, P.
Tradizioni funebri a Sebha nel Fezzan.
Riv. di etnografia 21. 1967, p. 26-32.

Corso, R.   2530

Di un rito funerario africano e della sua interpretazione.
AION 3. 1930, p. 63-70.

Corso, R. 2531

Per gli studi folkloristici nelle nostre colonie africane.
ACSC 1. 1931, vol. 4, p. 168-179.

Corso, R. 2532

Ricerche etnografiche tra i tuàregh di Gat.
Riv. di antropologia 30. 1933-34, p. 507-509.

Corso, R. 2533

La diffusione geografica di una costumanza nuziale nell'Africa e il suo significato.
AION 7. 1934, p. 14-36.

Corso, R. 2534

Una costumanza libica ricordata da Erodoto e i suoi riscontri africani.
Riv. d'oriente 1934, dicembre, p. 249-250.

Corso, R. 2535

Nuovi elementi sul rito della posizione rannicchiata nell'etnografia africana.
Riv. di antropologia 31. 1935-37, p. 9-19.

Corso, R. 2536

Le recenti ricerche etnografiche nell'oasi di Gat.
ASIPS 25. 1936, vol. 4, p. 197-201.

Corso, R. 2537

I velati dell'oasi di Gat.
IdO 2. 1937, n. 18, p. 6-8.

Corso, R. 2538

Per l'etnografia dell'impero coniale fascista.
ASIPS 28. 1939, vol. 4, p. 381-399.

Corso, R. 2539

Il problema del velo dei tuareg al lume della etnografia comparata africana.
Riv. di antropologia 35. 1944-47, p. 432-434.

Corso, R. 2540

Le problème du voile des Touareg.
CR. Congrès international des sciences anthropologiques et ethnologiques 3. 1948(1960), p. 49-50.

Corso, R. 2541

Il velo dei tuàregh.
AION NS 3. 1949, p. 151-166.

Corso, R. 2542

I tuàregh della conca di Gat e loro caratteristiche costumanze.
Libia 1. 1953, n. 1, p. 91-102.

Costumi femminili nella 2543
Tripoli del seicento.
RdC 1/2. 1927/28, p. 59-69.

Crisolito, G. 2544

Spunti di folklore in Tripolitania.
RdC 4. 1930, p. 729-733.

Deonna, W. 2545

Ciste funéraire de Cyrénaïque.
Revue d'ethnographie et des traditions populaires 2. 1921, p. 13-15.

Fantoli, P. 2546

Gioielli arabi.
RdC 4. 1930, p. 874-883.

Gabelli, O.   2547

Usanze nuziali in Tripolitania.
RdT 2. 1925/26, p. 295-306, 351-362.

Gini, C.   2548

A Berber form of baseball.
CR. Congrès international des sciences anthropologiques et ethnologiques 2. 1938(1939), p. 263-264.

Gini, C.   2549

Rural ritual games in Libya.
Rural sociology 4. 1939, p. 283-299.

Gini, C.   2550

Considerazioni ed ipotesi sull'origine dell'"Om el Mahag" e, in generale, dei giuochi di "Battingball".
Genus 5. 1941, n. 1/2, p. 73-86.

Godard, J.   2551

Jours et semaines fastes à Brak.
BIS 6. 1955, n. 20, p. 89-90.

Godard, J.   2552

Croyances et coutumes du Fezzân.
BIS 7. 1956, p. 79-83.

Leone, E. de   2553

Conservazione e tutela delle arti
indigene.
RdC 8. 1934, p. 362-370.

Lorecchio, B.   2554

Usi e costumi degli ebrei libici.
Oltremare 3. 1929, p. 393-397.

Manetti, C.   2555

Usi e tradizioni degli arabi in Libia e nel Nord-Africa nell'allevamento del cavallo.
REAI 18. 1930, p. 533-553.

Mercier, M.   2556

Les idoles de Ghadamès.
Revue africaine 97. 1953, p. 17-47.

Mordini, A.   2557

La stregoneria presso i Tuâregh
Azgher.
AION 7. 1934, p. 44-49.

Mordini, A.   2558

Note etnografiche sul Sahara italiano.
BSGI 72. 1935, p. 351-362.

Mordini, A.   2559

Etnografia e fatti culturali.
SIFOG 1937, p. 449-491.

Narducci, G.   2560

La sezione etnografica del museo
libico di storia naturale di Tripoli.
ACSC 3. 1937, vol. 6, p. 160-167.

Narducci, G.   2561

Contributo a gli studi di etnografia libica.
Anthropologie 49. 1938, p. 596-597.

Narducci, G.   2562

Gli amuleti libici.
Annali del museo libico di storia
naturale 1. 1939, p. 407-416.

Narducci, G. 2563

Pani e dolci festivi della Libia.
Annali del museo libico di storia
naturale 2. 1940, p. 313-332.

Narducci, G. 2564

La mano di fatma e il numero 5 nelle
credenze nordafricane in genere e
libiche in particolare.
RSAI 4. 1941, p. 1027-1035.

Panetta, E. 2565

Tradizioni popolari della Cirenaica.
Lares 7. 1936, p. 276-289.

Panetta, E. 2566

Tradizioni popolari in Cirenaica:
nascita, circoncisione, riti funera-
ri.
ASIPS 25. 1936, vol. 3, p. 207-224.

Panetta, E. 2567

Tradizioni popolari in Cirenaica:
il matrimonio.
ACSC 3. 1937, vol. 6, p. 175-191.

Panetta, E. 2568

Su alcune costumanze popolari di
Bengasi.
RSO 24. 1949, p. 67-73.

Panetta, E. 2569

Studi italiani di etnografia e di
folklore della Libia.
Roma: IPS 1963.
(L'Italia in Africa. Serie scienti-
fico-culturale.)

Pâques, V. 2570

Le bélier cosmique - son role dans
les structures humaines et territo-
riales du Fezzân.
Journal. Société des africanistes
26. 1956, p. 211-253.

Pâques, V. 2571

L'arbre cosmique dans la pensee po-
pulaire et dans la vie quotidienne
du nord-ouest africain.
Paris: Institut d'Ethnologie 1964.

Peters, E. 2572

Some structural aspects of the feud
among the camel-herding bedouin of
Cyrenaica.
Africa. London 37. 1967, p. 261-282.

Pfalz, R. 2573

Arabische Hochzeitsbräuche in Tripolitanien.
Anthropos 24. 1929, p. 221-227.

Piccioli, A. 2574

L'arte coloniale.
RdC 10. 1936, p. 727-747.

Placido, N. 2575

L'artigianato indigeno a Tripoli.
L'Italia coloniale 11. 1934, p. 109-
111.

Queirolo Ghelli, E. 2576

Matrimoni tripolini.
RdC 1/2. 1927/28, p. 71-89.

Queirolo Ghelli, E. 2577

Maternità, usi e costumi tripolini.
RdC 3. 1929, p. 116-123.

Rackow, E. 2578

Das Beduinenkostüm in Tripolitanien,
dargestellt am Beispiel des Nuâil-
Stammes.
Baessler Archiv 25. 1943, p. 24-50.

Ricard, P.   2579

Les arts tripolitains.
RdT 2. 1925/26, p. 203-235, 275-
292.

Scalella, L.   2580

Usi locali tripolini (il matrimonio
arabo).
AIn 46. 1927, p. 22-26, 231-234.

Scortecci, G.   2581

Crono e il deserto.
Illustrazione del medico 1961,
n. 179, gennaio.

Scotti, P.   2582

Etnologia del Fezzan.
Genova: Editrice L.U.P.A. 1949.

Serra, L.   2583

Su alcune costumanze dei berberi
ibāditi di Zuara (Tripolitania).
Atti del congresso di studi arabi e
islamici 3. 1966 (1967), p. 623-632.

Skarzynska, K.   2584

Moeurs et rites nuptiaux chez quelques groupes éthniques d'Égypte de
Nubie et de Libye, d'après les ré-
cents travaux arabes.
Folia orientalia 4. 1962, p.343-352.

Toschi, P.   2585

Musica popolare tripolina.
Lares 8. 1937, p. 136-138.

Toschi, P.   2586

Usanze e superstizioni dei corsari
tripolini.
Mediterranea (almanacco) 1950,
p. 225-228.

Tucci, G.   2587

Contributo alla conoscenza dei tuareg di Gat.
Riv. di etnografia 3. 1949, p. 1-11.

Woelfel, D.J.   2588

Nord- und Weissafrika.
Die grosse Völkerkunde. Ed. H.A. Bernatzik. Leipzig vol. 1. 1939, p. 225-
243.

Zanon, F.   2589

Le consuetudini matrimoniali presso
i beduini della Cirenaica.
AIn 54. 1936, p. 126-135.

Nomadism.

Abou-Zeid, A.M.   2590

The changing world of the nomads.
Contributions to Mediterranean sociology. Ed. J.G. Peristiany. Paris
1968, p. 279-288.

Bensch, P.   2591

Die Entwicklung des Nomadentums in
Afrika.
Göttingen 1949. Diss.

Berque, J.   2592

Nomads and nomadism in the arid zone.
International social science journal
11. 1959, p. 481-498.

Brehony, J.A.N.   2593

Semi-nomadism in the Jebel Tarhuna.
FSL 1960, p. 60-69.

Cauneille, A.   2594

Le nomadisme des Megarha (Fezzân).
TIRS 12. 1954, 2e sem., p. 41-69.

Cauneille, A.   2595

Les Hassouna, tribu du Fezzân.
BLS 6. 1955, n. 19, p. 31-49.

Cauneille, A.   2596

Le nomadisme des Zentân (Tripolitaine et Fezzân).
TIRS 16. 1957, 2e sem., p. 73-99.

Cauneille, A.   2597

Le nomadisme des Guedadfa, tribu de
Tripolitaine (Syrte).
BLS 9. 1958, n. 32, p. 338-353.

Cauneille, A.   2598

Les Goueyda d'Ouenzerik, tribu du
Fezzân.
BLS 11. 1960, n. 38, p. 161-173.

Cauneille, A.   2599

Le semi-nomadisme dans l'ouest libyen (Fezzân, Tripolitaine).
Arid zone research 19. 1963, p. 101-
112.

Clarke, J.I.   2600

Studies of semi-nomadism in North
Africa.
Economic geography 35. 1959, p. 95-
108.

Clarke, J.I.   2601

The Siaan: pastoralists of the Jefara.
FSL 1960, p. 52-59.

Dubief, J.   2602

Les Ifoghas de Ghadamès. Chronologie
et nomadisme.
IBLA 11. 1948, p. 141-158.

Dubief, J.   2603

Chronologie et migration des Iman-
ghasaten.
IBLA 13. 1950, p. 23-36.

L'économie pastorale   2604
saharienne. Carte no. 58:
Le Sahara des nomades 1:5000000.
Note documentaire 1953, n. 1730.

Herzog, R.   2605

Veränderungen und Auflösungserschei-
nungen im nordafrikanischen Nomaden-
tum.
Paideuma 6. 1956, p. 210-223.

Herzog, R.   2606

Sesshaftwerden von Nomaden.
Köln: Westdeutscher Verlag 1963.
(Forschungsberichte des Landes NRW.
1238.)

Herzog, R.   2607

Anpassungsprobleme der Nomaden.
Zs für ausländische Landwirtschaft
6. 1967, p. 1-21.

Johnson, D.L.   2608

The nature of nomadism: a comparative study of pastoral migrations in
south-western Asia and northern Africa.
Chicago: University of Chicago,   1.

Johnson, D.L.   2608

Dept. of Geography 1969.
(Research paper. 118.)

                                   2.

Kikhia, M.M.   2609

Le nomadisme pastoral en Cyrénaïque
septentrional.
Aix-en-Provence: La Pensée Universi-
taire 1968. Diss.

Monteil, V.   2610

The evolution and settling of the
nomads of the Sahara.
International social science journal 11. 1959, p. 572-585.

Nomades et nomadisme au   2611
Sahara.
Paris: UNESCO 1963.
(Arid zone research. 19.)

Pazzi, M.   2612

Riflessi sociali del nomadismo in
Libia.
RSAI 2. 1939, p. 847-852.

Peters, E.   2613

The ecology of Cyrenaican pastora-
lism.
University of Manchester: Dept. of
Social Anthropology nd.

Peters, E.   2614

The sociology of the bedouin of
Cyrenaica.
Oxford: Institute of Social Anthro-
pology 1951. Diss.

Plan d'étude sociologique   2615
d'une tribu nomade saharienne.
BIS 11. 1960, n. 38, p. 116-118.

Planhol, X. de   2616

Nomades et pasteurs.
Revue de géographie de l'est
1. 1961 - 8. 1968: passim.

Toni, Y.   2617

Social mobility and relative stability among the bedouins of Cyrenaica.
Bulletin de la société de géographie d'Égypte 36. 1963, p. 113-136.

Settlements.

Agostini, E. de   2618

Notizie sul cazà di el-Agelat.
Tripoli 1915.

Agostini, E. de   2619

Il castello di Tripoli.
RdC 9. 1935, p. 470-477.

Alpago-Novello, A. - Cabiati,   2620
O. - Ferrazza, G.

Relazione sul piano regolatore della città di Bengasi.
Milano 1930.

Amer, O.M. ben'   2621

A farming community for Cyrenaica.
Wash.: Catholic University of America, Graduate School of Engineering
and Architecture 1959. Diss.

Applicazione dell'ordinamen-   2622
to tributario dei municipi
della Libia. Governo Generale della
Libia. R. Prefettura di Tripoli.
Tripoli 1939.

Aurigemma, S.   2623

Demolizione delle mura della città
di Tripoli nel periodo settembre
1915-marzo 1916.
NA 2. 1916 (1918), p. 365-379.

Battistella, G.   2639

Nuove case per il popolo in Libia.
Libia 3. 1939, n. 12, p. 20-23.

Bono, F.   2647

Mizda, cuore della Ghibla.
Vie del mondo 15. 1953, p. 175-180.

Blake, G.H.   2640

The form and function of Misratah's
commercial centre.
Bulletin of the faculty of arts. University of Libya 2. 1968, p. 9-40.

Bono, F.   2648

Architettura popolare della Libia.
Libia 3. 1955, n. 1, p. 63-71.

Blake, G.H.   2641

Misurata: a market town in Tripoli-
tania.
Durham: Dept. of Geography 1968.
(Research papers series. 9.)

Borghi, M.   2649

Got-es-Sultan.
Napoli 1934.

Bonfiglio, E.   2642

A Tripoli dopo undici anni.
IdO 2. 1937, n. 5, p. 14-15, 20-22.

Brown, R.W.   2650

Two Libyan oases (Augila and Marada).
Mondo. C.W.Post College of Long
Island University 1968, n. 4, p. 1-
11.

Bonfiglio, E.   2643

Tripoli: armonia di tre architetture.
AIr 2. 1939, n. 3-4, p. 33-36.

Brulard, M.   2651

L'oasis de Ghât qui s'appela durant
dix ans Fort-Duveyrier.
Revue du Sahara 1958, n. 1, p. 20-
31.

Bonfiglio, G.   2644

L'attività municipale nella città di
Bengasi.
Empoli: Caparrini 1949.

Bulugma, H.M.R.   2652

The urban geography of Benghazi.
Durham: Dept. of Geography 1964.
Diss.

Boni, G. - Mariani, L.   2645

Relazione intorno al consolidamento
ed al ripristino dell'arco di Marco
Aurelio in Tripoli.
NA 1. 1915, p. 13-34.

Callegari, G.P.   2653

I villaggi libici.
Torino 1941.

Bono, F.   2646

Orientamenti di edilizia e urbanisti-
ca in Libia.
RdC 16. 1942, p. 1045-1049.

Campani, R.   2654

Vecchia Cirenaica.
Libia 2. 1938, n. 3, p. 32-34.

Caputo, G. 2655
Il consolidamento dell'arco di Marco Aurelio in Tripoli.
AIb 7. 1940, p. 46-66.

Cardella, E.P. 2656
Le opere pubbliche.
La rinascita della Tripolitania.
Milano 1926, p. 353-380.

Case popolari in Libia. 2657
AAI 2. 1939, vol. 1,
p. 321-325.

Ceriani, E. 2658
Cufra.
AIn 39. 1920, p. 97-125.

Chiauzzi, G.L. 2659
Ricerche su vari tipi di insediamenti trogloditici ancora in uso nel Gebel Garian libico.
Atti dell'accademia di scienze e lettere. Genova 1969.

Corò, F. 2660
Gusrat el Siagha. Il castello degli argentieri.
Oltremare 3. 1929, p. 437-440.

Corò, F. 2661
Come vidi Gadames nella rioccupazione del 1924.
RdC 5. 1931, p. 612-627, 697-713, 794-800.

Corò, F. 2662
Ghat, la sentinella sahariana.
AAI 1. 1938, vol. 1, p. 291-306.

Corò, F. 2663
I pittoreschi e originali funduchi della vecchia Tripoli.
Libia 2. 1938, n. 1, p. 19-23.

Corò, F. 2664
Una villa famosa nei dintorni di Tripoli.
Libia 2. 1938, n. 4, p. 29-34.

Corò, F. 2665
Alla scoperta dei vecchi "fondugh" tripolini.
Vie d'Italia 45. 1939, p. 201-210.

Corò, F. 2666
Il culto della vite in Tripolitania.
Libia 3. 1939, n. 8, p. 17-20.

Corò, F. 2667
Uaddan, la città santa della Giofra.
Libia 4. 1940, n. 1, p. 18-22.

Corò, F. 2668
Una Gadames in miniatura: Tunin.
Libia 4. 1940, n. 11-12, p. 11-13.

Corò, F. 2669
Le oasi di Derg e la loro storia millenaria.
Libia 5. 1941, n. 5-6, p. 11-14.

Cortese, E. 2670
Ieffren - Asabaa - Garian - Tarhuna.
ACGI 9. 1925, vol. 2, p. 87-91.

Despois, J.   2671

Les déplacements de villages dans le
Djebel Néfousa.
Revue tunisienne 1933, p. 263-284.

Despois, J.   2672

L'habitation dans le Djebel Néfousa.
Revue tunisienne 1934, p. 277-316.

Despois, J.   2673

Les greniers fortifiés de l'Afrique
du Nord.
Cahiers de Tunisie 1. 1953, p. 38-58.

Despois, J.   2674

Awdjila. Benghāzī. Al-Djaghbūb. Al-
Djufra. Ghadamès (Ghdāms). Ghat.
EIne.

Giani, R.   2675

Oasi e villaggi del sud.
AIr 2. 1939, n. 1, p. 27-32.

Guidi, G.   2676

Il restauro del castello di Tripoli.
AIb 5. 1933,p. 119-134.

Hagedorn, H.   2677

Siedlungsgeographie des Sahara-Raums.
Afrika-Spektrum 1967, n. 3, p. 48-
59.

Harris, J.   2678

Libyan government proposes big expenditure for housing.
International commerce 73. 1967,
n. 5, p. 9-10.

Harrison, R.S.   2679

Migrants in the city of Tripoli.
Geographical review 57. 1967,
p. 397-423.

Hefel, A.   2680

Der unterirdische Vielkammerbau in
Afrika und im Mittelmeergebiet.
Archiv für Völkerkunde 1. 1946,
p. 189-239.

Housing in Libya.   2681
Prepared for the government
of the Kingdom of Libya, Ministry
of Planning and Development.Vol.1.2.
Athens: Doxiadis Associates 1964.
(Document Dox-Lib-A 17.)

Housing in Libya: problems,   2682
policies, programmes.
Doxiadis Associates.
Ekistics 17. 1964, p. 328-335.

Howells, D.A.   2683

The human geography of El Grefe: a
settlement in Wadi el Agial, Fezzan.
Journal. Durham Coll. Geogr. Society
1959-60, n. 2, p. 3-10.

Khuja, M.A.   2684

Garian town.
FSL 1960, p. 120-123.

Khuja, M.A.   2685

The growth and functions of Tripoli,
Libya.
Durham: Dept. of Geography 1969.
Diss.

Kilian, C.   2686

Rhât, la ville qui se meurt.
L'illustration 1930, 1.2., p. 164-
167.

King, W.J.H.   2687

Lost oases of the Libyan Desert.
Geographical journal 72. 1928,
p. 244-249.

Lagana, G.   2688

Tripoli misteriosa.
AIn 35. 1916, p. 6-32.

Lenz   2689

Wiederaufbauplanung für Barce (Libyen).
Auslandskurier 1965, n. 6, p. 29-32.

Lewicki, T.   2690

Ḏiāḏŭ (Djado).
EIne.

Map of Tripoli.   2691
1:8 000.
Tripoli: Orient Bookshop 1960.

Marassi, A.   2692

L'oasi di Tauorga.
Firenze 1942.

Marchal, R.   2693

Urbanization problems in Libya with
special reference to Cyrenaica.
Correspondance d'orient. Études
1965/66, n. 8/9, p. 41-52.

Marchetti, U.   2694

Vecchia Libia e Libia nuova.
AIr 1941-42, n. 37, p. 83-90.

Marelli, M.   2695

Relazione al progretto di sistema-
zione dell'Arco di Marco Aurelio in
Tripoli.
AIb 5. 1933, p. 162-171.

Mari, F.P.   2696

L'ordinamento tributario dei municipi della Libia.
REAI 26. 1938, p. 414-425.

Marsa el Brega: a guide.   2697
Tripoli: Esso Standard
Libya nd.

Marthelot, P.   2698

Une ville aux chances successives,
Benghazi.
Bulletin de l'association des géographes français 1964, n. 328-329,
p. 32-41.

Meliczek, H.   2699

Socio-economic conditions of a Libyan village and proposals for future development.
Berlin: Technical University, Institute of Foreign Agriculture 1964.

Meliczek, H.   2700

Wirtschaftlicher und sozialer Wan-
del in Messa, einer Siedlung in der
Cyrenaica.
Zs für ausländische Landwirtschaft
7. 1968, p. 87-93.

Micacchi, R.   2701

L'Arco di Marco Aurelio in Tripoli
e la sistemazione della zona adia-
cente.
RdC 8. 1934, p. 824-839.

Migliorini, E.   2702

L'elemento europeo nelle citta nordafricane.
AION NS 3. 1949, p. 101-126.

Minami, K.   2703

Relocation and reconstruction of
the town of Barce, Cyrenaica, Libya,
damaged by the earthquake of 21 February, 1963.
Paris: UNESCO 1965.

Minervino, N. da   2704

Bengasi e il suo piano regolatore.
Vie d'Italia 40. 1934, p. 21-29.

Mueller-Westing, H.   2705

Der Siedlungshof in Libyen.
Prag 1941. Diss.

Newbold, D.   2706

More lost oases of the Libyan Desert.
Geographical journal 72. 1928,
p. 547-554.

Norris, H.T.   2707

Cave habitations and granaries in
Tripolitania and Tunisia.
Man 53. 1953, p. 82-85.

Nuovo dizionario dei comuni   2708
e frazioni di comune del
regno d'Italia. 13th ed.
Con l'aggiunta delle località della
Libia ...
Roma 1940.

Obst, J.   2709

Luftbild Gharian/Libyen. Zur Umwand-
lung einer troglodytischen Siedlung.
Erde 98. 1967, p. 169-172.

Ornato, G.Z.   2710

Tauorga e la sua bonifica.
IdO 2. 1937, n. 10, p. 22-23.

Ornato, G.Z.   2711

Tigrinna, baluardo d'italianità sul
Gebel Garian.
IdO 2. 1937, n. 5, p. 10-12.

Ornato, G.Z.   2712

Tripoli d'un tempo e Tripoli d'oggi.
IdO 2. 1937, n. 13, p. 22-23.

Paradisi, U.   2713

Ghadames porta magica del sud.
Vie del mondo 25. 1963, n. 5.

Pavese, G.   2714

Il nuovo volto di Derna.
IdO 2. 1937, n. 9, p. 14-15.

Piccioli, A.   2715

Ricordo di Gadames.
AIr 2. 1939, n. 1, p. 12-18.

Planning objectives for city 2716
and regional plans: Kingdom
of Libya. Preliminary report.
Whiting Associates International,
Inc. 1966.
v. Shiber, S.G. 1968 n. 2749,
    p. 726-731.

Planung des Wiederaufbaues   2717
der Stadt Barce in Libyen.
Bauamt und Gemeindebau 38. 1965,
p. 211-213.

Provisional town plan   2718
of Tripoli.
1:10 000 (1:5 000).
Tripoli: Libya Shell N.V. and the
Shell Company of Libya Ltd. 1959.

Quint, M. 2719
Djawf Kufra.
EIne.

Rava, C.E. 2720
Architettura coloniale.
AAI 1. 1938, vol. 3/4, p. 1293-1300.

Rava, M. 2721
Dobbiamo rispettare il carattere
dell'edilizia tripolina.
Oltremare 3. 1929, p. 458-464.

Rebsamen, H. 2722
Tripolis.
Geographica helvetica 18. 1963,
p. 319-328.

Regolamento edilizio per 2723
la città di Tripoli.
Municipio di Tripoli.
Tripoli 1936.

Rendiconti dell'anno ... 2724
Sezione Autonoma della Cassa
di Risparmio della Libia per le Case Popolari.
Tripoli.
1. 1938-

Ricci, L. 2725
Centri abitati e tribù nomadi.
CGEP 1923, p. 87-106.

Il rinnovamento della città 2726
di Tripoli negli anni XII e
XIII. Municipio di Tripoli.
Tripoli 1936.

Roberti, V. 2727
L'architettura libica e i nuovi
centri agricoli.
Emporium 88. 1938, p. 309-318.

Romanelli, P. 2728
Scavi e scoperte nella città di Tripoli.
NA 2. 1916 (1918), p. 301-364,
1922, fasc. 3, p. 103-111.

Romanelli, P. 2729
Restauri alle mura barbaresche di
Tripoli.
Boll. d'arte NS 2. 1922-23, p. 570-
576.

Romanelli, P. 2730
Vecchie case arabe di Tripoli.
Architettura e arti decorative 1924,
fasc. 5, p. 193-211.

Romanelli, P. 2731
Origini e sviluppi delle città tri-
politane.
Roma 1939.

Rossi, E. 2732
Tripolis (Ṭarābulus, Aṭrābulus).
EI.

Rossi, N. 2733
Il castello di Tripoli.
Vie d'Italia 43. 1937, p. 256-264.

Rubeis, A. de 2734
Ghat. La città sahariana.
RdC 3. 1929, p. 735-768.

Ruggiero, G. 2735

Notizie sulla regione dell'oasi di
Marada e di Abu-Naim (Cirenaica).
REAI 17. 1929, p. 508-535.

Sayegh, K.S. 2736

Sea terminal communities: Marsa el
Brega (Libya) - a case study.
(Oil and Arab regional development).
New York: Praeger 1968, p. 122-127.

Scarin, E. 2737

Tipi indigeni di insediamento umano
e loro distribuzione nella Tripolitania settentrionale.
ACSC 1. 1931, vol. 4, p. 24-44.

Scarin, E. 2738

Murzuch negli ultimi secoli.
Universo 14. 1933, p. 943-951.

Scarin, E. 2739

Descrizione delle oasi e gruppi di
oasi.
SIFOG 1937, p. 603-644.

Scarin, E. 2740

La Giofra e Zella (le oasi del 29°
parallelo della Libia occidentale).
Riv. geografica italiana 44. 1937,
p. 163-245.

Scarin, E. 2741

Insediamenti e tipi di dimore.
SIFOG 1937, p. 515-560.

Scarin, E. 2742

L'insediamento umano nella zona
fezzanese di Gat.
Riv. geografica italiana 44. 1937,
p. 1-59.

Scarin, E. 2743

Tipo di ricerche per l'insediamento
umano per un'oasi del Sahara.
Esempio: l'oasi di Gat.
ACSC 3. 1937, vol. 5, p. 124-134.

Scarin, E. 2744

Zuila.
Universo 19. 1938, p. 825-837.

Schapira, E. 2745

Neue Zweckbauten in Libyen. Italiens
"Novecento Stil" auf afrikanischem
Boden.
Afrika-Rundschau 2. 1936/37, p. 244-
246.

Schiassi, N. 2746

L'opera dell'I.N.C.I.S. nell'Africa
italiana.
AAI 5. 1942, vol. 2, p. 431-445.

Serrazanetti, A. 2747

Edilizia nuova. Le costruzioni nell'
Africa italiana.
Bologna 1936.

Shiber, S.G. 2748

Libya plans ...
Middle East business digest 11.
1967, n. 147, p. 50-54.

Shiber, S.G. 2749

Commentary on aspects of Libya
planning.
(Recent Arab city growth).
Kuweit: Kuweit Government Printing
Press 1968, p. 412-421.

Spalletti, P. 2750

Cufra.
RdC 5. 1931, p. 131-137.

Suter, K. 2751

Ghadames. Beitrag zur Anthropogeo-
graphie einer Oase der tripolitanischen Sahara.
Zs für Ethnologie 86. 1961, p. 1-22.

Suter, K. 2752

Die Wohnhöhlen und Speicherburgen
des tripolitanisch-tunesischen Berg-
landes.
Zs für Ethnologie 89. 1964,p.216-275.

Tucci, G. 2753

Conoscenza di Gat.
Rivista d'oriente 3. 1935, n. 2-3.

Valori, F. 2754

La nuova edilizia nelle provincie
di Bengasi, Derna e Misurata.
AIr 2. 1939, n. 3-4, p. 37-40.

La valorizzazione libica. 2755
Nuovi villaggi e borgate.
RdC 13. 1939, p. 1681-1685.

Veccia Vaglieri, L. 2756

Darna.
EIne.

Vergara-Caffarelli, E. 2757

Prigioni sotterranee scoperte nel
castello di Tripoli.
Libia 3. 1955, n. 2, p. 53-55.

Vinaccia, G. 2758

Direttive solari ed eoliche di urba-
nistica dell'Africa italiana.
AAI 5. 1942, vol. 1, p. 143-202.

Ward, P. 2759

Tripoli: portrait of a city.
Stoughton/Wisc.: Oleander Press
1969.

Weis, H. 2760

Murzuch - Blüte und Verfall einer
Saharametropole.
Bustan 5. 1964, n. 3, p. 22-36.

Wellard, J. 2761

Lost cities of the Libyan Sahara.
Geographical magazine 37. 1964/65,
p. 602-615.

Zander, F.C. 2762

The old "medinah" of Tripoli, Libya.
v. Shiber, S.G. 1968, n.2749,
    p. 731-732.

Zanon, F. 2763

L'oasi leggendaria del deserto
libico: Augila.
RdC 7. 1933, p. 860-870, 937-950,
8. 1934, p. 39-49.

Reggiori, F. 2764

Architetture per la nostra maggior
colonia.
Dedalo 1931, p. 1339-1361.

Economy.
Bibliography.
Current Information.

Bibliothek des Instituts 2765
fuer Weltwirtschaft Kiel.
Kataloge ...
Boston, Mass.: Hall 1966-68.

Sources bibliographiques   2766
de l'économie du Maghreb.
Maghreb 1968, n. 26, p. 53-60, n. 27,
p. 37-41, 1969, n. 31, p. 38-42.

Libyan economic and   2774
business review.
Faculty of Commerce and Economics,
University of Libya, Benghazi.
Benghazi.
3. 1967-   ianc

The Arab directory for   2767
commerce, industry and
liberal professions in the Arab
countries (le guide arabe). 22nd ed.
New York: International Publications Service 1968.

Marché tropicaux et   2775
méditerranéens.
Paris.
25. 1969-   ianc

Commercial directory.   2768
Chamber of Commerce and
Industry Tripolitania, Libya.
Tripoli.
1966-

Middle East business digest.   2776
Beirut/London/New York.
11. 1967-

Owen's commerce and travel   2769
and international register.
Africa...
London.
16. 1969-

Monthly bulletin.   2777
Chamber of Commerce and
Industry Tripolitania.
Tripoli.
14. 1966, n. 94-   ianc

Economic bulletin.   2770
Economic Research Division
of the Bank of Libya.
Tripoli.
9. 1969-   ianc
Index. 1. 1961-6. 1966.

Economy.
Statistics.

Etude mensuelle sur l'économie   2771
et les finances des pays
arabes. Centre d'Etudes et de Documentation Economiques, Financières
et Sociales.
Beyrouth.
10. 1967-

Allgemeine Statistik des   2778
Auslandes. Laenderberichte.
Statistisches Bundesamt Wiesbaden.
Stuttgart/Mainz: Kohlhammer.

Informazioni per il commercio   2772
estero. Istituto Nazionale
per il Commercio Estero.
Roma.
24. 1969-
                        ianc

An analysis of the value of   2779
imports of the Kingdom of
Libya 1955-66.
Tripoli: Census and Statistical
Dept. nd.

International commerce.   2773
U.S. Department of Commerce.
Bureau of International Commerce.
Wash.
75. 1969-

Der Aussenhandel des Aus-   2780
landes.
Statistisches Bundesamt Wiesbaden.
Libyen: 1958, n. 95, 1961, n. 164,
        1964, n. 218, 1967, n. 309.

Balance of payments for 2781
the years ...
Tripoli: Census and Statistical
Dept.
1954-

Bibliography of African 2782
statistical publications,
1950-1965.
New York: United Nations, Economic
Commission for Africa 1966.

Bollettino statistico dell' 2783
Africa italiana (notiziario
statistico).
Ministero dell'Africa Italiana.
Roma.
1. 1938 - 4. 1941.

Censimento industriale e 2784
commerciale 1937-1940.
Istituto Centrale di Statistica del
Regno d'Italia.
Roma 1940.
Vol. 1. Industrie alimentari 1937.

Census of employment and pro- 2785
duction in urban areas.
Part 1. Registration of premises in
which persons were gainfully occu-
pied during 1956.
Tripoli: Census and Statistical
Dept. 1957.

Economic bulletin. 2786
Statistical supplement.
Economic Research Division of the
Bank of Libya.
Tripoli.
1967, July-

Entwicklung der Wirtschaft 2787
Libyens in Zahlen.
Marktinformationsdienst der BfA
1966, n. A 889.

Estimates of gross national 2788
product 1964-66.
Tripoli: Census and Statistical
Dept. nd.

External trade indices 2789
1962-66.
Tripoli: Census and Statistical
Dept. 1968.

External trade statistics. 2790
Tripoli: Census and Statistical Dept. 1954-
1968 (1969).

Foreign trade statistics 2791
for Africa.
New York: United Nations, Economic
Commission for Africa.
Series A. Direction of trade
11. 1968-   1.

Foreign trade statistics ... 2791
Series B. Trade by commodity
10. 1965-

                                   2.

Harvey, J.M. 2792
Statistics. Africa. Sources for
market research.
Beckenham, Kent 1970.

A list of the statistical 2793
information and other
quantitative data existing in the
government records in Libya.
Tripoli: Census and Statistical
Dept. 1966.

Mascaro, T. 2794
L'organizzazione dei servizi sta-
tistici nelle colonie italiane.
ACSC 3. 1937, vol. 7, p. 25-50.

National income estimates 2795
1958.
Tripoli: Census and Statistical
Dept. 1959.

Notiziario statistico.   2796
v. Rassegna economica dell'
   Africa italiana.
   Roma.
   26. 1938-

Report of the survey of li-   2804
censed construction units.
Tripoli: Census and Statistical
Dept. 1967.

Preliminary results of in-   2797
dustrial census 1964.
a) Large manufacturing establish-
ments. b) Small manufacturing estab-
lishments. c)Mining and quarrying.
Tripoli: Census and Statistical
Dept. nd.

Report on the first phase   2805
of the household sample
survey (Benghazi town).
Tripoli: Census and Statistical
Dept. 1969.

Report of a preliminary   2798
survey of five important
service trades in Tripoli town.
Tripoli: Census and Statistical
Dept. 1966.

Report on the first phase   2806
of the household sample
survey (Tripoli town).
Tripoli: Census and Statistical
Dept. 1968.

Report of a preliminary   2799
survey of wholesale and
retail trade and five important service trades in Benghazi town.
Tripoli: Census and Statistical
Dept. 1966.

Report on the first phase   2807
of the household sample
survey (Tripoli and Benghazi).
Papers 3.4. Economically active population.
Tripoli: Census and Statistical
Dept. 1968-69.

Report of the annual survey   2800
of large manufacturing estab-
lishments.
Tripoli: Census and Statistical
Dept. 1965-
1967 (1968).

I risultati del censimento   2808
industriale e commerciale
in Tripolitania al 15 ottobre 1928.
Camera di Commercio, Industria ed
Agricoltura della Tripolitania.
Tripoli 1930.

Report of the industrial   2801
census 1958.
Tripoli: Census and Statistical
Dept. 1959.

Statistica del commercio   2809
estero delle colonie italiane.
Ministero delle Colonie.
Roma.
1933-34 (1936).

Report of the industrial   2802
census 1964.
Tripoli: Census and Statistical
Dept. 1966.

Statistica del movimento   2810
commerciale marittimo dell'
Eritrea, della Somalia italiana,
della Tripolitania e della Cirenaica.
Ministero delle Colonie.
Roma.   1.

Report of the preliminary   2803
survey of wholesale and
retail trade in Tripoli town.
Tripoli: Census and Statistical
Dept. 1966.

Statistica del movimento ...   2810
1921-22 (1926) - 1930-31 (1934).

Statistica del movimento 2811
commerciale marittimo delle
colonie. Importazione ed esportazio-
ne della Tripolitania, della Cirenaica ... Ministero delle Colonie.
Roma.
1931-32 (1936).

Statistical abstract. 2812
Tripoli: Census and Statistical
Dept. 1958-
1967 (1968).

Statistical summary. 2813
Tripoli: Census and Statistical
Dept. 1954-
1954-66.

Summary of external trade 2814
statistics.
Tripoli: Census and Statistical
Dept. 1956-

Trends in Libyan imports 2815
and exports 1962-68.
Part 1.2.
Tripoli: Census and Statistical
Dept. 1969.

Wholesale prices in Tripoli 2816
town.
Tripoli: Census and Statistical
Dept. 1967-

Finance.

Annual report of the board 2817
of directors.
Tripoli: Bank of Libya.
12. 1967/68-

Bank of Libya. 2818
Brief history of its first
decade 1956-1966.
Economic Research Division. Bank of
of Libya.
Tripoli 1967.

Bengur, A.R. 2819
Financial aspects of Libya's oil
economy.
Finance and development 4. 1967,
p. 56-64.

Bolzon (relatore) 2820
Relazione della commissione generale del bilancio della camera dei
fasci e delle corporazioni sullo
stato di previsione della spesa 1.
del Ministero dell'Africa Italiana

Bolzon (relatore) 2820
per l'esercizio finanziario dal 1.7.
1939 al 30.6.1940.
RdC 13. 1939, p. 625-638.

2.

Bongiovanni (relatore) 2821
Relazione della commissione generale del bilancio del senato del regno sullo stato di previsione della
spesa del Ministero dell'Africa
Italiana per l'esercizio 1.

Bongiovanni (relatore) 2821
finanziario dal 1.7.1939 al 30.6.
1940.
RdC 13. 1939, p. 639-648.

2.

Le budget libyen. 2822
Maghreb 1970, n. 40,
p. 12-14.

Le budget libyen 1969-70 2823
et le second plan quin-
quennal 1969-1974.
Maghreb 1969, . 34, p. 12-15.

Cantalupo, R.   2824

La relazione della giunta del bilancio.
Oltremare 3. 1929, p. 280-298.

Chandavarkar, A.G.   2825

Central banking in Libya.
Banker's magazine 189. 1960, n.1395,
p. 495-498.

Chandavarkar, A.G.   2826

Banking in Libya.
Banker 111. 1961, p. 628-633.

Currency, banking and finance   2827
in Libya.
Banker's magazine 178. 1954, n.1328,
p. 413-417.

Dajani, M.T.   2828

The development of public finance
in Libya 1944-1963.
Tripoli: Bank of Libya 1965.

Development budget. Libya.   2829
Tripoli: Ministry of Planning
and Development 1967-68.

Draft estimates of revenue   2830
and expenditure.
British Military Administration.
Tripoli nd.

L'économie libyenne à travers   2831
ses finances publiques.
Etude mensuelle sur l'économie et
les finances de la Syrie et des
pays arabes 9. 1966, n. 104, p. 60-
79.

Farley, R.   2832

A comment on the so-called problem
of inflation in Libya.
Tripoli: Ministry of Planning and
Development 1964.

Glinstra Bleeker, R.J.R. van   2833

Controlling inflation.
Tripoli: Ministry of Planning and
Development 1964.

Inflation in Libya.   2834
National Bank of Libya.
Economic Research Dept.
Tripoli 1961.

Lavault, P.   2835

Financement international de l'équi-
pement de la Libye.
Paris: CHEAM 1956.
(Publication 2582.)

Libya. Increasing monetary   2836
expansion and greater private
investment.
Middle East business digest 10. 1966,
n. 145, p. 14-16.

Manunta, U.   2837

La cassa di risparmio della Libia.
AAI 6. 1943, vol. 2, p. VII-XXIV.

Moghaizel, J.   2838

Le secret bancaire.
Assurances. Banques. Transports
2. 1966, p. 1213-1235.

Niccoli, U.   2839

La politica finanziaria.
La rinascita della Tripolitania.
Milano 1926, p. 239-257.

Pellegrineschi, A.V.   2840

L'opera della cassa di risparmio
della Libia.
AAI 3. 1940, vol. 4, p. 453-461.

Report. Libyan Currency   2841
Commission.
London.
1. 1952/53-

Sakkaf, M.   2842

The creation of the National Bank
of Libya.
L'Egypte contemporaine 48. 1957,
p. 1-25.

Tivaroni, J.   2843

Le finanze delle colonie.
Genova 1936.

Wiedensohler, G.   2844

Der Schutz deutscher Privatinvesti-
tionen in Libyen.
Hamburg: Verlag Weltarchiv 1965.

Economy. General.

Aethiopien, Libyen, Sudan.   2845
Statistisches Bundesamt
Wiesbaden.
Stuttgart/Mainz: Kohlhammer 1961.
(Afrikanische Entwicklungsländer.
3.)

Agata, C. de   2846

L'economia del Sahara libico.
REAI 27. 1939, p. 161-170.

Africa's relations with the   2847
major economic structures.
Tunis: Sécretariat d'État aux
Affaires Culturelles et à l'Information 1963.

Agostino Orsini di Came-   2848
rota, P. de

Gli studi economici coloniali in
Italia.
ACSC 1. 1931, vol. 6, p. 29-54.

Allegrini, A.   2849

Tendenze e criteri de diritto coloniale in materia doganale e loro
applicazione in Libia.
AIn 36. 1917, p. 120-137, 165-179,
219-252.

Ammar, B.J.   2850

Libya forges ahead: a review of
economic progress.
Arab world 1969, n. 22, p. 3-5, 7.

Andrews, A.M.   2851

Libya has buying power.
International commerce 73. 1967,
n. 5, p. 4-6.

Annual report on development   2852
activities.
National Planning Council.
Tripoli.
1963/64 (1964)-

Appeals for aid from abroad   2853
to help Libyan development.
United Nations bulletin 16. 1954,
p. 44-45.

Arani, A.   2854

Aspetti attuali dell'economia della
Libia.
ACSC 2. 1934, vol. 6, p. 424-446,
REAI 22. 1934, p. 950-968.

Arias, G.   2855

Il commercio marittimo e il credito.
La rinascita della Tripolitania.
Milano 1926, p. 461-485.

Arsharuni, N.A.   2856

Livija.
Moskva: Mysl' 1965.

Attiga, A.A.   2857

The second plan. Shift from investment to regular production.
Financial times 1969, 6.3., p. 19.

L'attività svolta durante   2858
il 1937-XV-XVI da Consiglio
e Ufficio Coloniale dell'Economia
Corporativa per le Provincie di
Bengasi e Derna.
REAI 26. 1938, p. 453-461.

L'attività svolta durante   2859
l'anno 1938.
Ufficio dell'Economia Corporativa
per le Provincie di Bengasi e Derna.
REAI 27. 1939, p. 882-890.

Attività svolta dal 1o luglio 2860
1939 al 28 ottobre 1939.
Ufficio dell'Economia Corporativa
di Derna.
REAI 28. 1940, p. 188-193.

Attività svolta dal 1.7.1939   2861
al 29.2.1940.
Ufficio dell'Economia Corporativa
di Misurata.
REAI 28. 1940, p. 285-289.

Aurigemma, S.   2862

Un marchese di Cavour, intendente
delle saline di Zuara.
Libia 3. 1955, n. 3, p. 45-48.

Ayler, M.F.   2863

Jefren and Abu Ghaylah silica sand,
Tripolitania.
Bulletin. Ministry of Industry. Tri-
poli 1965, n. 1.

Ayler, M.F.   2864

Phosphate deposits of Tripolitania,
Libya.
Bulletin. Ministry of Industry. Tri-
poli 1965, n. 3.

Aymo, J.   2865

L'économie de Ghadamès.
Paris: CHEAM 1958.
(Publication 2878.)

Azzam, I.   2866

Libyan survey.
The Egyptian economic and political
review 6. 1960, n. 8, p. 8-11.

Basic data on the economy   2867
of Libya.
Wash.: GPO 1961.
(World trade information service,
part 1. 61-10.)

Bengur, A.R.   2868

La Libye: ressources pétrolières,
finances publiques et développement.
Finances et développement 4. 1967,
n. 1, p. 68-76. Le commerce du Levant 7. 1967, n. 83, p. 24-27.

Benyoussef, A.   2869

Populations du Maghreb et communauté
économique à quatre.
Paris: Société d'Edition d'Enseignement Superieur 1967.
(Developpement économique. 12.)

Berreby, J.J.   2870

Libya faces prosperity.
New outlook 3. 1960, n. 9, p. 7-14,
50.

Bhaskara Rao, P.A. 2871

Outlook for Indo-Libyan trade.
Foreign trade review 2. 1967,
p. 93-107.

Bodrero, P. 2872

Sul regime doganale per la Tripolitania e la Cirenaica.
Roma 1919.

Bollettino della Camera di 2873
Commercio, Industria ed Agricoltura della Tripolitania.
Tripoli.
16. 1941-

Bollettino delle cooperative 2874
di consumo di Tripoli-Misura-
ta-Bengasi-Derna.
Tripoli.
1. 1940-

Bono, S. 2875

Intense relazioni economiche fra
l'Italia e la Libia (1.). Gli italiani nel progresso economico e sociale della Libia (2.).
Italiani nel mondo 23. 1967, n. 14,
p. 6-9, n. 15, p. 6-9.

Bono, S. 2876

Le relazioni commerciali fra i
paesi del Maghreb e l'Italia nel
medioevo.
Tripoli: Istituto Italiano di Cultura 1967.

Bottomley, A. 2877

Economic growth in a semi-nomadic
herding community. Tripolitania.
Economic development and cultural
change 11. 1963, p. 407-419.

Brulard, M. 2878

Aperçu sur le commerce caravanier
Tripolitaine-Ghat-Niger.
BLS 9. 1958, p. 37-48.

Brulard, M. 2879

Le commerce caravanier au Fezzân au
XIXe siècle.
BLS 9. 1958, n. 31, p. 202-217.

Bruni, G. 2880

L'azienda autonoma annonaria libica
nel primo anno di gestione 29 agosto
1939-XVII- 31 agosto 1940-XVIII.
Tripoli 1941.

Business firms - Libya. 2881
August 1968.
Wash.: U.S. Dept. of Commerce. Bu-
reau of International Commerce 1968.
(Trade list.)

Business organizations - Libya. 2882
Wash.: GPO 1963.
(Overseas business reports 63-116.)

Camilla, S. 2883

Il gedâri libico.
REAI 29. 1941, p. 670-674.

Castaldi, A. 2884

Alcune industrie tripoline.
RdC 1/2. 1927/28, p. 121-136.

Catalogo ufficiale. 2885
Fiera campionaria di Tripoli.
Tripoli 1929.

Cerbella, G. 2886

Commercio e marineria della Repubblica di Venezia in un rapporto del
console d'Italia del 1862.
Libia 4. 1956, n. 3-4, p. 45-60.

Chandavarkar, A.G.   2887

The economic development of Libya.
Indian economic journal 9. 1961,
p. 69-74.

Cirenaica.   2888
Camera di Commercio,
Industria ed Agricoltura della Cire-
naica, Bengasi.
Messina 1928.

Clarke, J.I.   2889

Economic and political changes in
the Sahara.
Geography 46. 1961, p. 102-119.

Clarke, J.I.   2890

Libya takes her place in the world.
Geographical magazine 42. 1969,
n. 2, p. 87-91.

Le colonie italiane e le   2891
isole italiane dell'Egeo.
Notiziario geografico-economico.
Roma 1935.

Commercial code of Libya.   2892
np 1967.

Les conditions du développe-   2893
ment économique de la Libye.
Problèmes economiques 1960, n. 676.

Consistenza delle ditte.   2894
Ufficio dell'Economia Cor-
porativa di Derna.
REAI 27. 1939, p. 1306-1307.

Cook, C.   2895

Libya: problems and prospects of an
expanding economy.
New Africa 10. 1968, n. 3/4, p. 7-8.

Coppolino, A.   2896

Raccolta delle disposizioni doganali in vigore in Libia al 1o ottobre
1932. Governo della Cirenaica.
Bengasi 1932.

Corò, F.   2897

Cacce indigene in Tripolitania dall'
antichità ad oggi.
ACSC 1. 1931, vol. 4, p. 202-209.

Corò, F.   2898

La cantina sociale di Tripoli.
Oltremare 6. 1932, p. 366-368.

Corò, F.   2899

Libya restituta. Bilancio di un
quinquennio.
AIr 2. 1939, n. 3-4, p. 11-16.

Corò, F.   2900

La storia dell'artigianato libico
attraverso i tempi e le dominazioni.
Libia 1. 1953, n. 1, p. 113-118.

Corò, F.   2901

Il commercio caravaniero fra la
la Libia ed i paesi dell'Africa
centrale.
Africa. Roma 16. 1961, n. 2, p. 87-
90.

Costa, G.   2902

La scuola-bottega d'arte orafa di
Sugh el-Muscir.
Libia 2. 1954, n. 1, p. 97-98.

Dal deserto il rilancio 2903
economic libico.
Costruttori italiani nel mondo
12. 1966, n. ?52, p. 3-12.

Despois, J. 2904
Aperçu sur l'économie libyenne.
Études sur la Libye septentrionale.
Annales de géographie 71. 1962,
n. 385, p. 334-335.

The development of Libya. 2905
Sunday Herald Tribune 1964,
8.3., special section.

Duncan-Peters, S. 2906
Libya: a market for U.S. products.
Wash.: GPO 1962.
(Country market survey.)

Duncan-Peters, S. 2907
Living conditions in Libya.
Wash.: GPO 1962.
(Overseas business reports 62-16.)

Eastern muhafadat inventory. 2908
Prepared for the government
of the Kingdom of Libya, Ministry of
Planning and Development. Vol. 1-7.
Athens: Doxiadis Associates 1966.
(Document Dox-Lib-A 65.)

Eastern muhafadat planning 2909
regional report.
Athens: Doxiadis Associates 1968.
(Document Dox-Lib-A 163.)

Eckman, C.M. 2910
Array of U.S. producer, consumer
goods could be sold in Libya.
International commerce 73. 1967,
n. 5, p. 12-13.

The economic development 2911
of Libya. Report of a mission
organized by the International Bank
for Reconstruction and Development
at the request of the government of
Libya.
Baltimore: Johns Hopkins Press 1960.

Economic survey in 1965 for 2912
the six countries of the
North African subregion.
New York: United Nations, Economic
Commission for Africa 1966.
(E/CN.14/NA/ECOP/5.)

Economic survey of Africa. 2913
Vol. 2. North African
subregion.
New York: United Nations, Economic
Commission for Africa 1968.
(E/CN.14/403.)

L'économie de la Libye. 2914
Notes et études documen-
taires 1968, n. 3525.

Establishing a business 2915
in Libya.
Wash.: GPO 1963. 1968.
(Overseas business reports 63-116.)
(Overseas business reports 68-56.)

Fantini, O. 2916
Produzione, consumi e blocco dei
prezzi nel regno e nella Libia.
REAI 29. 1941, p. 611-615.

Farrell, J.D. 2917
La Libia dopo il petrolio.
Spettatore internazionale 2. 1967,
n. 4-5, p. 577-592.

Farrell, J.D. 2918
Libya strikes it rich.
Africa report 12. 1967, April,
p. 8-15.

Fels, E.   2919

Die Entwicklung Tripolitaniens.
PGM 80. 1934, p. 324-328.

Fenwick, P.   2920

Fortunes of Libya.
Geographical magazine 36. 1963/64,
p. 547-558.

Five-year economic and social   2921
development plan 1963-1968.
Kingdom of Libya, Ministry of
Planning and Development.
Tripoli: Poligrafico Libico 1963.

The food processing industries   2922
of North Africa. Part 1.
New York: United Nations, Economic
Commission for Africa 1967.
(E/CN.14/INR/145.)

Foreign trade regulations   2923
of the Kingdom of Libya.
Wash.: GPO 1965.
(Overseas business reports 65-29.)

Gesellschafts- und   2924
Investitionsrecht in Libyen.
Mitteilungen. BfA 17. 1967, n. 34.

Gherrim, B.   2925

L'economia libica come elemento in-
tegrante dell'economia imperiale.
ASIPS 25. 1936, vol. 4, p. 444-450.

Glinstra Bleeker, R.J.R. van   2926

A tentative strategy of development
for Libya.
Tripoli: Ministry of Planning and
Development 1964.

Gorini, P.M.   2927

Motoaratura in Cirenaica.
AIn 40. 1921, p. 121-123.

Gorresio, V.   2928

La fiera di Tripoli in dodici anni
di attività.
RdC 12. 1938, p. 479-492.

Les grandes lignes de l'évolu-   2929
tion des importations entre
1955 et 1966, Libye.
Etude mensuelle sur l'économie et
les finances des pays arabes 10.
1967, n. 118, p. 41-47.

Graziani, R.   2930

Panorama economico della Cirenaica.
RdC 7. 1933, p. 294-307.

Grosso, P.   2931

Il Sahara libico e la sua economia.
AIr 2. 1939, n. 1, p. 23-26.

Hamouda, M.   2932

Les industries artisanales s'implan-
tent aux Fezzân en Libye.
Panorama (B.I.T.) 1966, n. 18, mai-
juin, p. 16-25.

Hemphill, D.B.   2933

Market in Libya for medicines, fertilizers seen.
International commerce 73. 1967, n.5,
p. 8-9.

Herzog, R.   2934

Ein Beitrag zur Geschichte des nordafrikanischen Karawanenhandels.
Welt des Islams 6. 1961, p. 255-262.

Hickmann, E.   2935

Die Wirtschaft des Auslandes. Vol.2.
Laos-Vietnam.
Darmstadt 1964.

Higgins, B.H.   2936

Entrepreneurship in Libya.
MEJ 11. 1957, p. 319-323.

Higgins, B.H.   2937

Economic development with unlimited
supplies of capital: the Libyan case.
(Economic development: principles,
problems and policies.)
London: Constable 1968, p. 818-838.

Hill, R.W.   2938

Some problems of the economic geo-
graphy in North Tripolitania.
Durham: Dept. of Geography 1960.
Diss.

Hilli, A.H. al   2939

Grundlagen, Stand und Entwicklungs-
möglichkeiten der Wirtschaft in
Libyen.
Köln: Westdeutscher Verlag 1961.

Husseini, S.   2940

Wirtschaftliche Entwicklung Libyens
seit der Unabhängigkeit.
Graz 1967.
Diss.

Import tariff system of Libya.   2941
Wash.: GPO 1962.
(World trade information service,
 part 2: operations reports 62-1.)

L'industrie de transformation   2942
en Libye. Résultats d'une enquête statistique de 1966.
Étude mensuelle sur l'économie et
les finances des pays arabes 10.
1967, n. 115, p. 48-55.

Information guide for those   2943
doing business outside the
United States of America. Libya.
New York: Price Waterhouse & Co.
1961.

Inventory report ...   2944
(... regional report,
master plan, layout plan, implemen-
tation report) submitted by
1) Architectural Planning Partner-
   ship, Copenhagen (muhafadahs: 1.

Inventory report ...   2944

   Al Jabal al Gharb, Az Zāwiyah),
2) Doxiadis Associates, Athens
   (muhafadahs: Banghāzī, Darnah,
   Al Jabal al Akhdar),   2.
3) McGaughy, Marshall, McMillan &

Inventory report ...   2944

   Lucas, Rome (muhafadahs: Al
   Khums, Misrātah),
4) Whiting International Associates,
   Rome (muhafadahs: Awbārī, Sabhah,
   Tarābulus).   3.

Inventory report ...   2944

Tripoli: Ministry of Planning and
Development 1966-

         4.

Inventory report for the   2945
muhafadah of El Khums
April-August 1966. Kingdom of Libya,
Ministry of Planning and Develop-
ment.
Rome: McGaughy, Marshall, McMillan
& Lucas nd.

Johns, R.   2946

Consolidation of the nation.
Financial times 1969, 6.3., p. 17.

Jong, H.W.N. de   2947

Libië als handelspartner.
Afrika. Den Haag 19. 1965, p. 140-
143.

Kermann, K.   2948

Libyen, ein vernachlässigter Handelspartner der Bundesrepublik Deutsch-
land.
Bremen: Bremer Ausschuss für Wirt-
schaftsforschung 1960.

Khokar, H.B.   2949

More emphasis on industry in the
second plan.
Financial times 1969, 6.3., p. 22.

Klitzsch, E.   2950

Mineral resources, petroleum and
gas resources and ground water in
Libya.
Tripoli: Ministry of Planning and
Development 1966.

Kurzmerkblatt Libyen.   2951
Neufassung ...
Mitteilungen. BfA 1963-

Laenderkurzberichte. Libyen.   2952
Statistisches Bundesamt
Wiesbaden.
Stuttgart/Mainz: Kohlhammer 1968-
(Allgemeine Statistik des Auslan-
des. 4.)

Laenderlexikon.   2953
Hamburgisches Welt-Wirt-
schafts-Archiv. Vol. 2.
Hamburg: Verlag Weltarchiv 1957.

Lavault, P.   2954

L'assistance technique des Nations
Unies en Libye.
Paris: CHEAM 1955.
(Publication 2583.)

Leone, E. de   2955

L'artigianato tripolitano e la sua
tradizionale conservazione.
Oltremare 8. 1934, p. 277-280.

Lessona, A.   2956

La produzione del sale nelle colonie italiane.
RdC 5. 1931, p. 163-174.

Lewicki, T.   2957

Średniowieczni pisarze arabscy o
bogactwach mineralnych Afryki i ich
eksploatacji.
Studia z Dziejów Górnictwa i Hut-
nictwa. Wrocław 11. 1967, p. 7-11.

La Libia e l'autarchia.   2958
AIr 3. 1940, n. 5, p. 1-26.

La Libia: un paese in svi-   2959
luppo.
Costruttori italiani nel mondo 15.
1969, n. 322, p. 3-11.

Libië is geen zandbak meer.   2960
Afrika. Den Haag 20. 1966,
p. 167-169.

Libya.   2961
Wash.: GPO 1969.
(Foreign economic trends 69-47.)

Libya: Egypt and the economy. 2962
Africa confidential 11. 1970,
n. 8, p. 1-3.

Libya: a Financial Times   2963
survey.
Financial Times 1969, 6.3., p. 17-
24.

Libya. Economic and commer- 2964
cial conditions in Libya.
Board of Trade. Commercial Relations
and Exports Dept.
London.
1952-1955 (1956).
(Overseas economic surveys.)

Libya. An economic survey. 2965
London: Barclays Bank D.C.O.
1960. 1962. 1965. 1967.

Libya. Trade mission report. 2966
International commerce 73.
1967, n. 5, p. 4-14.

Libya growth skyrockets. 2967
International commerce 75.
1969, n. 18, p. 27-29.

Libye: le 2 ème plan 2968
quinquennal de développement
1969-1974.
Le commerce du Levant 1970, n. 114,
p. 42-44.

Libye: la part de la C.E.E. 2969
ne présente que 40% du total
des importations.
Moniteur officiel du commerce international 1966, n. 517, p. 281-287.

Libye. Exercice 1963-1964. 2970
Bruxelles: Bureau Interna-
tional des Tarifs Douaniers 1963.
(Bulletin international des douanes.
51.)
Suppl. 1. 1964. Suppl. 2. 1965.

Libye. Nouvelle puissance 2971
pétrolière. Un marché en
évolution rapide, position de la
Suisse.
Lausanne/Zürich: Office Suisse
d'Expansion Commercial 1964.
(Rapport spécial, sér. A. 82.)

La Libye s'engage dans 2972
l'ère industrielle.
Le monde diplomatique 1968, n. 175,
p. 23-42.

La Libye et les sociétés 2973
étrangères.
Articles et documents 1960, n. 0922.

Libyen: puritanischer 2974
Nationalismus.
Internationales Afrika Forum
6. 1970, n. 1, p. 13-15.

Libyen: der Wettbewerb ist 2975
entbrannt.
Internationales Afrika Forum
5. 1969, n. 11, p. 634-636.

Libyen. Einfuhrlizenzpflich- 2976
tige Waren (Stand Oktober
1969).
Marktinformation. BfA 1969, n.C/768.

Libyen. Wirtschaftliche 2977
Entwicklung 1967.
Marktinformation. BfA 1968, n.A/941.

Libyens Aussenhandel in 2978
Zahlen.
Marktinformationsdienst der BfA
1962, n. A/481.

Das libysche Gesetz ueber 2979
Handelsvertreter. Libysierung
des gesamten Handels.
Mitteilungen. BfA 18. 1968, n. 63.

Licensing and exchange   2980
controls of Libya.
Wash.: GPO 1963.
(Overseas business reports 63-88.)

Lindberg, J.   2981
A general economic appraisal of Li-
bya.
New York: United Nations 1952.
(ST/TAA/K/Libya/1.)

Linss, H.P.   2982
Öl und Sand. Libyens Bemühungen um
eine gesunde Nationalwirtschaft.
Entwicklungsländer 3. 1961, p. 228-
231.

Lockwood, A.N.   2983
Libya, building a desert economy.
International concliation 1957,
n. 512, p. 313-378.

Lorenz, C.   2984
Significant rise in volume of trade.
Financial times 1969, 6.3., p. 21.

Mabro, R.   2985
La Libye, un état rentier ?
Projet 1969, n. 39, p. 1090-1101.

Maclachlan, K.   2986
Landed property and economic change
in Tripolitania.
Bulletin of the faculty of arts.
University of Libya 2. 1968, p. 85-
101.

Maghreb-Integration laeuft an. 2987
Mitteilungen. BfA 18. 1968,
n. 65.

Malfliet, E.   2988
Is Libye een interessant afzetgebied?
Tijd 1964, n. 39, p. 11-13.

Mallakh, R. el   2989
Affluence versus development in Li-
bya.
World today 24. 1968, p. 475-482.

Mallakh, R. el   2990
The economics of rapid growth:
Libya.
MEJ 23. 1969, p. 308-320.

Mallakh, R. el   2991
La programmazione in un'economia
con eccesso di capitali. Il caso
della Libia.   1.
Riv. internazionale di scienze
economiche e commerciali 16. 1969,

Mallakh, R. el   2991
p. 148-165.

                                  2.

Malov, J.A.   2992
Livija. Ekonomika i vnešnjaja tor-
govlja.
Moskva: Vneštorgizdat 1965.

Manifestazione internazionale, 2993
intercoloniale. Mostra coloniale dell'impero fascista. Fiera
di Tripoli.
Roma/Tripoli.
11. 1937: mostra coloniale 1-

Maratea, F.   2994
Panorama tripolitano nella stagione
della VI fiera coloniale.
RdC 6. 1932, p. 251-258.

Martel, A. 2995

Le commerce du natron au Fezzân
(1895-1899).
TIRS 20. 1961, p. 225-236.

Massi, E. 2996

Economia dell'Africa italiana
(l'economia italiana nel 1937).
Riv. internazionale di scienze
sociali 46. 1938, p. 434-458.

Mathieu, M. 2997

Quelques aspects de la mise en valeur
de la Cyrénaïque.
Correspondance d'orient. Études
1965/66, n. 8/9, p. 27-39.

Mazzei, J. 2998

La politica doganale coloniale e i
problemi che ne derivano.
ACSC 1. 1931, vol. 6, p. 72-92.

Mazzei, J. 2999

Italia e Africa settentrionale nel
problema economico mediterraneo.
Italia e Africa mediterranea. Firenze 1942, p. 147-260.

Melencamp, N.M. 3000

Market factors in Libya.
Wash.: GPO 1968.
(Overseas business reports 68-80.)

Memorandum on corporate, 3001
fiscal and other matters
affecting business enterprises in
Libya.
London: Price Waterhouse & Co. 1961.

El mercado de Libia. 3002
Madrid: Consejo Superior
de las Cameras Oficiales de Comercio,
Industria y Navegacion de España
1965.

Migliorini, E. 3003

Risorse economiche.
SIFOG 1937, p. 561-590.

Mining law. 3004
Ed. I.M. Hangari.
np 1966.

Mischi, L. 3005

Industrie manifatturiere e del mare
nella Libia orientale.
ACSC 3. 1937, vol. 8, p. 370-384.

Une mission du C.N.P.F. 3006
s'est rendue en Libye, pays
en pleine expansion.
Patronat français 1966, n. 262,
p. 16-22.

Modugno, M. 3007

Funzione autarchica della fiera di
Tripoli.
AIr 2. 1939, n. 2, p. 25-28.

Mondo afro-asiatico, 3008
numero dedicato alla fiera
internazionale di Tripoli:
3. 1965, febbr., p. 5-36 / IV.
4. 1966, febbr., p. 4-33 / V.
6. 1968, febbr.-marzo, p. 4-38 / VII.

Morgantini, A.M. 3009

Gli uffici della Camera di Commercio,
Industria e Agricoltura della Tripolitania, primo esempio di razionale
organizzazione amministrativa in Libia.
ACSC 2. 1934, vol. 6, p. 531-463.

Morgantini, A.M. 3010

Contributi dell'economia tripolitana
a quella della metropoli.
ACSC 2. 1934, vol. 6, p. 564-588.

Mortara, A.　　　　　　3011

Correnti di mano d'opera industriale
e commerciale verso la Libia e
l'A.O.I.
ACSC 3. 1937, vol. 7, p. 158-171.

Muller, J.　　　　　　3012

Forages au Fezzân.
Bulletin de la conféd. gén. du
commerce et de l'industrie en Tunisie 1950, n. 19, p. 1084-1095.

Musa, K.A.　　　　　　3013

Mise en valeur des ressources de la
Libye.
Forum du commerce international GATT
1967, n. 4, p. 12-13.

Napolitano, E.　　　　　3014

L'economia della Tripolitania in
rapporto all'economia nazionale.
Ente Autonomo Fiera Campionaria di
Tripoli.
Tripoli 1930.

Narducci, G.　　　　　　3015

Industrie nuove nelle colonie italiane. La concia delle pelli in Cirenaica.
AIn 36. 1917, p. 30-32.

Narducci, G.　　　　　　3016

Industrie e commercio della Cirenaica ed il loro avvenire nel "dopo
guerra".
AIn 37. 1918, p. 42-48, 86-99, 137-
144, 233-241.

Narducci, G.　　　　　　3017

Il commercio di Bengasi con le oasi
cirenaiche.
AIn 38. 1919, p. 253-255.

Narducci, G.　　　　　　3018

Nell'Africa mediterranea italiana.
L'artigianato.
IdO 1. 1936, n. 1, p. 24-25.

Narducci, G.　　　　　　3019

L'antico commercio delle Conterie
di Venezia ed il loro uso in Libia.
Annali del museo libico di storia
naturale 3. 1941, p. 251-260.

Nava, G.　　　　　　　3020

Una produzione nazionale saggiabile
sul litorale libico: il gelsomino.
REAI 28. 1940, p. 22-24.

Niccoli, E.　　　　　　3021

Le mellahe di Bu-Kammasch.
RdT 2. 1925/26, p. 35-49.

Niccoli, E.　　　　　　3022

Il problema industriale in Tripoli-
tania.
La rinascita della Tripolitania.
Milano 1926, p. 487-512.

Niccoli, E.　　　　　　3023

Le materie prime nella fiera campionaria di Tripoli.
RdC 1/2. 1927/28, p. 25-52.

Niccoli, E.　　　　　　3024

Le colonie italiane e la produzione
del magnesio.
RdC 4. 1930, p. 758-769.

Niccoli, E.　　　　　　3025

L'industria delle saline nelle colonie italiane.
ACSC 1. 1931, vol. 6, p. 164-184.

Niccoli, E.　　　　　　3026

Raffronto economico fra la Libia e
le colonie mediterranee francesi.
RdC 5. 1931, p. 585-600.

Note economiche dei 3027
governi coloniali.
Governo Generale della Libia.
v. Rassegna economica dell'Africa
italiana 26. 1938-

Objectives of the second 3028
five-year plan 1968-1973.
Kingdom of Libya.
Tripoli: National Planning Council
1967.

Official catalogue. 3029
Tripoli International Fair
1962. Compiled and ed. by Press and
Publicity Office, Tripoli International Fair.
Genova: Arti Poligrafiche Editoriale nd.

Oil boom improves Libya's 3030
market potential.
International commerce 70. 1962,
n. 39, p. 2-5.

Ordinamenti doganali della 3031
Tripolitania e Cirenaica ...
al 31 dicembre 1920.
Ministero delle Colonie.
Roma 1921.

Ortner-Heun, I. 3032
Das Entwicklungsland Libyen. 3rd ed.
Köln: BfA 1967.

Panunzio, S. 3033
Utilizzazione dell'energia del ven-
to in Tripolitania.
ASIPS 25. 1936, vol. 5, p. 133-173.

Pellegrineschi, A.V. 3034
Economia.
RdC 12. 1938 - 16. 1942 passim.

Pellegrineschi, A.V. 3035
Il lavoro italiano in Libia.
AIr 1943, n. 42, p. 33-44.

Il piano quinquennale di 3036
sviluppo economico libico.
Costruttori italiani nel mondo
1964, n. 202, 15.5.

Piccioli, A. 3037
La seconda fiera di Tripoli.
Oltremare 2. 1928, p. 25-27.

Piccioli, A. 3038
Il movimento artistico promosso in
Libia dal governo fascista.
L'impero coloniale fascista. Novara
1936, p. 497-502.

Piccioli, A. 3039
La fiera di Tripoli.
AAI 1. 1938, vol. 2, p. 497-566.

Pistolese, G.E. 3040
Ascesa dell'artigianato libico.
AIr 2. 1939, n. 3-4, p. 22-24.

Prinzi, D.G. 3041
Caratteri dell'economia indigena
tripolitana.
ACSC 2. 1934, vol. 6, p. 792-802.

Prinzi, D.G. 3042
Note sulla economia del Fezzan.
Firenze 1934.
(Relazioni e monografie agrario-
coloniali. 29.)

Les problèmes économiques   3043
de la Libye.
Problèmes économiques 1962, n. 772,
p. 20-22.

Provini, M.A.   3044
Appunti di politica economica
coloniale.
Milano 1935.

Quadrotta, G.   3045
Sunto della relazione sull'arti-
gianato libico.
ACSC 3. 1937, vol. 8, p. 364-369.

Quadrotta, G.   3046
Sviluppo e realizzazioni dell'arti-
gianato in Libia.
REAI 25. 1937, p. 952-967.

Quadrotta, G.   3047
Disciplina economica dell'artigiana-
to e della piccola industria in
Libia.
REAI 26. 1938, p. 1424-1429.

Quadrotta, G.   3048
La XII fiera di Tripoli.
REAI 26. 1938, p. 402-413.

Quadrotta, G.   3049
Aspetti economico corporativi dell'
industria in Libia.
REAI 27. 1939, p. 814-826.

Quadrotta, G.   3050
Disciplina economica e sindacale
dell'artigianato in Libia.
Roma 1939.

Quadrotta, G.   3051
L'evoluzione dell'economia industria-
le libica.
REAI 27. 1939, p. 818-826.

Rapport de la mission C.E.A.   3052
de coordination industrielle
en Algérie, Libye, Maroc et Tunisie.
Tanger: Nations Unies, Commission
Economique pour l'Afrique 1964.

Rassegna d'oltremare,   3053
(il commercio italo africano).
Genova/Roma.
7. 1937-

ianc

Régnier, J.J.   3054
Libye (chronique économique).
AAN 7. 1968, p. 365-390, 8. 1969,
p. 541-563.

Relazione sull'attività   3055
svolta nel 1937-XV-XVI.
Istituto Fascista per l'Artigianato
della Libia.
REAI 26. 1938, p. 1477-1484.

Report.   3056
Public Development and Stabili-
zation Agency.
Tripoli 1952/54-

Report. Industrial co-ordina-   3057
tion mission to Algeria, Libya,
Morocco and Tunisia.
New York: United Nations, Economic
Commission for Africa 1964.
(E/CN. 14/248.)

Report of study of United   3058
States foreign aid in 10
Middle Eastern and African countries,
Turkey, ... Libya, ... submitted by
E. Gruening.
Wash.: GPO 1963.

Rossi, F.M. 3059
Le piccole industrie indigene.
La rinascita della Tripolitania.
Milano 1926, p. 513-519.

Rossi, P. 3060
Libye 64, un pays au feu de la fortune.
Jeune Afrique 1964, n. 175, p. 29-
43.

Roy, J.C. 3061
Un nouvel et puissant acheteur:
la Libye.
Gestion 6. 1963, p. 92-100.

Sacchetti, R. 3062
La centrale termo-elettrica di Barce
nella Cirenaica.
RdC 3. 1929, p. 387-391.

Sanders, J. 3063
Libya pushes ahead rapidly on port
improvement, roads, dams, schools.
International commerce 73. 1967,
n. 5, p. 11-12.

Satta Dessolis, A. 3064
Emigrazione ed espansione commer-
ciale italiana in Africa.
ACSC 2. 1934, vol. 4, p. 298-316.

Scandura, A. 3065
Soggettività dei pesi e delle misure
indigene dell'Africa italiana e loro
funzione economica.
REAI 28. 1940, p. 991-997.

Scarin, E. 3066
Le risorse economiche delle terre
italiane d'oltremare: Libia.
Riv. di commissariato e dei servizi
amministrativi militari 1940,
p. 246-265.

Schiffers, H. 3067
Die Sahara - das Reich der Fata
Morgana.
Internationales Afrika Forum
2. 1966, p. 186-192.

Serafy, S.el 3068
Fundamental changes in economic
structure.
Financial times 1969, 6.3., p. 18.

Sette anni di scambi 3069
tra Cirenaica ed Egitto.
Oltremare 4. 1930, p. 94-97.

Sharkasy, M.M. 3070
Guida per l'operatore economico in
Libia.
Tripoli: Libyaconsult 1967.

Sikta, A. 3071
Lo sviluppo economico della Libia.
Atti del convegno economico italo
africano 17. 1968, p. 21-30.
Levante 1968, dicembre, p. 5-24.

La situation économique 3072
de la Libye.
Notes et études documentaires 1953,
n. 1765. Perspectives 1953, 11.9.,
p. 1-11. Articles et documents 1959,
n. 0848, 1961, n. 1046.

Situation économique et poli- 3073
tique des anciennes colonies
italiennes.
Notes et études documentaires 1948,
n. 1025-1026.

Spaull, H. 3074
Grundsteine für Libyens Genossen-
schaften.
Internationale genossenschaftliche
Rundschau 50. 1957, p. 234-237.

Spoecker, J.   3075
Die wirtschaftliche Entwicklung
Libyens.
Zs für Wirtschaftsgeographie
6. 1962, p. 1-4.

Statement in parliament   3076
by the prime minister
introducing the draft of the five-
year plan, 1963-1968.
Tripoli: Ministry of Information
and Guidance 1963.

Stechschulte, R.F.   3077
Group visits Tripoli, Benghazi,
brings back specific proposals.
International commerce 73. 1967,
n. 5, p. 6-7.

Survey of economic and   3078
commercial conditions in
Morocco, Algeria, Tunisia, Tripoli-
tania and Cyrenaica, 1926-1927.
Department of Overseas Trade.
London: HMSO 1927.

Talha, L.   3079
Libye (chronique économique).
AAN 6. 1967, p. 513-560.

Teruzzi, A.   3080
Potenziamento autarchico della
Libia.
REAI 27. 1939, p. 1185-1191.

Tran Buu Khanh   3081
Les ressources pétrolières et
l'évolution sociale et économique
de la Libye.
Correspondance d'orient. Études
1965/66, n. 8-9, p. 53-61.

Il trentennale della Libia: 3082
1911-1941.
AIr 1941-42, n. 37, p. 1-99.

Treyer, C.   3083
Sahara 1956-62.
Paris: Société les Belles Lettres
1966.
(Publications de l'Université de
Dijon. 37.)

Turqman, T.T.   3084
Libya's oil wealth creates fast
growing economy.
International commerce 74. 1968,
n. 51, p. 13-16.

Vacca Maggiolini, E.   3085
La seconda fiera di Tripoli.
RdC 1/2. 1927/28, p. 599-605.

Valle, C. della   3086
L'industria in Libia tra il 1911 e
il 1940.
Libia 3. 1955, n. 3, p. 61-65, n. 4,
p. 45-65.

Vesci, I.   3087
Problemi e prospettive dell'economia
della Libia.
Italiani nel mondo 1960, gennaio,
p. 16-19.

Vigand, G.C.   3088
La XIII fiera di Tripoli.
REAI 27. 1939, p. 263-266.

Vigand, G.C.   3089
La mostra dell'artigianato libico ai
Mercati Traianei.
REAI 29. 1941, p. 574-578.

Virgilii, F.   3090
Il sistema tributario delle colonie
italiane.
ACSC 2. 1934, vol. 6, p. 164-175.

Weis, H.   3091
Schatzkammer Libyen - Wirtschafts-
wandlungen am Rande der Sahara.
Bustan 6. 1965, n. 2, p. 11-16.

Weltwirtschaft am Jahres-   3092
wechsel. Libyen.
Mitteilungen. BfA 10. 1960, n. 120-
20. 1970, n. 65.

Whitehead, K.D.   3093
Basic data on the economy of Libya.
Wash.: GPO 1964.
(Overseas business reports 64-112.)

Wirtschaftsentwicklung   3094
in Libyen.
Marktinformationsdienst der BfA
1963, n. A/626.

Die Wirtschaftslage Libyens   3095
1961/62.
Marktinformationsdienst der BfA
1962, n. A/523.

Wittschell, L.   3096
Die Entwicklung Tripolitaniens seit
der italienischen Besitzergreifung.
PGM 72. 1926, p. 166-172.

Woodmansee, W.C.   3097
The mineral industry of Libya.
Minerals yearbook. Wash.: GPO.
Vol. 4. 1965, p. 833-839.

Zambrano, C.   3098
Le industrie alimentari della Libia.
REAI 28. 1940, p. 731-737.

Zlitni, A.M. - Cowling, K.   3099
Exports, imports and consumption of
agricultural products in a rapidly
growing economy: the case of Libya.
Farm economist 11. 1966, p. 120-134.

Zucco, G.   3100
Bu Chemmasc.
Oltremare 2. 1928, p. 95-98.

Zucco, G.   3101
Tonnare e tonnaroti in Libia.
Oltremare 2. 1928, p. 365-369.

Zucco, G.   3102
Una nuova industria in Tripolitania.
I sali potassici di Pisida.
RdC 3. 1929, p. 718-734.

Zucco, G.   3103
Le tonnare nell'industria, nella
storia, nella letteratura e nell'
arte.
RdC 4. 1930, p. 152-163.

Oil Industry.

Ward, P.   3104
The Libyan oil industry: a reader's
guide.
Tripoli: Oasis Oil Co. of Libya 1967.

Arab oil review.   3105
A review of oil industry
published every monthend in Libya.
Tripoli 1964-

Oel.   3106
Zeitschrift für die Mineraloel-
wirtschaft.
Hamburg.
7. 1969-

World oil.   3114
Houston, Texas.
141. 1955-

Oil and gas international.   3107
London/Tulsa, Oklahoma.
9. 1969-

World petroleum.   3115
New York.
39. 1969-

Oil and gas journal.   3108
Tulsa, Oklahoma.
67. 1969-

Employment in oil-mining   3116
industries 1964.
Tripoli: Census and Statistical
Dept. nd

Petroleum.   3109
London.
31. 1968-

Employment in the petroleum   3117
mining industry in Libya 1964.
Tripoli: Census and Statistical
Dept. 1966.

Petroleum press service.   3110
London.
36. 1969-

Imports by oil companies   3118
1963-68.
Tripoli: Census and Statistical
Dept. nd

Petroleum times.   3111
London.
73. 1969-

Libye. Resultats de l'en-   3119
quête annuelle sur l'in-
dustrie petrolière.
Étude mensuelle sur l'économie et
les finances des pays arabes   12.
1969, n. 144, p. 31-41.

Proceedings. Libyan Association 3112
of Petroleum Technologists.
Tripoli: L.A.P.T.
1. 1965.
2. 1966.
3. 1967.

Petroleum development in   3120
Libya.
Benghazi: Petroleum Commission.
1954 through 1958. 1959.
1954 through mid-1961. 1961.
1954 through mid-1962. 1962.

Review of Arab petroleum   3113
and economics.
Baghdad.
2. 1966, n. 11-

Petroleum development in   3121
Libya.
Tripoli: Ministry of Petroleum
Affairs.
1954 through mid-1963. 1964.
1954 through 1964. 1965.

Report of the annual   3122
survey of petroleum
mining industry.
Tripoli: Census and Statistical
Dept.
4. 1969-

Alber, O.   3123
Erdöl und Erdgas in der Sahara.
Afrika-Spektrum 1967, n. 3, p. 38-
47.

Anderson, K.E.   3124
Pipelines in Libya.
Mechanical engineering 88. 1966,
n. 7, p. 42-45.

Azzam, I.   3125
Libya and oil.
Contemporary review 205. 1964,
p. 129-133.

Barthel, G.   3126
Ölmacht Libyen.
Deutsche Aussenpolitik 14. 1969,
p. 563-577.

Berreby, J.J.   3127
La Libye à l'heure du pétrole.
Politique étrangère 24. 1959,
p. 636-644.

Bianchi, F.   3128
Il petrolio della Libia.
Vicenza 1922.
Venezia 1938.

Bischoff, G.   3129
Der Stand der Erdölexploration in
Libyen.
Erde 93. 1962, p. 50-53.

Bowerman, J.N.   3130
Petroleum developments in North
Africa in 1965, 1966.
BAAPG 50. 1966, p. 1681-1703, 51.
1967, p. 1564-1586.

Brady, R.T.   3131
Libya. Petroleum developments in
North Africa 1965.
BAAPG 50. 1966, p. 1691-1700.

Braeuner, H.   3132
Erdöl in Libyen. Crude oil in Libya.
Nürnberg: Libyen-Verlag 1966.

Brown, R.W.   3133
A spatial view of oil development
in the desert: Libya in the first
decade 1955-1965.
New York: Columbia University 1969.
Diss.

Brundage, H.T.   3134
Libya becoming one of world's top
gas and oil exporters.
World oil 161. 1965, n. 3, p. 68-71.

Clarke, J.I.   3135
Oil in Libya: some implications.
Economic geography 39. 1963,
p. 40-59.

Clutter, L.W.   3136
Libya. Petroleum developments in
North Africa 1966.
BAAPG 51. 1967, p. 1571-1580.

Cole, H.M.   3137
Libyan petroleum legislation.
(North Africa. Basic oil laws and
concession contracts. Original
texts.)
Petroleum legislation. New York
1965.

Coulter, J.W.   3138
Libya's black gold.
Journal of geography 66. 1967,
p. 294-305.

Coup d'oeil sur l'actualité   3139
pétrolière mondiale. La
Libye.
Perspectives 1969, n. 1132, p. 1-11.

Crabbe, R.   3140
La Libye, un Texas africain.
Eurafrica 1967, n. 1-3, p. 15-17.

Davis, H.M.   3141
The Sidrah pipeline system.
Tripoli: Oasis Oil Co. of Libya
1962.

Décret-loi amendant la loi   3142
sur le pétrole (de 1955).
AAN 4. 1965, p. 667-677.

Desio, A.   3143
L'oro nero nel sottosuolo della
Libia.
Vie del mondo 22. 1960, p. 655-666.

Empis, P.   3144
La Libye supplantera-t-elle le Sahara comme fournisseur del'Europe
occidentale.
Revue pétrolière 1964, n. 1059,
p. 636-645.

Das Erdoelland Libyen.   3145
Kultur und Wirtschaft.
Essen: Gelsenkirchener Bergwerks AG
1968.

Esiste il petrolio in Libia ?   3146
AIn 39. 1920, p. 286.

Esso in Libya.   3147
Tripoli: Esso Standard Libya
1964.

Fellmann, W.   3148
Erdöl in Libyen.
Zs für angewandte Geologie 11. 1965,
p. 98-100.

Gabriel, E.   3149
Erdöl in Libyen.
Orient 1. 1960, p. 67-69.

Gaudio, A.   3150
La Libia nell'era del petrolio.
Universo 40. 1960, p. 997-1016.

Gaudio, A.   3151
La Libye à l'heure du pétrole.
Horizons 9. 1960, n. 108, p. 92-105.

Gaudio, A.   3152
L'oro nero del Sahara libico-algeri-
no.
Levante 11. 1964, n. 3-4, p. 63-80.

Gaudio, A.   3153
L'oro nero del Sahara.
Vie del mondo 27. 1965, p. 326-340.

Gaudio, A. 3154

Il miracolo del petrolio libico.
Universo 46. 1966, p. 937-958.

Gaudio, A. 3155

La Libye. Grande puissance pétrolière.
Eurafrica 1969, n. 9-10, p. 17-22.

Gaudio, A. 3156

La Libye, troisième producteur mondiale de pétrole.
France Eurafrique 21. 1969, n. 209,
p. 3-8.

Gelsenberg in Libyen. 3157
Öl. Zs für die Mineral-
ölwirtschaft 5. 1967, p. 145-150.

Gemmel, T.M. 3158

Esso Libya's gas project.
Review of Arab petroleum and economics 2. 1966, n. 4, p. 9-11.

Godard, J. 3159

Etat des recherches pétrolières en
Libye.
Orient 12. 1959, p. 71-75.

Grosse, M. 3160

Un nouveau producteur de pétrole:
la Libye.
Annales de géographie 72. 1963,
p. 231-232.

Hagemeier, M.E. 3161

Petroleum developments in North
Africa in 1964.
BAAPG 49. 1965, p. 1232-1256.

Hanisch, W. 3162

Tobruk - Libyens wichtigster Ölhafen
der Zukunft.
Seeverkehr 1966, p. 359-361.

Heatzig, G. - Michel, R. 3163

Petroleum developments in North Africa in 1967, 1968.
BAAPG 52. 1968, p. 1489-1511, 53.
1969, p. 1700-1727.

Heitmann, G. 3164

Libya: an analysis of the oil economy.
Journal of modern African studies
7. 1969, p. 249-263.

Heller, W. 3165

Die Änderungen des Erdölgesetzes von
1955.
Zs für Bergrecht 106. 1965, p. 308-
318.

Hullot, J.B. 3166

Le pétrole en Libye.
(Le pétrole en Afrique).
Revue française d'études politiques
africaines 1969, novembre, p. 17-60.

Johns, R. 3167

Brightest star in the world oil
production scene. Purposeful oil
policy.
Financial times 1969, 6.3., p. 20-
22.

Jong, H.W.N. de 3168

De aardoliewinning in Libië.
Afrika. Mededelingen van het Afrika
Instituut 15. 1961, p. 6-9.

Jost, P.P. 3169

Hoffnung für Libyen. Amerikaner und
Erdöl.
Das neue Journal 9. 1960, n. 5,
p. 19-22.

Kubbah, A.A.Q.   3170
Libya, its oil industry and economic system.
Baghdad: Arab Petro-Economic Research Centre 1964.

Lador, M. - Harry Wassall &   3171
Ass.
Libya. Petroleum developments in North Africa 1967.
BAAPG 52. 1968, p. 1495-1504.

Lador, M.   3172
Libya. Petroleum developments in North Africa 1968, 1969.
BAAPG 53. 1969, p. 1709-1717, 54. 1970, p. 1466-1473.

Leone, E. de   3173
Alcune verità storiche sul petrolio della Libia.
La Méditerranée de 1919 à 1939. Actes du colloque de Nice. Paris 1969, p. 53-58.

La Libia si annovera fra i   3174
grandi produttori di petrolio.
Rassegna della stampa estera (Banco di Roma) 23. 1968, p. 511-515.

Libya.   3175
(International outlook issue / 24th annual),
World oil 169. 1969, n. 3, p. 150-156.

Libyan petroleum law (no. 25   3176
of 1955).
Middle East law review 1. 1958, p. 38-44, 90-99, 119-120, 272-287, 328-340.

The Libyan petroleum law and   3177
regulations issued thereunder.
Tripoli: Fergiani Bookshop 1959.

Libye: nationalisation dans   3178
le secteur pétrolier.
Étude mensuelle sur l'économie et les finances des pays arabes 13. 1970, n. 152, p. 20-24.

La Libye, un désert riche en   3179
pétrole.
Problèmes economiques 1960, n. 656.

La Libye, un désert riche en   3180
pétrole ?
Bulletin hebdomadaire de la Krediet-bank 15. 1960, n. 24, p. 225-228.

La Libye à l'âge du pétrole.   3181
Afrique 1963, n. 29,
p. 22-25.

Libyen: mehr Geld fuer   3182
mehr Oel.
Internationale Afrika Forum 4. 1968, p. 659-661.

Marthelot, P.   3183
La révolution du pétrole dans un pays insuffisamment développé: la Libye.
Les cahiers d'outre-mer 18. 1965, n. 69, p. 5-31.

Michel, R.   3184
Petroleum developments in North Africa in 1969.
BAAPG 54. 1970, p. 1457-1483.

Obst, J.   3185
Die Erdölexploration in Libyen - Erfolge und Auswirkungen.
Erde 99. 1968, p. 265-277.

O'Donnell, J.P. 3186
Sand, rock are barriers to Libya's
big line.
Oil and gas journal 1966, 7.2.,
p. 110-115.

L'or noir de Libye. 3187
Europe Sud-est 1970, n. 73,
p. 12-18.

Ottolenghi, S. 3188
Lo scatolone di petrolio.
Vie d'Italia e del mondo 75.1969,
n. 2, p. 140-146.

Perrodon, A. 3189
Aperçu des principaux resultats ob-
tenus en Libye.
Bulletin de l'association française
des techniciens du pétrole 1960,
n. 142, p. 617-630.

Le pétrole dans l'économie 3190
libyenne.
Problèmes économiques 1966, n. 989,
p. 28-29.

Le pétrole de Libye. 3191
Perspectives 15. 1959,
n. 672. Articles et documents 1959,
n. 0886, 1960, n. 0959, 1966,
n. 1794.

Le pétrole de Libye concurrent 3192
du pétrole saharien.
Revue française d'énergie 11. 1959,
n. 112, p. 4-5.

Le pétrole et la Libye. 3193
Bulletin économique APS
1966, n. 69, p. 69-74.

Petroleum developments in 3194
Libya.
Men weekly 6. 1967, n. 45, p. 16-21.

Petroleum law amendment 3195
(revision of existing
concession agreements).
International legal materials
5. 1966, p. 442-461.

Plate, H. 3196
Erdöl wandelt die Wüste.
Hamburg: Baken-Verlag 1969.
(Bakenbücherei. 21.)

Portmann, H. 3197
Oil and oases in Libya.
Swiss review of world affairs
20. 1970, n. 4, p. 11-15.

Radice Fossati, E. 3198
La Libia e il petrolio.
Vie del mondo 29. 1967, p. 204-217.

Roccabella, A. 3199
Sotto le sabbie della Libia un mare
di petrolio.
Levante 10. 1963, n. 2, p. 26-32.

Salvatori, S. 3200
Cambia col petrolio il volto della
Libia.
Politica estera 1968, luglio-agosto,
p. 27-31.

Schafer, S.J. - Terry, C.E. 3201
Libya. Petroleum developments in
North Africa 1964.
BAAPG 49. 1965, p. 1244-1250.

Shaw, R.C.   3202
Essor de la production du pétrole
en Libye.
La revue pétrolière 1965, octobre,
p. 61-65.

The Sirtica pipeline and   3203
terminal system.
Tripoli: Mobil Oil Libya nd.

Situation de l'industrie   3204
petrolière en 1967.
Étude mensuelle sur l'économie et
les finances des pays arabes 1968,
octobre, p. 37-47.

Smith, J.P. - Naylor, W.V.   3205
History of oil development in Libya.
BAAPG 50. 1966, p. 635.

Talha, L.   3206
Le pétrole et l'économie libyenne.
AAN 5. 1966, p. 153-234.

Tuetsch, H.   3207
Oil in Libya.
Swiss review of world affairs 9.
1960, n. 11, p. 13-15.

Turine, A.   3208
Een nieuw petroleumrijk: Libye.
Tijdschrift voor belgische Handel
1960, n. 6, p. 9-14.

Un atout de premier plan,   3209
le pétrole.
Syrie et monde arabe 1970, n. 196,
p. 38-43.

Vor das Oel hat Allah   3210
die Angst gesetzt.
Weltbild 15. 1960, n. 15, p. 6-9.

Wells, M.J.   3211
Libya's most isolated field nears
operation.
World petroleum 37. 1966, n. 9,
p. 24-26, 29-30.

Wells, M.J.   3212
ESSO in Libya - Atsham to gas ex-
port.
World petroleum 38. 1967, n. 3,
p. 40-45.

Agriculture.

Catalogo di memorie, rela-   3213
zioni e documenti di ca-
rattere prevalentemente economico
esistenti presso il centro di docu-
mentazione. Osservatorio di Economia Rurale.   1.

Catalogo di memorie, ...   3213
Firenze: Istituto Agronomico per
l'Oltremare 1969.

                                    2.

Catalogo generale delle   3214
pubblicazioni 1966.
Firenze: Istituto Agronomico per
l'Oltremare 1966.
Supplemento fino al 31 marzo 1968
del ... 1968.

Contributo ad una biblio-   3215
grafia italiana sulla Libia
con particolare riferimento all'
agricoltura ed argomenti affini,
(fino al settembre 1952).
Firenze: Istituto Agronomico per
l'Oltremare 1953.

FAO documentation. 3216
Current index.
Rome: FAO Documentation Center.
1967-

Special index. 3217
Rome: FAO Documentation Center
1966-
DC/SP 1. FAO technical assistance
 reports (1951-65).
DC/SP 2. Fisheries (1945-66). 1.

Special index. 3217
DC/SP 3. FAO/UNDP (SF) project re-
 ports (1963-66).
DC/SP 4. Forestry (1945-66).
DC/SP 5. Plants (1945-66).
DC/SP 6. Animals (1945-66). 2.

Special index. 3217
DC/SP 7. Nutrition (1945-66).
DC/SP 8. Land and water (1945-66).
DC/SP 9. Rural institutions (1945-
 66).
DC/SP 10. Statistics (1945-66). 3.

Zanutto, S. 3218
Saggio di bibliografia giuridico-
agraria coloniale. Anni 1937, 1938,
1939.
Roma 1940.

Agricultural statistics 3219
estimates for Tripolitania
1950-59.
Tripoli: Nazirate of Agriculture
1960.

Agricultural statistics in 3220
Cyrenaica 1954-1958.
Benghazi: Nazirate of Agriculture nd.

Agricultural statistics for 3221
Cyrenaica 1959.
Tripoli: Nazirate of Agriculture
1960.

Agricultural statistics 3222
in Libya.
Tripoli: Ministry of Agriculture
1963.

Babic, B. 3223
Development of agricultural stati-
stics.
Rome: FAO 1967.
(Report 2355.)

Census of Agriculture 1960. 3224
Report and tables.
Tripoli: Ministry of Agriculture
1962.

Dilwali, C.K. 3225
Report on the pilot project for
central tabulation of the agricultural census data for the United
Kingdom of Libya by electronic
computers. 1.

Dilwali, C.K. 3225
Rome: FAO 1962.

2.

Évolution de la production 3226
agricole durant les années
1956-1966.
Syrie et monde arabe 15. 1968, n.171,
p. 62-67.

Kohli, D.R. 3227
System of agricultural statistics in
Libya.
v. Lectures presented ... 1968, n.20,
 p. 143-146, n.3404.

Kroeller, E.H. 3228
Lectures on agricultural statistics.
Rome: FAO 1959.

Kroeller, E.H.   3229

Agricultural statistics in Libya.
Rome: FAO 1962.
(Report 1480.)

Market returns (quantities   3230
and prices) of the fonduks
in Cyrenaica.
Benghazi: Nazirate of Agriculture
1958.

Mascaro, T. - Palloni, G.   3231

Primo censimento delle aziende agricole metropolitane della Libia al
21 aprile 1937.
AAI 1. 1938, vol. 2, p. 641-663.

Meat production in Cyrenaica   3232
1955-1958.
Benghazi: Nazirate of Agriculture nd.

Meat production in Libya.   3233
Tripoli: Ministry of Agriculture.
1. 1963-

Monthly bulletin of agri-   3234
cultural statistics.
Tripoli: Nazirate of Agriculture nd.

Production of olive oil,   3235
wine, milk, eggs, wool,
hides/skins and honey in Cyrenaica
1955-1958.
Benghazi: Nazirate of Agriculture nd.

Report of the 1960 world   3236
census of agriculture.
Vol. 1, part B. Census results by
countries.
Rome: FAO 1967.

Retail prices of agricultural   3237
commodities in Libya in 1965.
Tripoli: Ministry of Agriculture nd.

Situazioni statistiche della   3238
colonizzazione agraria in
Tripolitania 1914-1929.
Camera di Commercio, Industria e
Agricoltura della Tripolitania.
Tripoli 1930.

Some agricultural statistics-   3239
Libya. 1965-66 and 1966-67.
Tripoli: Ministry of Agriculture
1968.

Some data on agricultural   3240
statistics in Libya. Estima-
tes made in 1964/65.
Tripoli: Ministry of Agriculture nd.

The use of fertilizers in   3241
1964.
Tripoli: Ministry of Agriculture
1965.

Wholesale prices of certain   3242
agricultural commodities
April 1964-March 1965.
Tripoli: Ministry of Agriculture nd.

Yearly bulletin of price   3243
statistics.
Tripoli: Ministry of Agriculture.
1964 (1965).

Abu-Oaf, S.   3244

Legal rights on tribal land and
water rights in the pilot area (El
Useta and El Hania, Jebel el Akhdar).
Tripoli: NASA 1967.

Abu-Oaf, S.   3245

Legal aspects of tribal lands and
settlements in Libya.
Rome: FAO 1969.
(DTLSP 4,3.)

Abu Sharr, I.   3246

Crop agronomy and improvement in
Cyrenaica.
Rome: FAO 1962.
(Report 1577.)

Adragna, A.   3247

Improvements of fishing methods.
Rome: FAO 1965.
(Report 2082.)

L'agricoltura e la pastorizia 3248
indigena in Tripolitania nel
1930.
REAI 19. 1931, p. 340-346.

The agricultural economy of   3249
Libya.
Wash.: U.S. Dept. of Agriculture
1956.

Agricultural education and   3250
training in Algeria, Libya,
Malta ...
Rome: FAO 1963.

Agriculture in the North   3251
African subregion.
Economic bulletin for Africa 9.
1969, n. 2, p. 51-77.

Agriculture is the most   3252
likely sector for
resources development.
Financial times 1969, 6.3., p. 23.

Ahmad, N.A.   3253

Die ländlichen Lebensformen und die
Agrarentwicklung in Tripolitanien.
Heidelberg: Geographisches Institut
der Universität 1969.
(Heidelberger geogr. Arbeiten. 25.)

Allan, J.A.   3254

Recent developments in agriculture
in Libya with special reference to
areas close to Tripoli.
Bulletin of the faculty of arts.
University of Libya 3. 1969, p.37-

Allan, J.A.   3255

Some recent developments in Libyan
agriculture.
Middle East economic papers. Beirut
1969, p. 1-17.

Alwan, A.S.   3256

A field study of the customary
system of land tenure and related
problems in the mutassarrifia of
Agedabia.
Benghazi 1963.

Animal husbandry, production   3257
and health. Country study
1966. Libya.
Rome: FAO, Animal Production and
Health Division 1966-67.

Anni XII - XVIII.   3258
Ente per la Colonizzazione
della Libia.
Roma 1940.

Arif, M.   3259

Agricultural education in North East
Africa.
Rome: FAO 1965.

Arif, M.   3260

Report on visit to Libya, 17 April -
8 May 1967.
Cairo: FAO Regional Office 1967.

Arnott, N.M.H.   3261

Improvement of the sheep industry.
Rome: FAO 1959.
(Report 1123.)

Arnott, N.M.H.   3262

Livestock production.
Rome: FAO 1963.
(Report 1653.)

Asciak, J.J.   3263

Fishery administration and planning.
Rome: FAO 1964.
(Report 1858.)

Ballico, P.   3264

Il convegno agricolo di Misurata
(Tripolitania), 3-4 luglio 1954.
RAST 48. 1954, p. 218-234.

Ballico, P.   3265

Le esperienze italiane di avvaloramento agricolo in Tripolitania ed
in altri paesi d'oltremare e le prospettive della colonizzazione agricola.
Universo 38. 1958, p. 57-80.

Ballico, P.   3266

Gli italiani e la valorizzazione
agricola della Libia.
Italiani nel mondo 26. 1970, n. 18,
p. 3-7.

Barbosi, G.   3267

Die Entwicklung der Kolonisation in
Libyen.
Italien-Jahrbuch 1939, p. 175-189.

Barbosi, G.   3268

Cooperative agricole per i coloni
della Libia.
Atti del convegno di studi coloniali
2. 1947, p. 298-301.

Bartolozzi, E.   3269

Il regime del credito agrario nelle
colonie italiane.
REAI 21. 1933, p. 552-570.

Bartolozzi, E.   3270

Esempi di abitazioni rurali per agri-
coltori libici.
RAST 51. 1957, p. 413-424.

Bartolozzi, E.   3271

Esempi di costruzioni rurali nella
Tripolitania.
RAST 51. 1957, p. 299-312.

Basilici, C.   3272

L'armata del lavoro (il nuovo ciclo
della colonizzazione in Libia).
AAI 1. 1938, vol. 3-4, p. 745-760.

Bastawi, N.   3273

Home economics in the development of
tribal lands and settlements project.
Rome: FAO 1969.
(DTLSP 4,6.)

Battistella, G.   3274

Il credito agrario in Cirenaica.
REAI 22. 1934, p. 608-617.

Battistella, G.   3275

Il credito agrario in Tripolitania.
REAI 22. 1934, p, 587-607.

Battistella, G.   3276

Le crédit agricole en Libye.
Crédit agricole 1939, p. 431-441.

Battistella, G. 3277

Il credito agrario e fondiario in Africa. Cassa di Risparmio della Libia. Vol. 1.2.
Tripoli/Roma 1941.

Bellucci, A. 3278

Impressioni sulle attuali condizioni agricole.
CGEP 1923, p. 123-134.

Berardinis, G. de 3279

Aspetti economici della colonizzazione demografica in Libia.
AAI 4. 1941, vol. 2, p. 405-473.

Bignami, P. 3280

Tra i colonizzatori in Tripolitania.
Bologna 1931.

Bonacelli, B. 3281

L'antica cereacoltura africana.
ACSC 1. 1931, vol. 2, p. 134-145.

Boothby, D.G. 3282

Livestock development.
Rome: FAO 1970.
(Report 2836.)

Borlaug, N.E. 3283

Preliminary report of the third international spring wheat yield nursery 1966-67. Locations yield in kilos per hectare.
Rome: FAO 1968.

Bottomley, J.A. 3284

Agricultural credit in Tripolitania.
University of Virginia 1961. Diss.

Bottomley, J.A. 3285

The effect of the common ownership of land upon resource allocation in Tripolitania.
Land economics 39. 1963, p. 91-95.

Bourgois, F. 3286

The present situation of the Libyan fisheries.
Rome: FAO 1958.
(Report 817.)

Briotti, J. 3287

Il "waqf" in Libia.
Roma 1936.

Brown, R.W. 3288

Libya's rural sector.
Africa report 12. 1967, April, p. 16-18.

Buren, H.T. van 3289

The sponge fishing industry in Libya, Africa.
Wash.: GPO 1949.
(Fishery leaflet. 341.)

Buru, M. 3290

Derna - a study in local agriculture.
FSL 1960, p. 77-84.

Cairano, V. di 3291

L'invasione delle cavallette in Tripolitania nel 1932.
REAI 20. 1932, p. 977-1018.

Canady, H.M. 3292

Agricultural economy of Libya.
Wash.: GPO 1956.
(Foreign Agriculture Service. Miscellaneous. 1.)

Cappelletti, F. - Meliczek, H. 3293
Singh, H.

Prospects and proposals for land
settlement projects in Fezzan.
Rome/Tripoli: FAO 1966.

Cappelletti, F.   3294

Land settlement in western and
southern regions of Libya, formerly
Tripolitania and Fezzan.
Rome: FAO 1967.
(Funds-in-trust for Libya. 94.)

Cappelletti, F.   3295

Land settlement in western and
southern governates of Libya, formerly Tripolitania and Fezzan.
Rome: FAO 1967/69.
(DTLSP 4,4.)

Carbonara, P.   3296

Recenti aspetti della colonizzazione demografica della Libia.
Architettura 1939, n. 4, p. 249-
261.

Carocci Buzi, V.   3297

Agricoltura tropicale e subtropica-
le con particolare riferimento all'
Africa italiana.
Firenze 1938.
(Biblioteca di studi coloniali. 3.)

Cattaneo, V.   3298

Il contratto colonico nel quadro
della colonizzazione demografica
della Libia.
RSAI 6. 1943, p. 10-30.

Cavazza, F.   3299

La politica della colonizzazione.
La rinascita della Tripolitania.
Milano 1926, p. 187-237.

Cavazza, F.   3300

Importanza sociale della pastorizia
in Libia.
REAI 25. 1937, p. 771-780.

Cillis, E. de   3301

La colonizzazione agraria in Tripolitania. Impressioni di un viaggio e
di una relazione.
AIn 43. 1924, p. 103-109.

Cillis, E. de   3302

La valorizzazione agraria.
La rinascita della Tripolitania.
Milano 1926, p. 417-459.

Cles, F.O. von   3303

Libyen als kolonisatorische Leistung.
Revolution im Mittelmeer. Ed. P.
Schmidt. Berlin 1940, p. 93-110.

Coldefy, F.   3304

Notes sur la propriété terrienne au
Fezzân.
Paris: CHEAM 1946.
(Publication 2050.)

La colonizzazione della   3305
Cirenaica. Istituto Agricolo
Coloniale, Firenze. 2nd ed.
Roma: Tipografia del Senato 1947.

Colonizzazione demografica in-   3306
tensiva in Libia. Note istrutti-
ve per i coloni. Ente per la Colonizzazione della Libia.
Tripoli 1941.

La colonizzazione in Tripoli-   3307
tania nel 1923. Ufficio di
Colonizzazione del Governo della
Tripolitania.
RdT 1. 1924/25, p. 3-40.

Colucci, M.   3308

La proprietà fondiaria in Cirenaica.
CGEP 1923, p. 143-158.

Colucci, M. 3309
Il regime della proprietà fondiaria
nell'Africa italiana. Vol. 1. Libia.
Bologna 1942.
(Manuali coloniali.)

Corò, F. 3310
Il miracolo della colonizzazione
nell'oasi di Gadames.
Libia 4. 1940, n. 10, p. 9-12.

Cravino, A. 3311
Vedute economiche della Tripolitania.
Milano 1927.

Cultivation of the olive tree 3312
in Libya.
Rome: FAO, Plant Production and Protection Division 1963.

Curis, G. 3313
Studio sulla proprietà fondiaria in
Libia.
Napoli 1920.

Dalmasso, G. 3314
La viticoltura in Cirenaica.
Annali dell'Accademia di Agricoltura
di Torino 109. 1966-67, p. 81-116.

Damiano, A. - Parrini, U. 3315
L'agrumicoltura in Tripolitania.
RAST 55. 1961, p. 369-381.

Damiano, A. - Parrini, U. 3316
La coltivazione dell'arachide in
Tripolitania.
RAST 55. 1961, p. 156-162.

Damiano, A. - Parrini, U. 3317
La coltivazione della patata in Tri-
politania.
RAST 55. 1961, p. 301-308.

Damiano, A. 3318
List of species of noxious insects
recorded for Libya until 1960.
Tripoli: Nazirato dell'Agricoltura,
Sezione di Entomologia 1961.

Damiano, A. 3319
Prove di lotta mediante aereo contro
la mosca delle olive in Tripolitania.
RAST 56. 1962, p. 374-380.

Damiano, A. 3320
Rassegna dei principali casi entomo-
logici osservati in Tripolitania nel
1960.
RAST 56. 1962, p. 21-37.

Damiano, A. 3321
I parassiti dannosi all'olivo in Tri-
politania.
RAST 57. 1963, p. 447-462.

Damiano, A. 3322
Gli acari degli agrumeti in Tripoli-
tania.
RAST 58. 1964, p. 354-361.

Damiano, A. 3323
Contributo alla conoscenza della
Carpocapsa pomonella L. in Tripolita-
nia.
RAST 58. 1964, p. 214-227.

Damiano, A. 3324
Contributo alla conoscenza della Ca-
sama innotata Walker, Lepidottero
Limantriide dannoso all'Acacia
karroo in Tripolitania.
RAST 59. 1965, p. 143-148.

Damiano, A.   3325

Osservazioni sulle piante ospiti
secondarie della Ceratitis capitata
Wied, condotte in Tripolitania nel
1964.
RAST 59. 1965, p. 482-485.

Damiano, A.   3326

Osservazioni sulla biologia della
Cacaecimorpha pronubana Hub. in Tri-
politania.
RAST 60. 1966, p. 164-177.

Damiano, A.   3327

Prove di lotta contra il Dacus oleae
Gml. e la Pericerya purchasi Maskell
condotte in Tripolitania (Libia) durante il 1964 con nuovi insetticidi
fosforganici.
RAST 60. 1966, p. 49-52.

Damiano, A.   3328

Contributo alla conoscenza della
biologia della Sesamia cretica Led.
(Lepidoptera Agrotidae) in Tripolitania.
RAST 61. 1967, p. 261-270.

Damiano, A.   3329

Evaluation of some new organic-
phosphorus compounds against fruit-
fly in Tripolitania.
Rome: FAO 1967.

Damiano, A.   3330

Olive pests in Tripolitania and control methods.
Rome: FAO 1967.

Damiano, A.   3331

Principali parasitti animali dannosi
alle piante da frutto in Tripolitania.
RAST 62. 1968, p. 357-370.

Damiano, A.   3332

Contributo alla conoscenza dell'
entomo-fauna libica.
RAST 63. 1969, p. 129-139.

Demiruren, A.S.   3333

Improvement of sheep and goat pro-
duction.
Rome: FAO 1966.
(Report 2164.)

The desert locust situation   3334
in Northwest Africa and
neighbouring countries - May 1968 to
April 1969.
Rome: FAO Plant Production and Protection Division 1969.

Despois, J.   3335

Colonisation italienne en Libye.
Paris: CHEAM 1941.
(Publication 57.)

Deux colonisations: Djefara   3336
tripolitaine et Tunisie
centrale.
Afrique française 44. 1934, p. 679-
681, 731-734.

Dibbs, J.L.   3337

Fishery policy and administration.
Rome: FAO 1960.
(Report 1289.)

Din Noah, S. el   3338

Extension, education and training
for the development of land settlements in Libya.
Rome: FAO 1969.
(DTLSP 4,5.)

Dowson, V.H.W.   3339

Date production.
Rome: FAO 1961.
(Report 1263.)

Eberhard, A.   3340

Farm implements.
Rome: FAO 1963.
(Report 1645.)

Eldblom, L. 3341

Structure foncière: organisation et structure sociale. Une étude comparative sur la vie socio-économique dans les trois oasis libyennes de Ghat, Mourzouk et particulière- 1.

Eldblom, L. 3341

ment Ghadamès.
Lund: Uniskol 1968.
(Meddelande från Lunds Universitets Geografiska Institution. Avhandlingar 55.) 2.

Elwy, E.A. 3342

Report on a mission to Libya, 14 September - 21 November 1966.
Rome: FAO 1967.

Emeish, A. 3343

Grades, standards and quality control in Libya.
v. Lectures presented ... 1968, n.7, p. 49-54.

Emmrich, C.O. 3344

Outlook for production and trade of selected horticultural products in Mediterranean countries. Report on Libya.
Rome: FAO 1967.

Enix, J.R. 3345

A feasibility study of grain storage and mixed feed manufacturing in Libya. Agency for International Development. 1.
Springfield, Va.: Clearing House for

Enix, J.R. 3345

Federal Scientific and Technical Information 1963.

2.

Ezzat, M.A.W. 3346

Development of tribal land and settlement project in Libya.
Benghazi 1963.

Fantoli, A. 3347

Le antiche colonizzazioni della Libia nei rapporti con l'ambiente fisico.
RdC 7. 1933, p. 780-795.

Fantoli, A. 3348

Le isole del golfo di Bomba e le prime basi della colonizzazione greca in Cirenaica.
Universo 37. 1957, p. 1051-1066.

Farouky, S.T. 3349

Report on the present status of agricultural education in Libya.
Cairo: FAO Regional Office 1963.

Ferree, P.J. 3350

Libya - profile of a promising farm market.
Foreign agriculture 6. 1968, n. 48, p. 7-9.

Finocchiaro, M. 3351

La colonizzazione e la trasformazione fondiaria in Libia attraverso le sue fasi 1914 - 1966.
Roma 1968.

Fioretti, G. 3352

La colonizzazione agraria in Libia.
RdC 12. 1938, p. 1047-1061.

Une formule nouvelle de 3353
collaboration démographique
à forme corporative. L'essor agricole de la Cyrénaïque.
Renseignements coloniaux 1932, p.432-437.

Francesco-Menotti, G. de 3354

Il demanio pubblico nelle colonie libiche.
Annali dell'Istituto di Scienze Giuridiche, Economiche, Politiche e Sociale della R. Università di Messina 1/2. 1927.

Franchi, A.   3355

Pastorizia e zooproduzione in Cirenaica.
REAI 16. 1928, p. 377-401.

Fratepietro, C.   3356

Agricoltura e politica coloniale in
Tripolitania.
Foggia 1932.

Fujinami, N.   3357

Report of travel to Libya from 7 -
10 August 1967.
Rome: FAO 1967.

Gabrielli, A.   3358

Natura giuridica delle concessioni
agrarie in Libia.
Riv. di diritto agrario 1942, p.214-
231.

Galpin, S.H.   3359

Processing, grading and packing of
agricultural produce with special reference to the Derj project.
Rome: FAO 1966.
(Funds-in-trust for Libya. 2.)

Gaudio, A.   3360

Plan de développement rural en Tunisie et en Libye.
Mediterranea 1964, n. 3-4, p. 196-
207.

Ghonemy, M.R. el   3361

The development of tribal lands and
settlements in Libya.
Information on land reform, land
settlement and co-operatives (FAO)
1965, n. 1, p. 20-31.

Ghonemy, M.R. el   3362

Land policy in the Near East. Proceedings of the Development Center
on Land Policy and Settlement for
the Near East. Tripoli 16-28.10.1965.
Rome: FAO for the government of
Libya 1967.

Gnecco, A.   3363

Aspetti di diritto agrario libico.
Milano 1939.
(Pubblicazioni dell'Istituto di
 Diritto Agrario. R. Università di
 Roma. 3.)

Godard, J.   3364

Le djebbad du Fezzân. D'après une
enquête menée à Mourzouk en 1950
par l'auteur.
Cahiers de Tunisie 5. 1957, p. 45-
55.

Godard, J.   3365

La condition du djebbad au Fezzân.
Paris: CHEAM 1958.
(Publication 2851.)

Goetzsche, N.O.   3366

A report on the initial planning of
a municipal abattoir in Tripoli,
Libya.
Rome: FAO 1961.

Grasselli Barni, A.   3367

Il villaggio del Guarscià e la colonizzazione cirenaica.
Roma 1928.

Gregorio, D. de   3368

La conquista della terra in Libia.
Palermo 1940.

Grober, J.   3369

Die medizinischen, hygienisch-tech-
nischen und sozialen Hilfsmittel
der italienischen Ackerbausiedlun-
gen im Mutterlande und in den Kolo-
Jena 1941.   └nien.

Grumblat, W.E.H.   3370

Marketing, grading and inspection
of agricultural products.
Rome: FAO 1964.
(Report 1870.)

Guatelli, M.   3371

Profili economici della colonizzazione intensiva demografica in Libia.
REAI 28. 1940, p. 13-17.

Guidotti, R.   3372

Agrumicoltura in Tripolitania.
RAST 49. 1955, p. 113-116.

Haddad, A.   3373

Grain storage in Libya.
v. Lectures presented ... 1968,
    n. 9, p. 64-66.

Haider, M.S.   3374

Cadastral survey and land registra-
tion in Libya.
Rome: FAO 1969.
(DTLSP 4,2.)

Hajjaji, S.A.   3375

The land use patterns and rural
settlement in the Benghazi plain.
Durham: Dept. of Geography 1969.
Diss.

Harding, C.F.   3376

Improvement of flaying and curing
of hides and skins.
Rome: FAO 1956.
(Report 441.)

Herbicide trials for the   3377
control of Cynodon dactylon
in olive trees plantation.
Rome: FAO 1967.
Tripoli: Ministry of Agriculture
1967.

Herkommer, J.   3378

Die Kolonisation Libyens.
Freiburg i.B. 1941. Diss.

Herzog, R.   3379

Kritische Bemerkungen zur nordafrikanischen Pfluggrenze.
Veröffentlichungen des Instituts für
deutsche Volkskunde Berlin 13. 1957,
p. 198-213.

Hill, R.W.   3380

Agriculture and irrigation of the
Tripolitanian Jefara. Vol. 1-3.
Durham: Dept. of Geography 1960.
Diss.

Hilmi, H.A.   3381

Report on a visit to Libya.[Forestry]
Rome : FAO 1967.

Hoorn, G.C. van   3382

Improvements of hides, skins, leather
and leather articles.
Rome: FAO 1958.
(Report 975.)

Hoorn, G.C. van   3383

Establishment and operation of a
pilot tannery.
Rome: FAO 1964.
(Report 1902.)

Horticulture in the Mediterra-   3384
nean area. Outlook for production and trade.
Rome: FAO 1968.
(Commodity bulletin series. 42.)

Ibrahim, M.F.   3385

The cooperative movement in Libya.
Rome: FAO 1968.
(Report 2466.)

Jawhary, S.H. el   3386

Land settlement program in Libya.
Rome: FAO/United Nations 1966.
(World land reform conference.
Country paper Libya.)

Jawhary, S.H. el   3387

Present land settlement policy and
projects in Libya.
v. Ghonemy 1967, n. 3362, p. 137-151.

Jibouri, H.A. al   3388

Field crop production and improve-
ment in Cyrenaica.
Rome: FAO 1965.
(Report 2055.)

Jibouri, H.A. al   3389

Objectives of barley breeding in
Libya.
Rome: FAO 1965.

Jibouri, H.A. al   3390

Objectives of wheat breeding in
Libya.
Rome: FAO 1965.

Jibouri, H.A. al   3391

Wheat and barley improvement in
Libya.
Information bulletin ... FAO Regional Office Cairo 2. 1965, n. 3,
p. 1-4.

Jibouri, H.A. al   3392

Description and distribution of
wheat and barley varieties grown in
Libya.
Rome: FAO 1966.

Jibouri, H.A. al   3393

Field crop production and improve-
ment.
Rome: FAO 1966.
(Report 2133.)

Jibouri, H.A. al   3394

Note on wheat rusts in Libya.
FAO plant protection bulletin 14.
1966, n. 3, p. 58-59. Information
bulletin ... FAO Regional Office
Cairo 4. 1967, n. 1, p. 24-26.

Jibouri, H.A. al   3395

Wheat growing in Libya.
World crops 18. 1966, June, p. 25-
30.

Jones, J.R. - Tileston, F.M.   3396

Progress report on proposed land
reclamation and resettlement project near Bir el Ghnem, Tripolitania.
Wash.: USGS open-file report 1963.

Jongmans, D.G. - Jager Ger-   3397
lings, J.H.

Enkele sociaal-economische aspecten
van de landbouw in de oasen van de
Fezzan.   1.
Tijdschrift van het K. Nederlandsch

Jongmans, D.G. - ...   3397

Aardrijkskundig Genootschap 2. R.
77. 1960, p. 70-90.

                                    2.

Khan, M.H.   3398

Development of veterinary services.
Rome: FAO 1965.
(Report 1996.)

Klitzsche de la Grange, A.   3399

La proprietà fondiaria in Libia
(cenno storico).
RSAI 3. 1940, p. 121-129, 2. 1939,
p. 1327-1336.

Kranz, J.   3400

Plant disease in Cyrenaica.
FAO plant protection bulletin 10.
1962, p. 121-125.

Lanfry, J.   3401

Le mesurage du grain sur l'aire à
battre a Ghadamès.
IBLA 7. 1944, n. 28, p. 472-373.

Lanfry, J.   3402

Chronique de Ghadamès. Avant-propos:
autorité coutumière et droit
coutumier.
IBLA 8. 1945, n. 32, p. 367-383.

Lassoued, H.   3403

Alfa as a raw material for the manu-
facture of pulp for paper making,
checking during processing.
Cairo: FAO Regional Office/UNESCO
1963.

Lectures presented at the   3404
National Training Center on
Agricultural Marketing Tripoli
30.9. - 26.10. 1967.
Tripoli: Ministry of Agriculture and
Animal Wealth, Dept. of Planning and
Agricultural Economics 1968.

La legislazione agraria dell'   3405
Africa italiana.
Osservatorio Italiano di Diritto
Agrario, Ministero dell'Africa Ita-
liana.
Roma 1941.

Le Houerou, H.N.   3406

Improvement of natural pastures and
fodder resources.
Rome: FAO 1965.
(Report 1979.)

Leone, E. de   3407

La colonizzazione dell'Africa del
Nord (Algeria, Tunisia, Marocco,
Libia). Vol. 1.2.
Padova: CEDAM 1957-60.

Leone, G.   3408

Le dune mobili della Tripolitania ed
i risultati ottenuti con l'opera di
rimboschimento (1925).
RdT 1. 1924/25, p. 385-410.

Leone, G.   3409

Colonizzazione rurale di popolamento
in Tripolitania.
REAI 17. 1929, p. 448-464.

Leone, G.   3410

Le provvidenze di governo per la bonifica agraria e per la colonizzazione di popolamento in Tripolitania.
Roma 1930.

Leone, G.   3411

Osservazioni e deduzioni sulle possibilità agricole in Tripolitania in
relazione al clima.
ACSC 1. 1931, vol. 6, p. 250-262.

Leone, G.   3412

La tecnica adottata per l'avvaloramento forestale delle dune mobili
della Tripolitania ed i risultati
conseguiti.
Roma 1931.   1.

Leone, G.   3412

(Le colonie di diritto dominio. 6.)
REAI 19. 1931, p. 811-830.

                                    2.

Leone, G.   3413

La colonizzazione agraria della Tripolitania settentrionale nel suo
primo ventennio.
Roma 1933.

Leone, G.   3414

Le coltivazioni agrarie e gli ordinamenti aziendali nella Libia.
ASIPS 25. 1936, vol. 4, p. 389-400.

Le Riche, J.E.   3415

The management of public lands in
Libya.
Land tenure 1956, p. 632-633.

Lethielleux, J.   3416

La moisson au Fezzân.
IBLA 10. 1947, n. 39, p. 243-269.

Lethielleux, J.				3417

Au Fezzân: le calendrier agricole.
IBLA 11. 1948, p. 73-82.

Levi, C.				3418

L'alfa e lo sparto della Libia.
ASIPS 25. 1936, vol. 4, p. 367-381.

Libya. Libyan - London		3419
universities joint research
project, (Libyan university - London
university joint research project
on Libya). General report.
Benghazi: University of Libya 1969-
London: University of London,	1.

Libya. Libyan - London ...	3419
School of Oriental and African Stu-
dies 1969-
Vol. 1. Agriculture and the economic
		development of Libya.	2.
Vol. 2. Maps. Libya crop survey maps

Libya. Libyan - London ...	3419
		and general land use maps
		with an analysis of the agri-
		culture of western Libya by
		computer maps.		3.
Vol. 3. Tabulated data from question-

Libya. Libyan - London ...	3419
		naire surveys of Libya 1966/
		67 and western Libya 1967/68.
Vol. 4. A select map and air photo
		bibliography of Libya with
		special reference to coastal
		Libya.			4.

Lionti, R.				3420

Prove di coltivazione della barbabie-
tola da zucchero in Tripolitania.
RAST 54. 1960, p. 782-791.

List of plant diseases recorded 3421
in Libya.
Ministry of Agriculture and Animal
Wealth, Plant Protection Dept.,Libya.
Rome: FAO 1967.

Love, J.S.				3422

Tobacco production.
Rome: FAO 1961.
(Report 1330.)

MacLachlan, K.S.			3423

The Wadi Caam project: its social
and economic aspects.
FSL 1960, p. 70-76.

Mainardi, G.L.			3424

La pastorizia in Cirenaica.
CGEP 1923, p. 135-142.

Maize herbicides trial.		3425
Ministry of Agriculture and
Animal Wealth, Plant Protection Dept.
Libya.
Rome: FAO 1969.

Malan, F.				3426

Le tappe della colonizzazione demografica in Libia.
RSAI 3. 1940, p. 292-294.

Manetti, C.				3427

Aspetti della colonizzazione berbera
nell'Africa settentrionale.
AAI 4. 1941, vol. 1, p. 85-119.

Manetti, O.				3428

Culture, cereali e frutteti in Cirenaica.
AIn 39. 1920, fasc. 1.

Manzoni, G.				3429

Tecnica del consolidamento delle
dune in Cirenaica.
ACSC 2. 1934, vol. 6, p. 755-766.

Manzoni, G. 3430

Dati sull'opera di rimboschimento e
di ricostituzione di boschi dete-
riorati in Cirenaica.
REAI 23. 1935, p. 26-46.

Mariani, M. 3431

La coltivazione di frumenti duri
nella Cirenaica settentrionale.
RAST 51. 1957, p. 438-445.

Maroi, F. 3432

Il diritto agrario e il problema
della colonizzazione.
ASIPS 25. 1936, vol. 4, p. 433-443.

Marroni, U. 3433

L'agricoltura irrigua in Tripolitania.
RAST 48. 1954, p. 319-324.

Marshall, W.E. 3434

Annual report. Dept. of Forests.
Tripoli.
1958-59.
1959-60.

Marshall, W.E. 3435

Forestry in Tripolitania.
FSL 1960, p. 101-110.
Tripoli 1961.

Martin, H. 3436

Observations on the Mediterranean
fruit fly on citrus in Tripolitania,
Libya in 1952/53.
FAO plant protection bulletin
1. 1953, n. 9, p. 132-136.

Martin, H. 3437

Olive psyllid in Libya, 1953/54.
FAO plant protection bulletin
2. 1954, p. 184-186.

Martin, H. 3438

Scale insects on citrus in Tripolitania.
FAO plant protection bulletin
2. 1954, p. 113-116.

Martin, H. 3439

Pests and diseases of date palm in
Libya.
FAO plant protection bulletin
6. 1958, p. 120-123.

Martin, H. 3440

Plant protection.
Rome: FAO 1960.
(Report 1234.)

Marucchi, A. 3441

L'attività del Regio Istituto Sperimentale della Tripolitania.
AIn 35. 1916, p. 252-263.

Mason, I.L. 3442

Sheep breeds of the Mediterranean.
Farnham Royal, Bucks.: Commonwealth
Agricultural Bureaux 1967.

Mathieu, M. 3443

Quelques aspects de la vie rurale
traditionelle au Fezzân.
Correspondance d'orient. Etudes 1963,
n. 3, p. 18-35.

Maugini, A. 3444

L'agricoltura indigena.
CGEP 1923, p. 107-122.

Maugini, A. 3445

La pianura di Merg.
RdT 1. 1924/25, p. 245-264.

Maugini, A.   3446

L'avvaloramento agricolo della Libia sotto l'aspetto tecnico.
L'impero coloniale fascista. Novara
1936, p. 503-526.

Maugini, A.   3447

Riflessioni sull'agricoltura libica.
RAST 51. 1957, p. 3-18.

Maugini, A.   3448

L'avvaloramento e la colonizzazione.
Vol. 1. L'opera di avvaloramento
agricolo e zootecnico.
Roma: IPS 1969.
(L'Italia in Africa. Serie economi-
  co agraria. 1.)

Mazzarelli, G.   3449

I campi di pesca delle acque della
Libia, esplorati con la R.N. "Tri-
tone".
ASIPS 25. 1936, vol. 4, p. 314-319.

Mazzarelli, G.   3450

Come i banchi di spugne della Libia
vennero in possesso dello stato
italiano.
ASIPS 25. 1936, vol. 4, p. 320-321.

Mazzocchi, G.B.   3451

Allevamento della pecora barbaresca
in Cirenaica e suo miglioramento.
RAST 48. 1954, p. 364-374.

Mazzocchi, G.B.   3452

Arboricoltura sul Gebel Garian
(Tripolitania).
RAST 48. 1954, p. 341-350.

Mazzocchi, G.B.   3453

Report of the activities carried
out in Tripolitania in close cooperation with the Dept. of Agriculture and private farmers from 1955-60.
Tripoli nd.

Mazzocchi, G.B.   3454

Preliminary considerations of agriculture in Libya with suggestions
for their improvement.
Tripoli 1961.

Mazzocchi, G.B.   3455

Production of fruit and vegetables.
Rome: FAO 1962. 1966.
(Report 1351. 2134.)

Mazzocchi, G.B.   3456

Improvement of grape production in
Libya. Observations and suggestions
for improvement.
Rome: FAO 1963.

Mazzocchi, G.B.   3457

Improvement of various nuts cultivation in Libya.
Rome: FAO 1963.

Mazzocchi, G.B. - Pucci, E.   3458

Indagine preliminare sul fabbisogno
di freddo di diverse specie arboree
da frutto in Tripolitania.
RAST 57. 1963, p. 370-394.

Mazzocchi, G.B.   3459

Practical consideration of almond
tree plantation in Tripolitania.
Rome: FAO 1963.

Meliczek, H.   3460

The socio-economic conditions of 200
EX ENTE farm households in Cyrenaica.
Benghazi/Rome: FAO 1965/66.

Meliczek, H.   3461

Socio-economic conditions of 227
households living on EX ENTE farms
in the pilot area of the FAO tribal
lands and settlement project in
Cyrenaica.
Benghazi/Rome: FAO 1966.

Meliczek, H. 3462

The development of government farms
in the eastern region of Libya.
Rome: FAO 1967/69.
(DTLSP 4,1.)

Merrill, N.W. 3463

Libya needs machinery to expand
farm output, canning, freezing will
depend on rise in production.
International commerce 73. 1967,
n. 5, p. 7-8.

Micheli, A. 3464

Esperimenti zootecnici in Cirenaica.
RAST 46. 1952, p. 74-85.

Micheli, A. 3465

Esperienze e problemi dell'olivicoltura in Cirenaica.
RAST 47. 1953, p. 66-75.

Micheli, A. 3466

Esperienze di agricoltura cirenaica.
RAST 48. 1954, p. 358-363.

Micheli, D. de 3467

Acqua, macchine e uomini nella
valorizzazione della Tripolitania.
Atti del convegno di studi coloniali
2. 1947, p. 324-330.

Milone, F. 3468

La messa a coltura della Gefara
tripolina.
BSGI 66. 1929, p. 372-390.

Mininni Caracciolo, M. 3469

Vigor di vita in Tripolitania.
AIn 46. 1927, p. 278-282.

Mininni Caracciolo, M. 3470

Colonizzazione e credito in Libia.
AIn 47. 1928, p. 32-36.

Mite species in Libya. 3471
Ministry of Agriculture,
Plant Protection Dept., Libya.
Rome: FAO 1967.

Montagnac, H. 3472

Report on the agricultural product
processing industries in North
Africa - Algeria, Libya, Morocco,
Tunisia.
Rome: FAO 1964.

Monteverde, G. 3473

Valorizzazione zootecnica delle
steppe sirtiche e marmariche.
REAI 24. 1936, p. 186-199, 317-335.

Moore, M. 3474

Fourth shore. Italy's mass colonisation of Libya.
London 1940.

Morgantini, A.M. 3475

Commercio e statistiche dei prodotti agrari della Tripolitania.
Agricoltura libica 1941, giugno-
luglio, p. 226-249.

Nafie, E. 3476

Development of poultry production.
Rome: FAO 1968.
(Funds-in-trust for Libya. 94.)

Narducci, G. 3477

Il problema dell'agricoltura
e della pastorizia in Cirenaica.
AIn 35. 1916, p. 309-312.

Narducci, G.   3478

La colonizzazione della Cirenaica
nell'antichità e nel presente.
Bengasi 1934.

Narducci, G.   3479

Storia della colonizzazione della
Cirenaica.
Milano 1942.

Nematodes control trial.   3480
Ministry of Agriculture and
Animal Wealth, Plant Protection
Dept., Libya.
Rome: FAO 1967.

Niccoli, E.   3481

Industrie derivate dall'agricoltura
in Tripolitania.
RdT 1. 1924/25, p. 93-106.

Nicola, G. de   3482

La colonizzazione romana e quella
fascista.
AAI 3. 1940, vol. 4, p. 409-444.

Nixon, W.J.   3483

A new slaughterhouse for Tripoli.
Rome: FAO 1964.
(Report 1899.)

Nodari, L.   3484

Il nuovo ciclo demografico della
valorizzazione agraria della Libia.
Atti dei convegni "Volta" 8. 1938
"L'Africa", p. 540-556.

Norme relative alla colonizza- 3485
zione in Libia.
Governo della Libia. Direzione Affari Economici e Colonizzazione.
Tripoli 1939.

La nuova legislazione   3486
sulla valorizzazione agraria
della colonia. Governo della Tripolitania.
Tripoli 1929.

Nuttonson, M.Y.   3487

The physical environment and agriculture of Libya and Egypt ... with
special reference to their regions
containing areas climatically and
latitudinally analogous   1.

Nuttonson, M.Y.   3487

to Israel.
Wash.: American Institute of Crop
Ecology 1961.
(Studies of the American Institute
 of Crop Ecology. 23.)   2.

Observations and recommenda-   3488
tions on marketing of
pickled sheepskins.
Gallagher International, Inc., Agency for International Development.
Springfield, Va.: Clearing House for
                                 1.

Observations and ...   3488

Federal Scientific and Technical
Information nd.

                                 2.

Obst, J.   3489

Statik und Dynamik in der Agrarland-
schaft des Jabal al Akhdar/Libyen.
Ein Beitrag zur Agrargeographie
semi-arider Gebiete.
Frankfurt a.M.: Johann Wolfgang   1.

Obst, J.   3489

Goethe-Universität 1969. Habilita-
tionsschrift.

                                 2.

Ongaro, G.   3490

Pastorizia e colonizzazione musulmana della Libia.
RSAI 2. 1939, p. 675-680.

Oram, P.A. 3491
Crop agronomy and improvement in
Tripolitania.
Rome: FAO 1959.
(Report 1144.)

Ornato, G.Z. 3492
I "ventimila" al lavoro nelle terre
libiche.
Vie d'Italia 45. 1939, p. 36-47.

Palloni, G. 3493
I contratti agrari degli indigeni
in Cirenaica.
Agricoltura coloniale 30. 1936,
p. 241-251, 308-310, 343-350, 428-
432, 460-471.

Palloni, G. 3494
I contratti agrari degli enti di
colonizzazione in Libia.
Firenze: Sansoni 1945.
(Pubblicazioni del Centro di Studi
  Coloniali. 28.)

Palloni, G. 3495
Considerazioni sull'avvaloramento
agrario in Cirenaica.
RAST 48. 1954, p. 350-357.

Pan, C.L. 3496
The prospects of growing rice and
other irrigated crops in Fezzan
province.
Rome: FAO 1961.
(Report 1359.)

Papers presented at the 3497
session of the Near East
Plant Protection Commission.
Rome: FAO Plant Production and Protection Division.
2. 1967 (6.-13.5.) Tripoli,
3. 1969 (21.-28.4.) Karachi.

Peanuts seeds dressing 3498
trials during 1961-1966.
Ministry of Agriculture and Animal
Wealth, Plant Protection Dept.,
Libya.
Rome: FAO 1967.

Petrovich, A. 3499
Capitale ed uomo nelle tre fasi della colonizzazione metropolitana libica.
REAI 27. 1939, p. 274-281.

Plant protection law no. 27, 3500
1968.
Ministry of Agriculture and Animal
Wealth, Plant Protection Dept.,
Libya.
Rome: FAO 1969.

Prasisto, V.T. 3501
System of land rights and taxation
in Tripolitania.
Tripoli 1963.

Present status of diseases 3502
in Libya.
Ministry of Agriculture and Animal
Wealth, Plant Protection Dept.,
Libya.
Rome: FAO 1969.

Prinzi, D.G. 3503
Contratti agrari in Tripolitania.
RdC 7. 1933, p. 109-118, 191-200.

Prinzi, D.G. 3504
I rapporti di lavoro nella agricol-
tura indigena della Tripolitania.
Firenze 1936.
(Relazioni e monografie agrario-
  coloniali. 40.)

Prosdocimo, F. 3505
Il problema agrario-economico libico.
Atti del convegno di studi coloniali
2. 1947, p. 292-298.

Pryor, L.D. 3506
Aspects of afforestation with parti-
cular reference to eucalyptus.
Rome: FAO 1964.
(Report 1863.)

Pucci, E. 3507

Rassegna dei principali casi fitopa-
tologici osservati in Tripolitania.
RAST 54. 1960, p. 34-53.

Pucci, E. 3508

Prove di lotta contro diverse malattie delle piante eseguite presso il
centro agricolo di Sidi Mesri, Tripoli, Libia.
RAST 56. 1962, p. 156-170.

Pucci, E. 3509

Lista preliminare delle malattie delle piante osservate in Tripolitania
dal 1959 al 1964. Sintomi, danni,
lotta.
RAST 59. 1965, p. 337-375.

Pucci, E. 3510

"Pythium myriothylum" agente del
marciume dei baccelli di arachide in
Tripolitania.
RAST 63. 1969, p. 496-500.

Quilici, N. 3511

Ventimila coloni in Libia.
Emporium 88. 1938, p. 295-308.

Radha, A.N.K. 3512

Land tenure system in the northern
part of eastern region.
Rome: FAO 1967/69.
(DTLSP 4,7.)

Ramadan, M. - Fuad, J. 3513

Progress in wheat and barley improvement and production in Libya during
1965/69. Present and projected programmes and policies.
Rome: FAO 1969.

Rascovich, E.M. 3514

Analysis of marketing structure and
methods in Italy, Spain, Morocco and
Libya.
Cairo: FAO Regional Office 1960.

Rava, M. 3515

Esperienze e verità.
Oltremare 2. 1928, p. 213-216.

Report of the activities 3516
of the Plant Protection
Department.
Ministry of Agriculture and Animal
Wealth, Plant Protection Dept.,
Libya.
Rome: FAO 1967.

Report of the first FAO 3517
international technical
meeting on date production and processing, Tripoli, Libya 5.-11.12.
1959.
Rome: FAO 1960.

Report of the third session 3518
of the FAO Northwest African
Desert Locust Research and Control
Coordination Subcommittee, Tripoli,
Libya 2.-5.6. 1969.
Rome: FAO, Plant Production and Pro-
tection Division 1969.

Report on trials for weed 3519
control in peanuts.
Ministry of Agriculture and Animal
Wealth, Plant Protection Dept.,
Libya.
Rome: FAO 1969.

Report on trials of herbicides 3520
in tomato fields.
Ministry of Agriculture and Animal
Wealth, Plant Protection Dept.,
Libya.
Rome: FAO 1969.

Ricci, C. 3521

Grain handling equipment.
Rome: FAO 1962.
(Funds-in-trust for Libya. 69.)

Rio, E. del 3522

Nota sui lavori eseguiti dalla Sezione Tecnica de R. Ufficio Fondiario di Bengasi fino al 31 dicembre
1922.
Bengasi 1924.

Ritsch, W. 3523

Tripolitanien als Getreideland.
Wien 1940. Diss.

Rizzuti, A. 3524

Le concessioni agricole nelle colonie italiane.
Roma 1939.
(Collana di studi di diritto agrario "Ageo Arcangeli". 6.)

Robertson, E.I. 3525

Animal feeds.
Rome: FAO 1965.
(Report 1938.)

Romanelli, P. 3526

La vita agricola tripolitana attraverso le rappresentazioni figurate.
AIb 3. 1930, p. 53-75.

Rompietti, A. 3527

Le direttive tecniche dell'agricoltura tripolitana quali appaiono a
seguito dell'azione dell'Italia.
RAST 48. 1954, p. 324-341.

Rompietti, A. 3528

La colonizzazione contadina in Tripolitania.
RAST 55. 1961, p. 20-34.

Rossi, L. 3529

Le colture industriali della Libia.
REAI 26. 1938, p. 609-614.

Rossi, L. 3530

Panorama della colonizzazione libica.
REAI 26. 1938, p. 879-885.

Russo, M. 3531

L'agricoltura in Cirenaica. La funzione sperimentale dello stato nelle
fattorie.
AIn 37. 1918, p. 60-65.

Saitta, A. 3532

Il patrimonio zootecnico della Libia.
REAI 27. 1939, p. 1061-1068.

Saitta, A. 3533

Trent'anni di colonizzazione italiana in Libia.
REAI 29. 1941, p. 601-610.

Sanctis, G. de 3534

Repertorio di legislazione agraria
coloniale.
Roma 1943.
(Studi giuridici coloniali. 5.)

Santmyer, C. 3535

Libya's agricultural economy in brief.
U.S. Dept. of Agriculture.
Wash.: GPO 1966.
(Economic research service. Foreign
series 147.)

Sbordoni, R. 3536

Tripoli and Benghazi cold storages.
Rome: FAO 1958.
(Report 799.)

Schepis, G. 3537

Consistenza e distribuzione della
proprietà fondiaria rurale indigena
in Algeria, Tunisia e Tripolitania.
ASIPS 25. 1936, vol. 5, p. 345-382.

Serra, F. 3538

Appunti sul problema della colonizzazione in Cirenaica.
CGEP 1923, p. 159-180.

I servizi zootecnici in   3539
Tripolitania.
REAI 17. 1929, p. 76-94.

Il servizio veterinario   3540
militare della Tripolitania.
REAI 17. 1929, p. 312-335.

Il settore cartario nei prin-   3541
cipali paesi extraeuropei
del bacino mediterraneo. La Libia.
Cellulosa e carta 1964, n. 9.

Sgaier, K.   3542
The development of groundnuts in
Libya.
FSL 1960, p. 85-87.

Sgaier, K.   3543
Government policy for stabilization
of prices of agricultural products
in Libya.
v. Lectures presented ...1968, n.26,
   p. 177-178.

Shah, F.A.   3544
Report on the marketing of fruit
and vegetables in Libya.
Rome: FAO 1968.

Shah, F.A.   3545
Definition and importance of agricultural marketing.
v. Lectures presented ... 1968, n.1,
   p. 1-9.

Sherif, S.R.   3546
Some aspects of marketing in Libya.
Cairo: FAO Regional Office 1960.

Short notes on the biology   3547
of the codling moth in
Tripolitania.
Ministry of Agriculture and Animal
Wealth, Plant Protection Dept.,
Libya.
Rome: FAO 1967.

Siniscalchi, A.   3548
Aspetti demografico-sociali della
colonizzazione agraria in Libia.
AAI 6. 1943, vol. 1, p. 97-109.

Soghaier, A.A.K.   3549
Crop agronomy and improvement in
Cyrenaica.
Rome: FAO 1959.
(Report 1111.)

Soghaier, A.A.K.   3550
Crop agronomy and improvement in
Tripolitania.
Rome: FAO 1961.
(Report 1371.)

Spalletti, P.   3551
Contratti agricoli in Cirenaica.
RdC 3. 1929, p. 437-451, 573-597.

Statement (of the head) of the   3552
Libyan delegation.
v. Papers presented ... 1967, 1969,
   n. 3497.

Statera, V.   3553
La colonizzazione demografica della
Libia.
Roma 1942.

Stewart, J.H.   3554
Land and water resources of Tripolitania: a measurement of the land
and its potential.
Tripoli: USOM 1960.

Taussig, E.   3555

Hides, skins and leather industries.
Rome: FAO 1966.
(Report 2195.)

Taylor, A.R.   3556

Regional variations in olive cultivation in northern Tripolitania.
FSL 1960, p. 88-100.

Taylor, A.R.   3557

The olive in northern Tripolitania.
Vol. 1.2.
Durham: Dept. of Geography 1961.
Diss.

Taylor, S.M.   3558

Marketing and agricultural develop-
ment.
Rome: FAO 1965.
(Funds-in-trust for Libya 1.)

Taylor , W.J.V.   3559

Improvement of services to agricul-
ture.
Rome: FAO 1957.
(Report 641.)

Thrower, L.B.   3560

Banana growing in Derna/Cyrenaica,
Libya.
Rome: FAO 1960.

Trigona, G.   3561

Gli imboschimenti di duna nella
Libia occidentale.
ACSC 3. 1937, vol. 8, p. 343-354.

Tripolitania economica   3562
(la colonizzazione a tutto
il 1931). Camera di Commercio, Industria e Agricoltura della Tripolitania.
Tripoli 1931.

Tucci, F.   3563

La zootecnia nella (della) Tripoli-
tania.
RdT 1. 1924/25, p. 265-280.
La rinascita della Tripolitania.
Milano 1926, p. 521-533.

Vierzigtausend siedeln in   3564
Libyen.
Reichskolonialbund.
München 1940.

Vigano, G.C.   3565

Sviluppi della politica agraria in
Libia.
AIr 2. 1939, n. 3-4, p. 17-21.

Vitta, C.   3566

Il demanio coloniale in confronto
al demanio metropolitano.
ACSC 1. 1931, vol. 5, p. 240-246.

Vivoli, G.   3567

Problema ed ampiezza dell'irriguo
in Tripolitania.
Atti del convegno di studi coloniali
2. 1947, p. 243-250.

Voechting, F.   3568

Italienische Siedelung in Libyen.
Jahrbücher für Nationalökonomie und
Statistik 151. 1940, p. 129-162,
257-289.

Volpe, G.   3569

La formation de la petite propriété
dans les territoires libyques et les
fonctions du crédit agricole.
Crédit agricole 1939, p. 461-473.

Volta, R. dalla   3570

La nuova fase della colonizzazione
demografica in Libia.
Economia italiana 1939, marzo,
p. 291-301.

Volta, R. dalla   3571

La nouvelle phase de la colonisation
démographique en Libye.
Revue économique internationale
1939, avril, p. 25-35.

Social Conditions.
Labour.

Weis, H.   3572

Libyens grüner Wall. Aufforstung und
Wiederbesiedlung in der Cyrenaika
und in Tripolitanien.
Bustan 7. 1966, p. 17-24.

Abdeljaouad, A.   3579

Report on an I.L.O. contribution to
training programmes for labour administration officials in Iraq, Jor-
dan, Libya and Syria.
Geneva: ILO 1963.

Williamson, J.Q.   3573

Forestry education and training.
Rome: FAO 1964.

Anselmi, A.   3580

L'organizzazione delle assicurazioni sociali nelle colonie italiane.
ASIPS 25. 1936, vol. 4, p. 69-82.

Willimott, S.G. - Gilchrist, S. 3574
Frisby,M. - Clarke, J.I.

A development survey in Tripolitania.
World crops 13. 1961, p. 1-7, 131-
133, 191-193.

Arsharuni, N.A.   3581

Polozhenie rabochego klassa v Livii.
Narodui Azii i Afriki 1964, n. 1,
p. 37-43.

Wylie, G.M.   3575

Agricultural mechanization.
Rome: FAO 1965.
(Report 2060.)

Aslam, M.   3582

Report to the government of Libya
on labour legislation.
Geneva: ILO 1955.

Zagallaci, M.A.   3576

Role of credit in agricultural
marketing in Libya.
v. Lectures presented ... 1968, n.17,
    p. 122-126.

Assan, G.   3583

Donne di Libia.
Comunità 13. 1959, ottobre, p. 18-
21.

Zlitni, A.M. - Cowling, K.   3577

Exports, imports and consumption of
agricultural products in a rapidly
growing economy. The case of Libya.
Farm economist 11. 1966, n. 3,
p. 120-134.

L'assistenza sociale in Libia 3584
nell'anno 1939.
RSAI 3. 1940, p. 99-100.

Zucco, G.   3578

Risorse agricole della Cirenaica in
rapporto alla possibilità della loro
valorizzazione.
AIn 42.1923, p. 17-21, 31-38.

L'attività dell'Istituto Na-   3585
zionale Fascista della Previdenza Sociale per la colonizzazione demografica della Libia.
Roma 1939.

Basile-Giannini, R. - 3586
Pistolese, G.E.

Codice del lavoro dell'Africa italiana. Ministero dell'Africa Italiana.
Roma 1938. Suppl. 1. 1939.

Basile-Giannini, R. 3587
Gli assegni familiari nell'Africa
italiana.
RSAI 4. 1941, p. 540-548.

Bleuchot, H. 3588
Libye. Chronique sociale et culturelle.
AAN 5. 1966, p. 347-351, 6. 1967,
p. 408-414.

Bono, S. - Filesi, T. - 3589
Ziliotto, G.
Lavoro italiano in Africa e norme
per l'emigrazione.
Premesse al lavoro italiano in Afri-
ca. Roma 1958, p. 221-309.

Bottomley, A. 3590
Stability of income and employment
in an underdeveloped semi-desert
community.
Economia internazionale 17. 1964,
p. 301-316.

Cao-Pinna, M. 3591
Il razionamento in Libia.
REAI 29. 1941, p. 781-791.

La cassa mutua per i lavora- 3592
tori dell'industria e dell'
artigianato della Libia.
REAI 26. 1938, p. 426-428.

Castelbarco, G. 3593
L'ordinamento sindacale-corporativo
nella organizzazione delle colonie
italiane.
Milano 1934.

Changes in the social 3594
security scheme of Libya.
International labour review 86. 1962,
p. 586-589.

Charkiewicz, M. 3595
Labour force projections by sex and
age 1964-1978. ILO manpower assess-
ment and planning project for the
Kingdom of Libya.
Tripoli 1968.

Charkiewicz, M. 3596
Population trends in Libya, 1954-
1978. ILO manpower assessment and
planning project for the Kingdom of
Libya.
Tripoli 1968.

Culik, F. 3597
Notes on the agricultural employment
problems in Libya. ILO manpower
assessment and planning project for
the Kingdom of Libya.
Tripoli 1968.

Culik, F. 3598
Preliminary study on employment in
commerce in Libya. ILO manpower
assessment and planning project for
the Kingdom of Libya.
Tripoli 1968.

Culik, F. 3599
Preliminary study on employment in
transport, communication and storage
in Libya. ILO manpower assessment and
planning project for the Kingdom of
Libya.
Tripoli 1968.

Culik, F. 3600
Some aspects of future development
of manufacturing in Libya. ILO manpower assessment and planning project for the Kingdom of Libya.
Tripoli 1968.

Dajani, S.W. 3601
Family budget survey in Tripoli town
1962.
Tripoli: Central Statistics Office
1962.

Figuerda-Colon, A. 3602

Report to the government of Libya
on vocational training.
Geneva: ILO 1966.

Food balance sheet for 3603
Cyrenaica.
Benghazi: Nazirate of Agriculture
and Forests 1957.

Food balance sheet for 3604
Libya.
Tripoli: Census and Statistical
Dept. 1959.

Gatti, T. 3605

Gli aspetti antropologici, psicolo-
gici e statistici della criminalità
indigena della Libia.
Riv. di diritto penitenziario 1940,
p. 38-56.

Das Genossenschaftswesen 3606
in Libyen.
Archiv für Genossenschaftswesen
1. 1940, p. 52-68.

Giaccardi, A. 3607

L'ordinamento corporativo nelle
colonie italiane.
ACSC 1. 1931, vol. 5, p. 170-195.

Giaccardi, A. 3608

I corporativismo coloniale ed i più
recenti sviluppi dell'ordinamento
corporativo.
ACSC 2. 1934, vol. 5, p. 92-105

Giordani, I. 3609

Il problema delle assicurazioni private nelle nos·re colonie.
ASIPS 25. 1936, vol. 4, p. 83-91.

Gordon, D.O. 3610

Living costs and conditions in Libya.
Wash.: GPO 1957.
(World trade information service,
part 2 operations reports 57-19.)

Home economics in school and 3611
out-of-school programs.
FAO Nutrition Division.
Rome: FAO 1967.
(CEP report 40.)

Hull, W.J. 3612

Report to the government of Libya on
manpower and labour administration.
Geneva: ILO 1960.

L'Italia per i suoi 3613
sudditi musulmani.
RdC 12. 1938, p. 1177-1191.

Joukhadar, I. 3614

Report to the government of Libya on
labour legislation and labour administration.
Geneva: ILO 1966.

Kern, B. - Tamburi, G. 3615

Report to the government of Libya on
the administration of the National
Social Insurance Institution and the
investment of its funds.
Geneva: ILO 1964.

Krug, P. 3616

Veranderingen in de sociale structur
in Libië.
Tijdschrift van het K. Nederlandsch
Aardrijkskundig Genootschap 2. R.
53. 1963, p. 193-194.

Labour conditions in Libya. 3617
Wash.: GPO 1966.
(Labour digests 114.)

Labour force in Libya. 3618
Population census 1964,
paper no. 3.
Tripoli: Census and Statistical
Dept. nd.

Labour law in Libya. 3619
Royal decree embodying the
labour law.
Middle East law review 1. 1958,
p. 360-386.

Labour survey of North Africa. 3620
Geneva: ILO 1960.

Libya labour law of 1957. 3621
Beirut: Saba & Co. 1958.

Maghreb labor digest. 3622
A summary of labor news
of Algeria, Libya, Morocco ...
Los Angeles: University of Southern
California, School of International
Relations.
1. 1963-   ianc

Manpower and employment 3623
problems in Libya.
International labour review 85.
1962, p. 30-40.

Marsden, K. 3624
Report to the government of Libya
on the role of handicrafts in a
rapidly developing economy.
Geneva: ILO 1967.

Martin, Y. 3625
Les débuts du syndicalisme en Libye.
AAN 6. 1967, p. 279-293.

Massart, E. 3626
L'ordinamento sindicale della Libia.
ACSC 3. 1937, vol. 3, p. 109-118.

Mir, M.A. el 3627
Employment services in Libya.
Geneva: ILO 1961.

Mondaini, G. 3628
Colonie e corporativismo.
RdC 8. 1934, p. 919-936, 993-1005.

Mondaini, G. 3629
La partecipazione degli indigeni
all'onere tributario dell'Africa
italiana. 1. Libia (1912-1939).
REAI 27. 1939, p. 939-944.

Mondaini, G. 3630
Lavoro e legislazione sociale in
Libia (1912-1940).
RSAI 4. 1941, p. 133-138.

Monthly cost of living 3631
index for Tripoli town.
Tripoli: Census and Statistical
Dept.
1964-

Morgantini, A.M. 3632
Gruppi etnici e distribuzione della
ricchezza sul territorio di Tripoli.
Riv. di antropologia 35. 1944/47,
p. 438.

Nadeždin, A. 3633
Razvitie nacional'noj gosudarst-
vennosti v Livii.
Sovetskoe gosudarstvo i pravo
36. 1966, n. 2, p. 130-134.

Nair, A.N.K.   3634

Report to the government of the
Kingdom of Libya on the development
of a manpower information programme.
Geneva: ILO 1969.

Narducci, G.   3635

Polizia scientifica coloniale.
AIn 35. 1916, p. 216-219.

Nicholson, J.L.   3636

A survey of the living conditions
of Arab families in Tripolitania
in November-December 1950.
Revue de l'Institut International
de Statistique 22. 1954, p. 68-84.

Norman, J.   3637

Labor and politics in Libya and
Arab Africa.
New York: Bookman Associates 1965.

Note sur la situation en   3638
Libye.
np General Union of Libyan Students
1967.

Notiziario corporativo   3639
della Libia.
Governo della Libia.
Tripoli.
12. 1939-

Paleologos, J.T.   3640

Report to the government of Libya on
the extension of the social security
system.
Geneva: ILO 1954.

Paleologos, J.T.   3641

Report to the government of Libya on
the bringing into operation of the
social insurance law no. 53. of 1957.
Geneva: ILO 1959.

Paleologos, J.T. - Zampetti, G. 3642

Report to the government of Libya on
social insurance.
Geneva: ILO 1961.

Pergolesi, F.   3643

Corporativismo coloniale italiano.
Roma 1937.

Pergolesi, F.   3644

Diritto coloniale del lavoro.
Padova 1938.

Pergolesi, F.   3645

Istituzioni di diritto corporativo
aggiornate con la legislazione libica. 4th ed.
Bologna 1940.

Piccialuti, T.   3646

L'Istituto Nazionale Fascista della
Previdenza Sociale e la colonizza-
zione demografica in Libia.
REAI 26. 1938, p. 1088-1096.

Pirrò, C.   3647

La riforma dell'ordinamento sindacale della Libia.
RSAI 5. 1942, p. 5-11.

Poloni, C.   3648

Report on workers education in
Libya.
Geneva: ILO 1966.

Pozzolini, G.   3649

La mano d'opera indigena nelle aziende agrarie in Tripolitania.
Atti del convegno di studi coloniali
2. 1947, p. 253-257.

Prinzi, D. 3650
I contratti di lavoro nella colonizzazione demografica della Libia.
REAI 29. 1941, p. 753-771.

Profsoyuzui stran severnoi 3651
i severovostochnoi Afriki.
Moskva: Izd. VTSSPS Profizdat 1965.
(Profsoyuzui mira.)

Quadrotta, G. 3652
L'ordinamento corporativo in Libia.
IdO 2. 1937, n. 4, p. 5-9.

Rabochii klass i rabochee 3653
dvizhenie v stranakh Azii
i Afriki.
Akademija Nauk SSSR. Institut Narodov Azii.
Moskva: Nauka 1965.

Rabochii klass stran Azii 3654
i Afriki. Spravochnik.
Red. koll. A.A. Iskenderov ...
Moskva: Nauka 1964.

Report to the government of 3655
Libya on the technical and
clerical training centre, Tripoli.
Geneva: ILO/UNESCO 1961.

Rijn, C.P. van 3656
Report to the government of the
United Kingdom of Libya on a manpower information programme.
Geneva: ILO 1962.

Romano, E. 3657
Tutela del lavoro in Africa: il contratto d'impiego privato in Libia.
RSAI 3. 1940, p. 726-729.

Royal decree to promulgate 3658
a labour act. Dated 2.11.62.
Geneva: ILO 1964.
(Legislative series 3.)

Scaparro, M. 3659
Ordinamento sindacale-corporativo
della Libia.
Tripoli 1937.

Scaparro, M. 3660
Origini e sviluppi dell'ordinamento
corporativo libico.
REAI 25. 1937, p. 359-367.

Scaparro, M. 3661
Una associazione sindacale di lavoratori in Libia.
Tripoli 1941.

Sega, C. 3662
Rapporti di lavoro e ordinamento
corporativo nell'Africa italiana.
Milano 1938.
(Collana di studi coloniali. 5/6.)

Sega, C. 3663
Aspetti della regolamentazione
collettiva dei rapporti di lavoro
in Libia.
Riv. di diritto coloniale 2. 1939,
n. 1, p. 12-23.

Sega, C. 3664
Gli accordi collettivi economici e
l'ordinamento sindacale libico.
REAI 29. 1941, p. 94-97.

Sega, C. 3665
Il comitato corporativo della Libia
e le sue funzioni.
Riv. di diritto coloniale 4. 1941,
p. 99-107.

Social security and I.L.O.   3666
technical co-operation
in Libya.
International labour review 91. 1965,
p. 292-320.

Souriau, C.   3667

Libye. Chronique sociale et culturelle.
AAN 7. 1968, p. 302-328, 8. 1969,
p. 497-518.

Souriau, C.   3668

La société féminine en Libye.
Revue de l'occident musulman et de
la Méditerranée 1969, p. 127-155.

Sparshott, A.C.   3669

Report to the government of Libya on
the vocational rehabilitation and
employment of the disabled.
Geneva: ILO 1968.

Stilon de Piro, M.   3670

Report to the government of Libya on
the organisation of medical benefits
administered by the National Social
Insurance Institute.
Geneva: ILO 1966.

Thomas, F.C.   3671

The Libyan oil worker.
MEJ 15. 1961, p. 264-276.

Treydte, K.P.   3672

Genossenschaften in Libyen.
Hannover: Verlag für Literatur und
Zeitgeschehen 1970.
(Schriftenreihe des Forschungsinsti-
tuts d. Friedrich-Ebert-Stiftung.79.)

Vacca Maggiolini, E.   3673

L'opera dell'Istituto Nazionale
Fascista per l'Assicurazione contro
gli infortuni sul lavoro nell'Africa
italiana.
AAI 1. 1938, vol. 3/4, p. 1213-1224.

Valenzi, F.   3674

Legislazione fascista e corporativismo in colonia nei riflessi della
politica economica coloniale.
RdC 7. 1933, p. 16-24.

Vecchioni, B.   3675

L'opera dell'INFAIL nell'Africa
italiana.
REAI 28. 1940, p. 236-239.

Vocational rehabilitation   3676
and employment of disabled
persons in Libya.
International labour review 87.
1963, p. 376-378.

Wasfy, M.   3677

Social insurance in the Kingdom of
Libya.
International social security re-
view 20. 1967, p. 463-485.

Weis, H.   3678

Afrikas Flüchtlingsprobleme im 20.
Jahrhundert mit besonderer Berück-
sichtigung des nordafrikanischen
Raumes.
Bustan 8. 1967, p. 29-36.

Zampetti, G.   3679

Report to the government of Libya
on the first actuarial review of the
pension branch of the National Social Insurance Institution (INAS).
Geneva: ILO 1966.

Zuzik, M.B.   3680

Labor law and practice in the Kingdom of Libya.
Wash.: GPO 1966.
(Bureau of Labor Statistics report.
297.)

Communications.

Carta automobilistica   3681
della Libia.

1:2 000 000.
Roma: R.A.C.I. 1938.

Shell road map of Libya.   3682

1:2 000 000.
np, nd (1965).

Esso road map. Libya.   3683

1:3 000 000.
Tripoli: Esso Standard Libya Inc.
1965.

Afrique (Nord et Ouest)   3684
au

1:4 000 000.
Paris: Michelin et Cie. 1967.
(Carte Michelin. 153.)

Aeronautical chart catalogue   3685
ICAO. 8th ed.
Montreal: International Civil Avia-
tion Organization 1970.
(Doc 7101-Map/565/8.)

Catalog of aeronautical   3686
charts and related
publications.
Wash.: U.S. Coast and Geodetic Survey 1968.

USAF catalog of aeronautical   3687
charts and flight information
publications.
St. Louis, Mo.: Aeronautical Chart
and Information Center, United States Airforce 1965-

USAF aeronautical approach   3688
chart, code AC.

1:250 000.
St. Louis, Mo.: ACIC, USAF 1965-

R.A.F. tactical pilotage   3689
chart, series TPC.

1:500 000.
London: Directorate of Military
Survey 1968-

USAF pilotage chart,   3690
code PC.

1:500 000.
(Small size, large size).
St. Louis, Mo.: ACIC, USAF 1954-

Carte aéronautique du monde.   3691
Edition provisoire OACI au

1 000 000e.
Paris: Institut Géographique National 1958-

R.A.F. aeronautical chart.   3692

1:1 000 000.
(Based on U.S.A.F. world aeronauti-
cal chart).
London: War Office 1955-
(GSGS 4695.)

R.A.F. topographic navigation   3693
chart, series TNC.

1:1 000 000.
London: Directorate of Military
Survey 1962-

USAF operational navigation   3694
chart, code ONC.

1:1 000 000.
(Large size).
St. Louis, Mo.: ACIC, USAF 1961-

USAF world aeronautical   3695
chart, code WAC.

1:1 000 000.
St. Louis, Mo.: ACIC, USAF 1955-

World aeronautical chart   3696
I.C.A.O.

1:1 000 000.
Athens: Ministry of Communications,
Civil Aviation Administration, Aero-
nautical Information Service 1964-

Aeronautical information   3697
services provided by states.
25th ed.
Montreal: International Civil
Aviation Organization 1970.
(Doc 7383-AIS/503/25.)

Air navigation plan.   3698
Africa-Indian Ocean region.
13th ed.
Montreal: International Civil
Aviation Organization 1969.
(Doc 7474/13.)

Balbo, I.   3699
La litoranea libica.
Atti dei convegni "Volta" 8. 1938
"Africa", p. 1194-1207.

Branzoli Zappi, V.   3700
Magazzini generali e servizi por-
tuali in Libia.
Oltremare 8. 1934, p. 205-207.

Civil aviation law no. 47 of   3701
September 23, 1956.
Air laws and treaties of the world.
U.S. Congress. Senate. Committee on
Commerce. Wash. 1965, p. 1673-1698.

Corò, F.   3702
La rete stradale delle quattro pro-
vincie libiche e dei territori del
Sahara italiana.
AIr 2. 1939, n. 12, p. 13-18.

Corò, F.   3703
Un documento inedito sull'antico
commercio carovaniero fra Tripoli e
l'Uadai.
AAI 4. 1941, vol. 4, p. 1235-1258.

La costruzione e l'esercizio   3704
delle ferrovie in Tripolitania e in Cirenaica, dall'occupazione
al 30 giugno 1915.
Roma 1917.

Crino, S.   3705
I porti del lembo più meridionale
della Sicilia in rapporto alle
communicazioni con la Libia.
Riv. geografica italiana 29. 1922,
p. 124-134.

Dietze, E.R. - Wagenfuehr, K.   3706
Das Rundfunkwesen.
Berlin 1942.
(Afrika. 16.)

Es Sider marine terminal: 3707
port information and rules.
Tripoli: Oasis Oil Co. of Libya nd.

Flight information publi-   3708
cation (FLIP).
Europe and North Africa.
St. Louis, Mo.: ACIC, USAF 1969-

Gasbarri, C.   3709
Filatelia africana d'Italia.
Africa. Roma 24. 1969, p. 224-232.

Giglio, C.   3710
Transafricane.
RdC 5. 1931, p. 442-457.

Guida di rotta.   3711
Avioraduno internazionale
sahariano. Informazioni ai concor-
renti.
Tripoli.
4. 1939-

Information for the guidance   3712
of ships calling at Marsa
el Brega.
Tripoli: Esso Standard Libya 1965.

Jeppesen airway manual. 3713
Europe-Mediterranean.
Africa.
Frankfurt a.M.: Jeppesen and Co.
1965-

Klitsche de la Grange, A.K. 3714
Comunicazioni tra la Libia e
l'A.O.I.
RSAI 2. 1939, p. 914-918.

The Libyan maritime code. 3715
Benghazi 1956.
Tripoli 1967.

Lista, A.M. 3716
L'aviazione civile in Libia.
AIn 40. 1921, p. 82-85.

Luigioni, C. 3717
Il nuovo tronco della ferrovia
Bengasi-Derna.
RdC 1/2. 1927/28, p. 167-176.

Migliorini, E. 3718
Vie di comunicazione.
SIFOG 1937, p. 591-601.

Moltedo, A. - Bartolomeo, P. 3719
di

Il porto di Tripoli.
Riv. marittima 1924, trim. 2,
p. 623-635, trim. 3, p. 55-73.

La nuova aerostazione 3720
Idriss a Tripoli.
Costruttori italiani nel mondo 11.
1965, n. 233, p. 9-14.

Ongaro, G. 3721
Le comunicazioni libiche.
AIr 2. 1939, n. 3-4, p. 25-28.

Orlando, E. de 3722
Note sul porto di Derna.
CGEP 1923, p. 267-270.

Ornato, G.Z. 3723
La litoranea libica.
AIr 2. 1939, n. 12, p. 19-24.

Pellegrineschi, A.V. 3724
Le nuove strade della Libia.
RdC 7. 1933, p. 882-890.

Pellegrineschi, A.V. 3725
Trasporti sahariani.
Oltremare 8. 1934, p. 6-9.

Pellegrineschi, A.V. 3726
I francobolli dell'Africa italiana
ed il loro valore artistico e simbolico.
AAI 4. 1941, vol. 4, p. 1215-1232.

Port statistics Tripoli. 3727
Tripoli: Nazirate of Finance
and Economics, Statistics Division
nd.

Queirolo, E. 3728
La politica delle comunicazioni.
La rinascita della Tripolitania.
Milano 1926, p. 259-283.

Reconstruction of Benghazi   3729
harbour.
Engineering 195. 1963, n. 5063,
p. 610. Concrete and constructional
engineering 59. 1964, p. 173-175.

Les relations carovanières   3730
à travers le Sahara de
l'antiquité au seuil du XX siècle.
Le saharien 1965, n. 39, p. 26-32.

Report of the Africa -   3731
Indian Ocean regional
air navigation meeting.
Montreal: International Civil
Aviation Organization.
4. 1964-

Romagnoli, M.   3732
Il problema e la funzione dei trasporti in relazione allo sviluppo
delle nostre colonie.
ACSC 1. 1931, vol. 6, p. 114-136.

Salvadori, M. - Cortese, E.   3733
La Libia e le comunicazioni trans-
sahariane.
Oltremare 4. 1930, p. 230-233, 275.

Sirtica terminal port infor-   3734
mation and regulations.
Ras Lanuf, Libya, 1965.
Tripoli: Mobil Oil Libya 1965.

La strada litoranea della   3735
Libia.
Verona/Milano 1937.

Le strade della Cirenaica.   3736
REAI 20. 1932, p. 793-807.

Le strade della Tripolitania.   3737
REAI 18. 1930, p. 1229-1234.

Tchilinghirian, S.D. -   3738
Bernardelli, R.R.
Stamps of Italy used abroad. Vol.1.2.
London: Harris Publications 1963-64.

The telephone directory for   3739
Tripolitania and Fezzan 1966.
(Indicatore telefonico 1966).
Ministry of Communications, Posts
and Telecommunications Dept.
Tripoli: Orient Press nd.

Thomas, B.E.   3740
Motoring in the Sahara. The French
raids of 1951-1953.
Economic geography 29. 1953, p. 327-
339.

Transport in Libya.   3741
A general survey and study
of the means of communications. Pre-
pared for the government of the
Kingdom of Libya, Ministry of   1.
Planning and Development. Vol. 1.2.

Transport in Libya.   3741
Athens: Doxiadis Associates 1965.
(Document Dox-Lib-A23.)

2.

Valori, F.   3742
Il porto di Tobruch e la sua fun-
zione economica.
RdC 12. 1938, p. 705-711.

Vandelli, G.   3743
Catalogo dei francobolli di Libia
(1943-1962).
Tripoli: Author 1963.

Zucco, G. 3744

L'avvenire della Cirenaica è nella
creazione di un sistema portuario.
Oltremare 1. 1927, p. 14-16.

Zucco, G. 3745

La ferrovia da Bengasi a Merg.
Oltremare 2. 1928, p. 23-25.

Zucco, G. 3746

Il linguaggio simbolico dei francobolli libici.
RdC 3. 1929, p. 355-359.

Tourism.

Libyen. 3747
Turistische Karte.
Generaldirektion des Turismus in
Libyen.
Tripoli: The Directorate General of
Tourism 1967.

Town plan Benghazi. 3748
Bengasi: Tourism Dept.
Cyrenaica 1960.

Benghasi. Stadtplan. 3749
Generaldirektion des Turismus
in Libyen.
Tripoli: The Directorate General of
Tourism 1967.

Tourist map of Tripoli. 3750
1:8 000.
Tripoli: Orient Bookshop 1960.

Tripolis. Stadtplan. 3751
Generaldirektion des Turis-
mus in Libyen.
Tripoli: The Directorate General of
Tourism 1967.

Algerie, Tunisie, Tripoli- 3752
taine. Malte.
Paris 1930.
(Les guides bleus.)

Baedeker, K. 3753

Unteritalien, Sizilien, Sardinien,
Malta, Tripolis, Korfu. 17th ed.
Leipzig 1936.

Bertacchi, C. 3754

La Libia turistica.
REAI 26. 1938, p. 1293-1298.

Bonardi, C. 3755

Nuove mete del turismo coloniale.
Touring nel Fezzân.
Vie d'Italia 41. 1935, p. 485-496.

Bonardi, C. 3756

L'avvenire turistico della Libia.
Vie d'Italia 43. 1937, p. 434-437.

Braeuner, H. 3757

Tripolitania. 2nd ed.
Bayreuth: Afrika Verlag 1961.

Braeuner, H. 3758

Rom in Libyen.
Starnberg: Keller 1963.
(Foto-Auslese. 6.)

Braeuner, H.   3759

Fezzan.
Nürnberg: Libyen-Verlag 1964.

Cooper, R.   3760

Host of antiquities to attract the
tourist.
Financial times 1969, 6.3., p. 24.

Cyrenaica.   3761
Tourist guide-book.
United Kingdom of Libya. Province
of Cyrenaica.
Bengasi: Tourist Dept. 1959.

Fantoli, A.   3762

Guida della Libia. Touring Club Ita-
liano. P. 1. Tripolitania. P. 2.
Cirenaica.
Milano 1923.

Geisenheyner, M.   3763

Zu den Palmen Libyens. 10 000 Kilo-
meter durch Italien und Afrika.
München 1938.

Guide du tourisme   3764
automobile au Sahara.
Alger: Shell d'Algerie 1955.

Italia meridionale e insulare - 3765
Libia.
Milano 1940.
(Guida breve d'Italia. 3.)

Libia. Itinerari.   3766
Commissariato per il Turismo
in Libia, Roma.
Roma 1935.

Libya.   3767
Tourist guide.
Bologna/Tripoli nd (1957).

Libye - Libya.   3768
Sabena revue 29. 1964, n. 2,
p. 1-99.

Mondo afro asiatico   3769
1967, n. 4, aprile.
Numero speciale dedicato alla Libia
in occasione dell'anno turistico.

Ornato, G.Z.   3770

La soluzione del problema turistico
in Libia.
AIr 2. 1939, n. 3-4, p. 29-32.

Reisefuehrer durch Tripoli-   3771
tanien - Libyen.
Italpublic, Direktion für Tourismus.
Tripoli 1966.

Siala, B.   3772

Das Vereinigte Königreich Libyen -
ein lohnendes Urlaubsziel.
Westdeutsche Wirtschaft 11. 1960,
n. 3-4, p. 44-46.

This is Libya. Tourist guide.   3773
Tripoli: Universal Technical
Advertising Agency 1962.
Tripoli: Ministry of Information
and Culture 1967.

Tourism in North African   3774
countries.
New York: United Nations 1968.
(E/CN. 14/Trans/32.)

Tripoli. Useful information 3775
1961.
Tripoli: Tourist Office 1961.

Tuninetti, D.M. 3776
Cirenaica d'oggi. Guida turistica
illustrata della Cirenaica.
Roma 1933.

Valle, C. della 3777
L'opera del Touring Club Italiano
per le nostre colonie dal 1911 in
poi.
RdC 9. 1935, p. 154-160.

Vandelli, G. 3778
Leptis Magna: petit guide illustré.
Tripoli: Agence Libyenne de Publici-
té Internationale 1964.

Vergara Caffarelli, E. - 3779
Braeuner, H.

Leptis Magna.
Bayreuth: Afrika Verlag 1959.

Vergara Caffarelli, E. - 3780
Braeuner, H.

Sabratha.
Bayreuth: Afrika Verlag 1960.

Vicari, E. 3781
L'Ente Turistico ed Alberghiero del-
la Libia (E.T.A.L.).
AAI 5. 1942, vol. 4, p. 955-975.

Ward, P. 3782
Touring Libya.The western provinces.
London: Faber and Faber 1967.

Ward, P. 3783
Touring Libya. The southern provin-
ces.
London: Faber and Faber 1968.

Ward, P. 3784
Touring Libya. The eastern provinces.
London: Faber and Faber 1969.

Ward, P. - Pesce, A. 3785
Motoring to Nalut.
Tripoli: Oasis Oil Co. of Libya 1970.
(Oasis travel series. 1.)

Ward, P. - Lafeber, H. 3786
Sabratha. A guide for visitors.
Stoughton, Wisc.: Oleander Press
1970.

Williams, G. 3787
Green Mountain. An informal guide
to Cyrenaica and its Jebel Akhdar.
London: Faber and Faber 1963.

Geology.
Bibliography. Maps.

Baird, D.W. 3788
Geological bibliography of the
Murzuk basin region.
GAPSF 1969, p. 139-150.

Bibliography and index of 3789
geology exclusive of North
America.
Boulder/Colorado: Geological Society
of America.
33. 1969-

Desio, A.   3790

Bibliografia geologica della Libia
sino al 1936.
ASIPS 25. 1936, p. 25-39.

Heath, J.A.   3791

Bibliography of reports resulting
from U.S. Geological Survey partici-
pation in the United States technical assistance program, 1940-1965.
Geological Survey bulletin 1965,   1.

Heath, J.A.   3791

n. 1193, p. 20-21.

                                 2.

Maley, J.   3792

Synthèse bibliographique sur le quaternaire de la Libye désertique.
Bulletin de liaison. Association
sénégalaise pour l'étude du quaternaire de l'ouest africain 1969,
n. 22, p. 71-85.

Merabet, O.   3793

Bibliographie de l'Algérie du sud
(Sahara) et des régions limitrophes.
Bulletin. Service Géologique de l'Al-
gérie 1968, n. 37.

Geologic map and section of   3794
the Shati valley area,
Fezzan, Libya (1957-58).

1:100 000.
v. Goudarzi 1970, plate 7.
   n. 3843.

Geological map of Tripolitanian 3795
Jebel.

1:150 000.
University of Milan. Institute of
Geology.
v. Memoria della RIP 9. 1963.

Freulon, J.M. - Lefranc, J.P. - 3796
Lelubre, M.

Carte géologique de reconnaissance
du Sahara.

1:500 000.
Feuille N.G. 33 N.O. Sebha.   1.

Freulon, J.M. - ...   3796

Alger: Institut de Recherches Sahariennes 1954.
(Afrique 1:500 000. Carte de reconnaissance.)
                                 2.

Plauchut, B.   3797

Notice explicative sur la carte géologique du bassin du Djado 1:500000,
(feuilles Djado et Toummo).
Dakar: Bureau de Recherches Géologiques et Minières 1960.

Geologic map of the Kingdom   3798
of Libya.

1:2 000 000.
Compiled by L.C. Conant, G.H. Gou-
darzi.
Wash.: USGS 1964.   1.

Geologic map ...   3798

(Miscellaneous geologic investigations. Map I - 350 A.)

                                 2.

Geologic map of Libya.   3799

1:2000 000.
Compiled by L.C. Conant, G.H. Goudarzi.
v. Goudarzi 1970, plate 2.
   n. 3843.

Topographic and mineral-   3800
resources map of Libya.

1:2 000 000.
v. Goudarzi 1970, pate 1.
   n. 3843.

Tectonic and paleogeographic   3801
map of Libya and neighboring
countries.

1:2 000 000.
v. Goudarzi 1970, plate 6.
   n. 3843.

Carte géologique du nord-   3802
ouest de l'Afrique.

1:2 000 000.
Feuille 3. Sahara occidental.
Feuille 4. Sahara central.
Paris: C.N.R.S. 1962.

Geological map of Africa. 3803

1:5 000 000.
Prepared by the Association of African Geological Surveys (ASGA) ...
Paris: UNESCO 1964.

International tectonic map 3804
of Africa.

1:5 000 000.
Compiled under the aegis of the International Geological Congress ...
Paris: UNESCO 1968.

Raisz, E.J. 3805

Landform map of North Africa.
Scale 1 inch to 30 miles (approx.),
(1:5 000 000). United States Army.
Wash.: Quartermaster Research and
Development Center ... 1952.

Geology. General.

Allen, W.W. - Herriot, H.P. - 3806
Stiehler, R.D.

History and performance prediction
of Umm Farud field, Libya.
Journal of petroleum technology 21.
1969, p. 570-578.

Amato, A. 3807

Le formazioni geologiche della costa
cirenaica.
RdC 4. 1930, p. 671-682.

Behrend, F. - Klingner, F.E. 3808
Libyen.
Afrika. Berlin. Vol. 3,1. 1942,
p. 113-137.

Bellair, P. 3809
Diagramme minéralogique du Grand Erg
oriental d'El Oued à Ghadamès.
CR Société Géologique de France 1953,
n. 6, p. 99-101.

Bellair, P. 3810

La phonolite de Maharouga (Châti,
Fezzân).
CR Société Géologique de France 1957,
n. 13, p. 289-291.

Bellair, P. 3811

Les volcans du Sahara.
BLS 9. 1958, n. 31, p. 194-199.

Betrandi, M.D. - Burollet, 3812
P.F.

Geological outline of Libya.
BAAPG 44. 1960, p. 1245-1246.

Beuf, S. - Biju-Duval, B. - 3813
Stevaux, J. - Kulbicki, G.

Extent of "Silurian" glaciation in
the Sahara: its influences and consequences upon sedimentation.
GAPSF 1969, p. 103-116.

Brady, R.T. 3814

A review of the first dozen years of
petroleum exploration in northernmost Cyrenaica (1955-1967).
GANC 1968, p. 207-215.

Burollet, P.F. 3815

Field trip guide book of the excursion to Jebel Nefusa. (Saharan
symposium 1963).
Tripoli: PESL 1963.

Burollet, P.F. 3816

Reconnaissance géologique dans le
sud-est du bassin de Kufra.
RIFP 18. 1963, p. 1537-1545.

Burollet, P.F. 3817

Rôles des études sédimentologiques
dans la conduite de l'exploration.
Proceedings. World petroleum congress 6. 1963 (1964), p. 51-62.

Chiarugi, A.   3818

Le foreste pietrificate delle nostre
colonie: resultati acquisiti e programma di ricerche.
ACSC 1. 1931, vol. 3, p. 39-47.

Chiarugi, A.   3819

Distribuzione dei legni fossili della Libia in base ai recenti ritrovamenti.
ACSC 2. 1934, vol. 3, p. 262-265.

Cohen, A.J.   3820

Origin of the Libyan Desert silica-
glass.
Nature 183. 1959, n. 4674, p. 1548-
1549.

Colley, B.B.   3821

Libya. Petroleum geology and deve-
loment.
Proceedings. World petroleum congress 6. 1963 (1964), p. 1-10.

Collomb, G.R.   3822

Etude géologique du Jebel Fezzân et
de sa bordure paléozoique.
Paris: Compagnie Française des Pé-
troles 1962.
(Notes et mémoires. 1.)

Coltro, R.   3823

Il tema di ricerca petrolifera creta-
ceo superiore-eocene inferiore nel
bacino della Sirte (Libia).
Riv. mineraria siciliana 17. 1966,
p. 208-233.

Coltro, R.   3824

I temi di ricerca petrolifera sotto-
stanti alla trasgressione cretacea
nell'area sirtica (Libia).
Mem. Soc. Geol. Ital. 6. 1967, p.503-
515.

Conant, L.C. - Goudarzi, G.H.   3825

Stratigraphic and tectonic framework
of Libya.
BAAPG 51. 1967, p. 719-730.

Cornet, A.   3826

Reconnaissance géologique dans l'Erg
d'Oubari et la Hamada Zegher (Fezzân).
TIRS 6. 1950, p. 63-72.

Desio, A.   3827

Short history of the geological,
mining and oil exploration in Libya.
AANL. Memorie. Classe di scienze
fis. ... ser. 8, vol. 8. 1967, n. 4,
p. 79-123.

Desio, A.   3828

History of geologic exploration in
Cyrenaica.
GANC 1968, p. 79-113.

Directory of geologists,   3829
geophysicists and exploration
personnel in Libya.
Tripoli: PESL 1963.

Dixey, F.   3830

Geology, applied geology (mineral
resources) and geophysics in Africa.
A review of the natural resources
of the African continent. Paris 1963,
p. 51-100.

Favretto, L. - Morelli, G.L.   3831

Su di un minerale a strati misti
osservato tra i prodotti di argilli-
ficazione di una vulcanite (Cufra).
Rendiconti. Istituto Lombardo. Accademia di Scienze e Lettere ser. A.
98. 1964, p. 511-524.

Field trip guidebook of the   3832
excursion to Aouinet Ouenine.
(Saharan symposium 1963).
Tripoli: PESL 1963.

First Saharan symposium   3833
Tripoli - April 1963.
Petroleum Exploration Society of
Libya.
RIFP 18. 1963, n. 10. 11.

Fraser, W.W.   3834

Geology of the Zelten field, Libya,
North Africa.
Proceedings. World petroleum congress 7. 1967, vol. 2, p. 259-264,
294-297.

Furon, R.   3835

Géologie de l'Afrique.
Geology of Africa.
Paris: Payot 1960.
Edinburgh: Oliver and Boyd 1963.

Furon, R.   3836

Le Sahara. Géologie. Ressources minérales. 2nd ed.
Paris: Payot 1964.

Gillispie, J. - Sanford, R.M.   3837

The geology of the Sarir oil field,
Sirte basin, Libya.
Proceedings. World petroleum congress 7. 1967, vol. 2, p. 181-193,
289-297.

Goudarzi, G.H.   3838

A summary of the geologic history of
Libya.
Wash.: USGS 1959.
(Open file report 496.)

Goudarzi, G.H.   3839

Idri salt deposits, Fezzan province,
Libya.
Wash.:USGS 1962.
(Open file report 656.)

Goudarzi, G.H.   3840

Iron deposit of the Shatti valley
area of Fezzan province, Libya.
Wash.: USGS 1962.
(Open file report 657.)

Goudarzi, G.H.   3841

Pisida salt deposit, Libya.
Wash.: USGS 1962.
(Open file report 659.)

Goudarzi, G.H.   3842

Report on Marada, Pisida, Idri and
Tauorga salt deposits in Libya.
Wash.: USGS 1962.
(Open file report 658.)

Goudarzi, G.H.   3843

Geology and mineral resources of
Libya: a reconnaissance.
Wash.: GPO 1970.
(U.S. Geological Survey. Professio-
nal paper 660.)

Gualtieri, J.L.   3844

Exploration of the Jefren gypsum -
anhydrite deposit, Libya.
Wash.: USGS 1962.
(Open file report 660.)

Hecht, F. - Fuerst, M. -   3845
Klitzsch, E.

Zur Geologie von Libyen.
Geologische Rundschau 53. 1964,
p. 413-470.

Jacqué, M.   3846

Reconnaissance géologique du Fezzân
oriental.
Paris: Compagnie Française des Pé-
troles 1962.
(Notes et mémoires. 5.)

Kleinmann, B.   3847

The breakdown of zirkon observed in
the Libyan Desert glass as evidence
of its impact origin.
Earth and planetary science letters
5. 1969, p. 497-501.

Kleinsmiede, W.F.J. - Berg,   3848
N.J.

Surface geology of the Jabal al
Akhdar, northern Cyrenaica, Libya.
GANC 1968, p. 115-123.

Klitzsch, E.   3849

Geology of the north-east flank of
the Murzuk basin (Djebel Ben Ghnema-
Dor el Gussa area).
RIFP 18. 1963, p. 1411-1427.

Klitzsch, E.   3850

Zur Geologie am Ostrand des Murzuk-
beckens.
Oberrheinische geologische Abhandlungen 13. 1964, p. 51-73.

Klitzsch, E.   3851

Comments on the geology of the central parts of southern Libya and
northern Chad.
SCLNC 1966, p. 1-17.

Klitzsch, E.   3852

Geology of the northeast flank of
the Murzuk basin (Djebel Ben Ghnema-
Dor el Gussa area).
SCLNC 1966, p. 19-32.

Klitzsch, E.   3853

Road log to the central parts of
southern Libya.
SCLNC 1966, p. 75-87.

Klitzsch, E.   3854

Kurzer Überblick zur Geologie des
Gebietes Djebel ben Ghnema - Dor el
Gussa (Ostfezzan, Libyen).
v. Ziegert 1967, n. 704,
   p. 1-7.

Klitzsch, E.   3855

Der Basaltvulkanismus des Djebel
Haroudj, Ostfezzan/Libyen.
Geologische Rundschau 57. 1968,
p. 585-601.

Klitzsch, E.   3856

Outline of the geology of Libya.
GANC 1968, p. 71-78.

Klitzsch, E. - Pesce, A.   3857

Roadlog for the eleventh annual
P.E.S.L. fieldtrip to southwest Li-
bya.
GAPSF 1969, p. 151-154.

Lexique stratigraphique   3858
international.
Vol. 4. Afrique, fasc. 4a Libye.
Ed. P.F. Burollet.
Paris: Centre National de la Recher-
che Scientifique 1960.

Marchetti, M.   3859

Itinerari geologici in Cirenaica.
ACSC 2. 1934, vol. 3, p. 273-286.

Martin, A.J.   3860

Possible impact structure in
southern Cyrenaica, Libya.
Nature 223. 1969, n. 5209, p. 940-
941.

Massa, D. - Collomb, G.R.   3861

Observations nouvelles sur la région
d'Aouinet Ouenine et du Djebel
Fezzân (Libye).
Report. International geological
congress 21. 1960, pt.12,p. 65-73.

Mizutani, S. - Suwa, K.   3862

Orthoquarzitic sand from the Libyan
Desert.
Journal of earth sciences. Nagoya
University. Dept. of Earth Sciences
14. 1966, p. 137-149.

Mizutani, S. - Uemura, T. -   3863
Suwa, K.

Two types of sand grains in sands of
the Libyan Desert.
Journal of the Geological Society of
Japan 74. 1968, p. 144.

Muller-Feuga, R.   3864

Contribution à l'étude de la géologie, de la pétrographie et des ressources hydrauliques et minérales du
Fezzân.
Nancy 1952. Diss.

Pesce, A.   3865

Uau en Namus.
SCLNC 1966, p. 47-51.

Piccoli, G. 3866

Osservazioni geologiche sui fenomeni eruttivi della Tripolitania settentrionale.
Boll. Soc. Geol. Ital. 79. 1960, p. 165-196.

Piccoli, G. 3867

Ricerche geologiche e petrografiche sul vulcanismo della Tripolitania settentrionale.
Memorie. Istituti di Geologia e Mineralogia. Padova 24. 1963-64.

Pietersz, C.R. 3868

Proposed nomenclature for rock units in northern Cyrenaica.
GANC 1968, p. 125-130.

Roberts, J.M. 3869

Amal field.
BAAPG 52. 1968, p. 547.

Sanford, R.M. 3870

Sarir, Libya. Desert surprise.
BAAPG 52. 1968, p. 549.

Spring geological excursion 3871
1961, Tibesti-Tchad 17.3. - 20.3. Ed. R.S.M. Templeton.
Tripoli: PESL 1961.
(Field trip guide book.)

Stefanini, G. 3872

Struttura geologica della Cirenaica.
CGEP 1923, p. 1-8.

Stefanini, G. 3873

Cenni descrittivi a corredo dello schizzo geologico dimostrativo della Cirenaica.
CGEP 1923, p. 215-236.

Terry, C.E. - Williams, J.J. 3874

The Idris "A" bioherm and oilfield, Sirte basin, Libya - its commercial development, regional Palaeocene geologic setting and stratigraphy.
The exploration for petroleum in   1.

Terry, C.E. - Williams, J.J. 3874

Europe and North Africa. Ed. P. Hepple. London: Institute of Petroleum 1969, p. 31-48.

2.

Viganò, P.L. 3875

Studio geologico del Gebel Garian.
Milano: Università di Milano, Istituto di Geologia nd. Diss.

Williams, J.J. 3876

Geology of Augila area, Libya.
BAAPG 52. 1968, p. 568.

Williams, J.J. 3877

The sedimentary and ingenious reservoirs of the Augila oil field, Libya.
GANC 1968, p. 197-205.

Williams, M.A.J. - Hall, D.N. 3878

Recent expeditions to Libya from the Royal Military Academy, Sandhurst.
Geographical journal 131. 1965, p. 482-501.

Structural Geology.

Campbell, A.S. 3879

The Barce (Al Marj) earthquake of 1963.
GANC 1968, p. 183-195.

Cassinis, G.   3880

La crociera gravimetrica del R.
Sommergibile "Des Geneys". Anno 1935.
Riv. geomineraria 3. 1942, n. 2,
p. 36-38.

Coltro, R.   3881

Paleotettonismo nell'accumolo di
idrocarburi a vari livelli nel bacino della Sirte.
Riv. mineraria siciliana 18. 1967,
p. 77-94.

Digiesi, D.   3882

La carta magnetica della Libia recen-
temente compilata dall'Istituto Geografico Militare.
Geofisica pura e applicata 3. 1941,
p. 45-51.

Digiesi, D.   3883

La carta magnetica della Libia recen-
temente pubblicata dall'I.G.M. e cenni sui metodi seguiti e sugli strumenti impiegati.
Universo 22. 1941, p. 369-378.

Dubief, J.   3884

Résultats de mesures magnétiques au
Sahara (Algérie et Tripolitaine) en
1943.
Travaux de l'Institut de Météorologie et de Physique du Globe d'Algérie 1944, fasc. 6, p. 1-3.

Dubief, J.   3885

Carte provisoire de la déclinaison
magnétique sur la Libye et les pays
limitrophes à la date du 1.1.1945.
Travaux de l'Institut de Météorologie ... d'Algérie 1945,fasc.7,p.1-3.

Dubief, J.   3886

Résultats de mesures magnétiques
faites au Sahara algérien et en Tripolitaine de décembre 1943 à juin
1944.
Travaux de l'Institut de Météorologie ... d'Algérie1945,fasc.7,p.3-13.

Earthquake Libya 1963.   3887
Bulletin mensuel du bureau.
Union Géodesique et Géophysique International (UGGI bulletin) 1963,
p. 330-333.

Goodchild, R.G.   3888

Earthquakes in ancient Cyrenaica.
GANC 1968, p. 41-44.

Gordon, D.W. - Engdahl, E.R.   3889

An instrumental study of the Libyan
earthquake of February 21, 1963.
Earthquake notes, Eastern Section,
Seismic Society of America 34. 1963,
p. 50-56.

Gordon, D.W.   3890

Libyan earthquake of February 21,
1963. A report published by the U.S.
Dept. of Commerce, Coast and Geodetic Survey.
Wash. 1963.

Klitzsch, E.   3891

Die Strukturgeschichte der Zentralsahara.
Geologische Rundschau 59. 1970,
p. 459-527.

Knetsch, G.   3892

Ein Vergleich des tektonischen Mu-
sters im Sahara-Feld mit dem deutschen Saxonikum.
Geologische Rundschau 54. 1965,
p. 892-905.

Lipparini, T.   3893

Tectonics and geomorphology of Tri-
politania, Libya.
Bulletin. Ministry of Industry.
Tripoli 1965, n. 4.

Newman, P.   3894

Some well shoot problems in Libya.
RIFP 18. 1963, p. 1377-1388.

Report on the Barce (El Merj)   3895
earthquakes, February 1963.
Report submitted to the Libyan government.
Tripoli: Oil Industry Committee 1963.

Geomorphology.

Baru, M. 3896

Soil analysis and its relation to land use in el-Marj plain, Cyrenaica.
Bulletin of the faculty of arts.
University of Libya 2. 1968, p. 41-70.

Buedel, J. 3897

Die pliozänen und quartären Pluvial-zeiten der Sahara.
Eiszeitalter und Gegenwart 14. 1963, p. 161-187.

Caporiacco, L. di 3898

Osservazioni sul Deserto Libico.
Universo 15. 1934, p. 9-21.

Capot-Rey, R. 3899

Forschungen in der zentralen Sahara.
Klimageomorphologie de M. W. Mecke-lein.
Annales de géographie 70. 1961, p. 82-86.

Coque, R. 3900

Morphogenèse quaternaire du piémont méditerranéen du Djebel Akhdar (Cyrénaïque).
Annales de géographie 79. 1970, p. 375-385.

Crema, C. 3901

Le "seghife" particolarità morfolo-gica valliva dei dintorni di Tobruch.
ACGI 9. 1925, vol. 2, p. 91-96.

Dominicis, A. de 3902

Fattori pedogenetici, condizioni pe-dologiche e caratteri agrologici del-le sabbie aride della Tripolitania.
ASIPS 25. 1936, vol. 5, p. 252-260.

Fuerst, M. 3903

Hamada - Serir - Erg.
Zs für Geomorphologie 9. 1965, p. 385-421.

Fuerst, M. 3904

Bau und Entstehung der Serir Tibesti.
Zs für Geomorphologie 10. 1966, p. 387-418.

Fuerst, M. 3905

The Serir Tibesti, its form, material and development.
SCLNC 1966, p. 43-46.

Grove, A.T. 3906

Geomorphology of the Tibesti region with special reference to western Tibesti.
Geographical journal 126. 1960, p. 18-31.

Hagedorn, H. 3907

Landforms of the Tibesti region.
SCLNC 1966, p. 53-58.

Hey, R.W. 3908

The Pleistocene shorelines of Cyre-naica.
Quaternaria 3. 1956, p. 139-144.

Hey, R.W. 3909

The Quaternary and Palaeolithic of northern Libya.
Quaternaria 6. 1962, p. 435-439.

Hey, R.W. 3910

The geomorphology of the Jabal al Akhdar and adjoining areas.
GANC 1968, p. 167-171.

Hey, R.W.   3911

The Quaternary geology of the Jabal
al Akhdar coast.
GANC 1968, p. 159-165.

Hoevermann, J.   3912

Hangformen und Hangentwicklung zwischen Syrte und Tschad.
L'évolution des versants. Symposium
international de géomorphologie,
Liège-Louvain 1966. Liège 1967,
p. 140-156.

Hubert, P.   3913

Report dealing with the soil conditions of the ENTE farm settlement
area of Tolmeitha (Cyrenaica).
Benghazi 1963.

Kádár, L.   3914

La morfologia dell'altopiano del
Gilf Kebir.
BSGI 74. 1937, p. 485-503.

Kanter, H.   3915

Zwei wissenschaftliche Reisen.
Deutsche Hochschullehrer-Zeitung
7. 1959, n. 2, p. 13-17.

Kanter, H.   3916

Eine Reise in NO-Tibesti (Republik
Tschad) 1958.
PGM 107. 1963, p. 21-30.

Kanter, H.   3917

Die Serir Kalanscho in Libyen, eine
Landschaft der Vollwüste.
PGM 109. 1965, p. 265-272.

Kanter, H.   3918

Wüstenreise von Benghasi nach Kufra
1957-58.
Geographische Rundschau 17. 1965,
p. 155-162.

Klitzsch, E.   3919

Bericht über eine Ost-Westquerung
der Zentralsahara.
Zs für Geomorphologie 11. 1967,
p. 62-92.

Lipparini, T.   3920

Geomorfologia della regione dei
laghi del "Trona" nel deserto dell'
edeien (Fezzàn).
ACSC 3. 1937, vol. 5, p. 198-201.

Lustig, L.K.   3921

Appraisal of research on geomorphology and surface hydrology of desert environments.
Deserts of the world. Ed. W.G. Mac
Ginnies ... Tucson 1968, p. 128-130.

MacKee, E.D. - Tibbitts, G.C. 3922

Primary structures of a seif dune
and associated deposits in Libya.
Journal of sedimentary petrology
34. 1964, p. 5-17.

Marinelli, O.   3923

Sulla morfologia della Cirenaica.
Riv. geografica italiana 27. 1920,
p. 69-86.

Marinelli, O.   3924

I problemi morfologici della Cirenaica e la nuova carta al 50 000
dell'I.G.M.
Riv. geografica italiana 28. 1921,
p. 168-170.

Marinelli, O.   3925

La carta al 50 mila dell'Istituto
Geografico Militare e la morfolo-
gia della Cirenaica.
CGEP 1923, p. 237-240.

Marinelli, O.   3926

Le condizioni generali del rilievo.
CGEP 1923, p. 9-22.

Meckelein, W. 3927

Forschungen in der zentralen Sahara.
1. Klimamorphologie.
Braunschweig: Westermann 1959.

Mensching, H. 3928

Bergfussflächen und das System der
Flächenbildung in den ariden Subtro-
pen und Tropen.
Geologische Rundschau 58. 1968,
p. 62-83.

Migliorini, P. 3929

Recenti studi su particolari aspetti
geomorfologici della Libia.
Riv. geografica italiana 73. 1966,
p. 192-198.

Mónterin, U. 3930

Sulla trasformazione delle dune
trasversali in longitudinali nel
Sahara libico.
Atti della R. Accademia delle Scienze di Torino 70. 1934-35, p. 62-80.

Mónterin, U. 3931

Fenomeni d'erosione torrentizia del
periodo pluviale nel Deserto Libico
e nel Tibesti.
Riv. geografica italiana 46. 1939,
p. 13-25.

Montet, A. 3932

Les terrasses marines de la côte
nord de Cyrénaïque.
CR ... Société Géologique de France
1955, p. 256-258.

Moseley, F. 3933

Plateau calcrete, calcreted gravels,
cemented dunes and related deposits
of the Maallegh-Bomba region of Libya. 1.
Zs für Geomorphologie 9. 1965,

Moseley, F. 3933

p. 166-185.

Oomkens, E. 3934

Environmental significance of sand
dikes.
Sedimentology 7. 1966, p. 145-148.

Price, R. 3935

Soil survey of selected areas in the
eastern, western and southern governates of Libya.
Rome: FAO 1968/69.
(DTLSP 3,3.)

Romagnoli, M. 3936

La stato attuale delle conoscenze
sui terreni agrari delle nostre
colonie.
ACSC 2. 1934, vol. 6, p. 1186-1226.

Scarin, E. 3937

Cenni sulla morfologia del Fezzàn.
ASIPS 21. 1932, vol. 2, p. 459-460.

Shirlaw, D.W.G. - Willimott, 3938
S.G. - Clarke, J.I. - Frisby, M.E.
Soil survey of Tauorga region.
Durham: Dept. of Geography 1961.
(Special reports. 4.)

Smith, H.T.U. 3939

Eolian geomorphology, wind direction,
and climatic change in North Africa.
Amhurst, Mass.: University of Massa-
chusetts, Geology Dept. 1963.

Uhden, R. 3940

Beckenformen und
Dünengebiete der libyschen Wüste.
Festschrift für Carl Uhlig. Öhringen
1932, p. 106-128.

Vita-Finzi, C. 3941

Post-roman erosion and deposition in
the wadis of Tripolitania.
Publication. International Association of Scientific Hydrology 53.
2. 1960 (Helsinki), p. 61-64.

Vita-Finzi, C.   3942

Recent alluvial history of the
eastern Gebel, Tripolitania.
Cambridge University 1961. Diss.

Vita-Finzi, C.   3943

Carbon-14 dating of medieval allu-
vium in Libya.
Nature 198. 1963, n. 4883, p. 880.

Vita-Finzi, C.   3944

The Mediterranean valleys.
Cambridge UP 1969.

Willimott, S.G.   3945

Soils of the Jefara.
FSL 1960, p. 26-45.

Wittschell, L.   3946

Die Bedeutung äolischer Böden in
Nordafrika.
PGM 74. 1928, p. 344-347.

Wulf, G.R.   3947

Recent ripple marks at Giorgimpopoli,
Libya.
Journal of sedimentary petrology 33.
1963, p. 964-965.

Historical Geology.
Stratigraphy.

Amato, A.   3948

Il miocene superiore e le sue mani-
festazioni gassose nella pianura
tripolina.
ACSC 2. 1934, vol. 3, p. 287-297.

Arambourg, C. - Magnier, P.   3949

Gisements de vertébrés dans le bassin
tertiaire de Syrte, Libye.
CR hebdomadaires des séances. Académie des Sciences 252. 1961, p. 1181-
1183.

Arni, P.   3950

L'évolution des Nummulitinae en tant
que facteur de modification des
dépôts litteraux.
Mémoires. Bureau de Recherches Géologiques et Minières 1965,n.32,p.7-20.

Arnould-Saget, S. - Magnier, P.   3951

Découverte de dents de palaeomasto-
dontes dans la région de Zella.
CR ... Société Géologique de France
1961 (1962), p. 283-287.

Barr, F.T.   3952

Late Cretaceous planktonic foraminifera from the coastal area east of
Susa (Apollonia), northeastern Libya.
Journal of paleontology 42. 1968,
p. 308-321.

Barr, F.T.   3953

Upper Cretaceous stratigraphy of
Jabal al Akhdar,
northern Cyrenaica.
GANC 1968, p. 131-147.

Barsotti, G.   3954

Paleocenic ostracods of Libya (Sirte
basin) and their wide African distribution.
RIFP 18. 1963, p. 1520-1535.

Bellair, P. - Freulon, J.M. -   3955
Lefranc, J.P.

Découvertes d'une formation à vertébrés et végétaux d'âge tertiaire au
bord occidental du désert libyque
(Sahara oriental).   1.

Bellair, P. - Freulon, J.M. ... 3955

CR hebdomadaires des séances. Académie des Sciences 239. 1954, p. 1822-
1824.

2.

Burollet, P.F. - Magnier, P.   3956

Remarques sur la limite crétacé-tertiaire en Tunisie et en Libye.
Report. International geological congress 21. 1960, part 5, p. 136-144.

Burollet, P.F. - Klitzsch, E.   3957

Discussion sur la stratigraphie
libyenne. Discussion of Libyan stratigraphy.
RIFP 18. 1963, p. 1323-1329.

Burollet, P.F.   3958

Trias de Tunisie et de Libye, relations avec le trias européen et saharien.
Mémoires. Bureau de Recherches Géologiques et Minières 1963,n.15,p.482-
494.

Burollet, P.F.   3959

Remarques sur la néogène de Tunisie
et de Libye et ses rélations avec
les bassins voisins.   1.
Cursillos y conferencias. Instituto
"Lucas Mallada" de Investigaciones

Burollet, P.F.   3959

Geológicas. Madrid 1964, n. 9,
p. 199-202.

                                    2.

Burollet, P.F. - Byramjee, R.S. 3960

Shape and structure of Saharan Cambro-Ordovician sand bodies, paleocurrents and depositional environment.
BAAPG 48. 1964, p. 519-520.

Burollet, P.F. - Manderscheid,G.3961

Le crétacé inférieur en Tunisie et
en Libye.
Mémoires. Bureau de Recherches Géologiques et Minières 1965, n. 34,
p. 785-794.

Burollet, P.F.   3962

Sédimentologie du dévonien inférieur
en Libye.
Mémoires. Bureau de Recherches Géologiques et Minières 1965, n. 33,
p. 18-19.

Burollet, P.F.   3963

Remarques sur la stratigraphie du
Jebel Nefusa.
RIP 72. 1966, p. 1313-1317.

Burollet, P.F. - Manderscheid,G.3964

Le dévonien en Libye et en Tunisie.
International symposium on the Devonian system. Calgary vol. 1. 1967,
p. 205-213.

Burollet, P.F.   3965

Sédimentologie du dévonien inférieur
en Libye.
Mémoires. Bureau de Recherches Géologiques et Minières 1967, n. 33,
p. 205-213.

Burollet, P.F. - Byramjee, R.   3966

Etude sédimentologique des grès cambro-ordoviciens du Sahara libyen.
Paléocourants et milieu de depôt.
Report. International geological congress 23. 1968, abstracts vol.,p.227.

Burollet, P.F. - Byramjee, R.   3967

Sedimentological remarks on lower
Paleozoic sandstones of south Libya.
GAPSF 1969, p. 91-101.

Cesare, F. di - Franchino, A. - 3968
Sommaruga, C.

The Pliocene-Quaternary of Giarabub
Erg region.
RIFP 18. 1963, p. 1344-1362.

Collignon, M.   3969

Céphalopodes néocrétacés du Tinrhert
(Fezzân).
Annales de paléontologie 43. 1957,
113-136.

Combaz, A.   3970

Sur un nouveau type de microplanctonte cénobial fossile du gothlandien
de Libye, Deflandrastrum nov. gen.
CR hebdomadaires des séances. Académie des Sciences 255. 1962, p. 1977-
1979.

Cox, L.R.   3971

Tertiary bivalvia from Libya.
Palaeontology 5. 1962, p. 1-8.

Depitout, A.   3972

Étude des gigantostracés siluriens
du Sahara central.
Paris: C.N.R.S. 1962.
(Publications. Centre de Recherches
 Sahariennes. Série géologique. 2.)

Desio, A. - Rossi Ronchetti, C. 3973
Invernizzi, G.

Il giurassico dei dintorni di Jefren
in Tripolitania.
RIP 66. 1960, p. 65-113.

Desio, A. - Rossi Ronchetti, C. 3974

Sul giurassico medio di Garet el-
Bellàa (Tripolitania) e sulla posizione stratigrafica della formazione
di Tacbàl.
RIP 66. 1960, p. 173-190.

Desio, A. - Rossi Ronchetti, C. 3975
Viganò, P.L.

Sulla stratigrafia del trias in Tripolitania e nel sud-tunisino.
RIP 66. 1960, p. 273-322.

Desio, A. - Rossi Ronchetti, C. 3976
Pozzi, R. - Clerici, F. -
Invernizzi, G. - Pisoni, C. - Viganò,
                                   P.L.
Stratigraphic studies in the
Tripolitanian Jebel (Libya).
Milano 1963.
(Memoria della RIP. 9.)

Desio, A. - Rossi Ronchetti, C. 3977
Pozzi, R.

Osservazioni alla nota di P.F. Burollet "Remarques sur la stratigraphie du Jebel Nefusa".
RIP 72. 1966, p. 1319-1322.

Freulon, J.M.   3978

Stratigraphie du carbonifère du
Tassili n'Ajjer et du Fezzân occidental.
CR hebdomadaires des séances. Académie des Sciences 241. 1955, p. 1478-
1480.

Freulon, J.M.   3979

Étude géologique des séries primaires du Sahara central (Tassili
n'Ajjer et Fezzân).
Paris: C.N.R.S. 1964.
(Publications. Centre de Recherches
 sur les Zones Arides. Sér. géol. 3.)

Fuerst, M. - Klitzsch, E.   3980

Late Caledonian paleogeography of
the Murzuk basin.
RIFP 18. 1963, p. 1472-1484.

Fuerst, M.   3981

Die Oberkreide - Paleozän - Transgression im östlichen Fezzan.
Geologische Rundschau 54. 1965,
p. 1060-1088.

Fuerst, M.   3982

Die Paleozän - Eozän - Transgression
in Südlibyen.
Geologische Rundschau 58. 1968,
p. 296-313.

Gohrbandt, K.H.A.   3983

Some Cenomanian foraminifera from
northwestern Libya.
Micropaleontology 12. 1966, p. 65-
70.

Gohrbandt, K.H.A.   3984

Upper Cretaceous and lower Tertiary
stratigraphy along the western and
southwestern edge of the Sirte basin,
Libya.
SCLNC 1966, p. 33-41.

Gohrbandt, K.H.A. - Hottin-   3985
ger, L.

Der libysche Flosculina Limestone.
Eclogae Geologicae Helvetiae 60.
1967, p. 697-705.

Hammuda, O.S.   3986

Jurassic and lower Cretaceous rocks
of central Jabal Nefusa, north-
western Libya.
Tripoli: PESL 1969.

Hay, W.W.   3987

Coccoliths and other calcareous
nannofossils in marine sediments in
Cyrenaica.
GANC 1968, p. 149-157.

Haynes, J.   3988

Operculina and associated foraminifera from the Paleocene of the N.E.
Fezzan, Libya.
Contributions from the Cushman Foun-
dation for Foraminiferal Research
13. 1962, part 3, p. 90-97.

Hecht, F.   3989

Der paläozoische Unterbau Libyens.
Zs der deutschen geologischen Gesellschaft 117. 1965 (1968), p. 491.

Hecht, F.   3990

Der paläozoische Bau Libyens.
Erdöl und Kohle 20. 1967, p. 159-168.

Hoffmeister, W.S.   3991

Lower Silurian plant spores from
Libya.
Micropaleontology 5. 1959, p. 331-
334.

Jordi, H.A. - Lonfat, F.   3992

Stratigraphic subdivision and prob-
lems in upper Cretaceous - lower
Tertiary deposits in northwestern
Libya.
RIFP 18. 1963, p. 1428-1436.

Klitzsch, E.   3993

Die Gotlandium-Transgression in der
Zentral-Sahara.
Zs der deutschen geologischen Gesell-
schaft 117. 1965 (1968), p. 492-501.

Klitzsch, E.   3994

Ein Profil aus dem Typusgebiet got-
landischer und devonischer Schichten
der Zentralsahara (Westrand Murzuk-
becken, Libyen).
Erdöl und Kohle 18.1965, p. 605-607.

Klitzsch, E.   3995

Stratigraphic section from the type
areas of Silurian and Devonian stra-
ta at western Murzuk basin (Libya).
GAPSF 1969, p. 83-90.

Koeniguer, J.C. - Louvet, P.   3996

Sur la présence d'un bois de mélia-
cées dans le tertiaire du Fezzân
oriental: entandrophragmoxylon bou-
reaui Louvet.
Palaeobotanist 17. 1968, p. 33-35.

Lefranc, J.P.   3997

Stratigraphie des séries continentales intercalaires au Fezzân nord-
occidental (Libye).
CR hebdomadaires des séances. Académie des Sciences 247.1958,p.1360-63.

Lefranc, J.P.   3998

Le séries continentales intercalaires du Fezzân nord-occidental (Libye)
leur age et leur corrélations.
CR hebdomadaires des séances. Académie des Sciences 249.1959,p.1685-87.

Lefranc, J.P.   3999

Existence,au Fezzân nord occidental
(Libye), de lacunes et discordances
dans les séries du continental inter-
calaire.   1.
CR hebdomadaires des séances. Acadé-

Lefranc, J.P.   3999

mie des Sciences 249. 1959, p. 2345-
2347.

                                                  2.

Lehmann, E.P.   4000

Tertiary-Cretaceous boundary facies
in the Sirte basin, Libya.
Proceedings. International geological congress 22. 1964, part 3, p. 56-
73.

Lehmann, E.P. - Rozeboom, J.J.   4001
Waller, H.O. - Conley, C.D.

Microfacies of Libya.
Tripoli: PESL 1967.

Lehmann, J.P.   4002

Les stégocephales sahariens.
Annales de paléontologie 43. 1957,
p. 137-146. CR hebdomadaires des
séances. Académie des Sciences 245.
1957, p. 551-552.

Magnier, P.   4003

Etude stratigraphique dans le Gebel
Nefousa et le Gebel Garian.
CR ... Société Géologique de France
1963 (1964), p. 89-94.

Magnier, P.   4004

Le néogène du bassin de Syrte et du
sud de la Cyrénaïque (Libye).
Cursillos y coferencias. Instituto
"Lucas Mallada" de Investigaciones
Geológicas 1964, n.9, p. 193-198.

Mennig, J.J. - Vittimberga, P.   4005

Application des méthodes pétrogra-
phiques à l'étude du paléozoïque
ancien du Fezzân.
Paris: Compagnie Française des Pé-
troles 1962.
(Notes et mémoires. 2.)

Mennig, J.J. - Vittimberga, P.   4006
Lehmann, P.

Etude sédimentologique et pétrogra-
phique de la formation Ras Hamia
(trias moyen) du nord-ouest de la
Libye. RIFP 18. 1963,p. 1504-1519.

Oberlin, A. - Freulon, J.M. -   4007
Lefranc, J.P.

Etude minéralogique de quelques ar-
giles des grès de Nubie du Fezzân.
Bulletin de la Société Française de
Minéralogie ... 81. 1958,p. 1-4.

Oberlin, A. - Freulon, J.M.   4008

Etude minéralogique de quelques ar-
giles des séries primaires du Tassili n'Ajjer et du Fezzân.
Bulletin de la Société Française de
Minéralogie ... 81.1958, p. 186-189.

Pomeyrol, R.   4009

A catharsis on the term Nubian sand-
stone.
GAPSF 1969, p. 131-137.

Rasmussen, H.W.   4010

Astéroides du tertiaire inférieur de
Libye.
Annales de paléontologie 52. 1966,
p. 3-15.

Ratschiller, L.K.   4011

Sahara. Correlazioni geologico-lito-
stratigrafiche fra Sahara centrale e
occidentale.
Memorie del museo tridentino di
scienze naturali 16.1967,p. 53-293.

Rossi Ronchetti, C.   4012

Revisione della fauna neocretacica
della Libia, Fam. Trochidae, Colum-
bellinidae, Olividae.
RIP 65. 1959, p. 55-68.

Rossi Ronchetti, C. - Albanesi, 4013
                            C.
Fossili cenomaniani del
Gebel tripolitano.
RIP 67. 1961, p. 251-307.

Rossi Ronchetti, C.   4014

Variazioni e accrescimento relativo
in Exogyra overwegi von Buch del
maestrichtiano libico.
RIP 68. 1962, p. 193-243.

Roubet, C.   4015

Etat des recherches sur le quaternaire au nord et au nord-est de
l'Afrique (1967-1968).   1.
Bulletin de liaison. Association Sénégalaise pour l'Etude du Quaternai-

Roubet, C.   4015

re de l'Ouest Africain 1969, n. 22,
p. 55-70.

                                    2.

Salahi, D.   4016

Ostracodes du crétacé supérieur et
du tertiaire en provenance d'un son-
dage de la région de Zelten.
RIFP 21. 1966, p. 3-32.

Savage, R.J.G. - White, M.E.   4017

Two mammal faunas from the early Tertiary of central Libya.
Proceedings. Geological Society of London 1965, n. 1623, p. 89-91.

Schwarzbach, M.   4018

Das Alter der Wüste Sahara.
Neues Jahrbuch für Geologie und Paläontologie 1953, p. 157-174.

Seilacher, A.   4019

Sedimentary rhythms and trace fossils in Paleozoic sandstones in Libya.
GAPSF 1969, p. 117-123.

Selley, R.C.   4020

The Miocene rocks of the Marada and Jebel Zelten area, central Libya. A study of shoreline sedimentation.
Tripoli: PESL 1966.

Selley, R.C.   4021

The Miocene shoreline of Marada, Libya.
London: Imperial College, Dept. of Geology 1966.

Selley, R.C.   4022

Paleocurrents and sediment transport in nearshore sediments of the Sirte basin, Libya.
Journal of geology 75. 1967, p. 215-223.

Selley, R.C.   4023

Near-shore marine and continental sediments of the Sirte basin, Libya.
Proceedings. Geological Society of London 1968, n. 1648, p. 81-90.

Tedeschi, D. - Papetti, I.   4024

On the occurrence of Pseudolituonella in Libya.
Revue de micropaléontologie 7. 1964, p. 180-187.

Vittimberga, P. - Cardello, R.   4025

Sédimentologie et pétrographie du paléozoique du bassin de Kufra.
RIFP 18. 1963, p. 1546-1558.

Wood, L.E.   4026

Pseudo-oolites of northern Libya, their occurrence and origin.
Journal of sedimentary petrology 34. 1964, p. 661-663.

Wray, J.L.   4027

Palynology of Paleozoic rocks of Libya.
BAAPG 46. 1962, p. 284.

Wray, J.L.   4028

Paleozoic palynomorphs from Libya.
Special publication. Society of Economic Paleontologists and Mineralogists. Tulsa 11. 1964, p. 90-96.

Ziegert, H.   4029

Zur Pleistozän-Gliederung in Nordafrika.
Afrika-Spektrum 1967, n. 3, p. 5-24.

Hydrology.

Agostini, E. de   4030

Repertorio delle principali località di acqua (pozzi, sorgenti, cisterne) riconosciute in Cirenaica fino a tutto il 1926.
Bengasi 1927.

Agostini, E. de   4031

Primo elenco di aggiunte e varianti al repertorio delle principali località d'acqua riconosciute in Cirenaica fino a tutto il 1926.
Bengasi 1929.

Amato, A.   4032

Il bacino idrogeologico del Fueihat.
RdC 5. 1931, p. 175-189.

Amato, A.   4033

Problemi geoidrologici in Tripolitania.
RdC 6. 1932, p. 525-533.

Amato, A.   4034

Le acque sotterranee della pianura
tripolina.
ACSC 2. 1934, vol. 3, p. 297-300.

Ambroggi, R.P.   4035

Water under the Sahara.
Scientific American 214. 1966, n. 5,
p. 21-29.

Bellair, P.   4036

L'hydrogéologie du Sahara oriental
et le dessèchement du désert libyque.
Congrès géologique international
19. 1952 (1953), fasc. 8, p. 9-13.

Bertaiola, M.   4037

Ground water in the Azzahra - Annasi-
ra - Al Amiria area, Tripolitania.
Wash.: USGS 1961.
(Open file report.)

Breccia, A.E.   4038

Un mare interno fra la Cirenaica e
l'Egitto.
Scienza e tecnica 4. 1940, p. 453-
460.

Brown, L.A.   4039

Planning and policy guidelines for
water and soil development in Libya.
Tripoli 1963.

Burdon, D.J.   4040

The problem of water and soil in-
vestigation, development, utilization and conservation in Libya.
Cairo: FAO Regional Office 1964.

Burdon, D.J.   4041

Water development and conservation
in the Jabal Akhdar region in con-
junction with the project for the
development of tribal lands and
settlements in Libya.
Cairo: FAO Regional Office 1964.

Caponera, D.A.   4042

Water legislation.
Rome: FAO 1962.
(Report 1550.)

Carraro, A.   4043

Problemi idrologici della Libia
orientale.
ACSC 3. 1937, vol. 5, p. 195-198.

Castigliola, O.   4044

Sorgenti artesiane solfuree in Tripolitania.
REAI 20. 1932, p. 127-168.

Cederstrom, D.J. - Bertaiola, M. 4045

Ground-water resources of the Tripoli area, Libya.
Wash.: USGS Water Research Division
1960.

Ciric, D.   4046

Irrigation of settlement schemes in
Libya.
Rome: FAO 1968/69.
(DTLSP 3,4.)

Clap, V. - Meunier, J.L.   4047

Profondeur de trois des lacs de
l'Erg d'Oubari.
BLS 9. 1958, n. 32, p. 332-334.

Cooper, R.   4048
Development of water resources.
Financial times 1969, 6.3., p. 23-24.

Crema, C.   4049
L'estrazione delle acque sotterranee
in Tripolitania.
REAI 16. 1928, p. 625-628.

Crema, C.   4050
I problemi idrologici della Libia.
ACSC 1. 1931, vol. 3, p. 145-164.

Curran, C.D. - Dixey, F.   4051
Water projects in Libya.
Rome: FAO 1967.
(Funds-in-trust for Libya 408.)

Desio, A.   4052
Sugli spartiacque della Cirenaica.
BSGI 66. 1929, p. 19-22.

Desio, A.   4053
I due laghetti salati di Cufra nel
Sahara italiano.
BSGI 76. 1939, p. 740-746.

Desio, A.   4054
Underground waters and peopling of
arid and semi arid regions (Gefara
and Misurata regions).
Colloque géol. appl. Proche-Orient.
Ankara 1955 (1956), p. 243-252.

Doyel, W.W. - Maguire, F.J.   4055
Results of water investigations,
Benghazi area, Libya.
Wash.: USGS Water Research Division
1959.

Doyel, W.W.   4056
Water supply, Tobruk, Libya.
Wash.: USGS 1959.
(Open file report.)

Doyel, W.W. - Maguire, F.J.   4057
Ground-water resources of the Bengá-
si area, Cyrenaica, U.K. of Libya.
Wash.: GPO 1964.
(USGS water-supply paper. 1757-B.)

Drouhin, G.   4058
The problem of water resources in
North-west Africa.
Arid zone research 1. 1953, p. 9-41.

Dubief, J.   4059
Essai sur l'hydrologie superficielle
au Sahara.
Alger 1953.

Dubief, J.   4060
Le problème de l'eau superficielle
au Sahara.
La météorologie sér. 4, 1965, n. 77,
p. 3-32.

Eldblom, L.   4061
Quelques points de vue comparatifs
sur les problèmes d'irrigation dans
les trois oasis libyennes de Brâk,
Ghadamès et particulièrement Mourzouk.
                              1.

Eldblom, L.   4061
Lund studies in geography 22. 1961.
Svensk geografisk arsbok 37. 1961,
p. 124-145.

                              2.

Eldblom, L.   4062
Bewässerungsfragen in den drei libyschen Oasen Brak, Ghadames und Murzuk.
Afrika heute 1966, p. 352-358.

Eldblom, L.   4063

Notes on problems of irrigation in
three Libyan oases.
Ekistics 23. 1967, p. 199-202.

Everdingen, R.O. van   4064

The deeper ground water in Libya.
Bulletin. International Association
of Scientific Hydrology 7. 1962,
p. 33-39.

Fantoli, A.   4065

Le acque sotterranee in Tripolitania.
ACSC 1. 1931, vol. 3, p. 182-203.

Fantoli, A.   4066

L'acqua.
IdO 6. 1941, n. 4, p. 61-62.

Ferree, P.J.   4067

Libya strikes a new source of wealth
- water.
Foreign algriculture 1969, 14.7.,
p. 6-8.

Giocch el Chebir (la grotta   4068
del Lete).
REAI 16. 1928, p. 1073-1076.

Gunston, D.   4069

Making the Sahara fruitful.
African world 1967, October, p. 6-7.

Hellstroem, B.   4070

Per lo sfruttamento delle acque
sotterranee nel deserto libico.
Riv. geomineraria 3. 1942, n. 2,
p. 33-35.

Hill, R.W.   4071

Underground water resources of the
Jefara plain.
FSL 1960, p. 10-26.

Jones, J.R.   4072

Brief résumé of ground-water condi-
tions in Libya.
Wash.: USGS 1960.
(Open file report.)

Jones, J.R.   4073

Water for municipal use at Agedabia.
Wash.: USGS 1963.
(Open file report.)

Jones, J.R.   4074

Ground-water maps of the Kingdom of
Libya.
Wash.: USGS 1964.
(Open file report.)

Jones, J.R.   4075

Ground-water exploration and development in Libya.
Water well journal 20. 1966, p. 13-
16, 40.

Kambo, L.   4076

Problemi e studi di idraulica coloniale.
ASIPS 25. 1936, vol. 5, p. 209-236.

Klitzsch, E.   4077

Über den Grundwasserhaushalt der
Sahara.
Afrika-Spektrum 1967, n. 3, p. 25-37.

Klitzsch, E. - Baird, D.W.   4078

Stratigraphy and paleohydrology of
the Germa (Jarma) area, southwest
Libya.
GAPSF 1969, p. 67-80.

Krulc, Z. - Mladenovic, M.L.J.   4079

The application of geoelectrical
methods to groundwater exploration
of unconsolidated formations in semi-
arid areas, Bunayyah, Jardas al Abid.
Geoexploration 7. 1969, p. 83-95.

Lanfry, J. - Laperrousaz, A.   4080

Chronique de Ghadamès. L'eau d'irrigation.
IBLA 9. 1946, n. 36, p. 343-369.

Laurenti, S.   4081

Le acque artesiane in Libia.
AAI 1. 1938, n. 3/4, p. 919-940.

Leuenberger, R.   4082

Proposals for the development of the
ground-water resources for irrigation and domestic use and measures
for soil and water conservation in
the Tolmeitha farming area.
Benghazi 1963.

Leuenberger, R.   4083

Progress report no. 4 on water resources and water utilization in
northern Cyrenaica, Libya.
Rome: FAO 1964.
(Funds-in-trust for Libya 94.)

Leuenberger, R.   4084

Final report on water resources and
water utilization in northern Cyrenaica, Libya.
Appendix A. Report on water utilization in the pilot area of the   1.

Leuenberger, R.   4084

FAO - tribal lands and settlements
project of Cyrenaica.
Rome: FAO 1965.
(Funds-in-trust for Libya 94.)
                                  2.

Leuenberger, R.   4085

Water resources and water utiliza-
tion in northern Cyrenaica, Libya.
Rome: FAO 1965/69.
(DTLSP 3,1.)

Mancuso, V.   4086

Considerazioni ed analisi di acqua e
sali dei laghi di trona del deserto
dell'edeien.
ACSC 3. 1937, vol. 5, p. 201-205.

Map showing locations of water   4087
wells drilled by oil companies,
quality of water, and ground-water
contours, Libya.   1:2 000 000.
Compiled by R.O. van Everdingen,
1961-1962.
v. Goudarzi 1970, plate 13.

Migliaia di pozzi, di sorgen-   4088
ti e di cisterne costruiti o
riparati in tutta la Libia.
(Map 1:3 000 000).
Libia 3. 1939, n. 5, p. 2-10.

Monod, T.   4089

A propos du Lac des Vers ou Bahr ed-
Dûd (Libye).
Bulletin de l'IFAN sér. A, 31. 1969,
p. 25-41.

Muehlhofer, F.   4090

Bewässerungsfrage der Cyrenaika.
Beiträge zur Kolonialforschung
6. 1944, p. 130-148.

Newport, T.G. - Haddor, Y.   4091

Ground-water exploration in Al Marj
area, Cyrenaica, U.K. of Libya.
Wash.: GPO 1963.
(USGS water-supply paper. 1757-A.)

Niccoli, E.   4092

Il nuovo acquedotto di Tripoli.
AAI 1. 1938, vol. 3/4, p. 1319-1326.

Niccoli, E. - Casini, V.   4093

Le acque profonde nel sottosuolo
della Libia occidentale.
Chimica 1939, p. 614-625, 1940,
p. 392-400.

Niccoli, E. - Casini, V.   4094

Composizione chimica delle acque artesiane profonde nel sottosuolo della
Libia occidentale e loro utilizzazione a scopo di colonizzazione agraria.
AAI 3. 1940, vol. 3, p. 259-278.

Noble, N.D.   4095

The hydrogeology and groundwater resources of the Jebel al Akhdar,
northern Cyrenaica, Libya.
Rome: FAO 1966/69.
(DTISP 3,2.)

Ogilbee, W. - Vorhis, R.C. -   4096
Deghaies, F.

Ground-water resources of Al Mayah
area, Tripolitania.
Wash.: USGS 1962.
(Open file report.)

Ogilbee, W. - Vorhis, R.C. -   4097
Russo, A.

Ground-water resources of the Surman
area, Tripolitania, U.K. of Libya.
Wash.: USGS 1962.
(Open file report.)

Ogilbee, W. - Vorhis, R.C. -   4098
Tarhuni, H.A.

Ground-water resources of the Az Za-
wiyah area, Tripolitania.
Wash.: USGS 1962.
(Open file report.)

Ogilbee, W.   4099

Report on the ground-water potential
of an area near Gasr Bu Hadi, Libya.
Wash.: USGS 1962.
(Open file report.)

Ogilbee, W. - Tarhuni, H.A.   4100

Ground-water resources of the Qarah-
bulli area, Tripolitania.
Wash.: USGS 1963.
(Open file report.)

Ogilbee, W.   4101

Ground-water in the Sirte area,
Tripolitania, U.K. of Libya.
Wash.: GPO 1964.
(USGS water-supply paper. 1757-C.)

Pantanelli, E.   4102

Le risorse idriche della Cirenaica
in rapporto all'agricoltura ed alla
colonizzazione.
ASIPS 25. 1936, vol. 4, p. 460-468.

Pozzi e cisterne in   4103
Cirenaica.
IdO 2. 1937, n. 10, p. 12-13.

Provasi, T.   4104

Acque vive perenni in Libia.
Libia 4. 1940, n. 10, p. 18-20.

Report on prospects for the   4105
development of potable water
supplies from tube wells at Sirte.
H.T. Smith International. International Cooperation Administration.
np 1959.

Ricci, L.   4106

Nota complementare sull'idrografia
della Cirenaica.
Riv. geografica italiana 28. 1921,
p. 170-174.

Ricci, L.   4107

Cenni sull'idrografia.Nota complementare sull'idrografia della Cirenaica.
CGEP 1923, p. 23-32, 241-247.

Richter, N.B.   4108

Zur Hydrologie der zentralen Sahara.
Monatsberichte der deutschen Akademie der Wissenschaften zu Berlin
1. 1959, p. 744-747.

Richter, N.B.   4109

Beobachtung der Verdunstung an frei-
en Wasserflächen der zentralen Sahara.
Gerlands Beiträge zur Geophysik 69.
1960, p. 362-367.

Richter, N.B. 4110

Das hydrologische System der Krateroase Wau en-Namus in der zentralen
Sahara.
Acta Hydrophysica 6. 1960, p. 131-
162.

Romanelli, P. 4111

Primi studi e ricerche sulle opere
idrauliche di Leptis Magna e sull'
approvvigionamento d'acqua della
città.
RdT 1. 1924/25, p. 209-227.

Schiffers, H. 4112

Ein Meer unter der Sahara ?
Orion 6. 1951, p. 387-392.

Schiffers, H. 4113

Die Seen in der Sahara.
Erde 3. 1951, p. 1-13.

Schiffers, H. 4114

Wasserhaushalt und Probleme der
Wassernutzung in der Sahara.
Erdkunde 5. 1951, p. 51-60.

Schiffers, H. 4115

Das Wasser in der Sahara.
Bild der Wissenschaft 4. 1967, n. 9,
p. 748-758.

Sharaf, A.T. 4116

The hydrological divisions of the
northern belt of Libya.
Freiburger geographische Hefte 6.
1968, p. 33-50.

Shotton, F.W. 4117

Perched water supplies above the
main water table of the western
desert.
Water and water engineering 49.
1946, p. 257-263.

Stroppa, F. 4118

L'idrografia della Tripolitania e la
politica idraulica romana.
Riv. coloniale 1919, p. 489-526,
545-553.

Stuart, W.T. 4119

Significance of decline in ground
water levels in Tripolitania.
Tripoli: U.S. Operations Mission
to Libya 1960.

Tibbitts, G.C. 4120

Reconnaissance report on the hydro-
logy of the Gioda-Tarumin farm area.
Wash.: USGS 1957.
(Open file report.)

Tileston, F.M. - Swanson, L.E. 4121

Water and soil development flood
control on Wadi Megenin, Libya.
Tripoli: U.S. Operations Mission
to Libya 1962.

T'Leven, J.A. van 4122

Report on the seminar on water-
logging in relation to irrigation
and salinity problems, Lahore 16.-
28.11. 1964.
Rome: FAO 1965. (Report 1932.)

Tria, E. 4123

Le acque della Cirenaica e della
Marmarica.
Giornale di medicina militare 1942,
p. 500-532.

Uhlig, D. 4124

Das Tauorga-Project - ein Bewässe-
rungsvorhaben in Libyen.
Wasser und Boden 19. 1967, p. 16-20.

Underhill, H.W. - Atherton, M.J. 4125

A coastal ground water study in Libya and a discussion of a double
pumping technique.
Journal of hydrology 2. 1964, p. 52-
64.

Viezzer, C.   4126

Le acque salienti di Ghadames in
Tripolitania.
REAI 19. 1931, p. 1079-1109.

Vita-Finzi, C. - Vorhis, R.C.   4127

Man-made changes in the water resources of Tripolitania, Libya.
Publication. International Association of Scientific Hydrology 57.
1961 (Athens), p. 530-531.

Weis, H.   4128

Schatzgräber im Sandmeer. Wasser -
der Wüste grösster Reichtum.
Universum - Natur und Technik 11.
1956, p. 513-518.

Weis, H.   4129

Der Wasserhaushalt des Fezzan, der
südlibyschen Wüste und des Berglan-
des von Tibesti.
GWF. Gas - und Wasserfach 97. 1956,
p. 929-932, 1028-1030.

Weis, H.   4130

Wasser und Erdöl in Libyen. Wirt-
schaftswandlungen am Rande der Sahara.
GWF. Gas - und Wasserfach 103. 1962,
p. 1285-1292.

Hydrography.

Almagià, R.   4131

Il rilievo idrografico della Libia.
RdC 6. 1932, p. 40-42.

Carte édité par l'Institut   4132
Océanographique et Musée de
Monaco. No. 9. Dressée par G. Gier-
mann, sous la direction du M. Pfannenstiel ...
Bulletin de l'Institut Océanographique 1960, n. 1192. Annexe.

Catalog of nautical charts   4133
and publications.
Wash.: U.S. Naval Oceanographic
Office. (H.O. Pub. No. 1-N.)
Introduction, part 1.2., 5th ed.
1967/68. Region 5, W. Africa and the
Mediterranean, 6th ed. 1967.

Catalogo generale dei   4134
documenti nautici in vendita.
Carte e pubblicazioni.
Genova: Istituto Idrografico della
Marina 1968.
(I.I. 3138.)

Catalogue of Admiralty charts   4135
and other hydrographic
publications. 1968.
London: Hydrographer of the Navy
1968.
(N.P. 131.)

Catalogue-index des cartes   4136
et ouvrages qui composent
l'hydrographie française.
Fasc. A. Europe et Méditerranée.
Paris 1969.
(Service Hydrographique de la Marine. 4 A.)

Fantoli, A.   4137

Le isole della Tripolitania e della
Cirenaica.
Universo 37. 1957, p. 923-930.

Filjushkin, B.N.   4138

The state of oceanographical know-
ledge of the Mediterranean Sea.
Trudy Instituta Okeanologii 56.
1962, p. 294-306.

Indice delle carte della   4139
idrografia III.
Coste mediterranee. Libia - Egitto
Genova: Istituto Idrografico   ...
della Marina 1958.
(I.I.M. - carta n. 1203.)

The Mediterranean pilot.   4140
Vol. 5. The coasts of Libya,
Egypt, Israel ... 5th ed.
London: Hydrographer of the Navy
1961.
(N.P. 49.)

Méditerranée orientale. 4141
Vol. 2. Côtes de Libye,
d'Égypte ...
Paris: Service Hydrographique de la
Marine 1956. Correction fasc.4.1967.
(Instructions nautiques. 409.)

Miskoski, V.T. 4142
The African coastal charting programme of the United States of America.
International hydrographic review
44. 1967, p. 141-149.

Mittelmeer-Handbuch. 4143
3. Teil. Die Nordküste von
Afrika. 4th ed.
Hamburg: Deutsches Hydrographisches
Institut 1956. Nachtrag Nr. 4.1964,
Ergänzung 1967.
(Nautisches Buch. 2029.)

Niccoli, E. 4144
Le mellahe di Bu-Kammasch e la utilizzazione dell'energia solare per
la soluzione di un grande problema
chimico tecnico.
RdT 2. 1925/26, p. 35-50.

Pellegrineschi, A.V. 4145
Le coste della Libia. Natura e con-
figurazione generale.
RdC 6. 1932, p. 461-470.

Pfannenstiel, M. 4146
Erläuterungen zu den bathymetrischen
Karten des östlichen Mittelmeeres.
Bulletin de l'Institut Océanographi-
que 1960, n. 1192.

Portolano del Mediterraneo. 4147
Vol. 8. Coste di Libia,
Egitto ... 1st ed.
Genova: Istituto Idrografico della
R. Marina 1931.

Portolano del Mediterraneo. 4148
Vol. 3. Mediterraneo orien-
tale. Coste di Libia, Egitto ...
Genova: Istituto Idrografico della
Marina 1958.
(I.I. 3153.)

Riccardi, R. 4149
Lo stato attuale delle conoscenze
dei mari italiani.
ACGI 18. 1961, vol. 1, p. 323-362.

Sailing directions for the 4150
Mediterranean.
Vol. 4. Libya, Egypt ... 3rd ed.
U.S. Naval Oceanographic Office.
Wash.: GPO 1963.
(H.O. Pub. No. 55.)

Watson, J.A. - Johnson, G.L. 4151
The marine geophysical survey in the
Mediterranean.
International hydrographical review
46. 1969, p. 81-107.

Climate.

Affronti, F. - Rizzo, S. 4152
Comportamento delle configurazioni
di bassa pressione di tipo subtropi-
cale attraversanti il basso Mediterraneo.
Riv. di meteorologia aeronautica
30. 1970, n. 2, p. 39-50.

Alfuth, W.H. - Alsobrook, A.P. 4153
ABMA climatological ringbook. Part
7. Empirical frequency distribu-
tions of pressure, temperature and
air density at levels of constant
altitude, Tripoli, Libya. 1.

Alfuth, W.H. - Alsobrook, A.P. 4153
Redstone Arsenal, Alabama: Army
Ballistic Missile Agency 1961.
(Report RR-TR-61-11.)
2.

Alfuth, W.H. - Alsobrook, A.P. 4154
ABMA climatological ringbook. Part
10. Empirical frequency distribu-
tions of wind components at constant
altitude levels, Tripoli, Libya.
Redstone Arsenal, Alabama: Army 1.

Alfuth, W.H. - Alsobrook, A.P.   4154

Ballistic Missile Agency 1961.
(Report RR-TR-61-14.)

2.

Alfuth, W.   4155

Hochreichende Radiosondenaufstiege.
Tripolis/Libyen, 1951 - 1957.
Fachliche Mitteilungen. Geophysika-
lischer Beratungsdienst der Bundes-
wehr im Luftwaffenamt   1.

Alfuth, W.   4155

Part 1-4. 1968, n. 138-141,
part 5-7. 1969, n. 145-147.

2.

Buettner, K.   4156

Einige Strahlungsmessungen in der
tripolitanischen Sahara.
Meteorologische Zeitschrift 50. 1933,
p. 489-493.

Butzer, K.W.   4157

Climatic changes in the arid zones
of Africa during early to mid-Holo-
cene times.
Proceedings of the international
symposium on world climate.   1.

Butzer, K.W.   4157

Imperial College. World climate from
8 000 to 0 B.C. London 1966, p. 72-
83.

2.

Caporiacco, L. di   4158

Il problema del disseccamento del
Sahara al luce di taluni fatti bio-
geografici.
Riv. di biologia coloniale 1. 1938,
p. 91-109.

Climatological summary.   4159
United Kingdom of Libya.
Ministry of Communication, Meteoro-
logical Dept.
Tripoli.
1966, n. 143, April-

Dubief, J.   4160

Note sur l'évolution du climat saharien au cours des derniers millé-
naires.
Actes du congr. de l'Assoc. Intern.
pour l'Étude du Quaternaire 4. 1.

Dubief, J.   4160

1953 (1956), vol. 2, p. 848-851.

2.

Dubief, J.   4161

Le climat du Sahara. Vol. 1.2.
Alger: Institut de Recherches Sahariennes 1959-63.
(Université d'Alger. Institut de Recherches Sahariennes. Mémoire.)

Fantoli, A.   4162

Cenni elementari di meteorologia
con norme per l'uso dei principali
strumenti compilate per gli osser-
vatori coloniali.
Tripoli 1930.

Fantoli, A.   4163

Le notizie meteorologiche sulla
Tripolitania e Cirenaica nell'anti-
chità.
RdC 5. 1931, p. 638-646.

Fantoli, A.   4164

Il ghibli.
Oltremare 7. 1933, p. 208-209.

Fantoli, A.   4165

Clima.
SIFOG 1937, p. 95-119.

Fantoli, A.   4166

Le carte pluviometriche dell'Africa
italiana.
Libia occidentale 1:1 500 000.
Libia orientale   1:1 500 000.
AAI 3. 1940, vol. 4, p. 471-482.

Fantoli, A. 4167

Il clima della Libia nei suoi rapporti con gli insediamenti umani e con la colonizzazione.
AAI 5. 1942, vol. 3, p. 787-805.

Fantoli, A. 4168

La media normale delle pioggie di Tripoli.
Libia 2. 1954, n. 4, p. 17-20.

Fantoli, A. 4169

La più alta temperatura del mondo.
Riv. di meteorologia aeronautica 18. 1958, n. 3, p. 53-63.

Fantoli, A. 4170

I venti al suolo e in quota a Tripoli.
Riv. di meteorologia aeronautica 24. 1964, n. 2, p. 3-34.

Fantoli, A. 4171

Contributo alla climatologia della Tripolitania. P. 1. Riassunto dei risultati e tabelle meteorologiche e pluviometriche. 1967.
Roma: Ministero degli Affari Esteri

Fantoli, A. 4172

Osservazioni meteorologiche effettuate a Tripoli dal 1.1. 1937 al 30.6. 1939 con i climagrammi del periodo.
Roma: Ministero degli Affari Esteri 1967.

Fantoli, A. 4173

Contributo alla climatologia della Cirenaica. Riassunto dei risultati e tabelle meteorologiche e pluviometriche. 1968.
Roma: Ministero degli Affari Esteri

Fantoli, A. 4174

Contributo alla climatologia delle regioni interne della Libia.
Roma: Ministero degli Affari Esteri 1969.

Flohn, H. 4175

Warum ist die Sahara trocken ?
Zs für Meteorologie 17. 1966, p. 316-320.

Genoviè, L. 4176

Le condizioni climatiche della Libia.
Riv. geografica italiana 38. 1931, p. 36-38.

Gorini, P. 4177

Sull'importanza degli indici pluviometrici in Cirenaica.
Giornale degli economisti e riv. di statistica 64. 1924, p. 532-546.

Grimes, A.E. 4178

An annotated bibliography on climatic maps of Libya.
Wash.: U.S. Weather Bureau 1961.

Isnard, H. 4179

Esquisse du climat de la Libye.
Méditerranée 9. 1968, p. 247-260.

Kanter, H. 4180

Klimatographische Witterungsschilderung. Tripolitanien.
Annalen der Hydrographie und maritimen Meteorologie 68. 1940, p. 294-298.

Kemp, A.K. - Durrans, K.L. 4181

Expedition to Tibesti.
Weather 23. 1968, p. 331-338.

Kirk, T.H. 4182

Some synoptic features of an occurrence of low-level turbulence (Cyrenaica).
Meteorological magazine 92. 1963, p. 147-154.

Kirk, T.H.   4183

Discontinuities with reference to
Mediterranean and North African
meteorology.
Technical note. World Meteorological
Organization 1964, n. 64,vol.1,p.35-
48.

Klitzsch, E.   4184

Bericht über starke Niederschläge in
der Zentralsahara (Herbst 1963).
Zs für Geomorphologie 10. 1966,
p. 161-168.

Knoche, W.   4185

Zur Entstehung der Wüste Sahara.
Forschungen und Fortschritte 12.
1936, p. 24.

Koch, H.G.   4186

Erscheinungen der sommerlichen Grund-
schicht an der nordafrikanischen
Mittelmeerküste.
Wissenschaftliche Zs der Karl-Marx-
Universität Leipzig. Math. -   1.

Koch, H.G.   4186

naturwiss. Reihe 16. 1967, p. 589-
599.

                                     2.

Le Houérou, H.N.   4187

La désertisation du Sahara septentrional et des steppes limitrophes
(Libye, Tunisie, Algerie).
Annales algériennes de géographie
3. 1968, n. 6, p. 5-30.

Lunson, E.A.   4188

Sandstorms on the northern coast of
Libya and Egypt.
Professional notes. Meteorological
Office London 7. 1950, n. 102.

Mac Ginnigle, J.B.   4189

Dust whirls at Idris Airport on 31
May and 1 June 1964.
Meteorological magazine 93. 1964,
p. 313-316.

Mac Ginnigle, J.B.   4190

Dust whirls in north-west Libya.
Weather 21. 1966, p. 272-276.

Magazzini, G.   4191

The climate of Tripolitania.
Tripoli: Libyan Meteorological
Service 1960.

Mean monthly surface dry   4192
bulb temperature (in °C)
and standard deviation at 0000, 0600,
1200 and 1800 GMT and mean daily
maximum and minimum temperature for
each month.   1.
Station: Benina. Period of record:

Mean monthly surface ...   4192

1955-59.
Station: Idris. Period of record:
1955-59.
Tripoli: Libyan Meteorological Service nd.   2.

Morsellino, N.A.   4193

L'organizzazione meteorologica dell'
aeronautica nell'Africa italiana.
Riv. di meteorologia aeronautica
1937, ottobre, p. 31-46.

Mosna, E.   4194

Il clima.
CGEP 1923, p. 33-48.

Richter, N.B.   4195

Bestimmungen des nächtlichen Trans-
missionskoeffizienten der Atmosphäre
in der libyschen Sahara und an der
Küste Tripolitaniens.
Zs für Meteorologie 3. 1949, p. 303-
312.

Schiffers, H.   4196

Aridität im nördlichen Afrika.
Geographische Rundschau 17. 1965,
p. 57-62.

Weather in the Mediterranean. 4197
Great Britain. Meteorological
Office. Vol. 1-3. 2nd ed.
London: HMSO 1945-64.

World weather records 1951- 4198
60. Vol. 5. Africa.
U.S. Dept. of Commerce, ESSA.
Wash.: GPO 1967.

World-wide airfield summaries. 4199
U.S. Naval Weather Service.
Vol. 9, part 1: Africa (northern
half).
Springfield, Va.: Clearinghouse for
Federal Scientific and Technical
Information 1968.

Flora. Fauna.

Bioclimatic map of the 4200
Mediterranean zone.

1:5 000 000.
Paris: UNESCO 1963.
(Arid zone research. 21.)

Vegetation map of the 4201
Mediterranean region.

1:5 000 000.
Paris: UNESCO 1968.

Beaumont, J. de 4202
Sphecidae (Hym.) récoltés en Tripolitaine et en Cyrénaïque par M. Ken-
neth M. Guichard.
Bulletin of the British Museum. Natural history. Entomology 9. 1960,
n. 3, p. 221-251.

Béguinot, A. 4203
Le raccolte botaniche in Libia ed in
Egeo fatte dal dott. prof. Antonio
Vaccari durante le operazioni di
guerra ed i principali risultati ...
ACSC 2. 1934, vol. 3, p. 139-150.

Béguinot, A. 4204
Lo stato attuale delle conoscenze
sulla flora della Libia litoranea ed
interna.
ASIPS 25. 1936, vol. 4, p. 169-184.

Bernard, F. 4205
Biotopes habituels des Fourmis sahariennes de plaine, d'après l'abondan-
ce de leurs nids en 60 stations très
diverses.
BSHN 52. 1961, p. 21-40.

Bonacelli, B. 4206
Il silfio dell'antica Cirenaica.
Ministero delle Colonie.
Roma 1924.

Bonacelli, B. 4207
I tartufi libici.
RdC 1/2. 1927/28, p. 467-473.

Calciati, C. 4208
I paesaggi botanici.
CGEP 1923, p. 49-66.

Carullo, F. 4209
Il problema dei rimboschimenti in
Libia.
Catania 1936.

Carullo, F. 4210
I rimboschimenti della Tripolitania.
Un caso speciale di aridocoltura.
Riv. forestale italiana 1940, aprile,
p. 4-12.

Chiovenda, E. 4211
L'utilizzazione della flora sponta-
nea nelle nostre colonie.
ASIPS 25. 1936, vol. 4, p. 335-366.

Cortesi, F.   4212

Piante medicinali, aromatiche, da
essenze e da profumi della Tripolitania.
RdT 2. 1925/26, p. 99-120, 249-256.

Cortesi, F.   4213

Vegetazione e piante utili della
Libia.
Oltremare 7. 1933, p. 241-243.

Corti, R.   4214

Rapporto preliminare sulle ricerche
botaniche eseguite nel Fezzân.
BSGI 70. 1933, p. 752-761.

Corti, R.   4215

La vegetazione.
SIFOG 1937, p. 161-210.

Corti, R.   4216

La vegetazione dell'uadi Tanezzúft
(Gat).
ACSC 3. 1937, vol. 5, p. 36-42.

Denis, J.   4217

Les Araignées du Fezzân.
BSHN 55. 1964, p. 103-144.

Drar, M.   4218

Flora of Africa north of the Sahara.
A review of the natural resources of
the African continent. Paris 1963,
p. 249-261.

Erroux, J.   4219

Les céréales de l'Ouadi El Ajal
(Fezzân).
BSHN 43. 1952, p. 211-224.

Erroux, J.   4220

Des variétés de céréales au Fezzân.
BLS 3. 1952, n. 11, p. 13-21.

Erroux, J.   4221

Les blés du Fezzân.
BSHN 45. 1954, p. 302-317.

Erroux, J.   4222

Les orges du Fezzân.
BSHN 47. 1956, p. 74-83.

Funiciello, L.   4223

Il problema forestale in Tripolitania.
Riv. forestale italiana 1939, n. 2,
p. 27-36.

Guichard, K.M. - Quezel, P. -   4224
Zaffran, J.

Plantes de Tripolitaine et de Cyrénaïque recoltées ...
BSHN 52. 1961, p. 201-248.

Jany, E.   4225

Heinrich Barths Mitteilungen zur
Flora und Fauna Afrikas (1849-1855).
HBFA 1967, p. 224-307.

Kranz, J.   4226

A list of plant pathogenic and other
fungi of Cyrenaica (Libya).
Kew: Commonwealth Mycological Institute 1965.
(Phytopathological papers. 6.)

Lapidus, M.   4227

Les teignes en Tripolitaine, flore
et distribution comparées des teignes nord-africaines.
Paris 1950. Diss.

Le Houerou, H.N.   4228

Contribution à l'étude de la flore
de la Libye.(Province de Tripolitaine).
BSHN 51. 1960, p. 175-200.

Léonard, J.   4229

The 1964-65 Belgian trans-Saharan
expedition.
Nature 209. 1966, n. 5019, p. 126-
128.

Leone, G.   4230

Origin and reclamation of the dunes
of Tripolitania.
Desert research. Proceedings. International symposium held in Jerusalem 1952.Jerusalem 1953,p.401-404.

Maire, R.   4231

Flore de l'Afrique du Nord. Vol. 1-
13.
Paris: Lechevalier 1952-67.
(Encyclopédie biologique 33. ... -
  68.)

Manzoni, G.   4232

Flora forestale spontanea della
Cirenaica ed esperimentazione di
specie esotiche.
Riv. forestale italiana 1940,
febbraio , p. 4-22.

Meliu, A.   4233

Il silfio esiste ancora ?
Libia 1. 1937, n. 7, p. 8-13.

Messeri, A.   4234

Criteri e resultati dello studio
ecologico-anatomico dei legni del
Fezzàn.
ACSC 3. 1937, vol. 5, p. 42-47.

Messeri, A.   4235

Studio anatomico-ecologico de legni
secondario di alcune piante del
Fezzàn.
Nuovo giornale botanico italiano
45. 1938, p. 267-367.

Messines, J.   4236

La fixation et le reboisement des
sables en Tripolitaine.
Unasylva 6. 1952, n. 2, p. 51-59.

Miranda, D. de   4237

Il silfio: antica e misteriosa pianta della Cirenaica.
Oltremare 5. 1931, p. 138-142.

Ozenda, P.   4238

Flore du Sahara septentrional et
central.
Paris: C.N.R.S. 1958.

Quézel, P. - Zaffran, J.   4239

Deux Labiées nouvelles de Cyrénaïque.
BSHN 52. 1961, p. 219-224.

Tedeschi, C.   4240

Il silfio.
RdC 3. 1929, p. 1276-1292.

Terlizzi, L.   4241

I boschi della Cirenaica. Loro importanza geologica, fitografica,
idrica ed economico-sociale.
RdT (Libya) 3. 1927, p. 53-67, 148-
162.

Tortonese, E.   4242

Il litorale tripolino nei suoi
caratteri fisici e biologici.
Riv. di biologia coloniale 1. 1938,
p. 435-458.

Trotter, A.   4243

Esame generale della Tripolitania
sotto l'aspetto fisico.
La rinascita della Tripolitania.
Milano 1926, p. 41-58.

Trotter, A.   4244

Di alcune piante da sperimentare
nella valorizzazione dei terreni
sterili della Libia.
ACSC 1. 1931, vol. 6, p. 239-249.

Trotter, A.   4245

Modificazioni nella flora della Libia in rapporto al clima ed alla
utilizzazione.
ACSC 3. 1937, vol. 5, p. 76-79.

Vigodsky-de Philippis, A.   4246

Studio monografico del solenostemma
oleifolium (nect.) Bull. et Bruce
(S. Argel (Delile Hayne).
ACSC 3. 1937, vol. 5, p. 54-59.

Alongi, G. - Balboni, A.   4247

La tripanosomiasi del dromedario in
Tripolitania.
ACSC 2. 1934, vol. 7, p. 260-267.

Conti, G.   4248

Il servizio veterinario nell'Africa
italiana.
Roma: IPS 1965.
(L'Italia in Africa. Serie civile.
 2.)

Demougeot, E.   4249

Le chameau et l'Afrique du Nord romaine.
Annales. Économies. Sociétés. Civilisations 15. 1960, p. 209-247.

Etchécopar, R.D. - Huee, F.   4250

Les oiseaux du Nord de l'Afrique de
la Mer Rouge aux Canaries.
The birds of North Africa.
Paris: Boubée 1964.
London: Oliver and Boyd 1967.

Ghigi, A.   4251

Caratteri faunistici.
CGEP 1923, p. 67-74.

Ghigi, A.   4252

Elenco descrittivo del materiale
zoologico raccolto.
CGEP 1923, p. 249-262.

Ghigi, A.   4253

Problemi zoogeografici delle colonie italiane.
ASIPS 25. 1936, vol. 4, p. 265-272.

Higgs, E.S.   4254

North Africa and Mount Carmel: recent developments. Some Pleistocene
fauna of the Mediterranean coastal
areas.
Man 61. 1961, p. 138-139.

Higgs, E.S.   4255

Some Pleistocene faunas of the Medi-
terranean coastal areas.
Proceedings of the Prehistoric
Society 27. 1961, p. 144-154.

Higgs, E.S.   4256

A metrical analysis of some prehistoric domesticated animal bones
from Cyrenaican Libya.
Man 62. 1962, p. 119-122.

Higgs, E.S.   4257

Early domesticated animals in Libya.
Background to evolution in Africa.
Ed. W.W. Bishop. Chicago 1967,
p. 165-173.

Higgs, E.S.   4258

Faunal fluctuations and climate in
Libya.
Background to evolution in Africa.
Ed. W.W. Bishop. Chicago 1967,
p. 149-163.

Hufnagl, E.   4259

Libyan animals.
Stoughton, Wisc.: Oleander Press
1969.

Hufnagl, E.   4260

Libyan mammals.
Stoughton, Wisc.: Oleander Press
1969.

Jany, E.   4261

Die Vogelwelt von Derna (Cyrenaika)
im Sommer 1941.
Ornithologische Monatsberichte 49.
1941, p. 168-171.

Jany, E.   4262

An Brutplätzen des Lannerfalkens
(Falco biarmicus erlangeri Klein-
schmidt) in einer Kieswüste der
inneren Sahara (Nordrand des Serir
Tibesti) zur Zeit des Frühjahrs- 1.

Jany, E.   4262

zugs.
International ornithological congress 12. 1958 (1960), p. 343-352.

2.

Rainey, R.C.   4263

Meteorology and the migration of
desert locusts. Application of synoptic meteorology in locust control.
Technical note. World Meteorological Organization 1963, n. 54.

Scortecci, G.   4264

Relazione preliminare delle ricerche zoologiche eseguite nel Fezzàn
per conto della Reale Società Geografica.
BSGI 72. 1935, p. 279-291.

Scortecci, G.   4265

La fauna.
SIFOG 1937, p. 211-239.

Snow, D.W.   4266

A journey to the Fezzan.
Geographical magazine 27. 1954/55,
p. 222-231.

Toschi, A.   4267

La fauna della Libia e le sue possibilità venatorie.
AAI 4. 1941, vol. 2, p. 593-603.

Vinciguerra, D.   4268

Relazione preliminare sopra i risultati zoologici dell'esplorazione
dell'oasi di Giarabùb.
ACGI 10. 1927, vol. 1, p. 159-164.

Zavattari, E.   4269

La parassitologia delle colonie italiane e i suoi principali problemi.
ACSC 1. 1931, vol. 7, p. 124-141.

Zavattari, E.   4270

Prime linee della parassitologia
dell'oasi di Marada.
ACSC 2. 1934, vol. 7, p. 303-309.

Zavattari, E.   4271

Relazione preliminare sulle ricerche
di biologia sahariana compiute nel
Fezzàn.
BSGI 71. 1934, p. 318-327.

Zavattari, E.   4272

Lo stato attuale delle conoscenze
sulla zoogeografia della Libia.
ASIPS 25. 1936, p. 185-193.

Zavattari, E.   4273

Ambiente biologico generale.
SIFOG 1937, p. 139-159.

Medicine. Public Health.

Bollettino sanitario della   4274
Tripolitania.
Tripoli.
1953-

                                  ianc

Allain, Y.M.   4275

La bilharziose chez l'enfant.
Afrique médicale 6. 1967, p. 483-
487.

Angrisani, V.   4276

La nosologia della provincia orientale della Tripolitania con speciale
riferimento alla amebiasi e ad altre
infestioni protozoarie.
Annali di medicina navale e coloniale 66. 1961, p. 833-848.

Antoine, R. - Legroux, R.   4277

Caractéristiques de la pathologie
oculaire au Fezzân.
TIRS 5. 1948, p. 121-131.

Antonino, N.   4278

I tipi di Eberthelia typhi in Tripoli.
ACSC 2. 1934, vol. 7, p. 431-435.

Barakat, M.R.   4279

A nutrition education program in
schools.
Rome: FAO 1959.
(Report 1148.)

Barakat, M.R.   4280

A nutrition education program for
the schools in Libya.
Rome: FAO.
Progress report 1960. 1961.
Follow-up report 1962. 1963.   1.

Barakat, M.R.   4280

Final report for the period 1959-
1964. 1964.

Bucco, G. - Natoli, A.   4281

L'organizzazione sanitaria nell'
Africa italiana.
Roma: IPS 1965.
(L'Italia in Africa. Serie civile.
  1.)

Camis, M.   4282

Ricerche calorimetriche e chimiche
sugli alimenti degli indigeni nelle
colonie italiane.
ACSC 1. 1931, vol. 7, p. 405-412.

Castigliola, O.   4283

Organizzazione del servizio sanitario militare in Tripolitania.
ACSC 1. 1931, vol. 7, p. 29-55.

Chiodi, V. - Persano, E.   4284

Igiene coloniale ed il suo compito
di fronte al colono europeo ed all'
indigeno.
ACSC 1. 1931, vol. 7, p. 55-93.

Cicchitto, E.   4285

Nuovo contributo alla terapia del
tracoma con la soluzione chininica.
Riv. di biologia coloniale 2. 1939,
p. 43-52.

Ciotola, A.   4286

Un venticinquennio di organizzazione
sanitaria in Libia.
ASIPS 25. 1936, vol. 5, p. 410-421.

Ciotola, A.   4287

L'ispettorato centrale di sanità
della Libia e la sua opera in rapporto alla patologia locale del 1911 al
1951.   1.
Archivio italiano di scienze mediche

Ciotola, A.   4287

tropicale e di parassitologia 1953,
p. 109-135.

Coghill, N.F. - Lawrence, J. - 4288
Ballantin, J.D.

Relapsing fever in Cyrenaica.
British medical journal 1947,
n. 4505, p. 637-640.

Cooper, E.L.   4289

Relapsing fever in Tobruk.
Medical journal of Australia 1942.

Denti di Pirajno, A.   4290

A cure for serpents.
Überlistete Dämonen.
London: Deutsch 1955.
Düsseldorf: Diederichs 1955.

Dixon, C.W.   4291

Smallpox in Tripolitania 1946: an
epidemiological and clinical study
of 500 cases, including trials of
penicillin treatment.   377.
Journal of hygiene 46.1948, p.351-

Dogliatti, M.   4292

Incidenze dermatologiche in Cirenaica.
Dermatologia internationalis 4. 1965,
p. 134-136.

Dogliatti, M.   4293

Situazione epidemiologica, clinica,
profilattica e terapeutica della
lebbra in Cirenaica (Libia). Nostre
osservazioni durante il settennio
1959-1966.   1.

Dogliatti, M.   4293

Minerva dermatologica 42. 1967,
p. 491-505.

                                    2.

Fivoli, F.   4294

Malattie sessuali e lotta antivene-
rea in colonia.
ACSC 1. 1931, vol. 7, p. 239-267.

Foellmer, W.   4295

Besonderheiten der Geburtshilfe und
Gynäkologie in Libyen.
Der Landarzt 34. 1958, p. 136-140.

Foellmer, W.   4296

Probleme der Gesundheitsorganisa-
tion in Libyen.
Deutsche medizinische Wochenschrift
83. 1958, p. 1908-1911.

Foellmer, W.   4297

Deutsche Ärzte in entwicklungsfähi-
gen Ländern.
Deutsche medizinische Wochenschrift
85. 1960, p. 1462-1467.

Foellmer, W.   4298

Die Säuglings- und Kindersterblich-
keit und ihre Ursachen in einem
Entwicklungsland.
Deutsche medizinische Wochenschrift
85. 1960, p. 1993-1997.

Foellmer, W.   4299

Deutsche Ärzte für Entwicklungsländer.
Medizinische Monatsschrift 15. 1961,
p. 183-187.

Foellmer, W.   4300

Wie soll der Einsatz von deutschen
Ärzten und deutschem Pflegepersonal
im Gesundheitsdienst der Entwick-
lungsländer durchgeführt werden ?
Ärztliche Mitteilungen (Deutsches
Ärzteblatt) 46. 1961, p. 2202-2206.

Foellmer, W.   4301

Laktation, Laktationsamenorrhoe und
Schwangerschaft bei Frauen in einem
Entwicklungsland.
Geburtshilfe und Frauenheilkunde 22.
1962, p. 1391-1399.

Foellmer, W.   4302

Besonderheiten der Geburtshilfe und
Gynäkologie in Entwicklungsländern.
Archiv für Gynäkologie 198. 1963,
p. 594-609.

Foellmer, W.   4303

Ärzte in Nordafrika.
Deutsches Ärzteblatt 62. 1965,
p. 263-264.

Fossati, C.   4304

Osservazioni sulla patologia delle
parassitosi intestinali nei lattan-
ti e nei bambini della città di Bengasi (Libia) e sobborghi.
Giornale di malattie infettive e pa-
rassitarie 16. 1964, p. 521-527.

Fossati, C.   4305

Inchiesta dispensariale effettuate
in Cirenaica sulla frequenza dell'
infezione e della malattia tuberco-
lare in un gruppo di bambini conviventi e non conviventi con   1.

Fossati, C.   4305

tubercolotici.
Giornale italiano della tubercolosi
e delle malattie del torace 19.
1965, p. 87-92.

                                    2.

Fossati, C.   4306

Sull'idatidosi famigliare in Cirenaica.
Clinica pediatrica 47. 1965, p. 280-
287.

Fossati, C.   4307

Sulla mortalità infantile per tubercolosi polmonare nella Cirenaica
(Libia) dal 1959 al 1964 compreso.
Minerva pediatrica 17. 1965,
p. 1847-1850.

Fossati, C.   4308

Sulla possibilità e sulla frequenza
della silicosi polmonare tra gli
abitanti del Deserto Libico.
Medicina del lavoro 60. 1969, n. 2,
p. 144-149.

Franchini, G.   4309

Il parassitismo intestinale nelle
nostre colonie.
ACSC 2. 1934, vol. 7, p. 289-302.

Franchini, G.   4310

Le spirochetosi ricorrenti nelle
nostre colonie africane.
ACSC 3. 1937, vol. 9, p. 277-297.

Galeotti, G.   4311

L'alimentazione degli indigeni nelle
colonie e nei possedimenti italiani.
RSAI 4. 1941, p. 626-638.

Gaspare, L.   4312

La lotta antimalarica nel Fezzan.
ACSC 2. 1934, vol. 7, p. 226-229.

Gaudio, A.   4313

Farmacopea berbera sahariana. Studio
comparativo.
Libia 4. 1956, n. 1/2, p. 41-46.

Giordano, M. - Nastasi, A.   4314

Sulla febbre esantematica del litto-
rale mediterraneo in Tripolitania.
ACSC 2. 1934, vol. 7, p. 462-495.

Girolami, M. - Scotti, G.   4315

Contributo dell'Italia alla conoscenza della nosografia dell'Africa.
Roma: IPS 1963.
(L'Italia in Africa. Serie scientifi-
co-culturale.)

Giua, S.   4316

La lotta contro la tubercolosi in
Libia.
REAI 27. 1939, p. 734-736.

Grimm, M.   4317

Sprechstunden eines Arztes in der
Wüste.
Deutsche in Entwicklungsländern
(Schriften des Auslands-Kurier) 3.
1966, p. 63-67.

Gurevitch, J. - Hasson, E. - 4318
Margolis, E. - Poliakoff, C.

Blood groups in Jews from Tripolitania.
Annals of human genetics 19. 1955,
p. 260-261.

Hakim, H. 4319
Tripoli school of nursing, Libya,
North Africa.
International nursing review 7.
1960, n. 6, p. 39-42.

Infirmities among the citizen 4320
population in Libya.
Population census 1964. Paper no. 2.
Tripoli: Census and Statistical
Dept. nd.

Issawi, A. - Khatib, M. - 4321
Pont-Flores, M.

An assessment of the school feeding
and nutrition education program.
Rome: FAO 1964.

Kanter, H. 4322
Libyen - Libya. Eine geographisch-
medizinische Landeskunde. A geomedi-
cal monograph.
Berlin: Springer 1967.
(Medizinische Länderkunde. 1.   1.

Kanter, H. 4322
Geomedical monograph series. 1.)

                                  2.

Khalil, A. 4323
Three weeks in two Libyan villages.
International journal of health
education 3. 1960, p. 136-142.

Krpo, A. - Mansour, K. 4324
Some aspects and problems of trauma
in Libya experienced by the Centre
for Traumatology and Emergency Sur-
gery, Tripoli, for 1962-1964.
Tripoli: Ministry of Health 1965.

Lauersen, F. 4325
School feeding.
Rome: FAO 1957.
(Report 686.)

Libya and Malaria. 4326
Tripoli: Ministry of Health
1964.

Libya - nutrition survey of 4327
the armed forces and civilians.
Wash.: Interdepartmental Committee
on Nutrition for National Defense
1957.

Lione, J.G. 4328
Organizing an occupational health
program in an emerging nation.
Medical bulletin. Standard Oil Company 25. 1965, p. 272-278.

Lionti, G. 4329
Sulla assistenza ospedaliera, spe-
cialmente chirurgica, ai civili libici ed europei in Bengasi, dal 1920
al 1928.
Bengasi 1930.

Livi, L. 4330
Sulla fluttuazione stagionale dei
matrimoni, delle nascite e delle
morti in taluni gruppi etnici della
Cirenaica.
ACSC 2. 1934, vol. 4, p. 240-249.

Lollini, C. 4331
Del matrimonio precoce in Libia.
Libia 3. 1955, n. 1, p. 73-75.

Lollini, C. 4332
Esperienze di vaccinazione con il
B.C.G. in Tripolitania considerazioni sull'indice tubercolinico e sull'
allergia postvaccinale.
Lotta contro la tubercolosi 30.1960,
p. 580-596.

Magri, G.   4333

Panorama nosologico della Libia con
particolare riguardo ai fattori am-
bientali.
Archivio italiano di scienze mediche
coloniali 1942, nov., p. 393-409.

May, J.M.   4334

Libya. The ecology of malnutrition
in northern Africa.
Studies in medical geography 7. 1967,
p. 3-52.

Mazzolani, D.A. - Castigliola,   4335
O. - Gustinelli, E. - Cortesi,
G. - Castro, L. de

L'organizzazione sanitaria della
Tripolitania.
Tripoli 1931.

Mazzolani, D.A.   4336

L'amebiasi in Tripolitania.
ACSC 2. 1934, vol. 7, p. 332-336.

Mazzolani, D.A.   4337

La tubercolosi polmonare fra gli
ebrei di Tripoli.
ACSC 2. 1934, vol. 7, p. 539-543.

Menotti, A.   4338

Relative incidence of myocardial
infarction and cerebrovascular acci-
dents among Arabs of Tripolitania.
Acta cardiologica 18. 1963, p. 248-
253.

Modica, R. - Livadiotti, M. -   4339
Macaluso, A.S.

Incidenza della sicklemia, pregressa
malaria e distribuzione razziale
nell'oasi costiera di Tauorga.
Archivio italiano di scienze   1.

Modica, R. - Livadiotti, M. -   4339

mediche tropicale e di parassitologia 41. 1960, p. 595-604.

Morbidity statistics in   4340
government-hospitals.
Tripoli: Central Statistics Office
1956.

Moschini-Antinori, E. -   4341
Menotti, A. - Splendiani, G.

Hypertension and normal blood
pressure in Tripolitania.
Panminerva medica 4. 1962, p. 500-
505.

Nastasi, A.   4342

Le reazioni per la lue in Tripoli
in rapporto alla razza.
Riv. di biologia coloniale 2. 1939,
p. 279-294.

Le oasi di Giàlo e Cúfra.   4343
Relazione della commissione
sanitaria che visitò le oasi nel
febbraio-aprile 1934.
REAI 23. 1935, p. 129-156, 294-331.

Onorato, R.   4344

Ripercussione dei metodi sanitari
sulle popolazioni indigene della
Tripolitania.
REAI 19. 1931, p. 1282-1296.

Panetta, E.   4345

Note sulla protezione dell'infanzia
nella medicina popolare araba.
RSAI 6. 1943, p. 247-254.

Panetta, E.   4346

Medicina empirica e farmacologia della Libia.
Libia 2. 1954, n. 3, p. 47-55, n. 4,
p. 45-50, 3. 1955, n. 1, p. 77-92.

Penso, G.   4347

La Cirenaica dal punto di vista medico.
RSAI 5. 1942, p. 231-237.

Piccinini, P.   4348

La Tripolitania dal punto di vista
climatologico e talassoterapico.
ACSC 1. 1931, vol. 7, p. 172-179.

Piccinini, P.   4349

Come si sta attuando una biblioteca
di medicina coloniale italiana.
ACSC 3. 1937, vol. 9, p. 229-233.

Proposed regular programme   4350
and budget estimates for the
financial year ... Eastern Mediterranean. Libya ...
Geneva: World Health Organization.
1.1. - 31.12. 1968 (1966).
1.1. - 31.12. 1969 (1967).   1.

Proposed regular programme ... 4350

1.1. - 31.12. 1970 (1968).
1.1. - 31.12. 1971 (1969).
(Official records of the World
 Health Organization. 154. 163. 171.
 179.)   2.

Public health in Libya.   4351
Tripoli: Ministry of Information and Guidance nd.

Quadrone, E.   4352

Il primo autotreno sanitario sulle
piste del Fezzan e del Sahara italiano.
Libia 1. 1937, n. 5, p. 12-17.

Raffaele, O.   4353

Il granuloma ulceroso delle pudende
in Tripolitania.
ACSC 2. 1934, vol. 7, p. 427-430.

Richter, L.   4354

Beobachtungen über die Kinder und
Jugendlichen aus den Oasen des
Fezzan (Königreich Libyen).
Ärztliche Jugendkunde 53. 1962,
p. 205-224, 272-281.

Ritchie, J.A.S.   4355

Learning better nutrition. A second
study of approaches and techniques.
Chapter 6 to 11.
FAO nutritional studies 1968, n. 20,
p. 102-225.

Rizzuti, G.   4356

La malaria nelle nostre colonie
africane.
ACSC 1. 1931, vol. 7, p. 289-303.

Sanarelli, G.   4357

L'opera sanitaria.
La rinascita della Tripolitania.
Milano 1926, p. 381-397.

Sarnelli, T.   4358

La malattia del "Lâtah" in Tripolitania.
Giornale di medicina militare 1924,
fasc. 2.

Sarnelli, T.   4359

Il tracoma in rapporto alle razze in
Tripolitania.
Archivio di ottalmologia 31. 1924,
p. 416-421.

Sarnelli, T.   4360

La medicina coloniale in Italia.
Giornale di medicina militare 1926,
fasc. 8-9.

Sarnelli, T.   4361

La lotta al tracoma nel nord africano, con speciale riguardo alle
nostre colonie dirette e indirette.
Atti del congresso nazionale di medicina coloniale 2.1929, p. 254-269.

Sarnelli, T.   4362

Come difendersi dalle congiuntiviti.
Brevi norme per le popolazioni libi-
che. Edito a cura della "Comunità
Israelitica".
Bengasi 1930.

Sarnelli, T.   4363

Acque salutari miracolose dell'
Africa italiana.
IdO 2. 1937, n. 17, p. 6-8, n. 18,
p. 9-12.

Sarnelli, T.   4364

La grotta di Sīdī el-Magbūl (magia
e misticismo nella medicina indigena
delle nostre colonie).
BSGI 74. 1937, p. 473.

Sarnelli, T.   4365

L'etnoiatrica o medicina indigena.
Medicina e biologia 1. 1942, p. 395-
407.

Sarnelli, T.   4366

La medicina araba.
Medicina e biologia 4. 1946, p. 385-
427.

Sarnelli, T.   4367

Probabile esistenza a Tripoli del
"Libro dei semplici" di Aḥmad al-
Ghāfiqī (sec. XII).
Atti e memorie della accademia di
storia dell'arte sanitaria ser. 2,
vol. 13. 1947, p. 150-154.

Scortecci, G.   4368

Crono e il deserto.
Illustrazione del medico 1961,
n. 179, gennaio.

Selby Lowndes, R.M.   4369

Health visiting in Cyrenaica.
Nursing times 1953, 21.11., p. 1199-
1200.

Sirleo, L.   4370

Organisation des services sanitaires
civils en Libye.
CR des séances ... Institut Colonial
International 19. 1924, vol. 1,
p. 269-283.

Strecker, G.   4371

Das Gesundheitswesen in Libyen.
Hessisches Ärzteblatt 23. 1962,
p. 208-214.

Tedeschi, C.   4372

La medicina indigena nella Barca
orientale.
Oltremare 5. 1931, p. 376-379.

Testi, F.   4373

Cose viste e cose raccolte in Cirenaica dall'anno 1915 all'anno 1916.
ACSC 2. 1934, vol. 7, p. 583-595.

Thomasis, G. de   4374

Il sanitario "Generale Caneva" in
Tripoli.
Riv. della assistenza 1939, p. 255-
259.

Tripòdi, M.   4375

Malattie dominanti nella Tripolitania: osservazioni e problemi di
studio.
ASIPS 25. 1936, vol. 5, p. 425-433.

Valensi, L.   4376

Calamités démographiques en Tunisie
et en Méditerranée orientale aux
XVIIIe et XIXe siècles.
Annales. Économies. Sociétés. Civilisations 24. 1969, p. 1540-1561.

Vallegiani, L.   4377

Relievi clinico-statistici sulla tubercolosi di primo accertamento in
Tripolitania.
Lotta contro la tubercolosi 29. 1959,
p. 1256-1266.

Vermeil, C.   4378

Présence de Bulinus contortus Mi-
chaud à Rhat, Fezzân.
Annales de parasitologie 1951,
p. 415-419.

Vermeil, C.   4379

Contribution à l'étude des Bilharzioses au Fezzân (Libye).
Bulletin de la société des sciences naturelles de Tunisie 5. 1952,
p. 185-194.

Vermeil, C. - Tournoux, P. -   4380
Tocheport, G. - Noger, C. -
Schmitt, P.

Premières données sur l'état actuel des Bilharzioses au Fezzân, Libye.
Annales de parasitologie 27. 1952,
p. 499-538.

Vermeil, C.   4381

Contribution à l'étude des Culicides du Fezzân (Libye).
Bulletin de la société de pathologie exotique et de ses filiales 1953,
p. 445-454.

Weinand, J.   4382

Befinden, Heilen, Ernähren. H. Barths Angaben aus dem Gebiet seiner grossen Reise.
HBFA 1967, p. 308-360.

Whiteman, J.   4383
Food and nutrition amongst school children of a Libyan oasis.
Nutrition 18. 1964, n. 1, p. 14-18.

The work of WHO.   4384
1967. Geneva 1968.
1968. Geneva 1969.
1969. Geneva 1970.
(Official records of the World Health Organization. 164. 172. 180.)

Wustmann, I.   4385
Beduinenkinder in der libyschen Wüste.
Ärztliche Jugendkunde 55. 1965,
p. 417-433.

Yang, Y.H.   4386
Food and nutrition policy.
Rome: FAO 1963.

Zavattari, E.   4387

Il duda, lo strano cibo dei Dauada del Fezzan.
Sapere 1. 1935, p. 235-237.

Zavattari, E.   4388

Condizioni sanitarie.
SIFOG 1937, p. 385-400.

Zavattari, E.   4389

Ambiente fisico e Schistosomiasi vescicale in Libia.
Riv. di biologia coloniale 1. 1938,
p. 5-27.

Addenda.

Afrika-Biographien.   4390
Forschungsinstitut der   (1627a)
Friedrich-Ebert-Stiftung.
Bonn/Bad Godesberg 1967-

Bachmann, P.   4391
'Alī Muṣṭafā al-Miṣurātī.   (2165a)
Ein libyscher Schriftsteller der Gegenwart.
Deutscher Orientalistentag (ZDMG Suppl. 1.) 17. 1968, p. 623-630.

Ben Sassi, K.   4392
Rencontre des hommes de   (2166a)
lettres et écrivains maghrébins,
Tripoli 15-19 mars 1969.
IBLA 1969, n. 124, p. 321-327.

Breton, H.   4393
La Libye républicaine.   (1650a)
Essai d'analyse d'un changement politique.
AAN 8. 1969, p. 359-373.

Brinke, J. 4394
(82a)
Libye (Libyen).
Lidé a Země. Praha 17. 1968, p. 321-
324.

Les données de base de 4395
l'économie libyenne. (2905a)
Syrie et monde arabe 1969,
n. 189, p. 53-62.

Du Pasquier, R. 4396
La Libye en plein essor. (2907a)
Journal de Genève 1969, 12., 13.,
14., 15., 17. 3.

Falchi, N. 4397
Le peuplement rural des (3346a)
provinces libyques.
Travail agricole 1939, février,
p. 80-106.

Gaudio, A. 4398
Le Sahara des africains. (512a)
Paris: Julliard 1960.
(Collection histoire et voyages.)

Gaudio, A. 4399
Les civilisations du Sahara. (512b)
Verviers: Gérard 1967.
(Marabout Université. 42.)

Herald, G.W. 4400
The Libyan oil revolt. (1687a)
The new leader 52. 1969,
29.9., p. 5-8.

Lentin, A.P. 4401
Le putsch des gentlemen (1706a)
(Libye).
Nouvel observateur 1969, 8-14.9.,
p. 8-14.

Le Tourneau, R. 4402
Libye. Chronique politique. (1707a)
AAN 8. 1969, p. 393-397.

Libya's new golden age. 4403
Oil: lifestream of (2967a)
progress 18. 1968, n. 4,
p. 2-9.

Libyens Wirtschaftsprobleme. 4404
Afrika-Informations- (2978a)
dienst 2. 1959, n. 11,
p. 194-197.

Loi relative à la protection 4405
du droit d'auteur (no.9, (2189a)
de 1968).
Le droit d'auteur 82. 1969, p. 116-
121.

La nationalisation et la 4406
nouvelle politique pétro- (3019a)
lière en (de la) Libye.
Syrie et monde arabe 1969, n. 191,
p. 24-28. Le pétrole et le gaz arabe
1969, 1.11., p. 3-7.

Nobili Massuero, F. 4407
La Tripolitania economica nel (3026a)
1922.
Riv. di politica economica 1923,
p. 744-752.

Pace, B. 4408
Fouilles dans le Fezzân. (1161a)
La renaissance 17. 1934,
p. 140-144.

Pautard, A. 4409
Libye: les militaires au (1744a)
pouvoir.
Revue française d'études politiques
africaines 1969, n. 46, p. 9-12.

Peters, E.L. 4410
(2470a)
Aspects of the family
among the bedouin of Cyrenaica.
Comparative family systems. Ed.
M.F. Nimkoff. Boston 1965, p. 121-
146.

Proclamation constitutionelle 4411
de la République Arabe (1822a)
Libyenne (11 décembre 1969).
AAN 8. 1969, p. 942-946.

Roucek, J.S. 4412
(3060a)
Emerging Libya.
New Africa 7. 1965, n. 3, p. 10-11.

Scarin, E. 4413
(3065a)
La situazione economica del
Fezzàn e le sue possibilità.
Economia 1934, p. 440-450.

Slousch, N. 4414
(2420a)
L'ethnographie juive de
l'Afrique du Nord.
Bulletin de la Société de Géographie d'Égypte 10. 1921, p. 255-260.

Smith, D.J. 4415
(1000a)
A socketed axehead of
iron.
Antiquity 36. 1962, p. 138.

Talha, L. 4416
(3079a)
L'économie libyenne depuis
les découvertes pétrolières.
AAN 8. 1969, p. 203-284.

Toni, Y. 4417
(2426a)
Tribal distribution and
racial relationship of the ancient
and modern peoples of Cyrenaica.
Annals of the faculty of arts. Ain
Shams University. Cairo 8. 1963,
p. 153-191.

Vulterini, E. 4418
(1909a)
La giustizia penale in
Tripolitania.
Riv. penale 1924, p. 84-100.

Index of Authors and Editors.

Rosenthal, E.   1592.
Roselli Cecconi, M.   150.
Rosenbaum, E.   996.
Ross, D.W.   372.
Rossi, E.   797, 798, 1268, 1297,
   1309, 1318-1329, 1767, 1958,
   2047, 2128-2130, 2202-2204, 2415,
   2732.
Rossi, F.   3059.
Rossi, G.   1448.
Rossi, L.   3529, 3530.
Rossi, M.   1197.
Rossi, N.   2733.
Rossi, P.   539, 3060.
Rossi Ronchetti, C.   3973-3977,
   4012-4014.
Roubet, C.   4015.
Roucek, J.S.   4412.
Rouleau, E.   1768.
Rowe, A.   997, 998.
Roy, J.C.   3061.
Rozeboom, J.J.   4001.
Rubeis, A. de   2734.
Rubinacci, R.   1330, 1331, 1771.
Ruggieri, R.   478, 2048.
Ruggiero, G.   2735.
Rumeau, A.   247.
Rummel, J.F.   2284, 2285.
Russo, A.   4097.
Russo, M.   1449, 2049, 3531.

S

Sabatini, A.   2483-2488.
Sabki, H.M.   1772.
Sacchetti, R.   2205, 3062.
Sacerdoti, A.   1332.
Sa'dawiyah, A. al   854.
Sagal, V.E.   82.
Saint Pereuse   de   1593.
Saitta, A.   3532, 3533.
Sakka, H.O. el   2286.
Sakkaf, M.   2842.
Salahi, D.   4016.
Salama, P.   799, 1000.
Saliheen al-Houni, A. al   117.
Salter, J.C.   1594.
Salvadori, M.   3733.
Salvatori, S.   3200.
Salvemini, G.   1450.
Sanarelli, G.   4357.
Sanctis, G. de   3534.
Sanders, J.   3063.
Sandford, K.S.   1959.
Sandri, S.   1451, 1452.
Sanford, R.M.   3837, 3870.
Sani, M.   1453.
Sanità, G.   2050, 2051.
Sansone, L.   1454.

Santmyer, C.   3535.
Santoro, G.   1595.
Sanz y Diaz, J.   541.
Sarnelli, T.   2131-2135, 2416-2418,
   4358-4367.
Sasnett, M.   2287.
Sassani, A.H.K.   2288.
Satta Dessolis, A.   3064.
Sattin, F.   687-690.
Savage, M.A.   1333.
Savage, R.J.G.   4017.
Savoia Aosta, A. di   337, 406,
   1452.
Sayegh, K.S.   2736.
Sbordoni, R.   3536.
Scaglione, E.   1455.
Scala, E.   1456, 1596.
Scalamandré, G.   248.
Scalella, L.   2580.
Scalfaro, G.   1597.
Scandura, A.   1893-1895, 3065.
Scaparro, M.   3659-3661.
Scarin, E.   249, 338, 407-409, 479,
   691, 1960, 2419, 2737-2744, 3066,
   3937, 4413.
Schaefer, H.   1198.
Schafer, S.J.   3201.
Schanzer, C.   1457.
Schapira, E.   2745.
Schepis, G.   3537.
Schiassi, N.   2746.
Schiffers, H.   339-344, 410- 413,
   441, 450, 480-482, 542-544, 3067,
   4112-4115, 4196.
Schleucher, K.   445.
Schmidt, H.W.   1599.
Schmitt, P.   4380.
Schubarth-Engelschall, K.   483,484.
Schuhmacher, D.   1387.
Schwarzbach, M.   4018.
Scialhub, G.   2136.
Scichilone, G.   969.
Scortecci, G.   2581, 4264, 4265,
   4368.
Scotti, G.   4315.
Scotti, P.   2582.
Sears, S.W.   1600.
Seeger, W.   1482.
Sega, C.   3662-3665.
Segert, S.   295.
Seibert, J.   1199, 1200.
Seilacher, A.   4019.
Seklani, M.   2420.
Selby Lowndes, R.M.   4369.
Selley, R.C.   4020-4023.
Sepmeyer, J.   2287.
Serafy, S. el   3068.
Sergi, S.   1201, 1202, 2489-2492.
Sergio, R.   1896.